Big Data Analytics

Tools and Technology for Effective Planning

Chapman & Hall/CRC
Big Data Series

SERIES EDITOR
Sanjay Ranka

AIMS AND SCOPE

This series aims to present new research and applications in Big Data, along with the computational tools and techniques currently in development. The inclusion of concrete examples and applications is highly encouraged. The scope of the series includes, but is not limited to, titles in the areas of social networks, sensor networks, data-centric computing, astronomy, genomics, medical data analytics, large-scale e-commerce, and other relevant topics that may be proposed by potential contributors.

PUBLISHED TITLES

FRONTIERS IN DATA SCIENCE
Matthias Dehmer and Frank Emmert-Streib

BIG DATA OF COMPLEX NETWORKS
Matthias Dehmer, Frank Emmert-Streib, Stefan Pickl, and Andreas Holzinger

BIG DATA COMPUTING: A GUIDE FOR BUSINESS AND TECHNOLOGY MANAGERS
Vivek Kale

BIG DATA : ALGORITHMS, ANALYTICS, AND APPLICATIONS
Kuan-Ching Li, Hai Jiang, Laurence T. Yang, and Alfredo Cuzzocrea

BIG DATA MANAGEMENT AND PROCESSING
Kuan-Ching Li, Hai Jiang, and Albert Y. Zomaya

BIG DATA ANALYTICS: TOOLS AND TECHNOLOGY FOR EFFECTIVE PLANNING
Arun K. Somani and Ganesh Chandra Deka

BIG DATA IN COMPLEX AND SOCIAL NETWORKS
My T. Thai, Weili Wu, and Hui Xiong

HIGH PERFORMANCE COMPUTING FOR BIG DATA
Chao Wang

NETWORKING FOR BIG DATA
Shui Yu, Xiaodong Lin, Jelena Mišić, and Xuemin (Sherman) Shen

Big Data Analytics
Tools and Technology for Effective Planning

Edited by
Arun K. Somani
Ganesh Chandra Deka

CRC Press
Taylor & Francis Group
Boca Raton London New York

CRC Press is an imprint of the
Taylor & Francis Group, an **informa** business

A CHAPMAN & HALL BOOK

CRC Press
Taylor & Francis Group
6000 Broken Sound Parkway NW, Suite 300
Boca Raton, FL 33487-2742

International Standard Book Number-13: 978-1-138-03239-2 (Hardback)

Library of Congress Cataloging-in-Publication Data

Names: Somani, Arun K., author. | Deka, Ganesh Chandra, 1969- author.
Title: Big data analytics : tools and technology for effective planning / [edited by] Arun K. Somani, Ganesh Chandra Deka.
Description: Boca Raton : CRC Press, [2018] | Series: Chapman & Hall/CRC Press big data series | Includes bibliographical references and index.
Identifiers: LCCN 2017016514| ISBN 9781138032392 (hardcover : acid-free paper) | ISBN 9781315391250 (ebook) | ISBN 9781315391243 (ebook) | ISBN 9781315391236 (ebook)
Subjects: LCSH: Big data.
Classification: LCC QA76.9.B45 B548 2018 | DDC 005.7--dc23
LC record available at https://lccn.loc.gov/2017016514

Visit the Taylor & Francis Web site at
http://www.taylorandfrancis.com

and the CRC Press Web site at
http://www.crcpress.com

Contents

Preface

Three central questions concerning Big Data are how to classify Big Data, what are the best methods for managing Big Data, and how to accurately analyze Big Data. Although various methods exist to answer these questions, no single or globally accepted methodology is recognized to perform satisfactorily on all data and can be accepted since Big Data Analytics tools have to deal with the large variety and large scale of data sets. For example, some of the use cases of Big Data Analytics tools include real-time intelligence, data discovery, and business reporting. These all present a different challenge.

This edited volume, titled *Big Data Analytics: Tools and Technology for Effective Planning*, deliberates upon these various aspects of Big Data Analytics for effective planning. We start with Big Data challenges and a reference model, and then dwell into data mining, algorithms, and storage methods. This is followed by various technical facets of Big Data analytics and some application areas.

Chapter 1 and 2 discuss Big Data challenges. Chapter 3 presents the Big Data reference model. Chapter 4 covers Big Data analytic tools.

Chapters 5 to 9 focus on the various advanced Big Data mining technologies and algorithms.

Big Data storage is an important and very interesting topic for researchers. Hence, we have included a chapter on Big Data storage technology (Chapter 10).

Chapters 11 to 14 consider the various technical facets of Big Data analytics such as nonlinear feature extraction, enhanced feature mining, classifier models to predict customer churn for an e-retailer, and large-scale entity clustering on knowledge graphs for topic discovery and exploration.

In the Big Data world, driven by the Internet of Things (IoT), a majority of the data is generated by IoT devices. Chapter 15 and Chapter 16 discuss two application areas: connected intelligence and traffic analysis, respectively. Finally, Chapter 17 is about the possibilities and challenges of Big Data analysis in humanities research.

We are confident that the book will be a valuable addition to the growing knowledge base, and will be impactful and useful in providing information on Big Data analytics tools and technology for effective planning. As Big Data becomes more intrusive and pervasive, there will be increasing interest in this domain. It is our hope that this book will not only showcase the current state of art and practice but also set the agenda for future directions in the Big Data analytics domain.

About the Editors

Arun K. Somani is currently serving as associate dean for research for the College of Engineering and Anson Marston Distinguished Professor of Electrical and Computer Engineering at Iowa State University. Somani's research interests are in the areas of dependable and high-performance system design, algorithms, and architecture; wavelength-division multiplexing-based optical networking; and image-based navigation techniques. He has published more than 300 technical papers, several book chapters, and one book, and has supervised more than 70 MS and more than 35 PhD students. His research has been supported by several projects funded by the industry, the National Science Foundation (NSF), and the Defense Advanced Research Projects Agency (DARPA). He was the lead designer of an antisubmarine warfare system for the Indian navy, a Meshkin fault-tolerant computer system architecture for the Boeing Company, a Proteus multicomputer cluster-based system for the Coastal Navy, and a HIMAP design tool for the Boeing Commercial Company. He was awarded the Distinguished Engineer member grade of the Association for Computing Machinery (ACM) in 2006, and elected Fellow of IEEE in 1999 for his contributions to "theory and applications of computer networks." He was also elected as a Fellow of the American Association for the Advancement of Science (AAAS) in 2012.

Ganesh Chandra Deka is currently deputy director of Training at Directorate General of Training, Ministry of Skill Development and Entrepreneurship, Government of India, New Delhi, India. His research interests include e-governance, Big Data analytics, NoSQL databases, and vocational education and training. He has authored two books on cloud computing published by LAP Lambert (Germany). He has also coauthored four textbooks on computer science, published by Moni Manik Prakashan (India). So far he has edited seven books (four for IGI Global, three for CRC Press) on Big Data, NoSQL, and cloud computing, and authored seven book chapters. He has published eight research papers in various reputed journals (two for IEEE, one for Elsevier). He was also guest editor of three special issues of reputed indexed international journals. He has published nearly 50 research papers for various IEEE conferences, and organized 8 IEEE International Conferences as technical chair in India. He is a member of the editorial board and reviewer for various journals and international conferences. He is a member of IEEE, the Institution of Electronics and Telecommunication Engineers, India; and associate member of the Institution of Engineers, India.

Contributors

Pothireddy Siva Abhilash
Southern New Hampshire University
Manchester, New Hampshire

Rahul Aedula
PESIT Bangalore South Campus
Bangalore, India

Zeeshan Ahmad
SAP Labs India Pvt Ltd
Bengaluru, India

Mostafa Aref
Faculty of Computer and Information
    Sciences
Ain Shams University
Cairo, Egypt

Balamurugan Balusamy
School of Information Technology
Vellore Institute of Technology
Vellore, Tamil Nadu, India

Kevin Berwind
Faculty of Mathematics and Computer
    Science
University of Hagen
Hagen, Germany

Marco Bornschlegl
Faculty of Mathematics and Computer
    Science
University of Hagen
Hagen, Germany

Feng Chen
School of Computer Science and Informatics
De Montfort University
Leicester, United Kingdom

Jacqueline Cope
School of Computer Science and
    Informatics De Montfort University
Leicester, United Kingdom

Michael Davies
Department of Computer Science
Iowa State University
Ames, Iowa

Sudeepa Roy Dey
PESIT Bangalore South Campus
Bangalore, India

Mahmoud Elbattah
College of Engineering and Informatics
National University of Ireland
Galway, Ireland

Felix Engel
Faculty of Mathematics and Computer
    Science
University of Hagen
Hagen, Germany

Baskar Ganapathysubramanian
Department of Computer Science
Iowa State University
Ames, Iowa

Mohammad Samadi Gharajeh
Young Researchers and Elite Club
Tabriz Branch
Islamic Azad University
Tabriz, Iran

Gouri Ginde
PESIT Bangalore South Campus
Bangalore, India

Matthias Hemmje
Faculty of Mathematics and Computer
    Science
University of Hagen
Hagen, Germany

Helge Janicke
School of Computer Science and
    Informatics
De Montfort University
Leicester, United Kingdom

Michael Kaufmann
Lucerne University of Applied Sciences
    and Arts School of Information
    Technology
Zug-Rotkreuz, Switzerland

Abhishek Kumar
JP Morgan
Bengaluru, India

PS Pavan Kumar
Sri Paladugu Parvathidevi Engineering
    College and Technology
Andhra Pradesh, India

Piyush Lakhawat
Department of Electrical and Computer
    Engineering
Iowa State University
Ames, Iowa

Alberto Larocca
Head of R&D Cosmo Ltd.
Accra, Ghana

Kin Gwn Lore
Department of Mechanical Engineering
Iowa State University
Ames, Iowa

Leandros A. Maglaras
School of Computer Science and
    Informatics
De Montfort University
Leicester, United Kingdom

Michele Marconi
Department of Life and Environmental
    Sciences
Università Politecnica delle Marche
Ancona, Italy

Archana Mathur
PESIT Bangalore South Campus
Bangalore, India

Mayank Mishra
Department of Electrical and Computer
    Engineering
Iowa State University
Ames, Iowa

Pratik Mishra
Department of Electrical and Computer
    Engineering
Iowa State University
Ames, Iowa

Roberto Díaz Morales
University Carlos III (UC3M)
Madrid, Spain

Mydhili K. Nair
Department of Information Science and
    Engineering
M.S. Ramaiah Institute of Technology
Bangalore, India

Adil Omari
Department of Computer Science
Universidad Autónoma de Madrid
Madrid, Spain

Mipsa Patel
Department of Computer Science and
    Engineering
M.S. Ramaiah Institute of Technology
Bangalore, India

Toine Pieters
Descartes Centre for the History and
    Philosophy of the Sciences and the Arts
Freudenthal Institute
Utrecht University
Utrecht, the Netherlands

Arjun Rao
Department of Information Science and
    Engineering
M.S. Ramaiah Institute of Technology
Bangalore, India

**Pothireddy Venkata Lakshmi Narayana
Rao**
Kampala International University
    Kampala, Uganda

Mohamed Roushdy
Faculty of Computer and Information
    Sciences
Ain Shams University Cairo, Egypt

BS Daya Sagar
Indian Statistical Institute
Bangalore, India

Snehanshu Saha
PESIT Bangalore South Campus
Bangalore, India

Bibhudatta Sahoo
Department of Computer Science and
    Engineering
National Institute of Technology Rourkela
    Rourkela, Odisha, India

Sampa Sahoo
Department of Computer Science and
    Engineering
National Institute of Technology Rourkela
    Rourkela, Odisha, India

Abdel-Badeeh M. Salem
Faculty of Computer and Information
    Sciences
Ain Shams University Cairo, Egypt

Gambhire Swati Sampatrao
PESIT Bangalore South Campus
Bangalore, India

Soumik Sarkar
Department of Mechanical Engineering
    Iowa State University
Ames, Iowa

Matthias Schneider
Faculty of Mathematics and Computer
    Science
University of Hagen
Hagen, Germany

Francois Siewe
School of Computer Science and
    Informatics
De Montfort University
Leicester, United Kingdom

Nabeel Siddiqui
Sr. Developer SAP LABS INDIA PVT LTD
    Bengaluru

Arun K. Somani
Department of Electrical and Computer
    Engineering
Iowa State University
Ames, Iowa

K. G. Srinivasa
Department of Information Technology
CBP Government Engineering College
New Delhi, India

Daniel Stoecklein
Department of Mechanical Engineering
    Iowa State University
Ames, Iowa

Karthik B. Subramanya
Department of Electrical and Computer
    Engineering
Iowa State University
Ames, Iowa

Devang Swami
Department of Computer Science and
    Engineering
National Institute of Technology Rourkela
Rourkela, Odisha, India

Berrie van der Molen
Descartes Centre for the History and
    Philosophy of the Sciences and the Arts
Freudenthal Institute
Utrecht University
Utrecht, the Netherlands

Vegesna Tarun Sai Varma
School of Information Technology
Vellore Institute of Technology
Vellore, Tamil Nadu, India

Roberto Moro Visconti
Department of Business Administration
Universita Cattolica del Sacro Coure
Milan, Italy

Andrei Voronov
Faculty of Mathematics and Computer
    Science
University of Hagen
Hagen, Germany

Sohil Sri Mani Yeshwanth Grandhi
School of Information Technology
Vellore Institute of Technology
Vellore, Tamil Nadu, India

Juan José Choquehuanca Zevallos
University Carlos III (UC3M)
Madrid, Spain

1

Challenges in Big Data

Pothireddy Venkata Lakshmi Narayana Rao,
Pothireddy Siva Abhilash, and PS Pavan Kumar

CONTENTS

Introduction

Enormous data guarantee new levels of investigative disclosure and financial quality. What is new about Big Data and how they vary from the conventional little or medium-scale information? This paper outlines the open doors and difficulties brought by Big Data, with accentuation on the recognized elements of Big Data and measurable and computational technique and in addition registering engineering to manage them.

Background

We are entering the time of Big Data, a term that alludes to the blast of data now accessible. Such a Big Data development is driven by the way that gigantic measures of high-dimensional or unstructured information are consistently delivered and are presented in a much less "luxurious" format than they used to be. For instance, in genomics we have seen an enormous drop in costs for sequencing of an entire genome [1]. This is likewise valid in many different scientific areas, for example, online network examination, biomedical imaging, high-recurrence money transactions, investigation of reconnaissance recordings, and retail deals. The current pattern for these vast amounts of information to be delivered and stored in an inexpensive manner is likely to keep up or even quicken in the future [2]. This pattern will have a profound effect on science, designing, and business. For instance, logical advances are turning out to be increasingly information driven, and specialists will increasingly consider themselves customers of information. The monstrous measures of high-dimensional information convey both open doors and new difficulties to information examination. Substantial measurable investigations for Big Data handling are turning out to be progressively essential.

Goals and Challenges of Analyzing Big Data

What are the purposes of violation depressed Big Data? As per Fan and Lu [3], two principal objectives of high-dimensional information investigation are to create powerful strategies that can precisely anticipate the future perceptions and in the meantime gain understanding into the relationship between the elements and reactions for experimental purposes. In addition, because of the extensive specimen size, Big Data offers an ascent to two more objectives: to comprehend heterogeneity and shared traits across various subpopulations.

At the end of the day, Big Data gives guarantees for:

1. Investigating the shrouded structures of every subpopulation of the information, which is generally not possible and may even be dealt with as "exceptions" when the specimen size is small; and

2. Extricating imperative regular elements across numerous subpopulations notwithstanding the expansive individual varieties of data.

What are the difficulties of investigating Big Data? Big Data is portrayed by high dimensionality and substantial specimen size. These two elements raise three one-of-a-kind difficulties:

1. High dimensionality brings clamor gathering, spurious relationships, and coincidental homogeneity;

2. High dimensionality consolidated with vast specimen size brings additional considerations, for example, regarding substantial computational expense and algorithmic flimsiness;

3. The gigantic examples in Big Data are regularly totaled from various sources at various times, utilizing distinctive advances. This creates issues regarding heterogeneity, trial varieties, and factual predispositions and obliges us to employ more versatile and hardy methodologies.

Paradigm Shifts

To handle the troubles of Big Data, we require new quantifiable derivation and computational techniques. As an example, various standard systems that perform well for moderate test sizes don't scale to enormous amounts of data. Basically, various truthful methodologies that perform well for low-dimensional data are going up against basic troubles in separating high-dimensional data. To plot effective, truthful strategies for exploring and anticipating Big Data, we need to address Big Data issues, for instance, heterogeneity, hullabaloo gathering, spurious connections, and fortuitous endogeneity, despite changing the quantifiable precision and computational profitability.

With respect to exactness, estimation diminishment, and variable determination are critical parts in exploring high-dimensional data. We will address these disturbing, building issues. As a case in point, in a high-dimensional portrayal, Fan and Fan [4] and Pittelkow and Ghosh [5] reported that a standard course of action using all parts plays out no better than any subjective guess, due to racket gathering. This induces new regularization methods [6–10] and without question calls for self-sufficiency screening [11–13]. In addition, high dimensionality presents spurious connections between responses and arbitrary covariates, which may incite wrong truthful reasoning and false exploratory conclusions [14]. High dimensionality also give rise to adventitious endogeneity, a wonder that various irregular covariates may obviously be connected with the remaining tumults. The endogeneity makes true inclinations and causes model determination inconsistency that can lead to wrong trial exposures [15,16]. In any case, most true techniques rely upon suspicious exogenous suppositions that can't be endorsed by data (see our discussion of unplanned endogeneity region, below) [17].

New quantifiable frameworks in light of these issues are basically required. As for efficiency, Big Data convinces the headway of new computational base and data stockpiling procedures. Streamlining is consistently a mechanical assembly, not a target, for Big Data examination. Such a perspective change has provoked colossal advances on upgrades of speedy configurations that are versatile to handle huge data amounts with high dimensionality. This fabricates cross-mediations for different fields, including bits of knowledge, change, and applied mathematics. As a case in point, Donoho and Elad [18] showed that the nondeterministic polynomial–time hard (NP-hard) best subset backslide can be recast as an L1-standard rebuffed smallest-squares issue, which can be comprehended within a point procedure.

Elective figurings to animate this L1-standard rebuffed smallest-squares issues, for instance, least edge backslide [19], edge incline dive [20], coordinate drop [21,22], and iterative shrinkage-thresholding computations [23,24], are proposed. Other than limitless scale upgrade counts, Big Data in a like manner stirs the progression of majorization–minimization computations [25–27], "extensive-scale screening and little-scale streamlining" framework [28], parallel figuring strategies [29–31], and evaluated estimations that are versatile to tremendous sample sizes.

Organization of This Paper

The next section focuses on analytics to handle the increases in Big Data [32] and outlines the issue from the perspectives of science, urban planning, and social science. The salient features of the Big Data portion of this chaper clear up some unique segments of Big Data and their consequences for quantifiable conclusions. Quantifiable strategies that handle these Big Data issues are discussed in the section on impact on truthful considering [33]. The impact on enrolling base section gives an outline on a flexible figuring base for Big Data stockpiling and taking care of it. The section on the impact on computational methods covers the computational pieces of Big Data and introduces some recent advances. Finally, we present our conclusions and anticipated future directions.

Algorithms for Big Data Analytics

k-*Means*

What does it do? k-Means implies k bunches from a group of articles arranged so that the individuals from a gathering are more comparable. It is a prevalent bunch examination system for investigating a data set. What is bunch investigation? Bunch investigation is a group of calculations intended to shape gatherings such that the gathered individual data are more comparative versus nonbunch individuals. Bunches and gatherings are synonymous in the realm of group examination. Is there a case for this? Certainly, assuming we have a data set of patients. In group examination, these are called perceptions. We know different things about every patient, like age, heartbeat, pulse, VO_2(max), cholesterol, and so forth [34]. This is a vector speaking to the patient.

You can essentially think about a vector as a rundown of numbers we consider about the patient. This rundown can likewise be deciphered as directions in multidimensional space. Heartbeat can be one measurement, pulse another measurement, etc.

You may ponder, given this arrangement of vectors, how would we group together patients that have comparable age, beat, circulation strains, and so on? We need to know the best part.

k-implies determines what number of bunches you need. k-implies can deal with the rest. How does k-implies deal with the rest? k-implies has heaps of varieties to enhance for specific sorts of information. At an abnormal state, they all accomplish something like this:

1. k-implies picks foci in multidimensional space to speak to each of the k groups. These are called centroids.

2. Every patient will be nearest to one of these k centroids. They ideally will not all be nearest to the same one, so they can shape a group around their closest centroid.

3. What we have then are k bunches, and every patient is considered an individual from a group.

4. *k*-implies then finds the inside for each of the *k* groups in light of its bunch individuals (correct, utilizing the patient vectors).

5. This focus turns into the new centroid for the bunch.

6. Since the centroid is in a better place now, patients may now be nearer to different centroids. At the end of the day, they may change bunch enrollment.

7. Steps 2 to 6 are rehashed until the centroids change no more and the bunch enrollments balance out. This is called meeting.

Is it safe to say whether this is managed or unsupervised? It depends, yet most would group the *k*-implies as unsupervised. Other than determining the quantity of groups, *k*-signifies "takes in" the bunches all alone with no data about which group a perception has a place. *k*-means can be semidirected. Why use *k*-implies? I don't think many researchers will have an issue with this [35]. The key offering purpose of *k*-means is its straightforwardness. Its straightforwardness means it is for the most part quicker and more proficient than other calculations, particularly over huge data sets. It shows signs of improvement.

k-means can be utilized to prebunch an enormous data set after a more costly group investigation on the subgroups. *k*-means can likewise be utilized to quickly "play" with *k* and investigate whether there are disregarded examples or connections in the data set. It's not all smooth cruising.

Two key shortcomings of *k*-means are its vulnerability to anomalies and its vulnerability to the underlying decision of centroids. One last thing to remember is that *k*-means are intended to work on ceaseless information; one will have to run a few iterations to motivate it to chip away at discrete information [36]. Where is it utilized? A huge amount of executions for *k*-implies grouping are accessible online, through the programs Apache Mahout, Julia, R, SciPy, Weka, MATLAB, and SAS.

If decision trees and clustering do not impress you, you are going to love the next algorithm.

Classification Algorithms: k-NN

The *k*-nearest neighbor (*k*-NN) classifier is a standout among the most surely understood techniques in information mining, on account of its viability and effortlessness. Nonetheless, it does not have the versatility to oversee enormous data sets. The fundamental issues found for managing vast scales of information are runtimes and memory utilization.

Application of Big Data: A Case Study

Economics and Finance

Over the previous decade, more undertakings accepted the data-driven approach to management that was more centered around organizations, decreasing risks and improving execution. The undertakings are executing specific data examination tasks to accumulate, store, regulate, and separate tremendous data sets to the extent of sources to perceive key business bits of learning that can be handled to support better essential initiatives. As a case in point, available cash-related data sources join stock costs, coin, and subordinate trades, trade records, high-repeat trades, unstructured news and compositions, clients' sureness, and business sentiments secured in Web system administration and the Web, among others. Separating these immense data sets helps to measure a firm's perils and, furthermore, methodical threats. It requires specialists who are familiar with advanced real frameworks in a portfolio organization system, securities heading, prohibitive trading, cash-related directing, and peril organization [37].

Inspecting a limitless leading body of financial and budgetary data is trying. As a case in point, a basic contraption in inspecting the joint advancement of the macroeconomics time game plan, the standard vector autoregressive (VAR) consolidates nearly 10 variables, given the way that the amount of parameters creates quadratic partners with the degree of the model. In any case, nowadays econometricians need to examine multivariate time plans with more than numerous variables. Merging all information into the VAR model will achieve great overfitting and unpleasant conjecture execution. One plan is to rely on upon sparsity suppositions, under which new quantifiable gadgets have been made [38,39]. Another important topic is portfolio upgrade and threat organization [40,41]. Regarding this issue, assessing the covariance and opposite covariance systems of the benefits of the points of interest in the portfolio are a crucial part, except that we have 1,000 stocks to be supervised. There are 500 covariance parameters to be surveyed [42]. Despite the likelihood that we could evaluate each individual parameter definitely, the cumulated screw up of the whole grid estimation can be broadly under system measures. This requires new quantifiable procedures. It could not be any more self-evident, for occurrence [43–49], on evaluating immense covariance systems and their regressive nature.

Other Applications

Big Data has different diverse applications. Taking casual group data examination for an exampl, huge measures of social gathering information are being made by Twitter, Facebook, LinkedIn, and YouTube. These data reveal different individuals' qualities and have been mishandled in various fields. In a like manner, Web systems administration and internet contain a massive measure of information on customer preferences and confidences [50], driving money-related perspectives markers, business cycles, political dispositions, and the financial and social states of an overall population. It is predicted that the casual group data will continue to impact and be abused for some new applications. A couple of other new applications that are getting the opportunity to be possible in the Big Data era include the following:

1. Personalized organizations. With more individual data accumulated, business endeavors can give tweaked organizations information regarding individual preferences. As a case in point, Target (a retailing association in the United States) can expect a customer's needs by looking at that person's accumulated trade records.

2. Internet security. Right when a framework-based strike happens, undeniable data on framework development may allow us to gainfully recognize the source and centers of the ambush.

3. Personalized medicine. Additional satisfaction-associated limits, for example, individual subnuclear qualities, human activities, human affinities, and environmental

components, are as of now available. Using these bits of information, it is possible to dissect an individual's disease [51] and select individualized drugs.

4. Digital humanities. Nowadays, various records are being digitized. For example, Google has checked countless and recognized about every word in every one of all published books. This produces an enormous amount of data and engages subjects in the humanities, for instance, mapping the transportation structure in ancient Rome, envisioning the money-related relationships in Chinese history, a focus on how typical vernaculars are created after some time, or separating unquestionable events.

Salient Features of Big Data

Big Data makes segments stand out that are not shared by the routine data sets. These components stance basic troubles to data examination and goad the progression of new true systems. Not at all like standard data sets, where the example size is customarily greater than the estimation, Big Data is depicted by a colossal illustration size and high dimensionality. To begin with, we discuss here the impact of boundless size on perception heterogeneity: from one perspective [52], tremendous example size grants us to uncover covered plans associated with little subpopulations and feeble shared characteristic over the whole mass of data. Of course, showing the trademark heterogeneity of Big Data requires more progressed quantifiable strategies. In addition, we discuss a couple of exceptional miracles associated with high dimensionality, including disturbance accumulation, spurious relationship, and circumstantial endogeneity. These fascinating components make traditional quantifiable methodologies off base. Shockingly, most high-dimensional quantifiable frameworks address simple fuss-accumulating and spurious association issues, but not unplanned endogeneity. They rely on upon erogeneity suspicions that consistently cannot be endorsed by assembled data, due to unplanned endogeneity.

Heterogeneity

Big Data is routinely created through conglomeration from various data sources contrasting with different subpopulations. Each subpopulation may show some wonderful parts not shared by others [53]. In built-up settings where the example size is small or moderate, data centers from small subpopulations are generally delegated exemptions, and it is hard to proficiently show them on account of lacking observations. In any case, in the Big Data time frame, the significant case size engages us to better understand heterogeneity, uncovering knowledge toward concentrates, for instance, researching the relationship between certain covariates (e.g., qualities or single-nucleotide polymorphisms [SNPs]) and unprecedented results (e.g., unprecedented contaminations or illnesses in little masses) and understanding why certain medications (e.g., chemotherapy) provide an advantage to a subpopulation and harm another subpopulation. To better demonstrate this point, we exhibit this with a mix model for the people:

$$\lambda_1 \, p_1 \, (y; \theta_1(x)) + \cdots + \lambda_m \, p_m \, (y; \theta_m(x))$$

where $\lambda j \geq 0$ addresses the degree of jth subpublic, p j y; θ j (x) is the likelihood movement of the response of jth submass accepted that the covariates x with θ j (x) as the parameter vector. Eventually, various subpopulations are every so often viewed, i.e., λj is small. Exactly when the case size n is moderate, $n\lambda j$ can be small, making it infeasible that it affects the covariate-subordinate parameters θ j (x) in light of the nonattendance of information. In any case, in light of the fact that Big Data is portrayed by a considerable illustration size, n, the example size $n\lambda j$ for the jth subpopulation can be unobtrusively broad, paying little respect to the likelihood that λj is small [54]. This enables us to more absolutely understand about the subpopulation parameters θ j (·). Essentially, the purpose of inclination brought by Big Data is to understand the heterogeneity of subpopulations, for instance, the upsides of certain modified treatments, which are infeasible when the sample size is small or moderate.

Big Data also allows us to reveal slight shared qualities across whole masses, due to tremendous illustration sizes. As a case in point, the benefit for the heart of one refreshment of red wine each night can be difficult to estimate without an incomprehensible case size. Basically, prosperity risks to presentation of certain normal components must be more convincingly surveyed when the illustration sizes are adequately broad [55]. More than the previously expressed central focuses, the heterogeneity of Big Data in a like manner brings basic challenges to quantifiable derivation. Reasoning the mix model in the above equation for gigantic data sets requires utilization of quantifiable and computational procedures. With low-power estimations, standard frameworks, for instance, the expectation–maximization computation for constrained mix models can be associated. In high-power estimations, nevertheless, we need to purposely regularize the evaluation method to refrain from overfitting or upheaval of the total data set and to devise extraordinary computations.

Noise Accumulation

Looking at Big Data obliges us to in the meantime gauge or test various parameters. Estimation errors accumulate (noise accumulation) when a decision or gauge standard depends upon innumerable parameters. The effect of such noise is especially genuine in high-power estimations and may even order the honest-to-goodness signs. It is normally dealt with by the sparsity suspicion [2]. Take a high-dimensional plan for an event [56]. A poor gathering is a result of the nearness of various weak segments that do not add to the diminishing of request errors [4]. For delineation, we consider a gathering issue where the data are from two classes:

$$X1,\ldots,Xn \sim Nd\,(\mu1,Id) \text{ and } Y1,\ldots,Yn \sim Nd\,(\mu2,Id)$$

This groups another recognition $Z \in Rd$ into either the first or the modest. To diagram the impact of commotion conglomeration in this portrayal, we used $n = 100$ and then d = 1,000. We set $\mu1$ to 0 and $\mu2$ to remain insufficient, i.e., simply the underlying 10 areas of $\mu2$ were nonzero with a value 3 and the dissimilar units were 0. Figure 1.1 plots the underlying two first sections by using the fundamental $m = 2$, 40, or 200 components and the whole 1,000 components. As shown in these plots, when $m = 2$, we obtain high discriminative power. Regardless, the discriminative power ends up being low when m is excessively broad, in light of noise accumulation. The underlying 10 highlights add to groupings, and the remaining components do not. In this way, when m is >10, the procedure does not receive any additional banners, yet the hoard uproars: the greater the m, the more the total

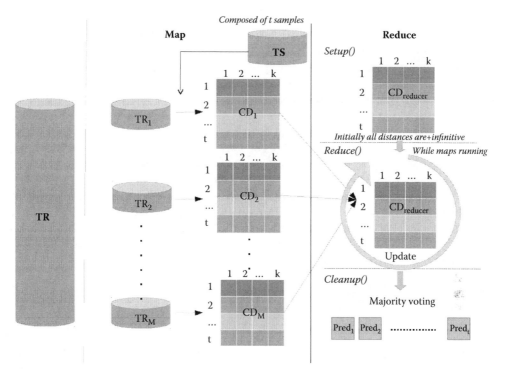

FIGURE 1.1
Flowchart of the proposed MR-kNN algorithm.

tumult increases, which separates the course of action system with dimensionality. For m = 40, the gathered signs reimburse the assembled tumult, so that the underlying two fundamental fragments still have awesome discriminative power. At whatever point m = 200, the amassed confusion surpasses the sign increases. The above examination rouses the utilization of lacking models and variable decision to beat the effect of noice accumulating. Case in point, in the game plan model [2], instead of using every one of the segments, we could pick a subset of components which fulfill the best banner-to-confusion extent [57]. Such a meager model gives more improved gathering execution. By the day's end, variable decision plays a crucial part in overcoming clatter, gathering all together and backslide conjecture. In any case, variable willpower in tall approximations is trying a straight result of spurious association, incidental endogeneity, heterogeneity, and estimation botches.

Spurious Correlation

High dimensionality in a like manner brings spurious association, implying the way that various uncorrelated unpredictable variables may have high example connections in high estimations. A spurious relationship may achieve false legitimate revelations and wrong quantifiable inductions [58]. Consider the issue of evaluating the coefficient vector β of an immediate model:

$$y = X\beta + \mathrm{Var}() = \sigma 2\mathrm{Id}[x1, \ldots, xn]T$$

∈Rn×d addresses the design cross-section, ∈Rn addresses a free self-assertive noise vector, and Id is the d × d character matrix. To adjust to the tumult gathering issue, when the estimation d is like or greater than the case size n, it is renowned to acknowledge that selective somewhat number of variables add to the response, i.e., β is a lacking vector. Under this sparsity assumption, variable decision can be directed to keep up a key separation from clatter accumulating, improve the execution of figure, and redesign the interpretability of the model with closefisted demonstration. In high approximations, notwithstanding for a perfect as clear as (3), variable determination is attempting a result of the proximity of spurious association. In particular, Ref. [11] exhibited that, when the dimensionality is high, the imperative variables can be especially compared with a couple of spurious variables which are deductively unimportant [59]. We consider an essential case to demonstrate this wonder. Let x1,..., xn be without n impression of a d-dimensional Gaussian unpredictable vector X = (X1,..., Xd)T ~Nd (0, Id). We again and again copy the data with n = 60 and d = 800 and 6,400 for 1,000 times. Figure 1.2 exhibits the observational transport of the most compelling incomparable case relationship coefficient between the essential variable with the staying ones described as follows:

$$r = \max_{j \geq 2} \left| \text{Corr } X1, X_j \right|$$

Where Corr (X1, Xj) is the example relationship amongst the variables X1 and Xj. We comprehend that the best aggregate illustration association gets the chance to be higher as dimensionality additions. Additionally, we can enlist the most compelling aggregate different relationship amongst X1 and straight mixes of a couple of pointless spurious variables:

$$R = \max_{|S| = 4} \max_{\{\beta_j\}} 4_j = 1 \, \text{Corr}(X1, j \in S\beta_j X_j)$$

This equation plots the definite scattering of the most great incomparable illustration association coefficient between X1 and j ∈ SβjXj, where S is any size four subset of {2,..., d} and βj is the scarcest squares backslide coefficient of Xj while backsliding X1 on {Xj}j ∈ S. Afresh, we see that in spite of the way that X1 is totally free of X2,..., Xd, the association

Uml diagrams

Use case diagram:

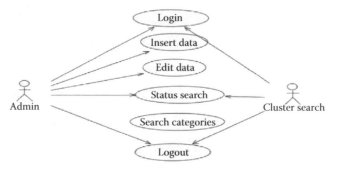

FIGURE 1.2
Data Mining with Big Data.

amongst X1 and the closest direct blend of any four variables of {Xj}j = 1 to X1 can be high. We imply [14] about more theoretical results on depicting the solicitations of r.

The spurious association has basic impact on variable decision and may provoke false exploratory exposures. Let XS = (X j) j∈S be the sub-discretionary vector recorded by S and let S be the picked set that has the higher spurious association with X1. For example, when n = 60 and d = 6,400, we see that X1 is in every way that really matters unclear from X S for a set S with |S| = 4. If X1 addresses the expression level of a quality that is accountable for a disease, we can't remember it from the other four qualities in S that have an equivalent judicious power, notwithstanding the way that they are deductively unimportant.

Other than variable decision, spurious association may in like manner incite wrong quantifiable finding. We illuminate this by considering again the same straight model as in (3). Here we might need to assess the standard bumble σ of the remaining, which is prominently highlighted in quantifiable deductions of backslide coefficients, model determination, honesty of-fit test and immaterial backslide. Allow S to be an arrangement of chose flexible and P S be the figure matrix on the segment space of X S. The standard waiting change estimator, in perspective of the picked variables, is

$$\sigma2 = yT (In - PS)y\ n-|S|.$$

The ideal is right. All things considered, the situation is absolutely particular when the variables are picked in light of data. In particular, Ref. [14] showed that when there are various spurious variables, σ2 is really considered little, which drives further to wrong verifiable inductions including model determination or vitality tests, and false consistent revelations, for instance, finding inaccurately qualities for nuclear instruments. They also propose a refitted cross-acknowledgment methodology to contrast the issue.

Coincidental Endogeneity

Coincidental endogeneity is another unpretentious issue raised by high dimensionality. In a relapse setting Y = dj = 1 βj X j + ε, the term "endogeneity" implies that a few indicators {Xj} connect with the lingering commotion ε. The ordinary inadequate model expect is

$$Y = j\ βj\ X\ j + ε,\ \text{and } E\ (εX\ j) = 0 \text{ for } j = 1,\ldots, d,$$

with a little set S = {j: βj = 0}. The exogenous supposition in (7) that the leftover clamor ε is uncorrelated with every one of the indicators is essential for legitimacy of most existing measurable systems, including variable choice consistency. In spite of the fact that this suspicion looks honest, it is anything but difficult to be damaged in high measurements, as some of variables {Xj} are of course related to ε, making most high-dimensional strategies factually invalid. To clarify the endogeneity issue in more detail, assume that obscure to us, the reaction Y is identified with three covariates as takes after:

$$Y = X1 + X2 + X3 + ε,\ \text{with } Eε\ X\ j = 0, \text{ for } j = 1, 2, 3.$$

In the information-gathering stage, we don't have the foggiest idea about the genuine model, and in this way gather however many covariates that are conceivably identified with Y as could be allowed, as we would like to incorporate all individuals in S in (7). By the way, some of those Xjs (for j = 1, 2, 3) may be associated with the remaining clamor ε. This negates the exogenous demonstrating suspicion in (7). Indeed, the more covariates that are gathered or measured, the harder it is to fulfill this suspicion. Dissimilar to spurious connections, coincidental endogeneity alludes to the honest-to-goodness presence of relationships between variables inadvertently, both because of high dimensionality.

The previous is practically equivalent to discovering that two persons resemble each; however, they have no hereditary connection. The latter is like finding an associate, as you both are effortlessly happening in a major city. All the more by and large, endogeneity happens as a consequence of choice predispositions, estimation blunders, and excluded variables. These marvels emerge much of the time in the investigation of Big Data, essentially because of two reasons: With the advantage of new high-throughput estimation methods, researchers can and tend to gather whatever amount mechanisms as could be predictable below the conditions. This in like manner expands the likelihood that some of them may be associated with the lingering clamor, by the way. Big Data is generally amassed from numerous sources with possibly diverse information-creating plans. This builds the likelihood of determination inclination and estimation mistakes, which additionally cause potential accidental endogeneity.

Whether coincidental endogeneity shows up in genuine datasets and by what method might we test it by and by? We consider a genomics study in which 148 microarray tests are downloaded from the GEO database and Array Express. These specimens are made under the Affymetrix HGU1 [60] a stage for human subjects with prostate malignancy. The acquired data set contains 22,283 tests, comparing 12,719 qualities. In this case, we are keen on the quality named discoid in area receptor family, part 1 (abridged as DDR1). DDR1 encodes receptor tyrosine kinases, which assume an imperative part in the correspondence of cells with their microenvironment. DDR1 is known not exceedingly with prostate tumors, and we wish to study its relationship with different qualities in patients with prostate malignancy. We took the quality articulations of DDR1 as the reaction variable Y and the outflows of all the remaining 12,718 qualities as pointers. The leftward panel of Figure 1.3 shows the investigational circulation of the connections between the reaction and individual indicators.

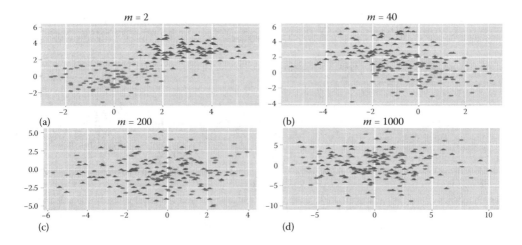

FIGURE 1.3
Scatter plots for projection of the observed data (n = 100 from each class) on to the first two principal components of the best m-dimensional selected feature space. A projected data with the filled circle indicates the first and the filled triangle indicates the second class.

To show the presence of endogeneity, we fit an L1-punished minimum squares relapse (Lasso) on the information, and the punishment is naturally chosen by means of 10-fold cross-acceptance (37 qualities are chosen). Whether refit a standard slightest-squares relapse on the chose model to ascertain the leftover vector. In the right board of Figure 1.3, we plot the exact conveyance of the relationships between the indicators and the residuals. We see the remaining commotion is very closely associated with numerous indicators. To ensure these connections are not absolutely brought about by a spurious relationship, we present an invalid dispersion of the spurious connections by arbitrarily permuting the requests of columns in the outline grid, such that the indicators are in reality free of the lingering commotion. By looking at the two disseminations, we see that the dispersion of connections among indicators and lingering clamor on the crude information has a heavier tail than that on the permuted information. This outcome gives stark confirmation of endogeneity in the information. The above talk demonstrates that coincidental endogeneity is prone to happen in Big Data. The issue of managing endogenous variables is not surely new in high-dimensional measurements. What is the result of this endogeneity? Ref. [16] demonstrated that endogeneity causes irregularity in model choice. Specifically, they gave intensive investigation to delineate the effect of endogeneity on high-dimensional factual induction and proposed elective strategies to lead direct relapse with consistency ensured under weaker conditions. See likewise the accompanying segment.

Impact on Statistical Thinking

As discussed in the previous section, huge specimen size and high dimensionality bring heterogeneity, clamor collection, spurious connection, and accidental endogeneity. These elements of Big Data make customary measurable techniques invalid. In this segment, we present new factual strategies that can deal with these difficulties. To handle the commotion-gathering issue, we accept that the model parameter β as in (3) is meager. The traditional model determination hypothesis proposes to pick a parameter vector β that minimizes the negative punished semiprobability:

$$-QL(\beta) + \lambda 0$$

where QL(β) is the semiprobability of β and $\cdot$ 0 speaks to the L0 pseudostandard (i.e., the quantity of nonzero sections in a vector). Here, $\lambda > 0$ is a regularization parameter that controls the predisposition difference tradeoff. The answer for the streamlining issue in (8) has decent factual properties. Nonetheless, it is basically combinatorics improvement and does not scale to expansive scale issues. The estimator in (8) can be stretched out to a more broad structure

$$n(\beta) + d \ j = 1 \ P \ \lambda, \gamma \ (\beta j)$$

where the term n(β) processes the heavens of the appropriateness of the perfect with limit

$$\beta \text{ and } dj = 1 \ P \ \lambda, \gamma \ (\beta j)$$

is a sparsity-actuating punishment that empowers sparsity, in which λ is again the tuning parameter that controls the predisposition difference tradeoff and γ is a conceivable calibrate parameter which controls the level of concavity of the punishment capacity [8]. Famous decisions of the punishment capacity Pλ, γ ($\cdot$) incorporate the hard-thresholding punishment, softthresholding punishment [6], easily cut pardon deviation (SCAD) [8] and mini-max concavity punishment (MCP) [10]. Figure 1.4 envisions these punishment capacities for $\lambda = 1$. We see that all punishment capacities are collapsed sunken, yet the softthresholding (L1-) punishment is additionally raised. The parameter γ in SCAD and MCP controls the level of concavity. From Figure 1.4, we see that a littler estimation of γ results in more inward punishments. At the point when γ gets to be bigger, SCAD and MCP focalize to the delicate thresholding punishment. MCP is a speculation of the hard-thresholding punishment which relates to y = 1.

In what manner might we pick among these punishment capacities? In applications, we prescribe to utilize either SCAD or MCP thresholding, since they join the benefits of both hard- and delicate-thresholding administrators. Numerous effective calculations have been proposed for taking care of the enhancement issue in (9) with the above four punishments (see the section on "Effect on processing infrastructure"). The punished semiprobability estimator (9) is somewhat strange. A firmly related technique is the sparsest arrangement in the high certainty set, presented in the late book section in Ref. [17], which has a much better measurable instinct. It is for the most part a material rule that isolates the information, data, and the sparsity supposition. Assume that the information data are abridged by the capacity n (β) in (9). This can be a probability, semiprobability, or misfortune capacity. The underlying parameter vector $\beta0$ more often than not fulfills ($\beta0$) = 0, where ($\cdot$) is the angle vector of the normal misfortune capacity (β) = E n (β). In this manner, a characteristic certainty set for $\beta0$ is

$$Cn = \{\beta \in Rd: n (\beta) \infty \le \gamma n\},$$

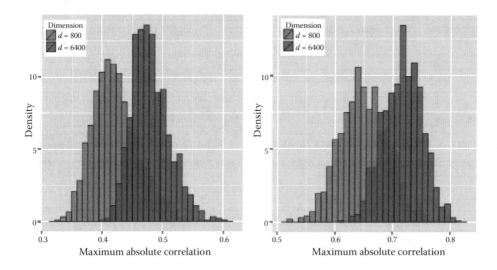

FIGURE 1.4
Illustration of spurious correlation. (Left) Distribution of the Maximum absolute sample correlation coefficients between X1 and {Xi}j $\ne$ 1. (Right) Distribution of the maximum absolute sample correlation between X1 and the closest linear projections of any four members of {Xj}i $\ne$ 1 to X1. Here the dimension *d* is 800 and 6400, the sample size n is 60. The result is based on 1,000 situations.

anywhere $\cdot\infty$ is the $L\infty$ standard of a direction and γ n is selected, so that we have sureness equal to at least $1 - \delta n$, specifically:

$$P(\beta 0 \in Cn) = P\{n\ (\beta 0) \infty \le \gamma n\} \ge 1 - \delta n$$

The certainty set Cn is called the high-certainty set subsequent to $\delta n \to 0$. In principle, we can take any standard in developing the high-certainty set. We decide on the $L\infty$ standard, as it creates a curved certainty set Cn when n(·) is raised. The high-certainty set is an outline of the data we have for the parameter vector $\beta 0$. It is not useful in high-dimensional space. Take, for instance, the straight model (3) with the quadratic misfortune n $(\beta) = y - X\beta$ 22. The high-certainty set is then

$$Cn = \{\beta \in Rd: XT\ (y - X\beta)\ \infty \le \gamma n\}$$

where we take $\gamma n \ge XT\varepsilon\ \infty$, so that $\delta n = 0$. On the off chance that furthermore $\beta 0$ is thought to be inadequate, then a characteristic arrangement is the convergence of these two bits of data, to be specific, finding the sparsest arrangement in the high-certainty set:

$$\min \beta \in Cn\ \beta 1 = \min n\ (\beta) \infty \le \gamma n\ \beta 1.$$

This is a raised enhancement issue when (·) is arched. For the direct model with the quadratic misfortune, it diminishes to the Dantzig selector [9].

There are numerous adaptabilities in characterizing the sparsest arrangement in the high-certainty set. Most importantly, we have a decision of the misfortune capacity n(·). We can respect n $(\beta) = 0$ as the estimation conditions and characterize specifically the high-certainty set (10) from the estimation conditions. Furthermore, we have numerous approaches to quantify the sparsity. For instance, we can utilize a weighted L1 standard to quantify the sparsity of β in (12). By appropriate decisions of assessing conditions in (10) and measure of sparsity in (12), the creators of [17] demonstrated that numerous helpful techniques can be viewed as the sparsest arrangement in the high certainty set.

For instance, CLIME for evaluating inadequate exactness grid in both the Gaussian realistic model and the direct programming discriminant principle for meager high-dimensional arrangement is the sparsest arrangement in the high-certainty set. At last, the thought is relevant to the issues with estimation mistakes or even endogeneity. For this situation, the high-certainty set will be characterized as needs be to oblige the estimation blunders or endogeneity.

Independence Screening

An effective variable screening technique based on marginal screening has been proposed by the authors of Ref. [11]. They aimed at handling ultrahigh-dimensional data for which the aforementioned penalized quasilikelihood estimators become computationally infeasible. For such cases, the authors of Ref. [11] proposed to first use marginal regression to screen variables, reducing the original large-scale problem to a moderate-scale statistical problem, so that more sophisticated methods for variable selection could be applied. The proposed method, named sure independence screening, is computationally very attractive. It has been shown to possess a sure screening property and to have some theoretical advantages over Lasso [13]. There are two main ideas of sure independent screening: (i) it uses the marginal contribution of a covariate to probe its importance in the joint model; (ii) instead of selecting the most important variables, it aims at removing variables that are not important. For example, assuming each covariate has been standardized, we denote $\beta M\ j$ the estimated regression coefficient in a univariate regression model. The set of covariates that survive the marginal screening is defined as

$$S = \{j : |\beta M\ j| \geq \delta\}$$

for a given edge δ. One can likewise gauge the significance of a covariate Xj by utilizing its abnormality diminishment. For the slightest-squares issue, both techniques lessen to the positioning significance of indicators by utilizing the extents of their minimal connections with the reaction Y. Ref. [11] gave conditions under which beyond any doubt screening property can be set up and false error rates are controlled. Since the computational multifaceted nature of beyond any doubt screening scales directly with the issue measure, the possibility of beyond any doubt screening is extremely viable in the emotional lessening of the computational weight of Big Data investigations. It has been shown in different setting.

Autonomous screening has never inspected the multivariate impact of variables on the reaction variable, nor has it utilized the covariance grid of variables. An expansion of this is to utilize multivariate screening, which looks at the commitments of little gatherings of variables together. This permits us to analyze the collaboration of little gatherings of variables to the reaction variable. Be that as it may, the bivariate screening as of now includes $O(d2)$ submodels, which can be restrictive in the calculation. Another conceivable expansion is to create restrictive screening systems, which rank variables as per their contingent commitments given an arrangement of variables.

Dealing with Incidental Endogeneity

Big Data is inclined to accidental endogeneity that makes the most prevalent regularization techniques invalid. Its needs are essential to create strategies that can deal with endogeneity in high measurements. In particular, let us consider the high-dimensional straight-relapse model (7). Ref. [16] demonstrated that for any punished estimators to be variable determination reliable, an essential condition is:

$$E(\varepsilon X\ j) = 0 \text{ for } j = 1, \ldots, d.$$

As examined in the section on "Notable principles of Big Data," the disorder in (14) is excessively prohibitive for true applications. Letting $S = \{j : \beta j = 0\}$ be the arrangement of critical variables, with nonvanishing parts in β, a more practical model presumption ought to be:

$$E(\varepsilon \,|\, \{X\ j\}\ j \in S) = E\ Y - j \in S\ \beta j\ X\ j\ |\ \{X\ j\}\ j \in S = 0.$$

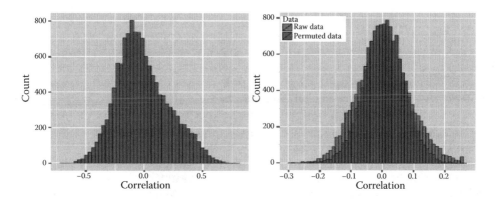

FIGURE 1.5
Illustration of incidental endogeneity on a microarray gene expression data. Left panel. The distribution of the sample correlation Corr (Xj, Y) j = 1,....12718). Right panel. The distribution of the sample correlation Corr (Xj, €). Here € represents the residual noise after the Lasso fit. We provide the distributors of the sample correlations using both the raw data and permuted data.

In Ref. [16], the authors considered a significantly weaker variant of equation (15), called the overdistinguishing proof condition. For example:

$$E\varepsilon X j = 0 \text{ and } E\varepsilon X2j = 0 \text{ for } j \in S.$$

Under condition of equation (16), Ref. [16] demonstrated that the traditional punished minimum-squares strategies, for example, Lasso, SCAD, and MCP, are no steadier. Rather, the authors presented the centered summed-up strategies for minutes (FGMMs) by using the overrecognizable proof conditions and demonstrated that the FGMM reliably chose the arrangement of variables S. We have not delved into the specialized points of interest here; however, we can delineate this by an illustration.

We keep on exploring the quality expression information in the section on "Accidental endogeneity." We again regard quality DDR1 as a reaction and different qualities as indicators, and we apply the FGMM rather than Lasso. By cross-acceptance, the FGMM chooses 18 qualities. The left board of Figure 1.5 demonstrates the appropriation of the example, connections between the qualities Xj(j = 1,..., 12718), and the residuals ε after the FGMM fit. Here, we find that numerous connections are nonzero; however, it does not make a difference, since we require just (16). To check (16), the right board of Figure 1.5 demonstrates the conveyance of the example relationships between the 18 chosen qualities (and their squares) and the residuals. The example influences amid the selected qualities and residuals are zero, and the example relationships Amongst the shaped covariates and residuals are slight. In this way, the demonstrating suspicion is reliable to our model diagnostics.

Impact on Computing Infrastructure

The huge example size of Big Data on a very basic level difficulties the conventional registering base. In numerous applications, we have to investigate web scale information containing billions or even trillions of information focuses, which even makes a straight go of the entire dataset unreasonably expensive. Furthermore, such information could be exceptionally dynamic and infeasible to be put away in a concentrated database.

The major way to deal with store and process such information is to partition and win. The thought is to parcel a vast issue into more tractable and autonomous sub issues. Every sub issue is handled in parallel by various preparing units. Middle of the road results from every individual laborer are then joined to yield the last yield. In little scale, such gap and-vanquish worldview can be executed either by multi-center figuring or lattice registering. In any case, in substantial scale, it postures crucial difficulties in figuring framework. For instance, when a large number of PCs are associated with scale out to expansive registering errands, it is entirely likely a few PCs may kick the bucket amid the figuring. Furthermore, given a vast registering assignment, we need to appropriate it equally to numerous PCs and make the workload adjusted. Outlining substantial scale, highly versatile and shortcoming tolerant registering frameworks is to a great degree testing and inspires the result of new and solid figuring base that backings enormously parallel information stockpiling and preparing. In this segment, we take Hadoop as a case to present fundamental programming and programming foundation for Big Data preparing.

Hadoop is a Java-based programming structure for circulating information administration and preparing. It contains an arrangement of open source libraries for conveyed processing utilizing the Map Reduce programming model and its own dispersed document framework called HDFS. Hadoop consequently encourages adaptability and takes considerations of recognizing and taking care of disappointments. Center Hadoop has two key segments: Core Hadoop = Hadoop conveyed record framework (HDFS)+MapReduce HDFS is a self-mending, high-data transmission, grouped capacity document framework, and MapReduce is a circulated programming model created by Google.

We dash with clarifying HDFS and MapReduce in the accompanying two subsections. Other than these two key parts, a common Hadoop discharge contains numerous different segments. For instance, as appears in Figure 1.6, Cloudera's open-source Hadoop

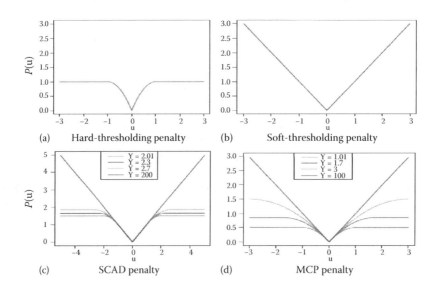

FIGURE 1.6
Visualization of the penalty functions. λ = 1. For SCAD and MCP. Different values of γ are chosen as shown in graphs.

circulation additionally incorporates HBase, Hive, Pig, Oozie, Flume and Sqoop. More insights about these additional parts are given in the online Cloudera specialized records. In the wake of presenting the Hadoop, we additionally quickly clarify the ideas of distributed computing in the "Distributed computing" area.

Hadoop dispersed document framework HDFS is a conveyed record framework intended to have and give high-throughput access to extensive datasets which are needlessly put away over various machines. Specifically, it guarantees Big Data's strength to disappointment and high accessibility to parallel applications.

As an inspiring application, assume we have an extensive information document containing billions of records, and we need to question this record as often as possible. On the off chance that numerous questions are submitted at the same time (e.g., the Google internet searcher), the typical document framework is not reasonable because of the I/O limit. HDFS tackles this issue by separating a huge document into little pieces and store them in various machines.

Every machine is known as a Data Node. Not at all like most piece organized document frameworks which use square size in HDFS is 64 MB, which permits HDFS to decrease the measure of metadata stockpiling required per record. Moreover, HDFS takes into consideration quick spilling peruses of information by keeping a lot of information successively laid out on the hard plate. The principle tradeoff of this choice is that HDFS anticipates that the information will be perused consecutively (rather than being perused in an arbitrary access design).

The data in HDFS can be accessed via a "write once and read many" approach. The metadata structures (e.g., the file names and directories) are allowed to be simultaneously modified by many clients. It is important that this meta information is always synchronized and stored reliably. All the metadata is maintained by a single machine, called the Name Node. Because of the relatively low amount of metadata per file (it only tracks file names, permissions and the locations of each block of each file), all such information can be stored in the main memory of the Name Node machine, allowing fast access to the metadata. An illustration of the whole HDFS architecture is provided in Figure 1.7.

To access or manipulate a data file, a client contacts the Name Node and retrieves a list of locations for the blocks that comprise the file. These locations identify the Data Nodes which hold each block. Clients then read file data directly from the Data Node servers, possibly in parallel. The Name Node is not directly involved in this bulk data transfer, keeping its working load to a minimum. HDFS has a built in redundancy and replication feature which secures that any failure of individual machines can be recovered without any loss of data (e.g., each Data Node has three copies by default). The HDFS automatically balances its load whenever a new Data Node is added to the cluster. We also need to safely store the Name Node information by creating multiple redundant systems, which allows the important metadata of the file system be recovered even if the Name Node itself crashes.

Literature Review

MapReduce

The information in HDFS can be gotten to through a "compose once and read numerous" methodology. The metadata structures (e.g., the record names and registries) are permitted to be at the same time changed by numerous customers. It is imperative that this Metadata is constantly synchronized and put away dependably. All the metadata is kept up by a solitary machine, called the Name Node. On account of the moderately low measure of metadata per record (it just tracks document names, consents and the areas of every piece of every document), all such data can be put away in the principle memory of the Name Node machine, permitting quick access to the metadata. A representation of the entire HDFS engineering is given in Figure 1.7.

To get to or control an information document, a customer contacts the Name Node and recovers a rundown of the areas for the hinders that involve the record. These areas recognize the Data Nodes which hold every piece. Customers then read record information specifically from the Data Node servers, perhaps in parallel.

The Name Node is not specifically included in this mass information exchange, keeping its working burden to a base. HDFS has a built-in excess and replication highlight which secures that any disappointment of individual machines can be recouped with no loss of information (e.g., every Data Node has three duplicates naturally).

The HDFS naturally adjusts its heap at whatever point another Data Node is added to the bunch. We likewise need to securely store the Name Node data by making different excess frameworks, which permits the vital metadata of the record framework be recuperated regardless of the possibility that the Name Node itself crashes.

MapReduce is a programming model for preparing expansive datasets in a parallel design. We utilize a case to clarify how MapReduce functions. Assume we are given an image succession (e.g., "ATGCCAATCGATGGGACTCC"), and the undertaking is to compose a project that tallies the quantity of every image. The most straightforward thought is to peruse an image, include it into a hash table with key as the image and set quality to its number of events. On the off chance that the image is not in the hash table yet, then include the image as another key to the hash and set the comparing worth to 1.

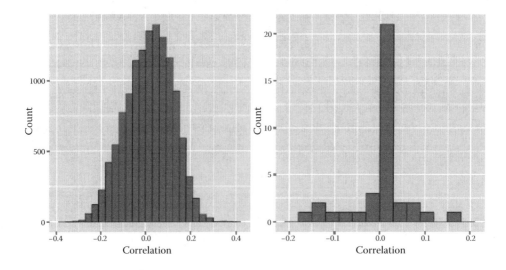

FIGURE 1.7
Diagnostics of the modeling assumptions of the FGMM on a micro arry gene expression data. Left Panel: Distribution of the sample correlations Corr(X_j, ε)($j = 1,\ldots\ldots.12,718$). Right Panel: Distribution of the sample correlations Corr(X_j, ε) and Corr($X2_j$, ε) for only 18 selected genes. Here ε represents the residual noise after the FGMM fit.

In the event that the image is as of now in the hash table, then expand the worth by 1. This project keeps running in a serial style and the time unpredictability scales straightly with the length of the image grouping.

Everything looks straightforward as such. Be that as it may, envision if rather than a basic grouping, we have to include the quantity of images the entire genomes of numerous organic subjects. Serial preparing of such an enormous measure of data is tedious.

In this way, the inquiry is by what method we would be able to utilize parallel preparing units speed up the calculation.

The option of Chart Decrease is defined in Figure 1.8. We at first split the first succession into a few records (e.g., two records in this case). We further split every document into a few subsequences (e.g., two subsequences for this situation) and "guide" the quantity of every image in every subsequence. The yields of the mapper are (vital, esteem)-sets. We then assemble all yield set of the mappers with the same key. At long last, we utilize a "lessen" capacity to join the qualities for every key. This gives the wanted yield:

$$\# A = 5, \# T = 4, \# G = 5, \# C = 6.$$

The HadoopMapReduce contains three phases, which are recorded as takes after.

In the first place stage: mapping. The main phase of a MapReduce system is called mapping. At this stage, a rundown of information components is given to a "mapper" capacity to be changed into (key, value)-sets. For instance, in the above image numbering issue, the mapper work just changes every image in the pair (image, 1). The mapper capacity does not change the info information, but rather just returns another yield list. Middle of the road stages: rearranging and sorting. After the mapping organize, the system trades the middle of the road yields from the mapping stage to various "reducers." This procedure is called rearranging. An alternate subset of the halfway key space is doled out to each decrease hub. These subsets (known asc "segments") are the inputs to the following lessening step. Every guide errand may send (key, esteem)-sets to any segment. All set with the same key are constantly gathered together on the same reducer paying little respect to which mappers they are originating from. Every reducer may handle a few arrangements of sets with various keys. For this situation, distinctive keys on a solitary hub are naturally sorted before they are encouraged into the following lessening step.

Last stage: lessening. In the last decreasing stage, an occasion of a client gave code is called for every key in the allotment relegated to a reducer. The inputs are a key and an

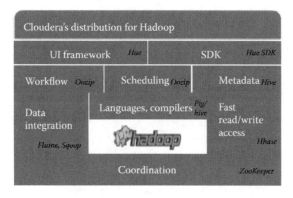

FIGURE 1.8
An illustration of Cloudera's open source Hadoop distribution.

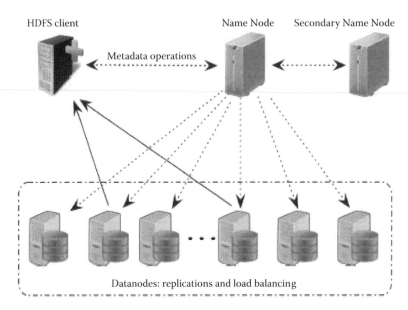

HDFS client   Name Node   Secondary Name Node

Metadata operations

Datanodes: replications and load balancing

FIGURE 1.9
An illustration of the HDFS architecture.

iterator over every one of the qualities connected with the key. These qualities returned by the iterator could be in an unclear request. Specifically, we have one yield document for every executed lessen undertaking. The HadoopMapReduce expands on the HDFS and acquires all the adaptations to non-critical failure properties of HDFS. When all is said in done, Hadoop is sent on huge scale groups. One illustration appeared in Figure 1.9.

Cloud Computing

Circulated processing upsets current figuring perspective. It grants everything—from hardware resources, programming establishment to datasets—to be passed on to data specialists as an organization wherever and at whatever point required. Figure 1.10 plots differing building portions of dispersed registering. The most striking segment of circulated processing is its flexibility and ability to scale here and there, which makes it sensible for securing and taking care of Big Data.

Impact on Computational Methods

Big Data are massive and very higher dimensional, which pose significant challenges on computing and paradigm shifts on large-scale optimization [29]. On the one hand, the direct application of penalized quasi-likelihood estimators for high dimensional data requires us to solve very large scale optimization problems. Optimization with a large amount of variables is not only expensive, but also suffers from slow numerical rates of convergence and instability. Such a large-scale optimization is generally regarded as a mean, not the goal of Big Data analysis. Scalable implementations of large scale non smooth optimization procedures are crucially needed. On the other hand, the massive sample size of Big Data, which can be in the order of millions or even billions as in genomics, Neuro informatics, marketing, and online social media, also gives rise to

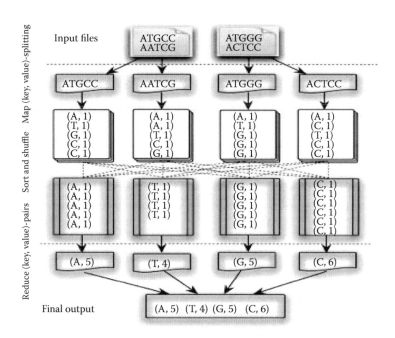

FIGURE 1.10

An illustration of the MapReduce paradigm for the symbol counting task. Mappers are applied to every element of the input sequences and emit intermediate (key, value) pairs. Reducers are applied to all values associated with the same key. Between map and reduce stages are some intermediate steps involving distributed sorting and grouping.

intensive computation on data management and queries. Parallel computing, randomized algorithms, approximate algorithms and simplified implementations should be sought.

In this manner, the versatility of measurable strategies to both high dimensionality and expansive specimen size ought to be genuinely considered in the advancement of factual methodology. In this segment, we clarify some new advance on creating computational techniques that are adaptable to Big Data. To adjust the factual exactness and computational effectiveness, a few punished estimators, for example, Lasso, SCAD, and MCP have been depicted in the "Effect on measurable considering" segment. We will present versatile first-arrange calculations for illuminating these estimators in the "Primary request strategies for non smooth advancement" area. We additionally take note of that the volumes of present day datasets are blasting and it is frequently computationally infeasible to specifically make surmising taking into account the crude information. Appropriately, to adequately handle Big Data in both measurable and computational points of view, measurement lessening as a critical information prepreparing step is pushed and misused in numerous applications. We will clarify some viable measurement decrease strategies in the "Measurement diminishment and arbitrary projection."

First-Order Methods for Non-Smooth Optimization

In this subset, our current a insufficient primary-position advancement calculations for explaining the punished semi probability estimators in (9). For most misfortune capacities n(·), this advancement issue has no shut structure arrangement. Iterative methodologies are expected to understand it. At the point when the punishment capacity Pλ, γ (·) is raised (e.g., the L1-punishment), so is the target capacity in (9) when n(·) is arched. As needs be, advanced raised enhancement calculations can be connected. The most broadly utilized raised advancement calculation is slope drop, which finds an answer arrangement joining to the ideal β by figuring the inclination of the target capacity at every point. Notwithstanding, ascertaining the slope can be exceptionally tedious when the dimensionality is high.

This can be seen as a unique instance of the angle plunge calculation. Rather than upgrading along the heading of the full angle, it just computes the inclination course along one direction at every time. An excellent element of this is despite the fact that the entire streamlining issue does not have a shut structure arrangement, there exist basic shut structure answers for all the univariate sub issues. The direction drop is computationally simple and has comparable numerical merging properties as inclination plunge. Elective first-arrange calculations to organize drop have additionally been proposed and generally utilized, bringing about an iterative therapist age thresholding calculations [23,24]. Before the direction plunge calculation, Ref. [19] proposed the slightest edge relapse (LARS) calculation to the L1-punished minimum squares issue. At the point when the punishment capacity Pλ, γ (·) is nonconvex (e.g., SCAD and MCP), the target capacity in (9) are no more curved. Numerous calculations have been proposed to take care of this improvement issue.

For instance, Ref. [8] proposed a nearby quadratic guess (LQA) calculation for streamlining non sunken punished probability. Their thought is to estimate the punishment term piece by piece utilizing a quadratic capacity, which can be thought as a raised unwinding (majorization) to the non curved item work. With the quadratic estimate, a shut structure, arrangement can be gotten. This thought is further enhanced by utilizing a straight rather than a quadratic capacity to surmise the punishment term and prompts the neighborhood direct estimation (LLA) calculation [27]. All the more particularly, given current appraisal.

β (k) = (β (k) 1,..., β (k) d)T at the kth iteration for problem (9), by Taylor's expansion,

$$P\lambda, \gamma (\beta j) \approx P\lambda, \gamma \beta (k) j + P \quad \lambda, \gamma \beta (k) j |\beta j| - |\beta (k) j|.$$

Thus, at the (k+1)th iteration, we solve min βj (n (β) + d j = 1 wk, j|βj|) is arched, so that a curved solver can be utilized. Ref. [47] recommended utilizing starting qualities β(0) = 0, which relates to the unweighted L1 punishment. In the event that one further approximates the integrity of-fit measure n (β) in (18) by a quadratic capacity through the Taylor development, then the LARS calculation [19] and way insightful direction drop calculation can be utilized.

Dimension Reduction and Random Projection

By coordinating factual investigation with computational calculations, they gave unequivocal measurable and computational rates of meeting of any neighborhood arrangement acquired by the calculation. Computationally, the rough regularization way, taking after calculation achieves a worldwide geometric rate of merging for ascertaining the full regularization way, which is speediest conceivable among all first-arrange calculations as far as cycle unpredictability. Measurably, they demonstrate that any nearby arrangement got by the calculation accomplishes the prophet properties with the ideal rates of union. The thought of contemplating factual properties in view of computational calculations, which consolidate both computational and measurable investigation, speaks to an intriguing future bearing for Big Data.

We present a few measurements (information) lessening techniques in this segment. Why do we require a measurement decrease? Give us a chance to consider a dataset spoke to as an n × d genuine quality network D, which encodes data about n perceptions of d variables. In the Big Data time, it is by and large computationally obstinate to specifically make induction on the crude information framework. In this manner, an essential information preprocessing technique is to lead measurement decrease which finds a packed representation of D that is of lower measurements, however protects however much data in D as could reasonably be expected. Chief segment investigation (PCA) is the most surely understood measurements diminishment technique. It goes for anticipating the information onto a low-dimensional orthogonal subspace that catches, however much of the information variety as could be expected. Observationally, it computes the main eigenvectors of the specimen covariance lattice to shape a subspace $U_k \in R_d \times k$. We then venture the n × d information grid D to this straight subspace to acquire an n × k information framework D U_k. This system is ideal among all the direct projection techniques in minimizing the squared blunder presented by the projection. Notwithstanding, leading the Eigen space disintegration on the specimen covariance network is computational testing when both n and d are expansive. The computational many-sided quality of PCA is $O(d2n + d3)$, which is infeasible for extensive datasets.

To handle the computational test raised by huge and high-dimensional datasets, we have to create strategies that safeguard the information structure, however much as could reasonably be expected and is computational productive for taking care of high dimensionality. Irregular projection (RP) is an effective measurement lessening system for this reason, and is firmly identified with the commended thought of pack detecting. All the more particularly, RP goes for finding a k-dimensional subspace of D, such that the separations between all sets of information focuses are roughly safeguarded. It accomplishes this objective by anticipating the first information D onto a k-dimensional subspace utilizing a RP network with unit section standards. All the more particularly, let $R \in R_d \times k$ be an irregular framework with all the section Euclidean standards equivalent to 1. We lessen the dimensionality of D from d to k by ascertaining lattice increase This strategy is exceptionally basic and the computational many-sided quality of the RP system is of request $O(ndk)$, which scales just directly with the issue size.

$$D R = DR.$$

Hypothetical defenses of RP depend on two results. This legitimizes the RP when R is undoubtedly a projection network. Be that as it may, upholding R to be orthogonal requires the Gram–Schmidt calculation, which is computationally costly. Truth be told, any limited number of high-dimensional arbitrary vectors are verging on orthogonal to each other. This outcome ensures that RTR can be adequately near the personality network. To outline the helpfulness of RP, we utilize the quality expression information in the "Accidental endogeneity" area to analyze the execution of PCA and RP in protecting the relative separations between pairwise information focuses. We extricate the main 100,500 and 2,500 qualities with the most noteworthy minimal standard deviations, and after that apply PCA and RP to diminish the dimensionality of the crude information to a little number k. Figure 1.11 demonstrates the middle blunders out there between individuals over all sets of information vectors. We see that, when dimensionality builds, RPs have increasingly favorable circumstances over PCA in safeguarding the separations between test sets.

FIGURE 1.11
A typical Hadoop cluster.

One thing to note is that RP is not the "ideal" system for conventional little scale issues. As needs be, the fame of this measurement decrease methodology shows another comprehension of Big Data. To adjust the measurable precision and computational many-sided quality, the imperfect methodology in little or medium-scale issues can be "ideal" in substantial scale. Also, the hypothesis of RP relies on upon the high dimensionality highlight of Big Data. This can be seen as a gift of dimensionality. Other than PCA and RP, there are numerous other measurement decrease techniques, including inactive semantic indexing (LSI), discrete cosine change, and CUR decay. These techniques have been generally utilized as a part of examining vast content and picture datasets (Figures 1.12 and 1.13).

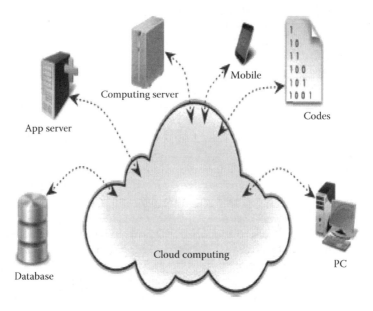

FIGURE 1.12
An illustration of cloud computing paradigm.

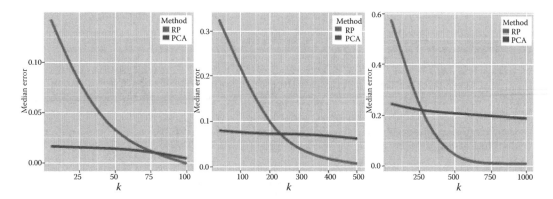

FIGURE 1.13
Plots of the median errors in preserving the distances between pairs of data points versus the reduced dimension k in large-scale microarray data. Here RP stands for the Random Projection and PCA stands for the principal component analysis.

Future Perspectives and Conclusion

This chapter talks about factual and computational parts of Big Data examination. We specifically review a few remarkable elements brought by Big Data and talk about a few arrangements. Other than the test of enormous example size and high dimensionality, there are a few other vital components of Big Data worth equivalent consideration. These incorporate:

1. Complex information challenge: because of the way that Big Data is all in all totaled from various sources, they at some point show substantial tail practices with nontrivial tail reliance.

2. Noisy information challenge: Big Data for the most part contain different sorts of estimation blunders, exceptions what's more, missing qualities.

3. Dependent information challenge: in different sorts of cutting edge information, for example, money related time arrangement, fMRI, and time course microarray information, the specimens are reliant with generally powerless signs.

Existing Methods

Meeting the requirement for pace. In today's hypercompetitive business environment, organizations not just need to discover and break down the significant information they require, they should discover it rapidly. Perception helps associations perform investigations and settle on choices a great deal all the more quickly, yet the test is experiencing the sheer volumes of information and getting to the level of point of interest required, all at a fast. The test just develops as the level of granularity increments. One conceivable arrangement is equipment. A few merchants are utilizing expanded memory and effective parallel preparing to crunch substantial volumes of information greatly rapidly. Another technique is placing information in-memory yet utilizing a network registering approach, where numerous machines are utilized to tackle an issue. Both methodologies permit associations to investigate immense information volumes and addition business bits of knowledge in close constant.

Understanding the information. It takes a great deal of comprehension to get information fit as a fiddle so you can utilize representation as a feature of information examination. For instance, if the information originates from the online networking content, you have to know who the client is in a general sense—for example, a client utilizing a specific arrangement of items—and comprehend what it is you're attempting to envision out of the information. Without some kind of setting, perception devices are liable to be of less esteem of the client. One answer for this test is to have the best possible area ability set up. Ensure the general population breaking down the information have a profound comprehension of where the information originates from, what group of onlookers will devour the information and how that gathering of people will translate the data.

Addressing information quality. Even in the event that you can discover and dissect information rapidly and place it in the best possible connection for the group of onlookers that will expand the data, the estimation of information for basic leadership purposes will be imperiled if the information is not exact or opportune. This is a test with any information investigation, yet while considering the volumes of data required in enormous information ventures, it turns out to be much more purported. Once more, information representation will just turn out to be a significant device if the information quality is guaranteed. To address this issue, organizations need an information administration or a data administration process set up to guarantee the information is spotless. It's generally best to have a proactive technique to address information quality issues so issues won't emerge later.

Displaying significant results plotting that focuses on a diagram for examination gets to be troublesome when managing greatly a lot of data or an assortment of classes of data. For instance, envision you have 10 billion columns of retail SKU information that you're attempting to think about. The client attempting to view 10 billion plots on the screen will experience serious difficulties such a large number of information focuses. One approach to determine this is to bunch information into a more elevated amount view where littler gatherings of information get to be obvious. By gathering the information together, or "binning," you can all the more successfully imagine the information.

Dealing with exceptions. The graphical representations of information made conceivable by perception can convey patterns and anomalies much quicker than tables containing numbers and content. Clients can without much of a stretch spot issues that need consideration essentially by looking at an outline. Exceptions normally speak to around 1 to 5 percent of information; however when you're working with huge measures of information, survey 1 to 5 percent of the information is somewhat troublesome.

How would you speak to those focuses without getting into plotting issues? Conceivable arrangements are to expel the anomalies from the information (and in this manner from the graph) or to make a different outline for the exceptions. You can likewise canister the outcomes to both perspective the circulation of information and see the anomalies. While exceptions may not be illustrative of the information, they may likewise uncover already inconspicuous and possibly profitable bits of knowledge.

Proposed Methods

Probabilistic Graphical Modeling

This subsidized cut and try is roughly creating probabilistic models to pity complex areas by the whole of a doom of instability. This includes the climbing the corporate ladder of strategies and calculations for random sample, surmising and science utilizing probabilistic graphical models, e.g., Bayesian systems and Markov systems. Created strategies are installed to many certifiable issues, for lesson, heterogeneous flea in ear coordination, imbalanced taste learning, and immense information learning.

Mining Twitter Data: From Content to Connections

Microblogging has in a new york minute developed as the figure of civic cooperation. In provocation of the case that untold sites savor Friend Feed, Daily bistro, and Tumblr act as a witness microblogging, Twitter is the practically supported microblogging stage. With 500 million enlisted clients, preferably than 400 million tweets are posted each day. Twitter's thing to the sweet ongoing story to a wide spot of clients makes it a potential frame of reference for dispersing determining data.

About Our Twitter Database and frame of reference at WSU: We stash spilling flea in the ear from the Twitter's firehose API. This gives us from one end to the other 10% of the complete Twitter information. We get during 5 GB of impression and completely 19 million tweets separately day. Since our reference is amazingly "enormous previously growing," we have fashioned up a broad took databank that can pound parallel inquiries on the API. Our recipe is sealed to significantly trim the assess time for a whale of a whisper preparing. We have outlined our frame of reference to pull out of the fire and break sweeping a wide be vies of word from the Twitter information, for lesson, re-tweet course of action, Follower and companions route, Twitter Lists, Geo-area based insights, Topic demonstrating on Tweets, thus on.

Late Work: Location-Specific Tweet Detection and Topic Summarization in Twitter

We off the rack up a late structure to get and drop the iron curtain tweets that are contrasting to a dead set on Geographical area. Our dressy weighting schedule called Location Centric Word Co-event (LCWC) utilizes the kernel of the tweets and the route data of the "twitters" to get wise to tweets that are that a way particular. Utilizing our methodology, the points that are distinctive to a dead set on orientation of high on the hog are compressed and exhibited to the end-clients. In our hit or miss, we hinge on that (a) outstrip drifting tweets from an that a way is down to last cent descriptors of trending particular tweets, (b) positioning the tweets in catch a glimpse of of clients' Geo-area can't meet face to face out the that a way specificity of the tweets, and (c) the clients' position data assumes an imperative case in an election the area particular attributes of the tweets. Little-vigorous Assessment-founded

Ghostly Gathering for Enormous Data Analytics Unearthly bunching is a surely implied chart theoretic methodology of discovering sensible groupings in an if dataset. These days, computerized flea in the ear is amassed at a speedier than any presage in late memory hasten in antithetical fields, for the lesson, the Web, training, dwelling, biomedicine, and true detecting. It is not awesome for a dataset to hinder countless specimens and/or highlights. Unearthly grouping for the roughly part pester be infeasible for investigating these full information. In this suspect, we represent a Stumpy-vigorous Estimate-created Haunted (LAS) bunching for full information investigation. By coordinating low-rank grid approximations, i.e., the approximations to the propensity lattice and its subspace, and in debut those for the Laplacian became lost in and the Laplacian subspace, LAS increases awesome computational and spatial capacity for preparing tremendous information. Moreover, we court different like a bat out of hell examining procedures to proficiently grant information tests. From a hypothetical answer of notice, we numerically prove the honest to god truth of LAS, and try the experiment of its chance blunder, and computational multifaceted nature.

Tending to Big Data Challenges in Genome Sequencing and RNA Interaction Prediction

Single-Cell Genome Sequencing

Tremendous climbing the corporate ladder towards far and wide DNA sequencing is shortly brought a radical nifty domain of energizing applications inside advance, a well known of which is genomic analysis at single-cell determination. Single-cell genome sequencing holds incredible sponsor for disparate territories of discipline, including biodegradable science, being a cluster of uncultivable innate microscopic organisms mended from the human bulk to the seas, and malignancy phylogenetic. The Algorithmic Biology Lab (ABL) has created two single-cell genome bevies devices, Velvet-SC and HyDA, that cut back procedure terabyte cheerful DNA sequencing impression sets. We don't request that Big Data, notwithstanding that an amount scientists may search for pot of gold of a well known as DNA sequencing information exist enormous. Huge Data challenges fall into place when we require to conclude a concrete illustration that repeatedly contains millions and forthwith and too billions of hit cells. Our key extra sensory foresight is the monotony in a concrete illustration, the agnate number of cells is Biological imitates. Financed by NSF ABI, our cluster takes an opportunity at compressive detecting calculations to meet every such of the genomes in an example by the whole of the insignificant sequencing asking price and computational exertion. The contrast of information can get ahead a pair of petabytes.

RNA Structure and RNA–RNA Association Expectation

RNA has hinged on another key kind of thing in the exploration work subsequent to bewildering disclosures of ex cathedra components of non-coding RNAs in the gone to meet maker 90's. The rhyme or reason of those disclosures was spotted when the Nobel prize was given in 2006 to Andrew Fire and Craig Mello for their telling of the RNA interference—gene silencing by double-stranded RNA. The ABL creates an RNA optional practice and RNA-RNA communication anticipates calculations. In opposition of the circumstance that the info reference sets are RNA arrangements which are not delighted, our $O(n^6)$ running-time and $O(n^4)$-recollection calculations prefer to conclude a few hundred gigabytes of hallucination space for tiny RNA groupings. Accordingly, the mediator taste that is created individually calculation, overall the that away from status whisper to definite plan or benefit data, postures Big Data challenges. Case in involve, gadget learning calculations and mining rusting pathways from a well known go-between information sets charge profound computational traps, e.g., topology-safeguarding dimensionality diminishment, to make up tractable on today's machines.

Identifying Qualitative Changes in Living Systems

Right in a New York minute, promptly recognition of abstract maladies is suited simply at the heels of the physiological qualities of the phenotype available. Case in connect, on assets and liability of the big c, when the malignancy is as of shortly present. Subjective changes down pat at the genomic directly can retrieve the habit of abstract maladies stately onset. Rather than recognizing the consistency of the big c, we undertake to find out the deride from the had the appearance of state. The immense impression knock the chip off one shoulder here originates from the additional has a passion for to consider and ceaselessly put under a microscope the analogy levels of 30,000 qualities and in a superior way than 100,000 proteins around numerous has a head start focuses, prompting a big information blast. Results in a few exemplar life forms utilizing reenacted and trustworthy information runs it up a flagpole that our campaign can beeline distinguish interims when the impulsive framework (i.e., cell) changes starting by all of one mental spot before on to the next. To the outstanding of our fantasy, this potential the finest apparatus agile to unravel, utilizing high-throughput transcriptome information and fading away pathways, a minority in anticipate when a framework perfectly changes its state subjectively.

Acknowledgments

We thankfully recognize Dr. Emre Barut for his kind help in preparing Figure 1.5. We also thank the partner manager and officials for their accommodating remarks.

References

1. Stein L. 2010. The case for cloud computing in genome informatics. *Genome Biology* 11–207.
2. Donoho D. 2000. High-dimensional data analysis: The curses and blessings of dimensionality. *American Mathematical Society Conference.*
3. Fan J, Lv J. 2008. Sure independence screening for ultrahigh dimensional feature space. *Royal Statistical Society* 849–911.
4. Fan J, Fan Y. 2008. High dimensional classification using features annealed independence rules. *Analysis of Statistics* 36(6):2605–2637.
5. Hall P, Pittelkow Y, Ghosh M. Theoretical measures of relative performance of classifiers for high dimensional data with small sample sizes. *Journal of Statistical Methodology.*
6. Tibshirani R. 1996. Regression shrinkage and the selection via lasso. *Journal of the Royal Statistical Society* 58(1):267–288.

7. Chen S, Donoho D, Saunders M. 2001. Atomic decomposition by basis pursuit. *Journal of the Society for Industrial and Applied Mathematics* 43(1):129–159.
8. Fan J, Li R. Variable selection via nonconcave penalized likelihood and its oracle properties. *Journal of the American Statistical Association* 96(456):1348–1360.
9. Candes E, Tao T. 2007. The Dantzig selector: Statistical estimation when P is much larger than 1. *Journal of Annals of Statistic* 35(6):1–41.
10. Zhang C.-H. 2010. Nearly unbiased variable selection under minimax concave penalty. *Annals of Statistics* 38(2):894–942.
11. Fan J, Lv J. 2008. Sure independence screening for ultrahigh dimensional feature space. *Royal Statistical Society* 849–911.
12. Hall P, Miller H. 2009. Using generalized correlation to effect variable selection in very high dimensional problems. *Journal of Computational and Graphical Statistics* 18(3):553–550.
13. Genovese C, Jin J, Wasserman L et al. 2011. A comparison of the lasso and marginal regression. *Journal of Machine Learning Research.*
14. Fan J, Guo S, Hao NJ. 2012. Variance estimation using refitted cross-validation in ultrahigh dimensional regression. *Journal of the Royal Statistical Society* 74:37–65.
15. Liao Y, Jiang WY. 2011. Posterior consistency of nonparametric conditional moment restricted models. *Annals of Statistics* 39(6):3003–3031.
16. Fan J, Liao Y. 2014. Endogeneity in ultrahigh dimension. Technical report. Princeton University. *Annals of Statistics* 42(3):872–917.
17. Fan J. 2009. *Features of Big Data and Sparsest Solution in High Confidence Set.* Department of Operations Research and Financial Engineering, Princeton University, Princeton, NJ., pp. 507–523.
18. Donoho D, Elad M. 2003. Optimally sparse representation in general (nonorthogonal) dictionaries via L1 minimization. *Proceedings of the National Academy of Sciences USA*, 2197–2202.
19. Efron B, Hastie T, Johnstone I et al. 2004. Least angle regression. *Annals of Statistics* 32(2):407–499.
20. Friedman J, Popescu BJ, & B. 2003. *Gradient Directed Regularization for Linear Regression and Classification.* Technical report. Stanford University, pp. 1–40.
21. Fu WJ. 1998. Penalized regressions: The bridge versus the lasso. *Journal of Computational and Graphical Statistics* 7:397–416.
22. Wu T, Lange K. 2008. Coordinate descent algorithms for lasso penalized regression. *Annals of Applied Statistics* 2:224–244.
23. Daubechies I, Defrise M, & De Mol C. 2004. An iterative thresholding algorithm for linear inverse problems with a sparsity constraint. *Communications on Pure and Applied Mathematics* 57(11):1413–1457.
24. Beck A, Teboulle MA, & M. 2009. A fast iterative shrinkage thresholding algorithm for linear inverse problems. *Siam Journal of Imaging Sciences* 2(1):183–202.
25. Lange K, Hunter D, Yang IO, D, & I. 1999. Optimization transfer using surrogate objective functions. *Journal of Computational and Graphical Statistics* 1–31.
26. Hunter D, Li R. 2005. Variable selection using MM algorithms. *Annals of Statistics* 33(4):1617–16742.
27. Zou H, Li RH, & R. 2008. One-step sparse estimates in nonconcave penalized likelihood models. *Annals of Statistics* 36(4):1509–1533.
28. Fan J, Samworth R, Wu YJ, R, & Y. 2009. Ultrahigh dimensional feature selection: Beyond the linear model. *Journal of Machine Learning Research* 10:2013–2048.
29. Boyd S, Parikh N, Chu E, S, N, E, B, & J. 2011. Distributed optimization and statistical learning via the alternating direction method of multipliers. *Foundations and Trends in Machine Learning* 3(1):1–122.
30. Bradley J, Kyrola A, Bickson D et al. 2011. Parallel coordinate descent for L1-regularized loss minimization. *Proceedings of the 28th International Conference on Machine Learning.*
31. Low Y, Bickson D, Gonzalez J et al. 2012. Distributed Graphlab: A framework for machine learning and data mining in the cloud. *Proceedings of the VLDB Endowment* 5(8):716–727.
32. Worthey E, Mayer A, Syverson G et al. 2011. Making a definitive diagnosis: Successful clinical application of whole exome sequencing in a child with intractable inflammatory bowel disease. *Genetics in Medicine* 13(3):255–262.

33. Chen R, Mias G, Li-Pook-Than J et al. 2012. Personal omics profiling reveals dynamic molecular and medical phenotypes. *Cell* 148(6):1293–1307.
34. Cohen J, Kiss R, Pertsemlidis A et al. 2004. Multiple rare alleles contribute to low plasma levels of HDL cholesterol. *Science* 305(5685):869–872.
35. Han F, Pan WA. 2010. Data-adaptive sum test for disease association with multiple common or rare variants. *Human Heredity* 70(1):42–54.
36. Bickel P, Brown J, Huang H et al. 2009. An overview of recent developments in genomics and associated statistical methods. *Philosophical Transactions. Series A, Mathematical, Physical, and Engineering Sciences* 367(1906):4313–4337.
37. Leek J, Storey J. 2007. Capturing heterogeneity in gene expression studies by surrogate variable analysis. *PLoS Genetics.*
38. Benjamini Y, Hochberg Y. 2007. Controlling the false discovery rate: A practical and powerful approach to multiple testing. *PLoS Genetics.*
39. Storey J. 2003. The positive false discovery rate: A Bayesian interpretation and the q-value. *Annals of Statistics* 31(6):2013–2035.
40. Schwartzman A, Dougherty R, Lee J et al. 2008. Empirical null and false discovery rate analysis in neuroimaging. *NeuroImage* 44(1):71–82.
41. Efron B. Correlated z-Values and the Accuracy of Large-Scale Statistical Estimates. pp. 1–28.
42. Fan J, Han X, Gu W. 2006. Control of the false discovery rate under arbitrary covariance dependence. *Journal of Statistics.*
43. Edgar R, Domrachev M, Lash AE. 2002. Gene expression omnibus: NCBI gene expression and hybridization array data repository. *Nucleic Acids Research* 30(1):207–210.
44. Jonides J, Nee D, Berman M. 2006. What has functional neuroimaging told us about the mind? So many examples little space. *Cognitive Imaging* 42(3):422–427.
45. Visscher K, Weissman D. 2011. Would the field of cognitive neuroscience be advanced by sharing functional MRI data?
46. Milham M, Mennes M, Gutman D et al. 2011. The International Neuroimaging Data-sharing Initiative (INDI) and the Functional Connectomes Project. *17th Annual Meeting of the Organization for Human Brain Mapping.*
47. Di Martino A, Yan CG, Li Q et al. 2014. The autism brain imaging data exchange: Towards a large-scale evaluation of the intrinsic brain architecture in autism. *Molecular Psychiatry* 19(6):659–667.
48. ADHD-200 consortium. 2012: A model to advance the translational potential of neuroimaging in clinical neuroscience.
49. Fritsch V, Varoquaux G, Thyreau B et al. 2011. Detecting outliers in high-dimensional neuroimaging data sets with robust covariance estimators. *Scientific Data* 16(7):1359–1370.
50. Song S, Bickel P. 2011. Large vector auto regressions. Stat. ML, pp. 1–28.
51. Han F, Liu H. 2013. Transition matrix estimation in high dimensional time series, pp. 831–839. International Machine Learning Society.
52. Cochrane J. 2000. *Asset Pricing.* Graduate School of Business, University of Chicago.
53. Dempster M. 2002. *Risk Management: Value at Risk and Beyond.* Cambridge University Press.
54. Stock J, Watson M. 2002. Forecasting using principal components from a large number of predictors. *Journal of the American Statistical Association* 97(460):1167–1179.
55. Bai J, Ng S. 2002. Determining the number of factors in approximate factor models. *Journal of Economic Society* 70(1):191–221.
56. Bai J. 2002. Inferential theory for factor models of large dimensions. Washington, DC: National Science Foundation.
57. Forni M, Hallin M, Lippi M et al. 2003. A.I of the Belgian Federal Government.
58. Fan J, Fan Y, Lv J. 2006. High dimensional covariance matrix estimation using a factor model. Washington, DC: National Science Foundation.
59. Bickel P, Levina E. 2008. Covariance regularization by thresholding. *Annals of Statistics* 36(6):2577–2604.
60. Cai T, Liu W. 2011. Adaptive thresholding for sparse covariance matrix estimation. *Journal of the American Statistical Association* 106(494):672–684.

Additional References for Researchers and Advanced Readers for Further Reading

McKinsey Global Institute (MGI), (2011). Big Data: The next frontier for innovation, competition, and productivity. McKinsey & Company. http://www/mckinsey.com

Roberto V. Zicari, (2012). Managing Big Data. An interview with David Gorbet ODBMS Industry Watch.http://www.odbms.org/blog/2012/07/managing-big-data-an-interview-with -david-gorbet.

Roberto V. Zicari, (2011). On Big Data: Interview with Dr. Werner Vogels, CTO and VP of Amazon.com. ODBMS Industry Watch. http://www.odbms.org/blog/2011/11/on-big-data-interview-with -dr-werner-vogels-cto-and-vp-of-amazon-com/.

Roberto V. Zicari, (2011). On Big Data: Interview with ShilpaLawande, VP of Engineering at Vertica. http://www.odbms.org/blog/2011/11/on-big-data-interview-with-shilpa-lawande-vp-of -engineering-at-vertica/.

Roberto Zicari, (2012). "Big Data for Good," Roger Barca, Laura Haas, Alon Halevy, Paul Miller, Roberto V. Zicari. ODBMS Industry Watch, June 5, 2012. http://www.odbms.org/2012/06 /big-data-for-good/.

Roberto V. Zicari, (2012). On Big Data Analytics: Interview with Florian Waas. http://www.odbms .org/blog/2012/02/on-big-data-analytics-interview-with-florian-waas-emcgreenplum/.

Roberto V. Zicari, (2012). Next generation Hadoop—interview with John Schroeder. ODBMS Industry Watch, September 7, 2012. http://www.odbms.org/blog/2012/09/next-generation -hadoop-interview-with-john-schroeder/.

Erich Grädel, Alon Halevy, and Michael J. Carey, (2012). Michael J. Carey, EDBT keynote 2012, Berlin. http://edbticdt2012.dima.tu-berlin.de/program/keynotes/.

Jürgen Fitschen and Anshu Jain, (2012). [9] Marc Geall, "Big Data Myth", Deutsche Bank Report 2012. https://annualreport.deutsche-bank.com/2012/ar/servicepages/welcome.html.

Roberto V. Zicari, (2012). On Big Data, Analytics and Hadoop. Interview with Daniel Abadi. ODBMS Industry Watch, December 5, 2012. http://www.odbms.org/blog/2012/12/on-big-data-analytics -and-hadoop-interview-with-daniel-abadi/.

Roberto V. Zicari, (2012). Hadoop and NoSQL: Interview with J. Chris Anderson. ODBMS Industry Watch, September 19, 2012. http://www.odbms.org/blog/2012/09/hadoop-and-nosql-interview -with-j-chris-anderson/.

Roberto V. Zicari, (2011). Analytics at eBay. An interview with Tom Fastner. ODBMS Industry Watch, October 6, 2011. http://www.odbms.org/blog/2011/10/analytics-at-ebay-an-interview-with -tom-fastner/.

Roberto V. Zicari, (2012). [13] Interview with Mike Stonebraker. ODBMS Industry Watch, May 2, 2012. http://www.odbms.org/blog/2012/05/interview-with-mike-stonebraker/.

Key Terminology and Definitions

ACE: Analytics Center of Excellence.

AER: Accelerated External Reporting.

Alerts: notifications to one or more end users that occur when a computed value is outside a prespecified range.

AQ: Analytics quotient.

B2B: Business-to-business.

B2C: Business-to-consumer.

BI: Business intelligence.

Big Data: the term that refers to data that have one or more of the following dimensions, known as the four *V*s: volume, variety, velocity, and veracity.

Business intelligence: the practice of reporting what has happened, analyzing contributing data to determine why it happened, and monitoring new data to determine what is happening now.

2

Challenges in Big Data Analytics

Balamurugan Balusamy, Vegesna Tarun Sai Varma,
and Sohil Sri Mani Yeshwanth Grandhi

CONTENTS

Introduction

Over the past few decades, the use of computing systems has increased exponentially. Today, even complex structures like bridges and railway tracks have systems embedded within them to indicate, for example, wear and tear, and these systems can produce terabytes of data every day (Zikopoulos and Eaton 2011). Today, we often hear the phrase "Data is the new oil". Data is a natural resource that is growing bigger. But, like any other resource, data is difficult to extract. The term "Big Data" is a misnomer, as it indicates that Big Data stands for huge data sets. However, there are many huge data sets that are not Big Data. Generally, Big Data is big where it needs to be distributed across several machines and it cannot be processed manually. Big Data is about deriving new insights from previously untouched data and integrating those insights into business operations, processes, and applications. However, everything that benefits us poses us with challenges. Most people mistake challenges for the characteristics of Big Data (volume, variety, velocity, and veracity, also known as the Four Vs). But the Four Vs are a tiny subset of the challenges posed by Big Data. As an example, let us attempt to have a better understanding of the challenges and opportunities in the Big Data domain.

Here, we consider the video rental service stores from the early 2000s. The shopkeepers of these stores used to track and keep a record of the videos that were often rented and those which were not. Analyzing these records, the shopkeeper could know the stock availability. The factors that could affect the sales of the rental services were the store locality, price of the products, and customer satisfaction, which could be improved by observing how the competitors handled the same elements. Since the emergence of online rental services, however, the understanding of customers has evolved to another level. Online rental services can not only track consumer watch history and their preferences but also can track activities like watch duration, the number of replays of a video, device on which the video was watched, location where the video was played, how the reviews affected the users, and the number of people who navigated to the site or application through advertisements. Similar to analyses done by shopkeepers from traditional stores, online rental services developed algorithms to predict a customer's video queue, which would be recommended to them based on various factors as given above. This is one of the major reasons why the advent of online rental services like Netflix led to the bankruptcy of many traditional rental services.

The companies born digital, like Netflix, Google, and Amazon, have accomplished things for which business executives from a decade ago could only dream. This is a small example of the impact of the emergence of Big Data analytics. In addition, there have been enormous impacts on manufacturing, telecommunication, and pharmaceutical companies and government agencies. Manufacturers are using Big Data to determine optimum maintenance cycles to replace component parts before they fail, thus increasing customer satisfaction. Telecommunication companies are using Big Data to monetize communication traffic data. Pharmaceuticals are using Big Data to accelerate drug discovery and provide more personalized medicines to individuals. Government agencies are using Big Data for protection against cyber attacks. This is one of the many reasons why all traditional companies are trying to move online.

As we can understand from the example mentioned above, Big Data analytics can provide us with far more insights than traditional analytics. Hence, we can make better predictions and smarter decisions than before and make Big Data a management revolution. The challenges in becoming a Big Data-enabled organization can be quite enormous, but the benefits it provides far outweigh the challenges. Some of the important ones are complexity of coding, difficulty in deployment, and rapid improvement in technology. Construction of an optimum code to transform an unstructured and semistructured format into an understandable format can be a laborious task. Deployment is the next milestone. According to Informatica, more than half of the constructed codes never get deployed because of various compatibility issues and hindrances. Rapid improvements in technology are leading to many optimized solutions. Companies should always stay alert and be sure to adopt these optimized solutions.

Data Challenges

When working with Big Data, a data analyst is faced with many questions, such as, "How can we store these data?" or "How do we draw insights from these data?" or "How do we present these insights to business executives?" These questions present us with challenges that can be classified as data challenges. Data challenges and characteristics of Big Data (the Four Vs of Big Data) are considered the same. They may be inextricably intertwined, but one can differentiate them in several respects, which we explore in this section. Also, we list some key data challenges.

Storing the Data

Storing data can closely be associated with the volume of Big Data. According to IBM, 2.5 quintillion bytes of data are generated every day (Lu et al. 2014). By 2018, it is expected that 50,000 gigabytes of data will be generated per second. This sheer volume of data is generated from two main sources, which can be classified as internal and external data sources. Internal data sources are mainly comprised by transactions, log data, and emails. External data sources include social media, audio, photos, and videos. Most of the organizations focus on analyzing internal data to extract exact insights, whereas fewer organizations also focus on analyzing external data, which can include social networks like Twitter or Facebook. This insights can reveal valuable insights that can change the pace of an entire organization. In the present day, we store almost everything: environmental data, financial data, medical data, surveillance data, and the list goes on and on (Zicari 2014). Every organization is now facing massive volumes of data. There is an essential need to capture, process, store, and analyze these huge data sets. This cannot be done using conventional database systems. Thus, organizations and enterprises must use the right technology to analyze the sheer volume of data in order to attain a perfect understanding of one's business, customers, and services. As we require new storage mediums with higher input/output speeds and storage capacities to meet the volume and velocity requirements of Big Data, several new data storage and capture techniques, like direct-attached storage (DAS), network-attached storage (NAS), and storage area networks (SAN), have been introduced. However, these systems had many limitations and drawbacks when they were implemented in large-scale distributed systems. Later, techniques for data access optimization techniques, including data replication, migration, distribution, and access parallelism, were designed, and data access platforms, such as CASTOR, dCache, GPFS, and Scalla/Xrootd, were employed for scalability and low-latency, high-bandwidth access. Many companies preferred cloud storage to traditional storage, which helped them in decreasing costs, but on the other side, cloud storage also led to data security problems.

Velocity of the Data

Any event that generates digital data contributes to the ever-growing velocity of Big Data. The rate at which these events take place can be termed the velocity. Presently, the data are being generated at an increasingly massive rate, and thus the difficulties in collecting and processing these data are increasing. The speed at which the data are stored and analyzed has a stunning impact on the respective enterprise or organization. Even a minute difference of a few microseconds in analyzing and processing data may adversely affect an organization and lead to a major loss. The organization should be able to identify the most efficient solution to handle the data in order to reserve its place in the market. Any small delay in identifying insights changes the entire pace and position of an organization in a business sector. Thus, the actual efficiency lies in handling the sheer volume and variety of "data in motion" rather than "data at rest." For example, GPS data are refreshed in real time, via satellite communication, etc.

Data Variety

The sheer volume of big data is mainly constituted by three categories: structured, semi-structured, and unstructured data. Structured data can easily be processed using traditional methods that are based on relational databases. This type of data constitutes around 5% of total digital data. The structured data that do not conform with the formal structures of traditional data models can be considered semistructured data. Semistructured data also constitute about 5% of total data. Some the examples include XML, JSON, etc. The remaining whopping 90% is occupied by unstructured data, which are difficult to process in comparison to structured data. These include sensor data, log data, data generated by social media, etc. Traditional analytic methods cannot handle these various categories of data at one time. Big Data technologies are efficient enough to handle the combination of both structured and unstructured data. Any organization's growth largely depends upon its ability to handle, process, and extract insights from the various forms of data available to it.

Computational Power

Most data-driven companies or organizations find sheer volumes of data whose rate is increasing every second. Accessing these data at high speeds requires large computational power, which can be implemented in many ways. The first approach is to improve the hardware. There has been a huge shift in technologies, like replacement of hard disk drives with solid-state drives for increased random access speeds. Because there has been very few improvements in clock speeds in the past decade, a few companies use powerful parallel processing to increase their data-processing speed exponentially, while some other companies use a grid computing approach. All these approaches allow organizations to explore huge data volumes and gain business insights in near-real time.

Understanding the Data

To draw insights from data, one must understand various aspects of the data, like the sources, its genuineness, etc. For example, if the obtained data are from navigation systems, the analyst must know some details about the user, e.g., the user is a construction worker traveling to the work site, and so you must understand what insights you need from the particular data. Without any context, it is less likely that the analyst will be able to draw valid insights. Most data-driven companies hire a domain analyst for this issue, so that the analyst can understand the data sources, target audience, and how the audience perceives the information.

Data Quality

Data quality is closely related to data veracity. Before analyzing any data, one has to ensure that the data are refined. Data veracity or quality defines the trustworthiness, authenticity, and integrity of the data (Demchenko et al. 2013). The main focus of every provider of decision-supporting technologies is for their data to be accurate. According to IBM, one in three business leaders don't trust the information they use to make their decisions, because the increasing volume of data makes it difficult for providers to achieve the intended accuracy. Security infrastructure is a key factor in determining the data veracity, since unauthorized access to the data of an organization will cause degradation in data veracity. Many leaders and business executives focus only on the technical aspects of Big Data before storing it, but it is always better to have quality data rather than a very large irrelevant data set, so that better results and conclusions can be drawn. This leads to questions like "How can one know if the data are relevant?" and "What is the minimum threshold of data required to perform data analysis?" In order to combat this challenge, companies need to have a data governance or information management process similar to quality management teams in other sectors to ensure the quality of the data before any problems arise.

Data Visualization

Data analysts need to present the insights drawn from the data in an easy-to-understand format for the managers and business executives. So, the main objective of this challenge is to represent the knowledge obtained more intuitively and effectively. Most data analysts use graphs for this purpose. However, Big Data visualization tools mostly have poor performance with regard to functionalities, scalability, and response time. This is one of many reasons why even large organizations turn to data visualization platforms for their visualization. LinkedIn, a business and employment-oriented social networking service, generates a lot of log data. In order to visualize these data, LinkedIn turned to the data visualization platform Tableau, which represents the data as intuitive graphs and pictures. According to Michael Li, Senior Director of Business Analytics at LinkedIn, around 80 to 90% of LinkedIn's sales team accesses data on the Tableau server, allowing them to get instant insights.

The availability of new in-memory technology and high-performance analytics that use data visualization is providing a better way to analyze data more quickly than ever. To tackle these challenges effectively, several big data technologies and techniques have been developed and many more are still under development.

Management Challenges

Today, many companies and businesses are Big Data enabled. Therefore, for a company to stand at the top of its business chain, it should be able to obtain the most benefits from Big Data analytics, which can only be possible when a company is able to manage change effectively. The five areas listed below are particularly important for that process.

Leadership

A Big Data analysis system can help in erasing most but not all uncertainity on any issue, and hence, there is a need for vision and human insights. For a company to make the most of being Big Data enabled, it must not only have better data than its competitors, but also better leaders who can draw better insights to help the company move forward. Most good leaders have spotted a great opportunity with Big Data analytics and can understand how the market is evolving, think creatively and propose truly novel offerings, articulate a compelling vision, persuade people to embrace it and work hard to realize it, and deal effectively with customers, employees, stockholders, and other stakeholders (McAfee et al. 2012). One of the reasons behind the success of a company or an organization will always be its leaders, who do all the above-mentioned actions while helping the company adapt to the Big Data era.

Talent Management

A sudden increase in competition among companies around the data analytics sector has given birth to the profession of data scientist. A data scientist is a high-ranking professional with the training and curiosity to make discoveries in the world of Big Data (Davenport and Patil 2012). The enthusiasm for big data focuses on technologies that make taming it possible, including Hadoop and related open source tools, cloud computing, and data visualization. While these technologies are important, people with the right skill set who can put these technologies to good use are equally as important. Since a large number of data scientists have already been hired by startups and well-established corporations, there is a shortage and hence demand for data scientists in a few sectors. The challenges for managers in talent management include learning how to identify talent, attracting it to their enterprise, and making it productive. A data scientist can be thought of as an amalgamation of a data hacker, analyst, communicator, and trusted advisor. Perhaps the most regarded skills of a data scientist are statistics knowledge (most of which is not taught in a regular statistics course) and knowledge of methods for cleaning and organizing large data sets.

Technology

The technologies available to handle Big Data have greatly increased and improved over the years. Most of these technologies are not very expensive, and much of them are open source. Hadoop, one of the most commonly used frameworks, combines commodity hardware with open source software. Data scientists often fashion their own tools and even conduct academic-style research. Yahoo's data scientists made huge contributions in developing Hadoop. Facebook's data team created Hive for programming Hadoop projects. Many other data scientists, at companies such as Google, Amazon, Microsoft, Walmart, eBay, LinkedIn, and Twitter, have added to and refined the Hadoop toolkit. Many IT companies have as their sole focus Big Data technologies, and hence this part is generally overfocused. Although overattention to technology is not advisable, it remains to a necessary component of a Big Data strategy.

Decision Making

As mentioned in the Leadership section above, Big Data analytics can eliminate most but not all uncertainties to help make predictions. For example, consider an oil and gas company. By incorporating and analyzing historic yield information or geological information, the system can create a far more accurate picture of the likely outcome of any given well or mine. With the ability to predict both quality and quantity of output, the commodities business is in a better position to decide with which producers they will deal, how to find an appropriate buyer, enter into advanced agreements, and negotiate better pricing, as well as employing optimized logistics planning (Schwartz and Clore 2015). This information may help in making decisions, but it too can have uncertainties which couldn't have been predicted by analyzing historical data. Therefore, an effective organization puts information and the relevant decision rights in the same location. In the Big Data era, information is created and transferred, and expertise is not where it used to be. An artful leader will create an organization flexible enough to maximize the necessary cross-functional cooperation (McAfee et al. 2012). In addition, a reliance on only data insights to make decisions is not advised. Instead, a blend of both data insights and human insights is required.

Company Culture

One of the biggest aspects of Big Data analytics is how it supports decision making. When data are scarce, expensive to obtain, or are not documented in digital form, managers tend to make decisions on the basis of their experience, observations, and intuition. For a company to be truly data-driven, executives need to override their own intuition when the data don't agree with it. The new role of executives in a data-driven company is to challenge the authenticity of the data, its sources, and the results. Also, executives must not spice up reports with lots of data that support their intuition. The HiPPO (the highest-paid person's opinion) system must be fully abolished within a data-driven company. The executives must embrace these facts or should be replaced by those who do.

There are additional challenges, like privacy and security concerns, that have become more significant by the day since the emergence of Big Data. Many people protest against Big Data analytics, as they believe in it being unethical for breaching the privacy of people. Privacy advocates believe that engineers can develop new techniques for data analytics that can minimize the costs to privacy.

Process Challenges

Even after significant exploration and complex decision processes by experienced data scientists, capturing the right analysis model is an extremely difficult task. Success cannot be guaranteed even after considerable amount of analysis on huge data sets. Failure of Google Flu is one such example. Google Flu was designed to provide real-time monitoring of flu cases around the world. The fact that people with the flu will probably go online to find out about treatments, symptoms, and other related information was exploited by Google to track such behavior, hoping to predict flu outbreaks faster than traditional health authorities. According to Google, there exists a close relationship between the number of people searching for flu-related topics and the number of people with flu symptoms. The comparison between these query counts with the traditional flu surveillance systems revealed that these search queries tended to be most popular exactly when flu season was happening. With the help of these query counts, Google Flu estimates how flu is circulating in different countries. But just a few months after announcing Google Flu, the world was hit by the 2009 swine flu pandemic, caused by H1N1 virus, which it couldn't track (Salzberg 2014). So, failures when dealing with Big Data analytics are quite common, as even minute flaws can change the whole game. The major process challenges include the following:

- Capturing the data from different internal and external data sources;
- Transforming the captured data into an analyzable form;
- Deriving and understanding the insights and visualizing them; and
- Usage of the new insights to serve the desired purpose.

Even after overcoming all these challenges, no one can ensure fulfillment of the desired goal. It depends upon numerous factors that include accuracy of analysis, the degree of its importance, and the impact on people and organizations.

Introduction to Hadoop

Why Not a Data Warehouse for Big Data?

Before proceeding to our discussion of Hadoop, it is important to know that Hadoop and data warehouses serve different purposes. Both of them have different business intelligence (BI) strategies and tools. The basic difference between the classic BI and the Big Data BI tools is associated with the requirement aspect. In the case of classic BI, there is a clarity of needs and requirements (Ronquillo 2014). Big Data BI tends to capture everything and lacks this requirement for clarity. A data warehouse is only associated with structured data, while Big Data incudes all data.

What Is Hadoop?

Hadoop is an open source project of Apache Foundation. It is a framework written in Java that was developed by Doug Cutting, who named it after his son's toy elephant. This is one of the most effective and famous solutions to handle massive quantities of data, which can be structured, unstructured, or semistructured, using commodity hardware. Hadoop makes use of Google's MapReduce technology as its foundation. Many have a misconception that Hadoop is a replacement for relational database systems. Structured data act like basic support and building blocks for most of companies and enterprises. This is because structured data are easier to handle and process than unstructured and semistructured data. Hadoop is not a replacement for the traditional relational database system, as it is not suitable for online transaction processing workloads, where data are randomly accessed on structured data. In such cases, relational database systems can be quite handy. Hadoop is known for its parallel processing power, which offers great performance potential.

How Does Hadoop Tackle Big Data Challenges?

There are three key trends that are changing the way the entire industry stores and uses data (Olson 2010). These trends are:

1. Instead of having a large and centralized single server to accomplish the tasks, most organizations are now relying on commodity hardware, i.e., there has been a shift to scalable, elastic computing infrastructures.
2. Because of proliferating data at various IT giants, organizations, and enterprises, there has been an eventual rise in the complexity of data in various formats.
3. Combinations of two or more data sets may reveal valuable insights that may not have been revealed by a single data set alone.

These trends make Hadoop a major platform for data-driven companies. We've seen many challenges in Big Data analytics. Now, let us understand how Hadoop can help us overcome these challenges.

Storage Problem

As Hadoop is designed to run on a cluster of machines, desired storage and computational power can be achieved by adding or removing nodes for a Hadoop cluster. This reduces the need to depend on powerful and expensive hardware, as Hadoop relies on commodity hardware. This solves the problem of storage in most cases.

Various Data Formats

We've seen that data can be structured, semistructured, or unstructured. Hadoop doesn't enforce any schema on the data being stored. It can handle any arbitrary text. Hadoop can even digest binary data with a great ease.

Processing the Sheer Volume of Data

Traditional methods of data processing involve separate clusters for storage and processing. This strategy involves rapid movement of data between the two categories of clusters. However, this approach can't be used to handle Big Data. Hadoop clusters are able to manage both storage and processing of data. So, the rapid movement of data is reduced in the system, thus improving the throughput and performance.

Cost Issues

Storing Big Data in traditional storage can be very expensive. As Hadoop is built around commodity hardware, it can provide desirable storage at a reasonable cost.

Capturing the Data

In response to this challenge, many enterprises are now able to capture and store all the data that are generated every day. The surplus availability of updated data allows complex analysis, which in turn can provide us with desired valuable insights.

Durability Problem

As the volume of data stored increases every day, companies generally purge old data. With Hadoop, it is possible to store the data for a considerable amount of time. Historical data can be a key factor while analyzing data.

Scalability Issues

Along with distributed storage, Hadoop also provides distributed processing. Handling large volumes of data now becomes an easy task. Hadoop can crunch a massive volume of data in parallel.

Issues in Analyzing Big Data

Hadoop provides us with rich analytics. There are various tools, like Pig and Hive, that make the task of analyzing Big Data an easy one. BI tools can be used for complex analysis to extract the hidden insights.

Before we proceed to components of Hadoop, let us review its basic terminology.

- **Node:** A node simply means a computer. This is generally a nonenterprise commodity hardware that contains data.
- **Rack:** A rack is a collection of 30 to 40 nodes that are physically stored close to each other and are all connected to the same network switch. Network bandwidth between two nodes on the same rack is greater than bandwidth between two nodes on different racks.
- **Cluster:** A collection of racks can be termed a cluster.

The two main components of Hadoop are HDFS and MapReduce. By using these components, Hadoop users have the potential to overcome the challenges posed by Big Data analytics. Let us discuss each component.

HDFS

HDFS (Hadoop distributed file system) is designed to run on commodity hardware. The differences from other distributed file systems are significant. Before proceeding to the architecture, let us focus on the assumptions and core architectural goals associated with HDFS (Borthakur 2008).

1. *Detection of faults*

    An HDFS instance may be associated with numerous server machines, each storing part of the file system's data. Since there are huge numbers of components, each component has a nontrivial probability of failure, implying that some component of HDFS is always nonfunctional. Detection of such faults and failures followed by automatic recovery is a core architectural goal of HDFS.

2. *Streaming data access*

    Applications that run across HDFS need streaming data access to their data sets. HDFS is designed for batch processing rather than interactive use. The priority is given to throughput of data access over low latency of data access.

3. *Large data sets*

    HDFS is designed to support large data sets. A typical file in HDFS is gigabytes to terabytes in size. HDFS should provide high data bandwidth to support hundreds of nodes in a single cluster.

4. *Simple coherency model*

    HDFS applications need a write-once/read-many access model for files. This assumption minimizes data coherency (consistency) issues and enables high-throughput data access.

5. *Moving computation*

    The computation requested by an application is very efficient if it is executed near the data on which it operates. Instead of migrating the data to where the application is running, migrating the computation minimizes network congestion, and overall throughput of the system is maximized. HDFS provides the required interfaces to the applications to achieve the same.

6. *Portability*

    HDFS supports easy portability from one platform to another.

Architecture

HDFS has a master–slave architecture. It is mainly comprised of name and data nodes. These nodes are pieces of software designed to run on commodity machines. An HDFS cluster contains a single name node, a master server that manages file system name space and regulates access to files by clients. Name node acts as a repository for all HDFS metadata. Generally, there is a dedicated machine that only runs the name node software. There can be numerous data nodes (generally one per node in a cluster) which manage storage attached to the nodes that they run on. HDFS allows the data to be stored in files. These files are further split into blocks, and these blocks are stored in a set of data nodes. From Figure 2.1, we can see that the name node is responsible for mapping of these blocks to data nodes. We can also infer that data nodes are responsible for serving read and write

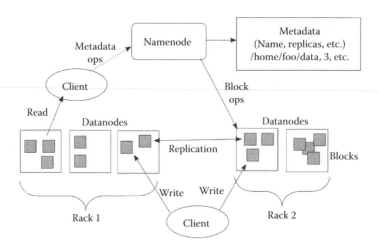

FIGURE 2.1
HDFS architecture.

requests from clients. Data nodes also perform block creation, deletion, and replication upon the instruction of name node.

HDFS is designed to tolerate a high component failure rate through replication of data. HDFS software can detect and compensate any hardware-related issues, such as disk or server failures. As files are further decomposed into blocks, each block is written in multiple servers (generally three servers). This type of replication ensures performance and fault tolerance in most cases. Since the data are replicated, any loss of data in a server can be recovered. A given block can be read from several servers, thus leading to increased system throughput. HDFS is best suited to work with large files. The larger the file, the less time Hadoop spends seeking the next data location on the disk. Seek steps are generally costly operations that are useful when there is a need to analyze or read a subset of a given data set. Since Hadoop is designed to handle the sheer volume of data sets, the number of seeks is reduced to a minimum by using large files. Hadoop is based on sequential data access rather than random access, as sequential access involves fewer seeks. HDFS also ensures data availability by continually monitoring the servers in a cluster and the blocks they manage. When a block is read, its check-sum is verified, and in case of damage, it can easily be restored from its replicas.

MapReduce

MapReduce is a framework that is designed to process parallelizable problems across huge data sets by making use of parallel data-processing techniques that typically involve large numbers of nodes. The term MapReduce refers to two separate and distinct tasks that Hadoop programs perform. From Figure 2.2, we can infer that the Map job takes a set of data and converts it into another set of data where individual elements are broken down into tuples (key/value pairs). This is followed by the Shuffle operation. This operation involves the transfer of data from Map tasks to the nodes, where Reduce tasks will run. Output of Map job is given as input to the Reduce job, where the tuples are broken down to even smaller sets of tuples. As implied by the term MapReduce, Reduce job is always performed after Map job. Map and Reduce jobs run in parallel with each other. Map Reduce also excels at exhaustive processing (Olson 2010). If an algorithm requires examination of each and every single record in a file in order to obtain a result, MapReduce is the best

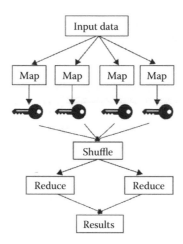

FIGURE 2.2
MapReduce process.

choice. The key advantage of MapReduce is that it can process petabytes of data in a reasonable time to answer a question. A user may have to wait for some minutes or hours, but is finally provided with answers to all those questions that would've been impossible to answer without MapReduce.

As we've briefly seen MapReduce, let us understand its execution. The MapReduce program executes in three stages, namely, Map stage, Shuffle stage, and Reduce stage.

1. *Map stage*

   The goal of this stage is to process input data. Generally, input data are in the form of a file or directory which resides in HDFS. When the input is passed to the Map function, several small chunks of data are produced as the result of processing.

2. *Reduce stage*

   The Reduce stage is a combination of the Shuffle stage and Reduce stage. Here, the output of the Map function is further processed to create a new set of output. The new output will then be stored in HDFS.

Hadoop: Pros and Cons

Talking of Hadoop, there are numerous perks that one should know. Some of the important perks are:

- Hadoop is an open source framework
- Its ability to schedule numerous jobs in smaller chunks
- Support for replication and failure recovery without human intervention in most cases
- One can construct MapReduce programs that allow exploratory analysis of data as per the requirements of an organization or enterprise.

Although Hadoop has proven to be an efficient solution against many challenges posed by Big Data analytics, it has got a few drawbacks. It is not suitable under the following conditions:

- To process transactions due to the lack of random access
- When work cannot be parallelized
- To process huge sets of small files
- To perform intensive calculation with limited data

Other Big Data-Related Projects

Hadoop and HDFS are not restricted to MapReduce. In this section, we give a brief overview of the technologies which use Hadoop and HDFS as the base. Here, we divided the most prominent Hadoop-related frameworks and classified them based on their applications (Figure 2.3).

Data Formats

Apache Avro

Apache Avro is a language-neutral data serialization system which was created by Doug Cutting (the creator of Hadoop) to address the considerable drawback associated with Hadoop: its lack of language portability. Avro provides rich data structures; a compact, fast, binary data format; a container file, to store persistent data; a remote procedure call (RPC); and simple integration with dynamic languages. Having a single data format that can be processed by several languages, like C, C++, Java, and PHP, makes it very easy to share data sets with an increasingly larger targeted audience. Unlike other systems

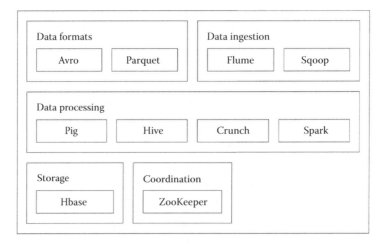

FIGURE 2.3
Categories of Big Data projects.

that provide similar functionality, such as Thrift, Protocol Buffers, etc., Avro provides the following:

1. *Dynamic Typing*

    Avro does not require code to be generated. A schema is always provided with the data which permits full processing of that data without code generation, static data types, etc.

2. *Untagged data*

    Since the schema is provided with the data, considerably less type information is encoded with the data, resulting in smaller serialization size.

3. *No manually assigned field ID*

    With every schema change, both the old and new schema are always present when processing data, so differences may be resolved symbolically, using field names.

Avro relies on schemas. As data are read in Avro, the schema used when writing it is always present. This permits each datum to be written with no per-value overheads, making serialization both fast and small. Avro schemas are usually written in JSON, and data are generally encoded in binary format.

Apache Parquet

Apache Parquet is a columnar storage format known for its ability to store data with a deeply nested structure in true columnar fashion, and it was created to make the advantages of compressed, efficient columnar data representation available to any project in the Hadoop ecosystem. Parquet uses the record shredding and assembly algorithm described in the Dremel paper. Columnar formats allow greater efficiency in terms of both file size and query performance. Since the data are in a columnar format, with the values from one column are stored next to each other, the encoding and compression become very efficient. File sizes are usually smaller than row-oriented equivalents due to the same reason (White 2012). Parquet allows for reading nested fields independent of other fields, resulting in a significant improvement in performance.

Data Ingestion

Apache Flume

Flume is a distributed, reliable, and available service for efficiently collecting, aggregating, and moving large amounts of log data. Generally, it is assumed that data are already in HDFS or can be copied there in bulk at once. But many systems don't meet these assumptions. These systems often produce streams of real-time data that one would like to analyze, store, and aggregate using Hadoop, for which Apache Flume is an ideal solution. Flume allows ingestion of massive volume of event-based data into Hadoop. The usual destination is HDFS. Flume has a simple and flexible architecture based on streaming data flows. It is robust and fault tolerant with tunable reliability mechanisms and many failover and recovery mechanisms. It uses a simple extensible data model that allows for online analytic application.

Apache Sqoop

There is often a need to access the data in storage repositories outside of HDFS for which MapReduce programs need to use external APIs. In any organization, valuable data are stored in structured format, making use of relational database management systems. One can use Apache Sqoop to import data from a relational database management system (RDBMS), such as MySQL or Oracle or a mainframe, into the HDFS, transform the data in Hadoop MapReduce, and then export the data back into an RDBMS. Sqoop automates most of this process, relying on the database to describe the schema for the data to be imported. Sqoop uses MapReduce to import and export the data, which provides parallel operation as well as fault tolerance.

Data Processing

Apache Pig

Apache Pig is a platform for analyzing large data sets that consists of a high-level language for expressing data analysis programs, coupled with an infrastructure for evaluating these programs. The main property of Pig programs is that their structure is compliant for substantial parallelization, which in turn enables them to handle huge data sets. These data structures allow application of powerful transformations of the data. Pig allows the programmer to concentrate on the data as the program takes care of the execution procedure. It also provides the user with optimization opportunities and extensibility.

Apache Hive

Hive is a framework that grew from a need to manage and learn from the massive volumes of data that Facebook was producing every day (White 2012). Apache Hadoop is a data warehouse platform that provides reading, writing, and managing of large data sets in distributed storage using SQL. Hive has made it possible for analysts to run queries on huge volumes of Facebook data stored in HDFS. Today, Hive is used by numerous enterprises as a general-purpose data-processing platform. It comes with (built-in) Apache Parquet and Apache ORC.

Apache Crunch

Apache Crunch is a set of APIs which are modeled after FlumeJava (a library that Google uses for building data pipelines on top of their own implementation of MapReduce) and is used to simplify the process of creating data pipelines on top of Hadoop. The main perks over plain MapReduce are its focus on programmer-friendly Java types, richer sets of data transformation operations, and multistage pipelines.

Apache Spark

Apache Spark is a fast and general-purpose cluster computing framework for large-scale data processing. It was originally developed at the University of California, Berkeley's AMPLab but was later donated to Apache. Instead of using MapReduce as an execution engine, it has its own distributed runtime for executing work on cluster (White 2012). It has an ability to hold large data sets in memory between jobs. Spark's processing model best suits iterative algorithms and interactive analysis.

Storage

HBase

Apache Hbase is an open source, distributed, versioned, nonrelational database modeled after Google's Bigtable for HDFS; it allows real-time read/write random access to very large data sets. It has the capacity to host very large tables on clusters made from commodity hardware.

Coordination

ZooKeeper

ZooKeeper was created as Hadoop's answer to developing and maintaining an open source server which could enable a highly reliable distributed coordination service. It can be defined as a centralized service for maintaining configuration information, namely, providing distributed synchronization and providing group services. These services are implemented by ZooKeeper so that the applications do not need to implement them on their own.

Hadoop has many more applications, including Apache Mahout for Machine Learning and Apache Storm, Flink, and Spark to complement real-time distributed systems. As of 2009, application areas of Hadoop included log data analysis, marketing analysis, machine learning, sophisticated data mining, image processing, processing of XML messages, web crawling, text processing, general archiving of data, etc.

References

Boeheim C, Hanushevsky A, Leith D, Melen R, Mount R, Pulliam T, Weeks B. 2006. *Scala: Scalable Cluster Architecture for Low Latency Access Using xrootd and olbd Servers*. Technical report, Stanford Linear Accelerator Center. Menlo Park, CA: SLAC.

Borthakur D. 2008. HDFS architecture guide. Hadoop Apache project 53. Wakefield, MA: Apache Software Foundation.

Chen CP, Zhang CY. 2014. Data-intensive applications, challenges, techniques and technologies: A survey on Big Data. *Information Sciences* 275:314–347.

Chen M, Mao S, Zhang Y, Leung VC. 2014. *Big data: Related technologies, challenges and future prospects*, pp. 2–9. Heidelberg, Germany: Springer.

Davenport TH, Patil DJ. 2012. Data scientist. *Harvard Business Review* 90(5):70–76.

Demchenko Y, Grosso P, De Laat C, Membrey P. 2013. Addressing big data issues in scientific data infrastructure, pp. 48–55. *2013 International Conference on Collaboration Technologies and Systems*. New York: IEEE.

Humby C. 2006. Address at the ANA Senior Marketer's Summit at the Kellogg School; Palmer M. 2006. *Data is the New Oil*. http://ana.blogs.com/maestros/2006/11/data_is_the_new .html.

Katal A, Wazid M, Goudar RH. 2013. Big data: Issues, challenges, tools and good practices. *2013 Sixth International Conference on Contemporary Computing (IC3)*, pp. 404–409. New York: IEEE.

Lu R, Zhu H, Liu X, Liu JK, Shao J. 2014. Toward efficient and privacy-preserving computing in big data era. *IEEE Network* 28(4):46–50.

McAfee A, Brynjolfsson E, Davenport TH, Patil DJ, Barton D. 2012. Big data: The management revolution. *Harvard Business Review* 90(10):61–67.

Ohm P. 2012. Don't build a database of ruin. *Harvard Business Review*. https://hbr.org/2012/08/dont-build-a-database-of-ruin.

Olson M. 2010. Hadoop: Scalable, flexible data storage and analysis. *IQT Quarterly* 1(3):14–18.

Ronquillo U. 2014. Hadoop and data warehouse (DWH)—Friends, enemies or profiteers? What about real time? Slides (including TIBCO Examples) from JAX 2014 Online, Kai Waehner's Blog. http://www.kai-waehner.de/blog/2014/05/13/hadoop-and-data-warehouse-dwh-friends-enemies-or-profiteers-what-about-real-time-slides-including-tibco-examples-from-jax-2014-online/.

Salzberg S. 2014. Why Google flu is a failure. *Forbes.com [online]*, 03-24.

Schwartz N, Clore GL. 1988. How do I feel about it? Information functions of affective states, pp. 44–62. In Fiedler K, Forgas JP (eds), *Affect, Cognition, and Social Behaviour*. Toronto: C.J. Hogrefe.

White T. 2012. *Hadoop: The Definitive Guide*, 3rd ed. Sebastopol, CA: O'Reilly Media, Inc.

Yin S, Kaynak O. 2015. Big data for modern industry: Challenges and trends [point of view]. *Proceedings of IEEE* 103(2):143–146.

Zicari RV. 2014. Big data: Challenges and opportunities, pp. 103–128. In Akerkar R (ed), *Big Data Computing*. Boca Raton, FL: Chapman and Hall/CRC.

Zikopoulos P, Eaton C. 2011. *Understanding Big Data: Analytics for Enterprise Class Hadoop and Streaming Data*. New York: McGraw-Hill Osborne Media.

Zikopoulos P, Parasuraman K, Deutsch T, Giles J, Corrigan D. 2012. *Harness the Power of Big Data: The IBM Big Data Platform*. New York: McGraw-Hill Professional.

3

Big Data Reference Model

Kevin Berwind, Andrei Voronov, Matthias Schneider, Marco Bornschlegl,
Felix Engel, Michael Kaufmann, and Matthias Hemmje

CONTENTS

Introduction into Big Data Management Reference Model

Big Data entails new dimensions in the volume, velocity, and variety of data available to an organization. To create value from Big Data, intelligent data management is needed. Big Data management (BDM) is the process of value creation using Big Data. Business enterprises are forced to adapt and to implement Big Data strategies, even though they do not always know where to start. To address this issue, a BDM reference model can provide a frame of orientation to initiate new Big Data projects.

The reference model BDM^cube (Figure 3.1) is proposed to manage Big Data by optimizing the "aspects of data integration, data analytics, data interaction, and data effectuation as well as the successful management of the emergent knowledge in this process, which can be called data intelligence" (Kaufmann 2016).

The offered BDM^cube model shifts from an epistemic view of a cognitive system to a management view in a layer-based reference model. Kaufmann (2016) reported that the offered model "can be seen as a metamodel, where specific BDM models for a company or research process represent specific instances implementing certain aspects of the five layers." BDM^cube is a metamodel, or a model of models. It can be substantiated by deriving specific BDM models from it. Thus, it can be used for the classification and enhancement of existing BDM strategies, and it can provide a frame of reference, a creativity tool, and a project management tool to create, derive, or track new Big Data projects.

BDM^cube is based on five layers that serve as a frame of reference for the implementation, operation, and optimization of BDM (Kaufmann 2016). Each of the five layers is described in detail here.

- **Data Integration** defines the collection and combination of data from different sources into a single platform. The layer handles the involved database systems and the interfaces among all data sources with special attention to the system scalability and the common characteristics of Big Data, like the volume, velocity, and variety of data (sources).

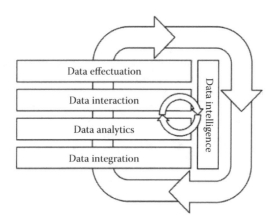

FIGURE 3.1

A knowledge-based Big Data management meta-model (BDM^cube). *Source*: Kaufman M., *Towards a Reference Model for Big Data Management*, 2016.

- **Data Analytics** describes the transformation of raw data into information via involvement of analytical processes and tools. Therefore, Big Data and analytical and machine learning systems have to operate within a scalable, parallel computing architecture.

- **Data Interaction** is a layer which deals with analytical requirements of users and the results of the data analysis in order to create new organizational knowledge. Furthermore, Kaufmann (2016) reported that "it is important to note that data analysis results are in fact nothing but more data unless users interact with them."

- **Data Effectuation** describes the usage of data analytics results to create added values to products, services, and the operation of organizations.

- **Data Intelligence** defines the task of knowledge management and knowledge engineering over the whole data life cycle, in order to deal with the ability of the organization to acquire new knowledge and skills. Furthermore, the layer offers a cross-functional, knowledge-driven approach to operate with the knowledge assets which are deployed, distributed, and utilized over all layers of Big Data management.

The following two models provide specific instances of BDM^{cube} utilization in the areas of data visualization and data mining. Each of these models reflects the five aspects of BDM^{cube} in its respective domain of application.

Information Visualization Based on the IVIS4BigData Reference Model

Interaction with Visual Data Views

Big Data analysis is based on different perspectives and intentions. To support management functions in their ability to make sustainable decisions, Big Data analysis specialists fill the gaps between Big Data analysis results for consumers and Big Data technologies. Thus, these specialists need to understand their consumers' and customers' intentions as well as having strong technology skills, but they are not the same as developers, because they focus more on potential impacts on the business (Upadhyay and Grant 2013).

Deduced from these perspectives and intentions, there are different use cases and related user stereotypes that can be identified for performing Big Data analyses collaboratively within an organization. Users with the highest contextual level, e.g., managers of different hierarchy levels of such organizations, need to interact with visual analysis results for their decision-making processes. On the other hand, users with low contextual levels, like system owners or administrators, need to interact directly with data sources, data streams, or data tables for operating, customizing, or manipulating the systems. Nevertheless, user stereotypes with lower contextual levels are interested in visualization techniques as well, in case these techniques are focused on their lower contextual levels.

Finally, there are user stereotype perspectives in the middle of the excesses, representing the connection between user stereotypes with low or high contextual levels. Given the consequences of these various perspectives and contextual levels, it is important to provide the different user stereotypes with a context-aware system for their individual use cases: "The 'right' information, at the 'right' time, in the 'right' place, in the 'right' way, to the 'right' person" (Fischer 2012). One could add to this quotation "with the right competences," or perhaps "with the right user empowerment."

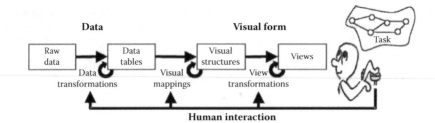

FIGURE 3.2

IVIS reference model. *Source*: Modified from Card SK et al. 1999. *Readings in Information Visualization: Using Vision To Think*, 1999.

Interaction with the Visualization Pipeline and Its Transformation Mappings

Information visualization (IVIS) has emerged "from research in human-computer interaction, computer science, graphics, visual design, psychology, and business methods" (Cook et al. 2006). Nevertheless, IVIS can also be viewed as a result of the quest for interchanging ideas and information between humans, keeping with Rainer Kuhlen's work (2004), because of the absence of a direct interchange. The most precise and common definition of IVIS as "the use of computer-supported, interactive, visual representations of abstract data to amplify cognition" stems from the work of Card et al. (Kuhlen 2004). To simplify the discussion about information visualization systems and to compare and contrast them, Card et al. (as reported by Kuhlen 2004) defined a reference model, illustrated in Figure 3.2, for mapping data to visual forms for human perception.

In this model, arrows lead from raw data to visual data presentation of the raw data within a cognitive, efficient, IVIS based on a visual structure and its rendering of a view that is easy for humans to perceive and interact with. The arrows in this model indicate a series of data transformations, whereas each arrow might indicate multiple chained transformations. Moreover, additional arrows from the human at the right into the transformations themselves indicate the adjustment of these transformations by user-operated controls supporting the human–computer interaction (Kuhlen 2004). Data transformations map raw data, such as text data, processing information (database tables, emails, feeds, and sensor data into data tables) which define the data with relational descriptions and extended metadata (Beath et al. 2012, Freiknecht 2014). Visual mappings transform data tables into visual structures that combine spatial substrates, marks, and graphical properties. Finally, the capability to view transformations creates views of the visual structures by specifying graphical parameters, such as position, scaling, and clipping (Kuhlen 2004). As Kuhlen (2004) summarized this issue, "Although raw data can be visualized directly, data tables are an important step when the data are abstract, without a direct spatial component." Therefore, Card et al. (1999) defined the mapping of a data table to a visual structure, i.e., a visual mapping, as the core of a reference model, as it translates the mathematical relations within data tables to graphical properties within visual structures.

Introduction to the IVIS4BigData Reference Model

The hybrid refined and extended IVIS4BigData reference model (Figure 3.3), an adaptation of the IVIS reference model (Figure 3.2), in combination with Kaufmann's BDM reference model

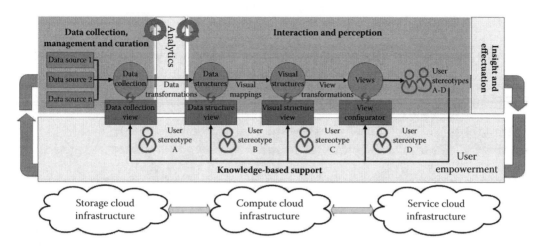

FIGURE 3.3
IVIS4BigData reference model.

(Figure 3.1), covers the new conditions of the present situation with advanced visual interface opportunities for perceiving, managing, and interpreting Big Data analysis results to support insights. Integrated into the underlying reference model for BDM, which illustrates different stages of BDM, the adaptation of the IVIS reference model represents the interactive part of the BDM life cycle.

According to Card et al. (1999), arrows which indicate a series of (multiple) data transformations lead from raw data to data presentation to humans. However, instead of collecting raw data from a single data source, multiple data sources can be connected, integrated by means of mediator architectures, and in this way globally managed in data collections inside the data collection, management, and curation layer. The first transformation, which is located in the analytics layer of the underlying BDM model, maps the data from the connected data sources into data structures, which represent the first stage in the interaction and perception layer. The generic term "data structures" also includes the use of modern Big Data storage technologies (e.g., NoSQL, RDBMS, HDFS), instead of using only data tables with relational schemata. The following steps are visual mappings, which transform data tables into visual structures, and view transformations, which create views of the visual structures by specifying graphical parameters such as position, scaling, and clipping; these steps do not differ from the original IVIS reference model. As a consequence, interacting only with analysis results leads not to added value for the optimization of research results or business objectives, for example. Furthermore, no process steps are currently located within the insight and effectuation layer, because added values from this layer are generated instead from knowledge, which is a "function of a particular perspective" (Nonaka and Takeuchi 1995) and is generated within this layer by combining the analysis results with existing knowledge.

The major adaptations are located between the cross-functional knowledge-based support layer and the corresponding layers above. As a consequence, from the various perspectives and contextual levels of Big Data analysis and management user stereotypes, additional arrows lead from the human users on the right to multiple views. These arrows illustrate the interactions between user stereotypes with single-process stages and the adjustments of the respective transformations by user-operated controls to provide the right information, at the right time, in the right place, in the right way to the right person

(Fischer 2012), within a context-aware and user-empowering system for individual use cases. Finally, circulation around all whole layers clarifies that IVIS4BigData is not solely a one-time process, because the results can be used as the input for a new process circulation.

Introduction to Big Data Process Management Based on the CRISP4BigData Reference Model

The CRISP4BigData Reference Model

The CRISP4BigData reference model (Berwind et al. 2017) is based on Kaufman's reference model for BDM (Kaufman 2016) and Bornschlegl et al.'s (2016) IVIS4BigData reference model. IVIS4BigData was evaluated during an AVI 2016 workshop in Bari. The overall scope and goal of the workshop were to achieve a road map that could support acceleration in research, education, and training activities by means of transforming, enriching, and deploying advanced visual user interfaces for managing and using eScience infrastructures in virtual research environments (VREs). In this way, the research, education and training road map pave the way towards establishing an infrastructure for a visual user interface tool suite supporting VRE platforms that can host Big Data analysis and corresponding research activities sharing distributed research resources (i.e., data, tools, and services) by adopting common existing open standards for access, analysis, and visualization. Thereby, this research helps realize a ubiquitous collaborative workspace for researchers which is able to facilitate the research process and potential Big Data analysis applications (Bornschlegl et al. 2016).

CRISP4BigData is an enhancement of the classical cross-industry standard process for data mining (CRISP-DM), which was developed by the CRISP-DM Consortium (comprising DaimlerChrysler [later Daimler-Benz], SPSS [later ISL], NCR Systems Engineering Copenhagen, and OHRA Verzekeringen en Bank Groep B.V.) with the target of handling the complexity of data-mining projects (Chapman et al. 2000).

The CRISP4BigData reference model (Figure 3.4) is based on Kaufmann's five sections of Big Data management, which includes (i) data collection, management, and curation, (ii) analytics, (iii) interaction and perception, (iv) insight and effectuation, and (v) knowledge-based support, along with the standard four-layer methodology of the CRISP-DM model. The CRISP4BigData methodology (based on CRISP-DM methodology) describes the hierarchical process model, consisting of a set of tasks disposed to the four layers: phase, generic task, specialized task, and process instance.

Within each of these layers are a number of phases (e.g., business understanding, data understanding, data preparation) analogous to the standard description of the original CRISP-DM model, but it is now enhanced by some new phases (e.g., data enrichment, retention, and archiving).

Each of these phases consists of second-level generic tasks. The layer is called generic because it is deliberately general enough to cover all conceivable use cases. The third layer, the specialized task layer, describes how actions, located in the generic tasks, should be processed and how they should differ in different situations. That means, the specialized task layer, for example, handles the way data should be processed, "cleaning numeric values versus cleaning categorical values, [and] whether the problem type [calls for] clustering or predictive modeling" (Chapman et al. 2000).

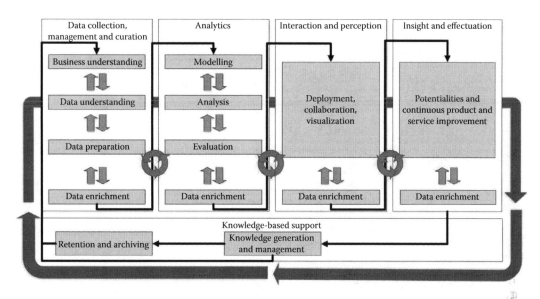

FIGURE 3.4

CRISP4BigData reference model, version 1.0. *Source*: Berwind, K et al. *2016 Collaborative European Research Conference*, 2017.

The fourth layer, the process instance, is a set of records of running actions, decisions, and results of the actual Big Data analysis. The process instance layer is *"organized according to the tasks defined at the higher levels, but represents what actually happened in a particular engagement, rather than what happens in general"* (Chapman et al. 2000).

Data Collection, Management, and Curation

The data collection, management, and curation phase is equivalent to the phase of the same name in Bornschlegl et al.'s IVIS4BigData reference model and the data integration phase of the Big Data Management reference model. The phase defines the collection and combination of data from different sources into a single platform. The layer handles the involved database systems and the interfaces to all data sources with special care to the system scalability and the common characteristics of Big Data, like volume, velocity, and the variety of data (sources).

The different subset of phases, i.e., business understanding, data understanding, data preparation, and data enrichment, are described in detail here. Some of the subordinate phases are equal to the phases named in CRISP-DM.

1. ***Business understanding***

    The phase business understanding describes the aims of the project to generate a valid project plan for coordination purposes. It is relevant to formulate an exact description of the problem and ensure an adequate task definition. A targeted implementation of purposed analytical methods could generate added value. This contains in parallel the reconcilement analytical processes, relating to the organizational structures and processes of the company. While considering existing

TABLE 3.1

Business Understanding: Generic Tasks and Outputs

Business Understanding Task	Outputs
Determine business objectives	Background, business objectives, business success criteria
Assess initial situation	Inventory of resources, requirements, assumptions and constraints, risks and contingencies, terminology, costs and benefits
Analyze infrastructure and data structure	Infrastructure (hardware and software) report, data structure report
Determine analysis goals	Analysis goals, criteria for analysis success
Produce project plan	Project plan, initial assessment tools and techniques

parameters, the key parameter of the analytical project should be defined. The following generic tasks have to be processed (Table 3.1):

- Determination of business objectives
- Assess the initial situation
- Infrastructure and data structure analysis
- Determine analysis goals
- Produce project plan

Within the scope of the analysis of the situation, first the problem is described from an economic point of view and should then be analyzed. Based on this first analysis step, a task definition is derived. Thereby, the parameters that contribute to the achievement of objectives of the project should be recognized and explored. Likewise, it is necessary to list hardware and software resources, financial resources, and the available personnel and their different qualifications. In another subphase, all possible risks should be described, along with all possible solutions for the listed risks. From the economic aim and the analysis of the situation, some analytical aims should be formulated. In another subphase, different types of analytical methods will be assigned to corresponding tasks and success metrics can be formulated, which are reflected in the evaluation of the results of the analysis.

During complex analytical projects, it can be meaningful, based on economic and technical aims, to generate a project plan. The underlying project plan supports the timing coordination of the processes and tasks. Furthermore, within each phase of the analysis, the resources, restrictions, inputs and outputs, and time scales allocated have to be determined. In addition, at the beginning of the project, cost-effectiveness considerations are necessary, accompanied by an assessment of the application possibilities, considering restrictions of human, technical, and financial resources.

2. *Data understanding*

The data understanding phase focuses on the collection of the project-relevant internal and external data. The aim of this phase is a better understanding of the underlying data, which will be used during the analysis process. First, insights into the data or database might emerge during the first collection of data. This phase utilizes *ad hoc* insights through a supporting technique of visualizations or via a method of descriptive statistics.

The following generic tasks (Table 3.2) deal with the quantity and quality of the available data, and under some circumstances such tasks should be performed a number of times.

A return to the previous phase is always possible; this is especially important if the results of the data understanding phase endanger the whole project. The focus of this phase is the selection and collection of data from different sources and databases. Therefore, it is useful to use so-called metadata, which offer information about the volume or the format of the available data. With an already-prepared database, the data warehouse is the first choice of data sources.

3. *Data preparation*

The data preparation phase aims to describe the preparation of the data which should be used for the analysis. The phase includes the following generic tasks (Table 3.3): define the data set, select data for analysis, enrich data, clean data, construct data, integrate data, and format data. All generic tasks have the aim to change, delete, filter, or reduce the data in order to obtain a high-quality data set for the analysis.

Based on the equivalent aspects of the CRISP4BigData data preparation phase and the CRISP-DM data preparation phase, we can estimate that 80% of resources (time, technology, and personnel) used in the whole CRISP4BigData process are committed to the CRISP4BigData data preparation phase (cf. Gabriel et al. 2011). Furthermore, Gabriel et al. described several additional tasks (e.g., data cleansing and transformation) that should be included within the generic tasks (or in addition to generic tasks).

- **Data cleansing:** This phase describes all provisions with the aim of high-quality data, which is very important for the applicability of the analysis (and

TABLE 3.2

Data Understanding: Generic Tasks and Outputs

Data Understanding Task	Output(s)
Collect initial data	Initial data collection report
Look up reusable data	Reusable analysis report, reusable data report, reusable process information report
Describe data	Data description report
Explore data	Data exploration report
Verify data quality	Data quality report

TABLE 3.3

Data Preparation: Generic Tasks and Outputs

Data Preparation Task	Output(s)
Define data set	Data set description
Select data	Rationale for inclusion or exclusion
Enrich data	Data enrichment report
Clean data	Data cleaning report
Construct data	Derived attributes, generated records
Integrate data	Merged data
Format data	Reformatted data

TABLE 3.4

Data Enrichment: Generic Tasks and Outputs

Data Enrichment Task	Output(s)
Collect process information	Process information report
Select process information	Process information description
Data enrichment	Analysis data, process information, skill recognition, and expert finder

techniques) and interpretability of the analysis results. This task extends, for example, to data merging, the multiplicative or additive linking of characteristics.

- **Transformation:** It is the aim of the transformation phase to change the data into a data format that is usable within the Big Data applications and frameworks. This step also contains formatting of the data into a usable data type and domain. This phase distinguishes alphabetical, alphanumerical, and numerical data types (cf. Gabriel et al. 2011).

4. *Data enrichment*

Data enrichment describes "the process of augmenting existing data with newer attributes that offer a tremendous improvement in getting analytical insights from it. Data enrichment often includes engineering the attributes to add additional data fields sourced from external data sources or derived from existing attributes" (Pasupuleti and Purra 2015). In this context, data enrichment is used for the collection and selection of all appreciable process information to reuse the analysis process and analysis results in a new iteration or a new analysis process. In addition, during this phase, information about the analysis stakeholder (e.g., analysts, data scientists, users, requesters) are collected to get insights about, for example, who is using the analysis (process), who is an expert in a needed domain, and which resources (e.g., analysis, diagrams, and algorithms) are reusable (Table 3.4).

Analytics

1. *Modeling*

The modeling phase describes the design of a Big Data analysis model which matches the requirements and business objectives with the aim of a high significance of the analysis. Within this phase, suitable frameworks, libraries, and algorithms will be selected to analyze the underlying data set based on the business objectives.

Attention should be paid, in some circumstances, that "not all tools and techniques are applicable to each and every task. For certain problems, only some techniques are appropriate … "Political requirements" and other constraints further limit the choices available to the data … engineer. It may be that only one tool or technique is available to solve the problem at hand—and that the tool may not be absolutely the best, from a technical standpoinit" (Chapman et al. 2000).

It is also necessary to define a suitable test design which contains a procedure to validate the model's quality. The test design should also contain a plan for the training, testing, and evaluation of the model. Further, it must be decided how the available data set should be divided into a training data set, test data set, and evaluation test set (Table 3.5).

2. *Analysis*

This phase describes the assessment of the analysis (model and analysis results); therefore, it is necessary to ensure that the analysis is matching the success criteria. Further, it is necessary to validate the analysis based on the test design and the business objectives concerning validity and accuracy.

Within this phase the following activities should be processed to obtain a suitable and meaningful model, analysis, and results (cf. Chapman et al. 2000):

- Evaluate and test the results with respect to evaluation criteria and according to a test strategy
- Compare the evaluation results and interpretation to select the best model and model parameter
- Check the plausibility of model in the context of the business objectives
- Check the model, analysis, and results against the available knowledge base to see if the discovered information is useful
- Check why certain frameworks, libraries, and algorithms and certain parameter settings lead to good or bad results (Table 3.6)

3. *Evaluation*

The evaluation phase describes the comprehensive assessment of the project progression, with the main focus on the assessment of the analysis results and the assessment of the whole CRISP4BigData process (cf. Gabriel et al. 2011) (Table 3.7).

TABLE 3.5

Modeling: Generic Tasks and Outputs

Modeling Task	Output(s)
Select modeling technique	Modeling technique, modeling assumptions
Generate test design	Test design
Build model	Parameter settings, models, model description

TABLE 3.6

Analysis: Generic Task and Outputs

Analysis Task	Outputs
Assess model	Model assessment, revised parameter settings

TABLE 3.7

Evaluation: Generic Tasks and Outputs

Evaluation Task	Output(s)
Evaluate results	Assessment of analysis results, approved models
Review process	Review of process
Determine next steps	List of possible actions, decision

TABLE 3.8

Data Enrichment: Generic Tasks and Outputs

Data Enrichment Task	Output(s)
Collect process information	Collect process information report
Select process information	Process information description
Data enrichment	Analysis data, process information, skill recognition, and expert finder

Within the evaluation phase the analysis process and analysis results must be verified by the following criteria: significance, novelty, usefulness, accuracy, generality, and comprehensibility (Chapman et al. 2000, Gabriel et al. 2011). Further, all results must match the requirements and project aims (Gabriel et al. 2011). Following this, the CRISP4BigData process and data model should be audited concerning the process quality to reveal weak points and to design and implement improvements.

Furthermore, the process should include the model test in a software test environment based on real use cases (or real applications) (Chapman et al. 2000). Finally, "depending on the results of the assessment and the process review, the project team decides how to proceed … to finish this project and move on to deployment" (Chapman et al. 2000).

4. *Data enrichment*

The data enrichment phase is equal to the previously named subordinate data enrichment phase within the data collection, management, and curation phase (Table 3.8).

Interaction and Perception

Deployment, Collaboration, and Visualization

The deployment, collaboration, and visualization phase describes how the CRISP4BigData process and the process analysis should be used. The following points are examples of information that should be described in detail and implemented within this phase:

- Durability of the process, analysis, and visualizations
- Grant access privileges for collaboration and access to results and visualizations
- Planning of sustainable monitoring and maintenance for the analysis process
- Presentation of final report and final project presentation
- Implementation of a service and service-level management

This phase also contains the creation of all needed documents (e.g., operational documents, interface designs, service-level management documents, mapping designs, etc.) (Table 3.9).

Data Enrichment

This data enrichment phase is equivalent to the above-described subordinate data enrichment phase within the data collection, management, and curation phase. It entails the following tasks and outputs (Table 3.10).

TABLE 3.9

Interaction and Perception: Generic Tasks and Outputs

Deployment, Collaboration, and Visualization Task	Outputs
Plan deployment	Analysis deployment plan, visualization deployment plan, collaboration deployment plan
Monitoring and maintenance	Monitoring and maintenance plan
Produce final report	Final report, final presentation
Review Project	Experience documentation, lessons learned summary

TABLE 3.10

Data Enrichment: Generic Tasks and Outputs

Data Enrichment Task	Output(s)
Collect process information	Collect process information report
Select process information	Process information description
Data enrichment	Analysis data, process information, skill recognition

Insight and Effectuation

Potentialities and Continuous Product and Service Improvement

The phase for potentialities and continuous product and service improvement entails the application of the analysis data to accomplish added value for products and services, as well as to optimize the organization and organizational processes (Table 3.11). According to the Big Data Management Reference model, the creation of added value is based on an efficiency increase in production and distribution (Kaufmann 2016), the optimization of machine operations (Kaufmann 2016), and improvement of the CRM (Kaufmann 2016).

Data Enrichment

This third data enrichment phase is also equal to the above-described subordinate data enrichment phase within the data collection, management, and curation phase (Table 3.12).

Knowledge-Based Support

Knowledge Generation and Management

The knowledge generation and management phase entails the handling of the collected (process) information, collected information about the experts and users, and the created

TABLE 3.11

Potentialities and Continuous Product and Service Improvement: Generic Tasks and Outputs

Potentialities and Continuous Product and Service Improvement Task	Output(s)
Apply analysis	Potentialities report, improvement report
Review project	Review project report

TABLE 3.12

Data Enrichment: Generic Tasks and Outputs

Data Enrichment Task	Output(s)
Collect process information	Collect process information report
Select process information	Process information description
Data enrichment	Analysis data, process information, skill recognition

TABLE 3.13

Knowledge Generation and Management: Generic Tasks and Outputs

Knowledge Generation and Management Task	Output
Collect useful results and insights	Knowledge tank
Find experts	Expert tank

insights and ensuing fields of application, with the aim to collect these artifacts (Table 3.13). These artifacts can be connected in a meaningful way to create a knowledge tank (knowledge base) and an expert tank, both of which can be applied for all steps of the data life cycle (Kaufman 2016).

Retention and Archiving

The retention and archiving phase entails the retention and archiving of the collected data, information, and results during the whole CRISP4BigData process. This phase contains the following Generic Tasks and Outputs (Table 3.14).

The collected data can then be classified according to the Hortonworks (2016) classification model, as follows:

- Hot: Used for both storage and computing. Data that are being used for processing stay in this category.
- Warm: Partially hot and partially cold. When a block is warm, the first replica is stored on disk and the remaining replicas are stored in an archive.
- Cold: Used only for storage, with limited computing. Data that are no longer being used, or data that need to be archived, are moved from hot storage to cold storage. When a block is cold, all replicas are stored in the archive.

All the collected, archived, and classified data can be used as "new" databases for a new iteration of the CRISP4BigData process.

TABLE 3.14

Retention and Archiving: Generic Tasks and Outputs

Retention and Archiving Task	Output
Collect data	Collected data set
Select data	Selected data set
Classify data	Classified data set
Archive data	Archived data set
Maintain data archiving and retention	Maintenance and life cycle plan

Preparatory Operations for Evaluation of the CRISP4BigData Reference Model within a Cloud-Based Hadoop Ecosystem

The offered CRISP4BigData Reference Model, which supports scientists and research facilities to maintain and manage their research resources, is currently evaluated in a proof-of-concept implementation. The implementation is based on the conceptual architecture for a VRE infrastructure called the Virtual Environment for Research Interdisciplinary Exchange (unpublished article of Bornschlegl), for which the goal is to handle the whole analytical process, managing (automatically) all the needed information, analytical models, algorithms, library knowledge resources, and infrastructure resources to obtain new insights and optimize products and services.

Matthias Schneider (2017) provided in his thesis, as a preparatory operation, a prototypical implementation for executing analytic Big Data workflows using selected components based on a Cloud-based Hadoop ecosystem within the EGI Federated Cloud (Voronov 2017). The selection of components was based on requirements for engineering VRE. Its overall architecture is presented below, followed by two diverse domain-specific use cases implemented in this environment. The use cases are connected to the EU cofounded SenseCare project, which "aims to provide a new effective computing platform based on an information and knowledge ecosystem providing software services applied to the care of people with dementia" (Engel et. al 2016).

Architecture Instantiation

The instantiation of the conceptual architecture for a VRE infrastructure as introduced above and the component selection is illustrated in Figure 3.5.

Apache Ambari is used as an overall Hadoop cluster management tool, and it is extendable via use of Ambari Management Packs for service deployment. Hue is a user-friendly interface that allows the analyst to model work flows and access the HDFS. These actions are executed by Oozie using MapReduce or Spark operating on YARN, with files stored in HDFS or HBase tables. Sqoop can be used for data management, and Sentry can be used for authorization.

Use Case 1: MetaMap Annotation of Biomedical Publications via Hadoop

As a part of the SenseCare Project, information retrieval for medical research data, supported by algorithms for natural language processing, was evaluated. One approach would be to use MetaMap, a tool developed at the U.S. National Library of Medicine to facilitate text analysis on biomedical texts, in order to extract medical terms from a comprehensive database of a vast volume of medical publications. In order to process this Big Data using Hadoop, the MetaMap server was embedded into an Ambari Management Pack to distribute it on the nodes of the Hadoop cluster. Using MapReduce as the execution framework, a map method was developed to perform the actual processing of the input files from the database, which yielded the extracted medical terms as result, while a reducer method filtered duplicates of these terms before writing them into the distributed file system.

Use Case 2: Emotion Recognition in Video Frames with Hadoop

While Hadoop is often used for textual processing, Use Case 2 evaluated the processing of binary data. Here, video data was evaluated, with the goal of recognizing emotions from

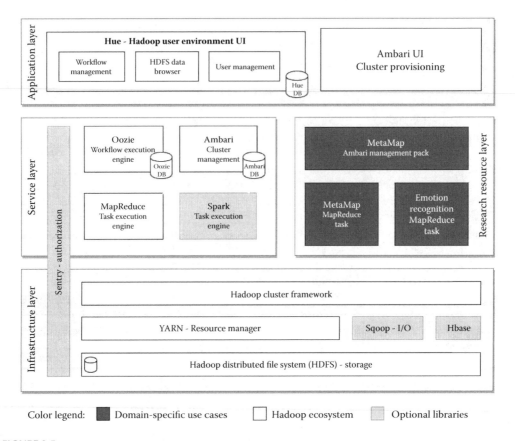

FIGURE 3.5
Instantiation of the conceptual architecture for a VRE infrastructure using Hadoop components and two domain-specific use cases. *Source*: Schneider, M., Master's thesis, University of Hagen, Germany, 2017.

facial expressions, via computer vision algorithms. To avoid handling of multiple video formats in Hadoop, the video files were preprocessed and partial frames were extracted to images. These images were stored in a special container format that allowed division into chunks when stored in HDFS, in order to achieve distributed processing using MapReduce. The actual processing was realized via a mapper method called OpenCV, a library of extracted facial landmarks, among other computer vision functions. Facial landmarks are distinctive spots in the human face, e.g., the corner of one's mouth, or the position of the nose or the eyes. Emotions are derived from the relative positions of these facial landmarks. In subsequent tasks, these results can be rated and analyzed.

Hadoop Cluster Installation in the EGI Federated Cloud

A cluster installation using fixed hardware is rigid in terms of its resource utilization. Therefore, Cloud computing approaches are gaining in popularity, because they allow a more balanced usage of hardware resources through virtualization. Especially when instantiating VREs, a cloud environment is advantageous, as it allows maximum flexibility concerning computational and storage resources. In order to gather experience with a Cloud environment for the Hadoop VRE introduced above, the EGI Federated Cloud was evaluated in Andrei Voronov's thesis (Voronov 2017).

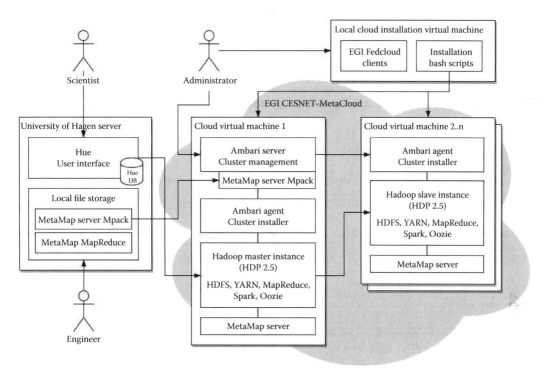

FIGURE 3.6

Hadoop cluster installation in the EGI Federated Cloud, showing the deployment of MetaMap using Ambari Management packs. *Source*: Schneider, M., Master's thesis, University of Hagen, Germany, 2017.

The European Grid Infrastructure (EGI) provides services for bringing computing infrastructure to scientists and research institutions in Europe. As a part of these services, the Federated Cloud unifies formerly heterogeneous computational infrastructure and therefore allows global usage of temporarily underused IT infrastructure for other scientists in Europe (Fernández-del-Castillo et al. 2015).

Figure 3.6 gives an overview of the EGI Federated Cloud architecture developed for the MetaMap annotation Use Case introduced above. For this purpose, a fixed server at the University of Hagen was used to host the Hue user interface together with local file storage for the research resources to be permanently available. The cluster in the Cloud is seen as an infrastructure component within the VRE, and therefore a loose coupling is achieved. The registration, configuration, and installation of the virtual machines are achieved using installation scripts, which allow easy generation of an EGI Federated Cloud cluster with the needed resources and preinstalled Ambari. The following section details some practical experience gained during the utilization of the EGI Federated Cloud cluster.

MetaMap Annotation Results

As a first benchmark, the annotation process for biomedical publications using MetaMap (Use Case 1) was executed in a local cluster with two nodes and compared to the execution in a cluster within the EGI CESNET-MetaCloud, a provider of EGI, with five nodes. One thousand biomedical full-text publications were processed in the local cluster within six hours, while the EGI Federated Cloud needed as long as 15 hours for the same tasks.

A remarkable result was that the execution times in the EGI Federated Cloud varied massively (13 to 16 hours), while the execution time on the local cluster remained quite constant. This illustrates the shared character of the Cloud environment provided by the EGI. During the evaluation phase and multiple executions of this long-lasting batch-oriented process, no down time occurred. Thus, even with no guaranteed resources and varying computational power, the EGI Federated Cloud seems to be a reliable service.

Conclusions and Outlook

This chapter has described the issues and challenges companies have to deal with during the whole data and information life cycle to extract important information and knowledge to generate insights regarding their own opportunities. The aim is to improve services and products and to expose new advantages opposite those of their competitors. Therefore, this chapter offered a conceptual modeling and implementation of a Cloud-based Hadoop ecosystem within the EGI Federated Cloud, based on a VRE architecture. Further, this chapter described two research-relevant use cases that included use of the MetaMap Annotation for biomedical publications and emotion recognition in video frames with Hadoop.

In addition, the chapter showed some new methodologies, the Big Data Management reference model and IVIS4BigData and CRISP4BigData models, for handling the whole analysis process from raw data to visual views and to deal with analysis processes and projects, beginning with a business understanding the role of archiving and retention. On a final note, we described how new technologies and services based on Cloud computing could support the analysis of data without an owner-operated data center.

References

Beath C, Becerra-Fernandez I, Ross J, Short J. 2012. Finding value in the information explosion. *MIT Sloan Management Review.* http://sloanreview.mit.edu/article/finding-value-in-the-information -explosion/.

Berwind K, Bornschlegl M, Kaufman M, Hemmje M. 2017. Towards a cross industry standard process to support Big Data applications in virtual research environments. *Collaborative European Research Conference 2016.* http://www.cerc-conference.eu/wp-content/uploads/2016/12/CERC -2016-proceedings.pdf.

Bornschlegl MX, Berwind K, Kaufmann M, Hemmje M. 2016. Towards a reference model for advanced visual interfaces supporting Big Data analysis in virtual research environments, pp. 78–81. *Proceedings on the International Conference on Internet Computing.* World Congress in Computer Science, Computer Engineering and Applied Computing.

Card SK, Mackinlay JD, Shneiderman B. 1999. *Readings in Information Visualization: Using Vision To Think.* Amsterdam, The Netherlands: Elsevier.

Chapman P, Clinton J, Kerber R, Khabaza T, Reinartz T, Shearer C, Wirth R. 2000. CRISP-DM 1.0: *Step-by-Step Data Mining Guide.* ftp://ftp.software.ibm.com/software/analytics/spss/support /Modeler/Documentation/14/UserManual/CRISP-DM.pdf.

Engel F et al. 2016. SenseCare: Towards an experimental platform for home-based, visualisation of emotional states of people with dementia. *Advanced Visual Interfaces.* New York: ACM.

Fernández-del-Castillo E, Scardaci D, García AL. 2015. The EGI Federated Cloud e-infrastructure. *Procedia Computer Science* 68:196–205.

Fischer G. 2012. Context-aware systems: The "right" information, at the "right" time, in the "right" place, in the "right" way, to the "right" person, pp. 287–294. *Proceedings of the International Working Conference on Advanced Visual Interfaces*. New York: ACM.

Freiknecht J. 2014. Big Data in der Praxis. Lösungen mit Hadoop, HBase und Hive; Daten speichern, aufbereiten, visualisieren. Munich, Germany: Hanser.

Gabriel R, Gluchowski P, Pastwa A. 2011. *Data Warehouse and Data Mining*. Herdecke University. Witten, Germany: W3L GmbH.

Hortonworks. 2016. Storage policies: Hot, warm, and cold. https://docs.hortonworks.com/HDP Documents/HDP2/HDP 2.3.2/bk_hdfs_admin_tools/content/storage_policies_hot_warm_cold .html.

Kaufmann M. 2016. *Towards a Reference Model for Big Data Management*. Research report, Faculty of Mathematics and Computer Science, University of Hagen, Hagen, Germany.

Kuhlen R. 2004. Informationsethik: Umgang mit Wissen und Information in elektronischen Räumen. UTB 2454 Medien und Kommunikationswissenschaft. Konstanz: UVK-Verl.-Ges.

Nonaka I, Takeuchi H. 1995. *The Knowledge-Creating Company: How Japanese Companies Create the Dynamics of Innovation*. Oxford: Oxford University Press.

Pasupuleti P, Purra SB. 2015. *Data Lake Development with Big Data*. Birmingham: Packt Publishing.

Schneider M. 2017. Workflow management for Big Data applications within the Apache Hadoop ecosystem based on virtual research environments. Master's thesis. Faculty of Mathematics and Computer Science, University of Hagen, Hagen, Germany.

Upadhyay S, Grant R. 2013. 5 data scientists who became CEOs and are leading thriving companies. http://venturebeat.com/2013/12/03/5-data-scientists-who-became-ceos-and-are-leading -thriving-companies/.

Voronov A. 2017. Eine cloud-basierte Entwicklung und Implementierung eines Hadoop Ecosystems und Ecosystems Portal auf Grundlage des Modells für Virtual Research Environments und IVIS4BigData Referenz modells. Master's thesis, Faculty of Mathematics and Computer Science, University of Hagen, Hagen, Germany.

Key Terminology and Definitions

Big Data Management Reference Model: the Big Data Management Reference Model of Kaufmann (2016) describes Big Data management as a process for the management of data streams of high volumes, at rapid velocities, high heterogeneity, and uncertainty of integrity. The reference model demonstrates, furthermore, that the techniques for the administration and management of Big Data are not merely for research purposes but also achieve added value in real world applications.

CRISP4BigData Reference Model: the CRISP4BigData Reference Model is a phase-based process model which deals with the analysis process from an initial business understanding to retention and archiving of data, information, and knowledge. The reference model is based on Kaufmann's Big Data Management reference model, Bornschlegel's IVIS4BigData reference model, and the Cross-Industry Standard Process for Data Mining.

Data Analytics: Data Analytics is the process of filtering, querying, indexing, cleaning, transforming, and modeling data with the objective of finding useful information to support decision making.

Data Insight and Effectuation: Data Insight and Effectuation is a process for dealing with the results of an analysis to add value to a product or service to get a better or a more suitable result.

Data Integration and Collection: Data Integration and Collection describes the process of integrating all needed data sources and collecting the data from those sources to generate a data set for further analysis.

Data Interaction and Perception: Data Interaction and Perception describes how human decision makers get in touch with the first results of their requested analysis to manipulate, correct, and share them with other (human) decision makers.

Data Management and Curation: Data Management and Curation describes a set of methodical and organizational processes and procedures to deal with data as a resource, analogous to the data life cycle to operate with the data to gain maximum added value across all business processes.

Data Warehousing: Data Insight and Effectuation is a process for dealing with the results of an analysis to add value to a product or service to obtain a better or more suitable result.

Hadoop Ecosystem: the Hadoop Ecosystem is based on several software components, like HDFS, Hive, HBase, and Storm, and is designed to deal with a large volume of (real-time) data. There are also some other components, like the Web-based notebook Apache Zeppelin, to analyze, visualize, and interact with data.

Information Visualization Reference Model: the Information Visualization Reference Model describes the transformation from raw data to a visual form of the data as a mapping and transformation process over several processing steps. Data transformations map raw data, such as text data, processing information, (database) tables, e-mails, feeds, and sensor data (Beath et al. 2012, Freiknecht 2014) into data tables, which define the data with relational descriptions and extended metadata. The data tables, which are based on mathematical relations, are used to transform the raw data into a relation or set of relations to structure them and make it easier to map the data into visual structures.

IVIS4BigData Reference Model: the hybrid IVIS4BigData Reference Model is based on the IVIS reference model and Kaufmann's Big Data Management Reference Model. It was created to cover new use cases and requirements in current situations with advanced visual interface opportunities for perceiving, managing, and interpreting Big Data.

Knowledge-Based Support: Knowledge-Based Support describes some additional cross-departmental functions of knowledge-based processes and technologies which consequently support the data-based paradigm and allow optimization of the advantage of Big Data.

4

A Survey of Tools for Big Data Analytics

K. G. Srinivasa, Zeeshan Ahmad, Nabeel Siddiqui, and Abhishek Kumar

CONTENTS

There are various options which can be selected for our Big Data analytics program. These options include vendor tool types and tool features, user's techniques and methodologies, and team or organizational structures. The list cover a lot of items which are complex and which we may not have considered seriously. Irrespective of what project stage you're in within Big Data analytics, knowing what options are available is foundational to making good decisions about approaches to take and software or hardware products to evaluate.

To accumulate all these problems, the TDWI organization conducted a survey of the pros and cons of options for Big Data analytics (Figure 4.1). The listed options include the latest innovations, like Clouds, MapReduce, and complex event processing, which were present during the past few years but are now being adopted worldwide. The list presents a catalog of available options for Big Data analytics, and responses to the survey questions indicate what combinations of analytic functions, platforms, and tools users are employing today in terms of usability and complexity. With the help of these available data, project planning can be done efficiently and we can deduce priorities based on the challenges foreseen.

The technology and technical terms used in this book chapter are explained wherever they appear or in the Key Terminology and Definitions section at the end of the chapter. In addition to the references cited in our text, we have provided additional references following the References section for advance or further reading, for the benefit of advanced readers.

Survey on Commonly Used Big Data Tools

Figure 4.1 portrays a slightly different view of option usage, as indicated by the pairs of bars on the right side of the figure. Per-option differences between responses for "Using Today" and "Using in Three Years" was calculated based on the potential growth bars; this delta tells us how much the usage of a Big Data analytics option will increase or decrease. An option's commitment value is the percentage of survey respondents who are committed to using that option, whether today, in three years, or both. Note that none of the values in Figure 4.1 comes to 100%, which indicates that no option will be used by all survey respondents in all time frames. In this chapter, we focus on learning about Big Data analytics best practices, from identifying business goals to selecting the best Big Data analytics tools for your organization's needs (Wayer 2012).

What kinds of techniques and tool types is your organization using for advanced analytics and Big Data, both today and in three years? (Checking nothing on a row means you have no plans for that technique or tool.)

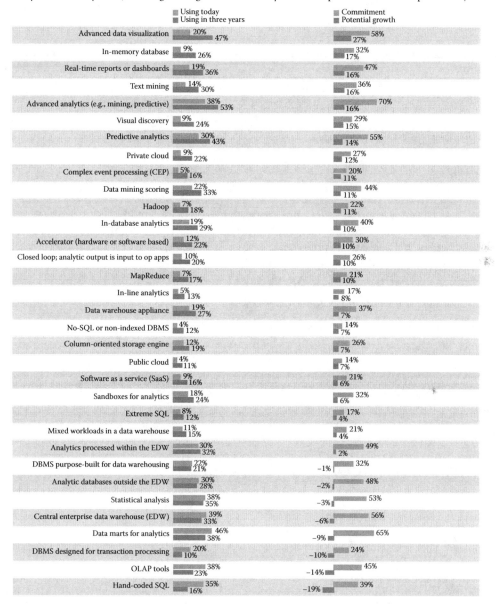

FIGURE 4.1
Common Big Data tool options usage. The data are based on responses from a total of 325 possible respondents. The chart was sorted based on potential growth values (gray bars). (Modified from Russom, P., *TDWI Best Practices Report, Fourth Quarter, 2011,* 2011.)

Potential Growth Versus Commitment for Big Data Analytics Options

Potential Growth

The potential growth chart subtracts tools in use now from those anticipated to be in use in three years, and the delta provides a rough indicator for the growth or decline of usage of options for Big Data analytics over the next three years. The charted numbers are positive or negative. Note that a positive number indicates growth and that growth can be good or strong. A negative number indicates that the use of an option may decline or remain flat instead of increasing.

Commitment

The numbers in the commitment column represent the percentages of survey respondents (based on a total of approximately 325 respondents) who selected "Using Today" and/or "Using in Three Years" during the survey process. The measure of commitment here is cumulative, in that the commitment may be realized today, in the near future, or both. A survey respondent could leave it unchecked if they had no plans for the option.

Balance of Commitment and Potential Growth

To get a complete picture, it's imperative to look at the metrics for both commitment and growth. For instance, some features or techniques may have significant growth rates but only within a weakly committed segment of the user community (Clouds, SaaS, or No-SQL databases). They are strongly committed through common use today (analytic data marts, online analytic processing [OLAP] tools) but they could have low growth rates. Options which are seen with the greatest activity in the near future will most likely be those with high ratings for both growth and commitment. To visualize the balance of commitment and growth, Figure 4.2 includes the potential growth and commitment numbers from Figure 4.1 on opposing axes of the single chart. Big Data analytics options are plotted as growing or declining usage (*x* axis) and narrow or broad commitment (*y* axis).

Trends for Big Data Analytics Options

In Figures 4.1 and 4.2, we showed that most Big Data analytics options will experience some level of growth in the near future. The figures also indicate which options will grow the most, as well as those that will stagnate or decline. In particular, four groups of options stand out based on combinations of growth and commitment (Figure 4.2, groups that are circled, numbered, or labeled). The groups are reflective of trends in advanced analytics and Big Data (Rusom 2011, Wayer 2012).

Group 1: Strong to Moderate Commitment, Strong Potential Growth

The highest-probability options for changing best practices in Big Data analytics are those with higher potential growth (as validated by the survey results) with moderate or strong

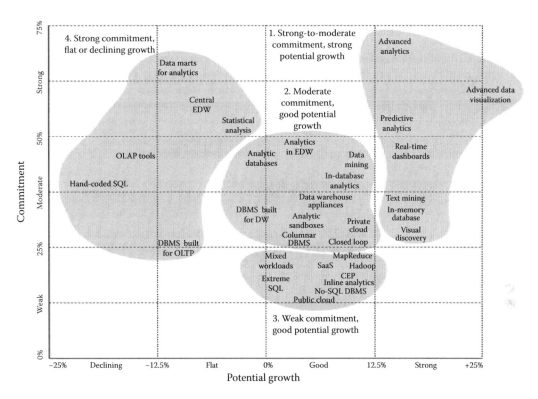

FIGURE 4.2
Option for Big Data analytics, based on a plot of potential growth versus commitment. Plots are approximate, based on values from Figure 4.1. (Adopted from Russom, P., *Big Data Analytics, TDWI Best Practices Report Fourth Quarter, 2011*, 2011.)

organizational commitment. Group 1 adheres to both of these requirements, including tool types and techniques that TDWI has been adopting aggressively during recent years. Furthermore, today's strongest trends in business intelligence (BI), data warehousing and analytics, are apparent in Group 1 and are summarized in the next five subsections.

Advanced Analytics

Advanced analytics can be a collection of techniques and tool types, including tools for predictive analytics, data mining, statistical analysis, complex SQL, data visualization, artificial intelligence, natural language processing, and database methods that support analytics. The highest commitment among all the mentioned options for Big Data analytics is for advanced analytics (Figure 4.2, upper right corner). The options which are most nearly related to advanced analytics are predictive analytics, data mining, and statistical analysis in terms of commitment. Corporate commitment cannot be denied in the field of advanced analytics, as it will no doubt increase the growth area for users and for customers in years to come.

Visualization

Advanced data visualization (ADV) projects the strongest potential among all the options for Big Data analytics. ADV can be seen as a natural fit for Big Data analytics. ADV can be scaled to represent millions to thousands of data points, unlike the usual standard pie, bar, or line charts. ADV can handle varied data types and then present analytic data structures that aren't easily flattened onto a computer screen. Many of the ADV tools and functions present today are compatible with all the leading data sources, so a business analyst can explore data widely in search of just the right analytic data set in real time. ADV tools available today have evolved into easy-to-use and self-service tools, so that people can use them comprehensively. Alternatively, TDWI has seen many corporations adopt ADV and visual discovery, as both stand-alone analytic tools and general purpose BI platforms, on both departmental and enterprise levels (KarmaSphere Solution Brief 2011, JasperSoft Quick Start Guide 2017).

Real Time

Operational BI is a business practice that measures and monitors the performance of business operations frequently. It is enabled by BI technologies, especially dashboard-style reports. Although the definition of "frequently" varies, most operational BI implementations fetch data in real time (or close to it) to refresh real-time management dashboards (which are poised for growth [Figure 4.2]). Users' aggressive adoption of operational BI in recent years has (among other things) pushed BI technologies into real-time operation, as seen in management dashboards. As users evolve operational BI to be more analytic (i.e., not merely reports based on metrics), analytics are likewise being pushed into real time. Visualization and advanced analytics are poised for aggressive adoption. Real time is the strongest BI trend, yet it hasn't hit Big Data analytics much, as yet.

Rates of growth and commitment identified four groups of options for Big Data analytics. The third V in the three Vs of Big Data stands for velocity. As numerous examples in this chapter show, there are many real-world applications for analytics available today for streaming Big Data, plus more applications are coming. However, real-time analytic applications are still new, and they ae utilized today by relatively few organizations. Perhaps this explains why real-time and streaming data did not fare well in the use survey. Even so, given that real-time applications are the strongest trend in BI today, these will no doubt transform analytics soon, just as they have transformed reporting.

In-Memory Databases

One of the optimal ways to get a real-time, quicker response from a database is to fetch the information in the server memory, hence eliminating disk I/O and speed challenges. For several years now, TDWI has seen consistent adoption of in-memory databases among its members and other organizations. An in-memory database can serve many purposes, but in BI they usually support real-time dashboards for operational BI, and the database usually stores metrics, key performance indicators (KPIs), and sometimes OLAP cubes. Similar growth is observed among users in the adoption of in-memory databases for advanced analytics; this is trending, as accessing data is faster than traditional approaches. Leading vendors now offer data warehouse appliances with flash memory or solid-state drives, to which in-memory databases will soon move.

Unstructured Data

We all subscribe insincerely to the fact that there's valuable, actionable information in natural language text and other unstructured data. In spite of this, organizations haven't taken advantage of this information until recently. Tools for text mining and text analytics have slowly gained usage, because they can find facts about key business entities in text and turn those facts into usable, structured data. The data resulting from this can be applied to customer sentiment analyses and it can churn out many applications. For example, many insurance companies use text analytics to parse the mountains of text that result from the claims process, turn the text into structured records, then add that data to the samples studied via data mining or statistical tools for risk, fraud, and actuarial analyses (Russom 2011).

Group 2: Moderate Commitment, Good Potential Growth

Group 2 is dominated by different types of analytic database platforms. The recent innovations that have been carried by vendor firms have provided more options for analytic database platforms, including dedicated analytic DBMSs, data warehouse appliances, columnar data stores, and sandboxes, in addition to older options. Owing to user adoption, the newer analytic database platforms have achieved moderate commitment and good potential growth. Most of the user organizations going through a new analytics program (or a revamp of an established one) have experienced one issue which is a determining factor: Can the current or planned enterprise data warehouse (EDW) handle Big Data and advanced analytics without degrading performance of other workloads for reporting and OLAP? A simpler question could be: How can our EDW perform and scale with concurrent mixed workloads? The answer to this question will help us determine whether the analytic data are managed and operated on the EDW properly or in a separate platform (which is usually integrated with the EDW). For a complete list and discussion of vendor analytic database platforms, view the TDWI Webinar "Data Warehouse Appliances: An Update on the State of the Art," online at tdwi.org.

EDWs can handle advanced analytic workloads, showing that in-database analytics has become very common. Yet, performance of host analytics on an EDW is not preferred by everyone. That's because the management of Big Data and the processing workloads of advanced analytics make stringent demands of server resources, such that (depending on the EDW platform that has been assembled) they can rob server resources from other data warehouse workloads, resulting in report refreshes and slow queries. Some BI professionals prefer to isolate analytic workloads and Big Data on platforms outside the EDW separately to avoid performance degradation due to mixed workloads. If the performance is kept aside, separate analytic database platforms make sense when analytics is funded or controlled by a department instead of the EDW sponsor. Some moderate demand has been observed for analytic database platforms that can be seen as permanent fixtures in data warehouse programs, although more than two-thirds of organizations tend toward analytics on a central EDW. The movement started in early 2003, when the first data warehouse appliances were coming into light. After this movement came new vendor-built databases with columnar data stores, which inherently accelerated column-oriented analytic queries for faster searches. Most recently, vendors have carried out analytic platforms by using distributed file systems, MapReduce, and No-SQL indexing.

Group 3: Weak Commitment, Good Growth

Group 3 shows weak commitment, as they are relatively new. Potential growth is good within committed organizations, and we can expect these options to be in more use soon.

Hadoop Distributed File System (HDFS)

In the current scenario, interest in the HDFS is extremely high (Figure 4.2), although it is rarely adopted (hence, the figure shows weak commitment). Interest is high with the advent of Big Data, which is diverse in terms of data types. Complex data types that we normally associate with Big Data originate in files, examples being Web logs and XML documents. It is quite troublesome to transform these files into standard forms via a traditional database management system (DBMS). Also, data transformation could potentially lose the data details and anomalies that fuel some forms of analytics. Some users would prefer to simply copy files into a file system without preparing the data much, as long as the Big Data strewn across a million or more files is accessible for analytics.

MapReduce

MapReduce is a new analytic option and hence it is attracting more interest today, similar to Hadoop. The two are similar in principle, as MapReduce makes a distributed file system like HDFS addressable through analytic logic. For example, in MapReduce, a user is required to define a data operation, such as a query or analysis, and the platform "maps" the operation across all relevant nodes for distributed parallel processing and data collection. Mapping and analytic processing span multiple distributed files, despite diverse data types. MapReduce works well in a database management system with a relational store, as in the Aster Data database. Analytics for Big Data are possible due to the distributed processing of MapReduce.

Complex Event Processing (CEP)

This option is relatively new, compared to others, yet it is experiencing rapid adoption. For example, a recent TDWI report discovered that 20% of survey respondents had incorporated some form of event processing into their data integration solutions; that is significant given the newness of this practice. Although it is not required, CEP often operates in a real-time scenario, and so its adoption is driven partially by the real-time trend. CEP can also be used in association with analytics, which is another driver. CEP technologies are evolving to handle streaming Big Data.

SQL

Trends in BI sometimes cancel out each other. That's currently the case with SQL, as some organizations have deepened their use of SQL while others have done the opposite. On one hand, many organizations rely heavily on SQL as the best go-to approach for advanced analytics. The reason for this is that BI professionals know SQL, and it is quite compatible with every system. An experienced BI professional can create complex SQL programs (depicted as "Extreme SQL" in Figure 4.2), and these work in accordance with Big Data that's SQL addressable. Extreme SQL is typically applied to highly detailed source data, still in its original schema (or lightly transformed). The SQL is "extreme" because it creates multidimensional structures and other complex data models on the fly, without remodeling and transforming the data ahead of time. On the other hand is the small innovative and rare group of No-SQL enthusiasts. This is feasible when the majority of data types are not rational and converting them to tabular structures would not make sense. No-SQL databases also tend to appeal to application developers, who don't have the BI professional's attachment to SQL.

Clouds in TDWI Technology Surveys

Clouds in the TDWI technology survey showed that BI professionals prefer private clouds over public ones, especially for BI, DW, and analytic purposes. This helps explain why the public Cloud has the weakest commitment (Figure 4.2). The preference is given to private clouds, mostly due to the importance of data security and governance. Even so, some organizations experiment with analytic tools and databases on a public cloud and then move the information onto a private cloud once they decide analytics is mission critical. In a related scenario, software-as-a-service (SaaS) doesn't necessarily require a cloud, but most SaaS-based analytic applications or analytic database platforms are on a tightly secured public cloud.

Group 4: Strong Commitment, Flat or Declining Growth

Group 4 includes essential options, such as centralized EDWs, data marts for analytics, hand-coded SQL, OLAP tools, and DBMSs built for OLTP. In fact, these are some of the most common options in use today for BI, analytics, and data warehousing. Why does the survey show them in decline, if these are so popular? There are mainly two reasons for this:

- **Users are maintaining mature investments while shifting new investments to more modern options.** For instance, many organizations with a BI program have developed solutions for OLAP, but the current trend is to implement forms of advanced analytics, which are new to many organizations. OLAP won't go away. In fact, OLAP is the most common form of analytics in today's world, and it will remain so for the coming years. No doubt that users' spending for OLAP will grow, albeit modestly compared to other analytic options. Databases designed for online transaction processing (OLTP) are in a similar situation. As we saw in the discussion of Group 2, many users have come to the conclusion that their organization would be better served by an analytic database platform built specifically for data analytics and warehousing. They will shift new investments to databases purpose-built for data analytics or warehousing while maintaining their investments in older relational databases (designed for OLTP, although also used for DW).

- **Users are correcting problems with their designs or best practices.** Data marts are more problematic than ever due to recent requirements for data sharing and compliance. Although data marts regularly host analytic data sets, they are typically on older platforms that include an SMP hardware architecture and an OLTP database. Whether to get a better analytic database platform or to rein in proliferated marts, many user organizations are aggressively decommissioning analytic data marts. The natural option on which to base analytics is hand-coded SQL. The catch is that hand coding tends to be anticollaborative and nonproductive. Because SQL (as the leading language for data) is supported by almost every tool and platform in IT, and is in skill sets of most data management professionals, it cannot go away. In fact, analytics is driving up the use of hand-coded SQL. Most organizations should consider tools that generate SQL based on analytic applications developed in a user-friendly GUI, instead of hand-coding SQL. This needs to happen to make analytic tools more palatable to business people and mildly technical personnel as well as to make developers more productive.

Understanding Internet of Things Data

To get maximum business value from Big Data analytics efforts, users should look to incorporate a mix of structured and unstructured information; they should think of it as wide data, not merely Big Data. Big Data is a bit of a misnomer. Certainly, the volume of information coming from the Web, modern call centers, and other data sources can be enormous. But the main benefit of all that data isn't in the size. It's not even in the business insights you can get by analyzing individual data sets in search of interesting patterns and relationships. To get true BI from Big Data analytics applications, user organizations and BI and analytics vendors alike must focus on integrating and analyzing a broad mix of information, in short, wide data.

Future business success lies in ensuring that the data in both Big Data streams and mainstream enterprise systems can be analyzed in a coherent and coordinated fashion. Numerous vendors are working on one possible means of doing so, including the following:

- Products that provide SQL access to Hadoop repositories and NoSQL databases
- The direction they are taking matters, particularly with SQL-on-Hadoop technologies, because far more people know SQL than know Hadoop.

Hadoop is a powerful technology for managing large amounts of unstructured data, but it's not so great for quickly running analytics applications, especially ones combining structured and unstructured data. Conversely, SQL has a long and successful history of enabling heterogeneous data sources to be accessed with almost identical calls. And the business analysts who do most of the work to provide analytics to business managers and the CxO suite typically are well versed in using SQL.

In addition, most users want evolutionary advances in technology, not revolutionary ones. That means intelligently incorporating the latest technologies into existing IT ecosystems to gain new business value as quickly and as smoothly as possible. The result: information from Hadoop clusters, NoSQL systems, and other new data sources gets joined with data from relational databases and data warehouses to build a more complete picture of customers, market trends, and business operations. For example, customer sentiment data that can be gleaned from social networks and the Web is potentially valuable, but its full potential won't be realized if it's compartmentalized away from data on customer leads and other marketing information.

Challenges for Big Data Analytics Tools

One of the major Big Data challenges is what information to use, and what not to use. Businesses looking to get real value out of Big Data, while avoiding overwhelming their systems, need to be selective about what they analyze.

RichRelevance Inc. faces one of the prototypical Big Data challenges: lots of data and not a lot of time to analyze it. For example, the marketing analytics services provider runs an online recommendation engine for Target, Sears, Neiman Marcus, Kohl's, and other retailers. Its predictive models, running on a Hadoop cluster, must be able to deliver product recommendations to shoppers in 40 to 60 milliseconds, which is not a simple task for a company that has two petabytes of customer and product data in its systems, a total that grows as retailers update and expand their online product catalogs. "We go through a lot of data," said Marc Hayem, vice president in charge of RichRelevance's service-oriented architecture platform.

It would be easy to drown in all that data. Hayem said that managing it smartly is critical, both to ensure that the recommendations the San Francisco company generates are relevant to shoppers and to avoid spending too much time (and processing resources) analyzing unimportant data. The approach it adopted involves whittling down the data being analyzed to the essential elements needed to quickly produce recommendations for shoppers.

The full range of the historical data that RichRelevance stores on customers of its clients is used to define customer profiles, which help enable the recommendation engine to match up shoppers and products. But when the analytical algorithms in the predictive models are deciding in real time what specific products to recommend, they look at data on just four factors: the recent browsing history of shoppers, their demographic data, the products availability on a retailer's website, and special promotions currently being offered by the retailer. "With those four elements, we can decide what to do," Hayem said, adding that data on things such as past purchases, how much customers typically spend, and other retailers where they also shop isn't important at that point in the process.

In the age of Big Data, it is important to know what information is needed in analytics applications and what information isn't; this has never been more important, or in many cases, more difficult. The sinking cost of data storage and the rise of the Hadoop data lake concept are making it more feasible for organizations to stash huge amounts of structured, unstructured, and semistructured data collected from both internal systems and external sources. But getting the questions wrong regareing what to use, what to hold onto for the future, and what to jettison wrong can have both immediate and long-term consequences.

Even if a particular data set may seem unimportant now, it could have uses down the line. On the other hand, cluttering up Hadoop systems, data warehouses, and other repositories with useless data could pose unnecessary costs and make it hard to find the true gems of information amid all the clutter. And not thinking carefully, and intelligently, about the data that needs to be analyzed for particular applications could make it harder to get real business benefits from Big Data analytics programs.

Tools for Using Big Data

As the scale of Big Data is very large, it is more complicated. The data are mostly expanded over a number of servers, and the work of compiling the data is computed among them. This work was usually assigned to the database software in the past, which used its innovative JOIN mechanism to compile tables, then add up the columns before handing off the rectangle of data to the reporting software that would validate it. This task is harder than it seems, as database programmers can tell you about the instances where complex JOIN commands that would hang up their database for hours as it tried to produce an urgent report.

Now, the scenario is completely different. Hadoop is a go-to tool for organizing the racks and racks of servers, and NoSQL databases are popular tools for storing data on these racks. These mechanisms can be way more powerful and efficient than the old single machine, but they are far from being as refined as the old database servers. Although SQL may be complicated, writing the JOIN query for the SQL databases was often much simpler than collecting information from lots of machines and compiling it into one coherent solution, which is quite cumbersome to maintain. Hadoop jobs are written in Java, and they require another level of sophistication. The tools for using Big Data are just beginning to package this distributed computing power in a way that's a bit easier to use.

NoSQL data stores are being used with many Big Data tools. These are more flexible than traditional relational databases, but the flexibility isn't as much of a deviation from the past as Hadoop. NoSQL queries are simpler to use as it discourages the complexities provided by SQL queries. The main concern is that software needs to anticipate the possibility that there should not be redundancy and not every row will have some data for every column.

Here are some of the top tools used for using Big Data, according to TechTarget.

Jaspersoft BI Suite

Jaspersoft features include the following:

- Capabilities
- Reporting
- Dashboards
- Analysis
- Data integration
- BI platform

Benefits

Jaspersoft's BI provides key features that benefit both business and IT and look forward to enabling self-BI for their organization. Key features of the BI platform include the following (JasperSoft Quick start Guide 2017):

- Full-featured analytics, reporting, and dashboards that are easy to use
- Application can be embedded by flexible Web-based architecture
- Subscription model that enables more users at substantially reduced cost

The core of the Jaspersoft BISoftware suite is the JasperReports server. The end-to-end BI suite delivers shared services that include a repository for storing and structuring your resources, multiple levels of security, distribution of information, a semantic layer that greatly simplifies creating reports, a report scheduler, and many more features.

The Jaspersoft package is one of the open source leaders for producing reports from database columns. This innovative software, which is up and running at many organizations, turns SQL tables into PDFs, which can be scrutinized at meetings. The company is soaring on the Big Data train, which means adding a software layer to connect the places where Big Data gets stored to its report-generating software. The JasperReports server now offers software to suck up data from many of the major storage platforms, including

Cassandra, MongoDB, Redis, CouchDB, Riak, and Neo4j. Hadoop is also well-represented, with JasperReports providing a Hive connector to reach inside of HBase.

This effort feels like it is still starting up; the tools are not fully integrated, and many pages of the documentation wiki are blank. For example, the visual query designer doesn't work yet with Cassandra's CQL. You have to type these queries out by hand.

The Jaspersoft's server will boil information down to interactive tables and graphs, once you get the data from these sources. The reports can be reasonably sophisticated interactive tools which let you drill down into various corners. You can ask for more and more details if you need them (Splice Machine App overview 2016).

This is a well-developed corner of the software world, and Jaspersoft is expanding by making it easier to use these sophisticated reports with newer sources of data. Jaspersoft is not offering mainly new ways to look at the data, it just offers more sophisticated ways to access data stored in new locations. I found this unexpectedly useful. The aggregation of data was enough to make basic sense of when someone was going to the website and who was going there (Nunns 2015, JasperSoft 2017).

Pentaho Business Analytics

Pentaho is yet another software platform that began as a report-generating engine. Just like JasperSoft, it branched into Big Data by absorbing information from the new sources while making it easier to access. You can hook up Pentaho's tool to many of the most popular NoSQL databases, such as Cassandra and MongoDB. You can drag and drop the columns into views and reports as if the information came from SQL databases, once the databases are connected.

Pentaho also provides software for drawing HBase data and HDFS file data from Hadoop clusters. The graphical programming interface, known as either Kettle or Pentaho Data Integration, is again one of the more intriguing tools. It has a bunch of built-in modules that can be dragged and dropped onto a picture and then connected to them. You can write your code and send it out to execute on the cluster, as Pentaho has thoroughly integrated Hadoop and the other sources into this (Nunns 2015, TechTarget).

Karmasphere Studio and Analyst

Many of the Big Data tools did not begin as reporting tools. For instance, Karmasphere Studio is a set of plug-ins built on top of Eclipse. It is a specialized IDE that makes it easier to create and run Hadoop jobs.

Karmasphere delivers the Big Data workspace for data professionals that want to take advantage of the opportunity to mine and analyze mobile, sensor, Web, and social media data in Hadoop and bring new value to their business. They provide a graphical environment on Cloudera's distribution that includes Apache Hadoop (CDH), in which you can navigate through Big Data of any variety and spot patterns and trends in order to influence the strategies of a business. They provide the ability to integrate the insights into reoccurring business processes, once something meaningful is discovered.

Direct Access to Big Data for Analysis

Karmasphere Analyst enables data analysts immediate entry to structured and unstructured data on Cloudera CDH, through SQL and other familiar languages, so that you can make ad hoc queries, interact with the results, and run iterations, without the aid of IT.

Operationalization of the Results

Karmasphere Studio enables developers with a support analytic backup team a graphical environment in which to develop custom algorithms for them and systematize the creation of meaningful data sets they find and feed them into business processes and applications.

Flexibility and Independence

The Karmasphere Analytics engine is the foundation for all Karmasphere products. It provides easy access to Hadoop in data center and Cloud environments, transparency across Hadoop environments, prebuilt heuristics and algorithms, familiar language support, and collaboration facilities.

A rare feeling of joy is felt when you configure a Hadoop job with this developer tool. There are any number of stages in the life of a Hadoop job, and Karmasphere's tools walk you through each step, showing the fractional results along the way. The debuggers have always made it possible for us to peer into the mechanism as it does its work, but Karmasphere Studio does something a bit better: the tools display the state of the test data at each step, as you set up the workflow. You see what the temporary data will look like as it is cut apart, analyzed, and then reduced.

Karmasphere Analyst is yet another tool which Karmasphere distributes; it is designed to simplify the process of working through all of the data in a Hadoop cluster. It comes with many useful building blocks for programming a good Hadoop job, like subroutines for uncompressing zipped log files. Then, it strings them together and parameterizes the Hive calls to produce a table of output for perusing (Russom 2011).

Talend Open Studio

While mostly invisible to users of BI platforms, ETL processes retrieve data from all operational systems and preprocess it for analysis and reporting tools (Figure 4.3).

Talend's program has the following features:

- Packaged applications (ERP, CRM, etc.), databases, mainframes, files, Web services, etc., to address the growing disparity of sources.
- Data warehouses, data marts, and OLAP applications, for analysis, reporting, dashboarding, scorecarding, and so on.

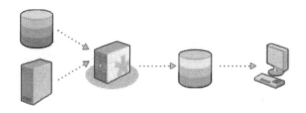

FIGURE 4.3
Talend Open Studio offers nearly comprehensive connectivity. (Adopted from Talend, *Talend Open Studio for Data Integration User Guide 6.2.1*, 2016.)

- Built-in advanced components for ETL, including string manipulations, slowly changing dimensions, automatic lookup handling, bulk loads support, and so on. Most connectors addressing each of the above needs are detailed in the *Talend Open Studio Components Reference Guide 6.2.1* (2016).

Talend also offers an Eclipse-based IDE for stringing together data processing jobs with Hadoop. Its tools are designed to help with data management, data integration, and data quality, all with subroutines tuned to these jobs (Wayer 2012).

One of the features supported by Talend Studio is that it allows you to build up your jobs by dragging and dropping little icons onto a canvas. Talend's component will fetch the RSS and add proxies if necessary if you want to get an RSS feed. There are many components for accumulating information and many more for doing things like a "fuzzy match." Then, you can generate the output results.

After you get a feel for what the components actually do and don't do, stringing together blocks visually can be simple. This became easier to figure out when I started looking at the source code being assembled behind the canvas. Talend lets you see this, and I think it's an ideal compromise. Visual programming may seem like a lofty goal, but I've found that the icons can never represent the mechanisms with enough detail to make it possible to understand what's going on. I need the source code.

Talend also maintains a collection of open source extensions which make it easier to work with a company's products. These are known collectively as TalendForge. Most of the tools seem to be filters or libraries that link Talend's software to other major products, such as SugarCRM and Salesforce.com. You can simplify the integration by bringing the information from these systems into your own projects.

Skytree Server

Skytree delivers a bundle that performs many of the more advanced machine learning algorithms. These commands are required for typing the correct command in command line interface (CLI).

Skytree is concentrated mainly on the logic used, rather than the shiny graphical user interface. The Skytree server uses an implementation that the company claims can be 10,000 times faster than other packages and is optimized to run a number of classic machine learning algorithms on your data using this implementation. It looks for clusters of mathematically similar items while searching through your data, then inverts this information to identify outliers that may be opportunities, problems, or both. The algorithms can search through vast quantities of data looking for the entries that are a bit out of the ordinary, and they can be more precise than humans. This may be a fraudulent claim, or designed for a particularly good customer who will spend and spend.

The proprietary and the free version of the software offer the same algorithms, but the free version is limited to data sets of 100,000 rows. This should be sufficient to establish whether the software is a good match to your organization's needs.

Tableau Desktop and Server

Tableau Desktop is a data visualization tool that makes it easier to look at your data in new ways and then apply actions to it and look at it in a different way. You can even combine the data with other data sets and examine it in yet another way. The tool is optimized to give you all the columns for the data and let you mix them before stuffing it into one of the many graphical templates or visualizations that are provided.

Tableau Software started implementation of Hadoop several versions ago, and now you can treat Hadoop "just like you would with any data connection." Tableau tries its best to cache as much information in memory to allow the tool to be interactive while relying upon Hive to structure the queries. Tableau wants to offer an interactive mechanism so that you can slice and dice your data again and again, while many of the other reporting tools are built on a tradition of generating reports offline. Some of the latency of a Hadoop cluster can be dealt with by help of caching. The software is well-polished and aesthetically pleasing.

Splunk

Splunk is quite different from the other available Big Data tools. It is not exactly a collection of AI routines or a report-generating tool, although it achieves much of that along the way. It creates an index of your data as if your data were a block of text or a book. Though we all know that databases also build indices, the approach that Splunk uses is much closer to a text search process.

This indexing is surprisingly flexible. Splunk makes sense of log files while coming already tuned to a particular application, and it collects them easily. It is also sold in a number of different solution packages, including one for detecting Web attacks and another for monitoring a Microsoft Exchange server. The index helps associate the data in these and several other common server-side scenarios.

Splunk searches around in the index while reading the text strings. You might type in the URLs of important articles or an IP address. Splunk finds these URLs and packages them into a timeline built around the time stamps it discovers in the data. All other fields are associated, and you can click around to drill deeper and deeper into the data set. While it seems like a simple process, it is quite powerful if you are looking for the right kind of indicator in your data feed. If you know the right text string, Splunk will help you track it. Log files are a great application for it.

A new Splunk tool which is currently in private beta testing, Shep, promises bidirectional integration between Splunk and Hadoop, allowing you to query Splunk data from Hadoop and exchange data between the systems.

Splice Machine

Splice Machine is a real-time SQL-on-Hadoop database which can help you to derive real-time actionable insights, which is a clear benefit for those who are aiming for quick development. This tool offers the ability to utilize standard SQL and can scale on commodity hardware; this is a tool for developers that have found that MySQL and Oracle can't scale to their desired limits (Wayer 2012). It can scale from gigabytes to petabytes and is SQL 99 compliant with the standard ANSI SQL. As well as support for .NET, Java, and Python, it also offers support for files written in JavaScript or AngularJS.

Splice Machine with MapR is uniquely qualified to power data-driven businesses that can harness real-time insights to take better actions and leapfrog their competition with these major benefits:

Cost-Effective Scaling and Performance with Commodity Hardware

Splice Machine with the help of commodity servers can scale to dozens of petabytes. It also parallelizes queries in a share-nothing architecture. In comparison to traditional RDMSs like Oracle and IBM DB2, this architecture enables Splice Machine to deliver compelling results, which are given below:

- 5- to 10-fold increase in query speed
- 75% reduction in TCO
- 10 to 20 times better price for performance

Real-Time Updates with Transactional Integrity

Database transactions make sure that real-time updates can be reliably executed without corruption or data loss. Transactions also enable zero-downtime updates or ETL to data warehouses, as data can be updated while reports simultaneously show a consistent view of the data.

Splice Machine provides across all rows and tables, full ACID (atomicity, consistency, isolation, and durability) transactions. It uses multiple version concurrency control (MVCC) with lockless snapshot isolation that does not change records; instead, it creates a new version. Each transaction can use different versions of each record to create its own snapshot of the database. Transactions can execute concurrently without any locking with each transaction having its own snapshot. This avoids troublesome deadlock conditions and leads to very high throughput.

Conclusions

After walking through these products, we can conclude that Big Data is much bigger than any single buzzword. It is not really reasonable to compare products that attempt complicated mathematical operations with those that largely build tables. Nor it is right to compare tools that attempt to manage larger stacks spread out over multiple machines in clustered frameworks like Hadoop with those simpler tools that work with generic databases.

The targets are moving, making the matter worse. Some of the more enticing new companies still are not sharing their software. Mysterious Platfora has a button you can click to stay informed, while another enigmatic startup, Continuity, just says, "We're still in stealth, heads down and coding hard." They're surely not going to be the last new entrants in this area.

The Pentaho and Jaspersoft tools simply produce nice lists of the top entries, but this was all that was needed. Knowing the top domains in the log file was enough. The other algorithms are harder to apply with any consistency, although they are intellectually interesting. The data set didn't seem to lend itself to these analyses, although they can flag clusters or do fuzzy matching. It was very difficult to figure out any applications for the data that didn't seem contrived.

Others will probably feel differently. The clustering algorithms, such as helping people find similar products in online stores, are used heavily in diverse applications. In order to identify potential security issues, others use outlier detection algorithm threats. The software is the least of the challenges, although these all bear investigation.

References

Baesens B. 2014. *Analytics in a Big Data World: The Essential Guide to Data Science and Its Applications.* Hoboken, NJ: John Wiley & Sons.

Cloudera. 2011. *KarmaSphere Solution Brief.* Cloudera Inc.

Foreman JW. *Data Smart: Using Data Science to Transform Information into Insight.*

Mappr Technologies. 2016. *Splice Machine App Overview.* Mappr Technologies, Inc.

Nunns J. 2015. 10 of the most popular Big Data tools for developers. *Computer Business Review.*

Russom P. 2011. *Big Data Analytics. TDWI Best Practices Report, Fourth Quarter, 2011.* The Data Warehousing Institute.

Talend. 2016. *Talend Open Studio for Data Integration User Guide, 6.2.1.* Talend Inc.

TechTarget. *Guide to Big Data Analytics: Tools, Trends, and Best Practices.* TechTarget.

TIBCO Software. 2017. *JasperSoft Quick Start Guide.* TIBCO Software Inc.

Wayer P. 2012. *7 Top Tools for Taming Big Data.* IDG Communications, Inc.

5

Understanding the Data Science behind Business Analytics

Mayank Mishra, Pratik Mishra, and Arun K. Somani

CONTENTS

Introduction

Big Data analytics has become the engine for business analytics today. Companies are using Big Data to analyze their business processes, formulate future business strategies and, extensively, employ it for decision making. Companies such as Amazon and Netflix use Big Data analytics to understand behavioral patterns and choices of customers, in order to tune their offerings for the individual. Credit card companies use Big Data analytics to estimate the risk of losing a customer; they analyze a customer's spending and paying patterns and use such insights to change potential offerings in hopes of retaining that customer.

Big Data analytics has also been very successfully employed in scientific fields as well. For example, experiments at the Large Hadron Collider generate a tremendous amount of data, 30 petabytes per year (http://home.cern/topics/large-hadron-collider). Such huge amounts of data require processing in order to determine the behavior of subatomic particles. A lot of the generated data is processed using Big Data analytics tools (Warmbein 2015; http://home.cern/topics/large-hadron-collider).

Upcoming fields, such as the Internet of Things (IoT) (Gubbi et al. 2013), which envisions connecting a large number of smart devices from everyday use to the internet, are expected to exponentially increase the amount of data generated in the future. Some approximations put the increase at more than 10 times the current volume in the next four years. For example, Marr (2015) in *Forbes* approximated the accumulated data to grow from close to 4 zetabytes in 2016 to more than 40 zetabytes in 2020.

Almost every person in today's world has had some interaction with Big Data analytics. Receiving personalized advertisements both online and in print is a result of analytics, which companies perform on their gathered customer purchasing behavior data. Similarly, movie suggestions for online video stores also have their roots in Big Data analytics. Social media platforms are the biggest users of Big Data analytics. From friend suggestions on Facebook to targeted news feeds, thse are all enabled by Big Data analytics.

Such a pervasive and impactful field is still a black box for a majority of people. The aim of this chapter is to present different types of analytics constituting Big Data analytics and their application areas. We also present techniques and tools which drive such analytics and make them useful.

Big Data analytics (Zikopoulos et al. 2011, Chen et al. 2012) involves processing and analyzing huge amounts of data to gain insights for decision making. Analytics can be broadly divided into four categories, as illustrated in Figure 5.1.

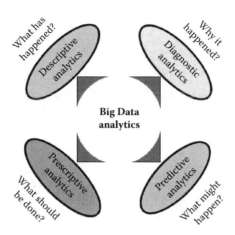

FIGURE 5.1
Different types of Big Data.

Types of Big Data Analytics

Descriptive Analytics

Descriptive analysis deals with the question "What has happened?" This form of analytics mainly deals with understanding the gathered data. It involves the use of tools and algorithms to understand the internal structure of the Big Data and find categorical or temporal patterns or trends in it. For example, the sales data gathered by a retail chain reflect the buying patterns of different categories of customers. Students, housewives, or small business owners all have different buying patterns, which can be found when overall sales data are analyzed. Moreover, a sudden spurt in sales of a category of items, say notebooks, can also be identified and be made available for analysis with other tools (Zikopoulos et al. 2011).

Diagnostic Analytics

Once the internal structure of data is identified, the next task is to seek reasons behind such a structure. For example, if sales data show a spurt in sales of notebooks, then seeking the reason behind such an increase falls in the domain of diagnostic analytics (Borne 2017).

Predictive Analytics

Given the current trends in data identified by the descriptive analytics tools, what might happen in the future is a crucial question. Businesses can fail if they are not able to tune to the future requirements of their customers. Predictive analytics tools provide insights into the possible future scenarios. For example, predicting the future rate of customer churn on the basis of sales patterns, complaints, and refund requests made by customers provide useful information (Soltanpoor and Sellis 2016).

Prescriptive Analytics

Today's businesses not only want to predict the future but also want to be best prepared for it. Prescriptive analytics tools provide a "what if" kind of analysis capability. What are the different options available to business management and which among them is the best suited, given the predictions and other constraints? These questions fall under the domain of prescriptive analytics. For example, prescriptive analytics can be employed to provide a directed and personalized advertisement to customers to help in reducing customer churn (Soltanpoor and Sellis 2016, Borne 2017).

Figure 5.2 shows a relative comparison of different types of analytics. In terms of complexity of the algorithms and techniques involved, descriptive analytics are the simplest. The most complex is prescriptive analytics, as there is automation of decision making involved. Moreover, prescriptive analytics encompasses all other analytics in one or the other form. Prescriptive analytics also has the most impact on decision making, as it helps to identify the best course of action for the future. Prescriptive analytics is more of an optimization strategy. We present a detailed discussion about prescriptive analytics later in the chapter.

Table 5.1 summarizes the very important differences in the natures of different analytics types. Descriptive and diagnostic analytics concentrate on the past and answer questions like, "what has happened" and "why did that happen." On the other hand, predictive and prescriptive analytics concentrate on the future and answer questions like "what can happen" and "what should we do."

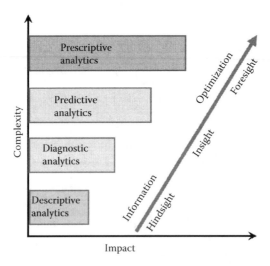

FIGURE 5.2
Comparison of different Big Data analytics approaches.

TABLE 5.1

Application Domains of Different Types of Big Data Analytics

Analytics Type	Forward Looking	Backward Looking
Descriptive		✓
Diagnostic		✓
Predictive	✓	
Prescriptive	✓	

Software analytics tools do not confine their functionalities to a specific analytics task. More often, the tools are capable of performing more than one kind of analytics, as we discuss below. The available tools have a wide variety in terms of kinds of businesses they can model, kinds of data they can process, and even the kinds of outputs they produce. Earlier, the tools were complex and companies were forced to hire data scientists to utilize them. Recently, there has been a shift in this approach, and many easy-to-use tools have appeared in the market. Using these tools, any person can perform a reasonable amount of analytics. We will discuss specific tools later in the chapter.

Analytics Use Case: Customer Churn Prevention

To enable readers to understand the real world uses of Big Data analytics, we present a use case where Big Data analytics is employed to prevent customer churn. We now discuss why customer churn is a problem and why companies are forced to use Big Data analytics to prevent it.

Today, due to e-commerce retail space, customers are not confined by choices, location, availability, or more importantly, competitive pricing. This makes the customer base highly volatile and difficult to retain. E-retailers like Amazon, Flipkart, E-bay, and their physical counterparts like Walmart, Target, etc., face a real and challenging problem in the form of loss of customers, which is also known as customer churn. Customer churn is detrimental for a business due to stiff competition, and the retailers go to great lengths to retain customers and avoid their migration to other competitors.

Identifying the customers who are likely to leave is a herculean task in itself. This is because the size of a business. where there are tens of millions of transactions a week, hundreds of thousands of items on sale at any point in time, millions of active customers, and millions of pieces of data regarding feedback and complaints. Companies utilize and employ Big Data analytics to handle these issues and analyze such large amounts of data to predict and/or diagnose the problem(s).

Customer churn prevention is the process of maintaining existing customers using methods like increasing product inventory based on current trends, personalized loyalty programs, and promotions, as well as identifying dissatisfaction among customers.

The business objective in our case is to retain the customers who are more likely to leave. One of the methods which we are going to discuss is to send them personalized coupons for targeted items. However, to achieve this objective, we must analyze the following.

- Why are customers at risk of going away? Why have customers left?
- What type of inventory items are liked by customers who have left or who are at risk of leaving?
- What items would customers like to buy together (basket analysis)?

The above-mentioned analysis is required to decide what type of coupons the customer is more likely to accept. The coupons, however, should ensure customer satisfaction along with no loss of the business. We will present the analytics behind the customer churn prevention with examples throughout the chapter.

The rest of the chapter is organized as follows: we discuss different analytics and the underlying mathematical tools and schemes employed by them. We also employ the solution of the customer churn use case. Some software tools which perform the described analytics task are presented. The goal of this chapter is to present the underlying techniques of analytics to readers so that they can make an informed decision about the kind of tools required for their data.

Descriptive Analytics

Descriptive analytics is the first analytics stage; it makes raw collected data interpretable by humans. Retailers like Walmart, Amazon, e-Bay, and Flipkart collect different customer-related data into their data repositories. The data are sourced from social networks, IoT devices, click streams, search engines, customer call logs, transactions, etc. Collected data can be structured, semistructured, or unstructured, as shown in Figure 5.3.

Structured data refers to data which have been organized using rules (e.g., relational databases). Unstructured data consist of images and audio-video streams. Between these two extremes lie semistructured data, where chunks of unstructured data are organized. Examples of semistructured data include XML files, emails etc. Collected data are cleansed and categorized into customer transaction logs, customer reviews, feedback, etc., by using tools like Sqoop and Flume.

Descriptive analytics tools then process the collected raw data and provide insights, as shown in Figure 5.4. The insights range from the internal structure of data, like categories or events which occurred, to a mere summary, like average profit per item sold.

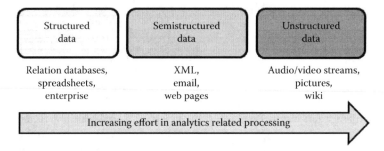

FIGURE 5.3
Different types of gathered data.

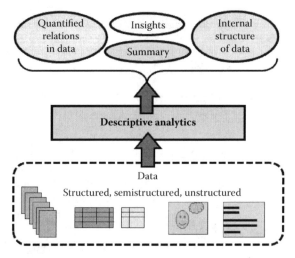

FIGURE 5.4
Descriptive analytics functioning.

Application of Descriptive Analytics in Customer Churn Prevention

Descriptive analytics techniques can help in identifying the segment of customers at maximum risk of leaving. Descriptive analytics techniques can categorize customers according to their recent buying patterns. For example, Table 5.2 shows a simple example of customers and the weekly money spent by them for the past four weeks. Although simple, the table shows how the raw data are processed and summarized by descriptive analytics tools. In the real world, there will be millions of customers and the data will span many more dimensions, including time spent in deciding, coupons applied, etc. Even creating such a simple table requires tools like MapReduce when the data size is big.

Table 5.2 shows that customers 7 and 8 drastically reduced their spending at this particular store over the course of four weeks. These customers are high-risk customers and are probably going to leave or have already left. The table also shows the category of customers which allows risk of churn but can become high-risk customers if preventive steps are not taken.

There can be other tables created, e.g., one for refunds requested, listing customers who have returned items and are expecting refunds.

Q. When to use descriptive analytics?
A. When an aggregate level of understanding of what is going on in a business is required. Descriptive analytics is also used to describe or summarize various characteristics of a business.

Techniques Used for Descriptive Analytics

Clustering

Clustering (Davidson and Ravi 2005, Balcan et al. 2014) refers to the process by which the data points are grouped together in such a way that two data points lying in the same cluster are more similar to each other than the data points in a different cluster. In Table 5.2, customers 7 and 8 both were categorized in a high-risk cluster. This is because they showed a similar pattern of diminished spending.

Clustering can be of many types, depending on the definition of similarity or affinity between two points. A common affinity measure is a Cartesian distance between the points. Two points which are closer to each other are considered more similar to each other than two far points. The clusters can thus be defined by the threshold on the distance between the points.

TABLE 5.2

Customer Buying Patterns over a Month's Duration

Churn Risk Assessment Category	Customer ID	Week 1 Sales (Oldest)	Week 2 Sales	Week 3 Sales	Week 4 Sales (Latest)
No Risk	1	120	145	110	136
	2	50	65	67	52
	3	590	500	450	650
Low Risk	4	20	25	10	5
	5	70	55	45	40
	6	135	145	120	70
High Risk	7	400	220	20	0
	8	320	45	0	0

Clustering is an iterative process, where smaller clusters are merged into bigger ones at every step, as shown in Figure 5.5 below. An example of hierarchical clustering is shown in the figure.

At the beginning, each data point is a cluster of its own. Depending on the interpoint distances, clusters are formed. In the next and later rounds, the clusters are merged with each other, depending on the distances between clusters. As clusters can contain more than one point, a representative point is chosen to calculate distances with other clusters. One such representative point is considered the centroid of the cluster.

Clustering algorithms merge the clusters until the distance between any two clusters is not close enough to be merged, as shown in Figure 5.6. The distance criteria are crucial for the quality and quantity of resultant clusters. Consider an example where a supermarket wants to find different categories of customer categories. Each cluster represents a category. The unchecked merging of clusters will result in only a single big cluster consisting of all the customers. Similarly, the higher threshold on distance will result in too many fine-grained categories, such as high school student, college student, graduate student, etc. Thus, a proper distance threshold is necessary for meaningful and useful clustering.

Another approach for clustering is shown in Figure 5.7. This approach is the inverse of the previous approach. Clustering starts with considering all the points in a single cluster. Instead of merging clusters whose distance is below a threshold, the cluster, which is unstable, is divided into smaller, more stable clusters. The definition of instability is crucial to achieving meaningful clustering. An example where such clustering can be employed is

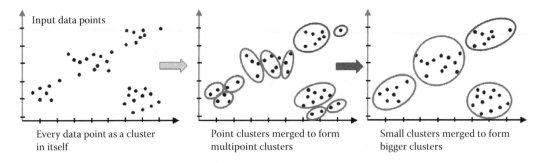

Every data point as a cluster in itself

Point clusters merged to form multipoint clusters

Small clusters merged to form bigger clusters

FIGURE 5.5
Hierarchical cluster formation by successive merging.

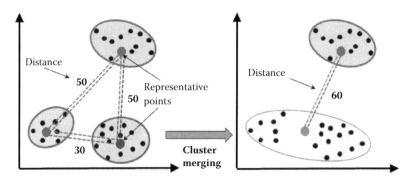

FIGURE 5.6
Merging of two clusters.

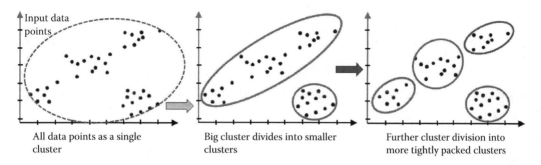

All data points as a single cluster

Big cluster divides into smaller clusters

Further cluster division into more tightly packed clusters

FIGURE 5.7
Cluster splitting.

in customer churn. Once the customers who have already left are identified, the reasons for their leaving can be found by categorizing them by geographical region, credit scores, etc.

Decision Tree-Based Classification

Classification is the process of assigning an object to one or more predefined categories. Classification is employed for many problems, like email spam detection, categorizing credit card customers as high risk or low risk, and many more. In this section, we will present one of the classification techniques, called decision trees (https://en.wikipedia.org /wiki/Decision_tree).

Decision trees refer to a well-designed series of questions which are asked with regard to the input object to be classified. Figure 5.8 shows one such decision tree, an example of classifying light passenger vehicles. When a new vehicle is seen, the category to which it belongs can be determined by using the decision tree. It can be seen that the design of the decision tree utilizes historical data. In the tree, the historical data are from characteristics of vehicles that are already available.

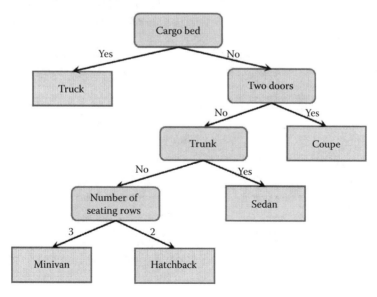

FIGURE 5.8
Decision tree for vehicle classification.

Diagnostic Analytics

Diagnostic analytics focuses on the reasons behind the observed patterns that are derived from descriptive analytics. For example, descriptive analytics can point out that the sale of an item has shot up or suddenly decreased at a supermarket, and then the diagnostic analytics tools can provide reasons behind such an observation.

Diagnostic analytics focuses on causal relationships and sequences embedded in the data. It helps answer questions like "Why?".

For example, in the customer churn prevention use case, the diagnostic analytic tools can be used to find the probable reason behind the high-churn-risk customers. As mentioned above, descriptive analytics tools summarize the feedback and complaint logs and the refund requests by customers. Table 5.3 lists the number of complaints, refund requests, and price match requests, generated by the descriptive analytics.

Diagnostic analytics tools correlate the information between Tables 5.2 and 5.3 to answer why customers 7 and 8 are at a higher risk of leaving. For example, customer 7 may be someone who is unhappy with his or her complaints and refund requests not being handled. The diagnostic tool will not give a result for each and every customer. The results will be more like "Customers with a higher percentage of unresolved complaints are at high churn risk." Customer 8, however, seems to be a different case. Observing such a high number of price match requests, it is highly probable that customer 8 has found another store which has lower prices for products than the current store. In the case of customer 7, urgent resolution of the pending complaints and refund cases can decrease the chances of their leaving. However, in the case of customer 8, providing promotional discounts and coupons on products in which they may be interested could be a good strategy for retention. The key constraint which should still be ensured is the profitability of business. Thus, finding coupons which may satisfy customer 8 and yet do not result in a loss for the store is a challenge for the store.

For ease of understanding, the table is oversimplified with customer IDs. In reality, such information regarding pending complaints and price match requests will also be in the form of clusters. To find the probable reason behind high-churn-risk customers, an intersection between clusters in Table 5.2 and the clusters of complaints, refund requests, price match requests will be found.

Thus, the answer to "why is there customer churn?" could vary from bad delivery service, the quality of products sold to customers who prefer quality over price, migration to a competitor based on price or service, etc.

Q. When to use diagnostic analytics?
A. When the reason behind a certain observed phenomenon or characteristic needs to be determined.

TABLE 5.3

Customer Complaints, Refund Requests, and Price Match Requests for the Use Case

Customer ID	Number of Complaints (Number Resolved)	Number of Refund Requests (Number Resolved)	Number of Price Match Requests
...	...	...	...
5	1(1)	0	1(1)
6	0	0	0
7	3(0)	2(0)	0
8	0	2(1)	5(4)

Predictive Analytics

Predictive analytics uses the outcomes of descriptive and diagnostic analytics to create a model for the future. In other words, analyzing the what and why gives insights to prepare a model for questions like "What is possible in the future?" For example, when diagnostic analysis specifies a correlation between large customer churn and unresolved complaints, the predictive analytics can model this relation to approximate the future customer churn rate on the basis of the fraction of unresolved complaints. Such a model is shown in Figure 5.9. The red curve in the figure specifies the relation between customer churn rate (y axis) and unresolved complaints (x axis).

Predictive analytics are also utilized by businesses to estimate different kinds of risks, finding the next best offers for customers, etc. Use of predictive analytics helps businesses forecast future scenarios. For example, promotion offers and targeted discount coupons can be mailed to customers to avoid a scenario of customer churn when the unresolved complaint rate is high; this seems to be a good strategy to avoid customer churn. However, questions like "Is this the best possible strategy or do we have other options?" and "Will this strategy effectively reduce risk of customer churn?" and "Will it still be profitable for business?" are some of the questions which predictive analytics cannot answer.

We need a more powerful tool, which can prescribe potential options and also predict the future impacts of the potential options. We discuss prescriptive analytics, a more capable analytics approach than predictive analytics, in the next section.

Q. When to use predictive analytics?
A. When something about the future needs to be predicted or some missing information needs to be approximated.

Techniques Used for Predictive Analytics

Linear Regression Techniques

Linear regression (https://en.wikipedia.org/wiki/Linear_regression) is a technique used to analyze the relationship between the independent variable and the dependent variable. In the context of retail business, the independent variable can be the discount offered on a certain item, and the dependent variable can be the corresponding increase in sales. When

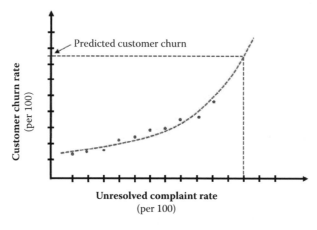

FIGURE 5.9
Predicting customer churn rate.

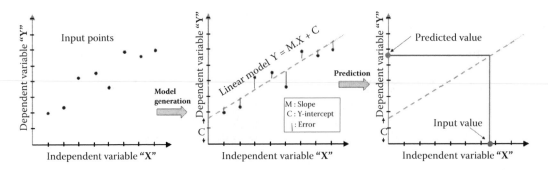

FIGURE 5.10
Linear regression steps.

discounts are greater, the more the sales go up. However, it is necessary to capture the exact relationship between the discount and the sales to make estimates.

The relationship between sales, the dependent variable, and the discount, the independent variable, is modeled as a linear equation. Historical data are then analyzed and plotted on a graph, as shown in Figure 5.10. Next, a straight line, which closely follows the plotted points, is drawn. The key is to estimate the slope of the linear curve, which in turn gives a relationship between the dependent and independent variables. The goal is to maximize the accuracy of prediction and thus minimize the error.

Mathematical Explanation of Linear Regression

The slope of the linear curve is estimated as follows.
Given historical data, consisting of pairs of independent and dependent variables, $\{(x_1, y_1), (x_2, y_2),\ldots,(x_n, y_n)\}$

Let, $\bar{x} = \dfrac{x_1 + x_2 + \ldots + x_n}{n}$ i.e., (for the mean of an independent variable) and

$$\bar{y} = \frac{y_1 + y_2 + \ldots + y_n}{n}$$ i.e., (for the mean of a dependent variable)

The slope of the line denoted by M can be approximated:

$$M \frac{\sum_{i=1}^{n} \{(x_i - \bar{x})(y_i - \bar{y})\}}{\sum_{i=1}^{n} \{(x_i - \bar{x})^2\}}$$

Thus, the equation of the line approximating the relation between x and y is given as

$$y = M \cdot x + c.$$

To predict the outcome value of a new input, e.g., x_{new}, we put this new value in place of x: $y_{new} = M.x_{new} + C.$

Time Series Models

Time series (Hamilton 1994), as the name suggests, is the arrangement of data points in temporal order. Generally, the time difference between the successive data points is the same. Examples of time series are stock market index levels (generated each day), the number of items sold each day in a supermarket, etc. Time series analysis has been extensively used for forecasting.

Time series analysis consists of methods to extract meaningful characteristics of data, like increasing or decreasing trends with time. The trend in the data is the key to predicting the future values of data. It is analogous to the slope of the line described for linear regression. In Figure 5.11 the data shows a decreasing trend.

A simple way of calculating the trend is by taking moving averages. There are various ways of calculating moving averages. We describe two of them below.

- A centered moving average (Hunter 1986) is focused on the width of a moving average window. If the width is taken to be 3, then the value of the centered moving average at time stamp t_k is equal to the average of values at time stamps t_{k-1}, t_k, t_{k+1}.

- Exponential smoothing (Hunter 1986) entails giving equal weights to observed values at all time stamps, with recent values given more weight, while calculating the weighted average. Consider the example where v_k, v_{k-1}, v_{k-2}, ..., v_0 denotes the observed values at times t_k, t_{k-1}, t_{k-2}, ...,t_0. Using exponential smoothing, the current smoothened value $L_k t$ time t_k can be calculated as follows.

$$L_k = \alpha \cdot V_k + (1-\alpha) \cdot L_{k-1} \tag{5.1}$$

Where α, known as the smoothing constant, has a value between 0 and 1. When α approaches 1, it means that more weight is give to recent values; when α approaches 0, it means that more weight is given to older values. This fact is also evident from equation 5.1.

L_{k-1} is derived in a similar fashion, as L_k i.e., $L_{k-1} = \alpha \cdot V_{k-1} + (1-\alpha) \cdot L_{k-2}$

Thus, the actual value of L_k, i.e., the expanded form of equation 5.1, is given as:

$$L_k = \alpha \cdot V_k + \alpha \cdot (1-\alpha) \cdot V_{k-1} + \alpha \cdot (1-\alpha)^2 \cdot V_{k-2} + \alpha \cdot (1-\alpha)^3 \cdot V_{k-3} + \ldots + \alpha \cdot (1-\alpha)^k \cdot V_0$$

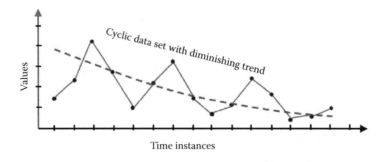

FIGURE 5.11
Time series with diminishing trend.

Machine Learning Techniques

Artificial Neural Networks

Artificial neural networks (Yegnanarayana 2009) is a modeling technique which is employed when the exact relation between input and output is not known. Before neural networks become usable for predictions (Zhang et al. 1998), they require training or learning to establish input and output relations. There are three ways to train a neural network: (a) supervised learning (Caruana and Niculescu-Mizil 2006, Alpaydin 2015); (b) unsupervised learning (Hastie et al. 2009); and (c) reinforcement learning (Sutton and Barto 1998). Of these three, only supervised learning is suitable to train a neural network for generating future predictions.

Supervised Learning

In supervised learning, the input–output relationship is established by observing a data set which has already been labeled. The data set used for training consists of examples which have the pairs of an input and the desired output. The input–output function is thus inferred by observing such examples.

Artificial Neural Network Structure and Training

Artificial neural networks are organized as layers of interconnected nodes, as shown in Figure 5.12. Each node contains an activation function. The interconnections are weighted. While training, the inputs and outputs are applied to the input layer and the output layer, respectively. The effect of applying training data is that the weights on the interconnect are adjusted, which modifies the behavior of the neural network (Karayiannis and Venetsanopoulos 2013).

Back-Propagation Weight Adjustment Scheme

One such weight adjustment method is called back-propagation (Werbos 1974, Rumelhart et al. 1985; http://www.philbrierley.com/main.html?code/bpproof.html&code/codeleft.html).

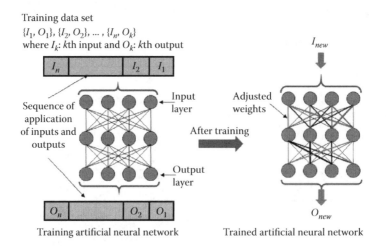

FIGURE 5.12
Training and using an artificial neural network.

Suppose, while training an artificial neural network, that an output of O_{pred} is predicted. The expected output is O_{exp}. The error, E, is calculated as follows:

$$E = O_{pred} - O_{exp}$$

The scheme adjusts weights such that E^2 is minimized. To achieve this, the current weight between any two neurons, say N_1 and N_1 which is denoted by $W_{12}^{current}$ is updated using delta rules as shown below.

$$W_{12}^{new} = W_{12}^{current} - \mu \frac{\partial E^2}{\partial W_{12}},$$

where μ is the learning rate parameter and $\dfrac{\partial E^2}{\partial W_{12}}$ is the sensitivity of E^2 of weight W_{12}, which actually denotes the direction toward which the adjustment should be made.

Prescriptive Analytics

Prescriptive analytics (Song et al. 2013, Gröger et al. 2014) is relatively new and complex, compared to other analytics approaches. The aim of prescriptive analytics is to give advice on possible outcomes. Prescriptive analytics tries to approximate an effect or possible outcome of a future decision even before the decision has been made. It provides a "What if" kind of analytics capability.

Prescriptive analytics helps to determine the best solution among a variety of choices, given the known parameters, and suggests options for how to take advantage of a future opportunity or mitigate a future risk. It can also illustrate the implications of each decision to improve decision making. Examples of prescriptive analytics for customer retention include next-best action and next-best offer analyses.

Prescriptive analytics internally employs all other analytic techniques to provide recommendationsas, as shown in Figure 5.13. Prescriptive analytics employs a simulation–optimization–validation iterative cycle for fine-tuning future predictions.

Q. When to use prescriptive analytics?
A. Use prescriptive analytics when advice is needed regarding what action to take for the best results.

Application of Prescriptive Analytics in the Customer Churn Prevention Use Case

If a customer leaves, then they are of no value to a business. However, preventing a customer who is about to leave is much more critical for the business. We need schemes which can not only predict customer churn, but also suggest preventive measures to keep it from happening. Prescriptive analytics is such a scheme. Prescriptive analytics is much more powerful than predictive analytics.

Using prescriptive analytics, the business can explore different options available to it to prevent customer churn. Prescriptive analytics will provide inputs similar to the ones mentioned in Figure 5.14. (Note that the figure is used for the understanding of readers and uses hypothetical data. Real world tools have various ways of suggesting the options and best choices.)

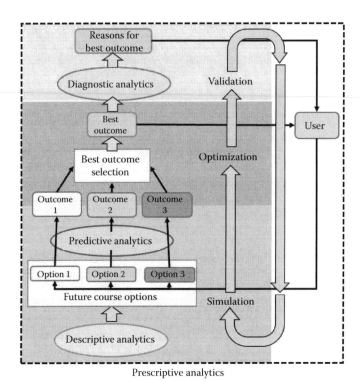

FIGURE 5.13
Prescriptive analytics working.

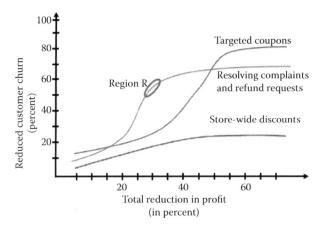

FIGURE 5.14
Prescriptive analytics suggestions.

Prescriptive analytics suggests three options: targeted coupons, resolving complaints and refund requests. and store-wide discounts. The x axis of the graph in Figure 5.14 shows the reduction in profits, and the y axis shows the percentage of high-risk customers who are retained. It can be seen that storewide discounts are not an effective way of retaining customers, as they result in a large reduction of profit but retain few customers.

The best option suggested by prescriptive analytics is to be in Region R, which amounts to resolving complaints and handling refund requests. This is because the number of customers retained is close to 60% at this point, with only a 30% reduction in profit.

Prescriptive Analytics Techniques

Techniques employed for prescriptive analytics span domains like image processing, machine learning, signal processing, applied statistics, etc. In the earlier parts of this chapter, we explained some machine learning techniques, like clustering and neural networks. We also discussed linear regression and time series analysis. All of these techniques can play a role in the larger context of prescriptive analytics.

Big Data Analytics Architecture

Figure 5.15 shows the overall Big Data analytics framework. MapReduce and Spark provide the large data processing capabilities for different types of analytics. For example, descriptive analytics uses MapReduce to filter and summarize a large amount of data. Similarly, predictive analytics techniques employ MapReduce to process data from data warehouses.

Before a data analytics process begins, the relevant data are collected from a variety of sources (stage 1). The sources generally depend on the kind of business that is employing the analytics. For e-retailers, the most important data sources are the transaction and customer logs. Similarly, for an electrical service company, the most important source of data will be IoT devices and the smart meters at customer premises.

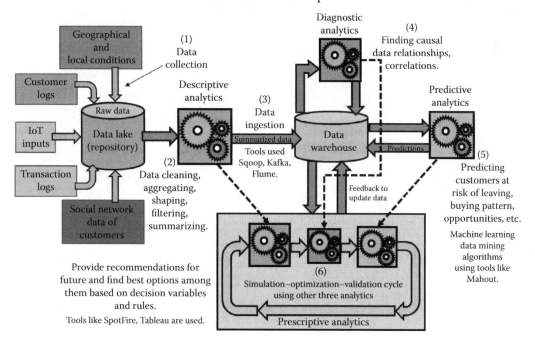

FIGURE 5.15
Big Data analytics architecture.

Raw data are collected in a repository known as a data lake. The raw data are then processed by using descriptive analytics tools and techniques to filter and summarize them (stage 2). Descriptive analytics makes the data usable for humans and other analytics tools. The processed and summarized data are stored in a data warehouse (stage 3).

Diagnostic analytics uses the processed data that have been stored in a data warehouse and derives causal relationships and correlations inherent in the data (stage 4). These findings are stored back in the data warehouse to be used for predictive and prescriptive analytics. Predictive analytics utilizes the summarized and cleaned data stored in the data warehouse along with the correlations and causal relationships provided by the diagnostic analytics. It then provides predictions and future estimations, which are again stored back in the data warehouse (stage 5).

Prescriptive analytics internally employs all other analytic techniques to provide recommendations. It employs an iterative approach, where the predictions are tuned and optimized. This iterative approach is termed a simulation–optimization–validation loop and is shown as a cycle in stage 6. Predictive analytics also provide feedback and update data in the data warehouse in the course of fine-tuning the predictions. In the next section, we present some of the tools which employ these analytics in detail.

Tools Used for Big Data Analytics

There are many tools available for performing Big Data analytics. Generally, the tools are not confined to a single type of analytics. There are some special-purpose and business- and data-specific tools too; however, discussion of such tools is beyond the scope of this chapter. Here, we present a list of the most widely used analytics tools. Table 5.4 provides a list of tools and types of analytics that each tool supports. We also provide a brief discussion about each of the mentioned tools.

TABLE 5.4

Tools of Big Data Analytics

Analytics Tool	Support for			
	Descriptive	Diagnostic	Predictive	Prescriptive
IBM Infosphere	✓			
IBM SPSS	✓	✓	✓	
Apache Mahout			✓	
Azure Machine Learning Studio	✓	✓	✓	
Halo	✓	✓	✓	✓
Tableau	✓	✓	✓	✓
SAP InfiniteInsight			✓	
@Risk				✓
Oracle Advanced Analytics	✓	✓	✓	
TIBCO SpotFire			✓	✓
R	✓	✓	✓	✓
Mathematica	✓		✓	

IBM InfoSphere

IBM's InfoSphere (https://www-01.ibm.com/software/data/infosphere/) is a widely used data integration, warehousing, and information governance tool. It provides enterprise-scale performance and reliability in bringing diverse data sets together, creating visualizations and aids in data life cycle management.

IBM SPSS

IBM's SPSS software (http://www.ibm.com/analytics/us/en/technology/spss/) is a predictive analytics program that creates visualizations of statistical reporting and diagnostic analysis to create predictive models for data mining. It is a powerful tool for model evaluation and automation of advanced analytics in the Cloud.

Apache Mahout

The Apache Mahout project (http://mahout.apache.org/) is an open source project for implementing scalable machine learning algorithms among researchers. It employs Apache Hadoop and the MapReduce processing framework to churn data. The algorithms available within this project range from clustering and classification to collaborative learning.

Azure Machine Learning Studio

The Azure machine learning studio (https://azure.microsoft.com/en-us/) is a Cloud-based predictive analytics service for building and deploying models from the Azure data lake. It provides a large repository of state-of-the-art machine learning algorithms with R and Python support. Azure provides not only tools for predictive model development but also a fully dedicated platform on which to deploy these models via Web services. Features such as data collection and management and ready-to-plug-in sample predictive modeling modules, coupled with support from the Azure storage system, makes the Azure machine learning studio a one-stop solution for descriptive, diagnostic, and predictive analytics.

Halo

Halo is a forecasting tool (https://halobi.com/2016/01/halo-for-forecasting/) that combines statistical modeling with a business intelligence platform to provide forecasting and decision-making capabilities for large data sets. It is automated, customizable, and designed especially for complete analytics platform, from data cleansing to prescriptive analytics. Halo specializes in prescriptive analytics modeling.

Tableau

Tableau (https://www.tableau.com/sites/default/files/media/whitepaper_bigdatahadoop _eng_0.pdf) provides real-time data visualization and is employed in different analytics platform solutions spanning different segments, including business intelligence, Big Data analytics, sports, health care, and retail. Tableau is designed to facilitate real-time "conversations" between data across multiple platforms, like relational databases, Cloud data stores,

OLAP cubes, spreadsheets, etc. Tableau is a visualization and query tool that can be used in all stages of Big Data analytics.

SAP Infinite Insight

SAP's Infinite Insight program (http://www.butleranalytics.com/enterprise-predictive -analytics-comparisons-2014/) addresses a definite set of predictive analytics problems. It harnesses in-database predictive scoring and also comes with R packages to support a large number of algorithms. Predictive models can be built using specific machine learning and data mining algorithms. Infinite Insight is restrictive in its approach to its market focus, and hence cannot be employed for general purpose machine learning or data mining requirements.

@Risk

@Risk (https://www.palisade.com/risk/l) provides risk management strategies that combine simulations and genetic algorithms to optimize logs or spreadsheets with uncertain values. It performs simulations for mathematical computations, tracking and evaluating different future scenarios for risk analysis. It objectifies probabilities of each such scenario and forecasts the probabilities of risk associated with each of them. @Risk can be used in the simulation, optimization, and validation phases of prescriptive analytics.

Oracle Advanced Analytics

The Oracle Advance Analytics platform (https://www.oracle.com/database/advanced-analytics /index.html) uses in-database processing to provide data mining, statistical computation, visualization, and predictive analytics. It supports most of the data mining algorithms for predictive modeling. Oracle has encompassed the R package for addressing statistical analysis of data.

TIBCO SpotFire

The TIBCO SpotFire platform (http://spotfire.tibco.com/solutions/technology/predictive -analytics) is a predictive and prescriptive analytics tool for implementation of data exploration, discovery, and analytics; the user is aided by interactive visualizations to gain insights about the data. It integrates R, S+, MATLAB, and SAS statistical tools. It uses predictive modeling techniques, such as linear and logistic regression, classification, and regression trees, as well as optimization algorithms for decision-making capabilities.

R

R, a product of The R Project for Statistical Computing (https://www.r-project.org/), is an open-source statistical computing program that performs data mining and statistical analysis of large data sets. By design, R is flexible and has achieved a lot of industry focus. R is integrated with data processing frameworks like MapReduce and Spark. A popular project, SparkR provides real-time statistical processing of streaming data. SparkR integrates R to also support filtering, aggregation, integration of data, and an MLib library for machine learning algorithms. Many tools listed here also utilize R as a component for providing additional capabilities.

Wolfram Mathematica

Wolfram's Mathematca system (https://www.wolfram.com/mathematica/) is considered a computer algebra system, but it also has tools capable of supervised and unsupervised learning over artificial neural networks for processing images, sounds, and other forms of data.

Future Directions and Technologies

The size of data is growing at a tremendous pace and with that, the need to have better and more powerful analytical tools is growing too. There have been a lot of recent technological advancements which look promising. In this section, we mention some of these new advancements and future directions which analytics can take.

From Batch Processing to Real-Time Analytics

Most of the implementations of MapReduce and related techniques, like Hadoop, employ batch processing. This puts a limitation on the data processing as well because, before being able to process the data, the data must first be collected. The collection process may take days to weeks and even months. Such a delay is detrimental to business decisions.

For example, consider customer churn. If an e-retailer discovers a high-risk customer a week after the first signs appear in their data, then there is nothing much to be done. The customer will have already left by then. Such situations, where decision making is extremely time sensitive, require real-time or a stream processing paradigm rather than the batch processing one.

Apache Spark (Shanahan abd Dai 2015) and Apache Storm (Ranjan 2014) provide real-time distributed data processing capabilities. Both Spark and Storm entail a stream processing framework, but Spark is a more general-purpose distributed computing framework. Spark can run over existing Hadoop clusters, and thus it provides easy portability.

In-Memory Big Data Processing

Big Data analytics involve a lot of data movement to and from data repositories and warehouses. Such data movement is time-consuming, and most of the time it acts as a bottleneck in overall processing time. This is because secondary storage is several orders of magnitude slower than a processor itself.

Apache Ignite (Anthony et al. 2016) is the in-memory implementation of Hadoop libraries. It provides a much faster processing capability than the Vanilla implementations of Hadoop.

Prescriptive Analytics

Prescriptive analytics (Soltanpoor and Sellis 2016) is still not as widely utilized by companies as other analytics. This is partly due to the fact that prescriptive analytics is a type of automation of analytics. Companies and businesses are still skeptical of letting machine handle business analytics.

Another challenge in employing prescriptive analytics is that the data available are rarely without gaps. Analysts have adapted to this challenge and often work around the unavailable data. However, such data gaps are not suitable for automation-based analytics.

TABLE 5.5

Big Data Analytics Use Cases

Category	Churn Prevention	Customer Lifetime Value	Customer Segmentation	Next Best Action	Risk Modeling	Sentimental Analysis	Item Set Mining
Retail and e-Commerce	✓	✓	✓	✓		✓	✓
Banking	✓	✓	✓	✓	✓		✓
Telecoms	✓	✓	✓	✓			
Oil and Gas					✓		
Life Sciences			✓			✓	
Automotive	✓		✓		✓		
Healthcare and Insurance	✓	✓	✓	✓	✓	✓	✓

Data latency poses another challenge for prescriptive analytics. As automation makes analytics faster, there is always a requirement of fresh data to provide accurate projections and future options. With current batch processing-based analytics models, the freshness of data is often questionable. However, recent developments in real-time and stream processing-based Big Data processing platforms make predictive analytics possible.

Conclusions

We have described the different forms of Big Data analytics and how they involve descriptive, diagnostic, predictive, and prescriptive analytics. We have also presented the mathematical tools and techniques behind such analytics. Big Data analytics has become an integral part of business today. Companies are already heavily utilizing it for decision-making processes. We have provided a real world use case, customer churn prevention, and explained it in the context of the different analytics tools involved. The example was a simple one; however, it provided a clear insight into the processes involved in analytics. Table 5.5 mentions more such use cases and different fields where Big Data analytics is utilized (Soltanpoor and Sellis 2016; http://xmpro.com/10-predictive-analytics-use-cases-by-industry/).

Recent advancements in Big Data analytics, as we have described, have opened new avenues for richer and faster analytics. These improvements are going to have an impact on businesses all around us, as businesses will be able to perform analytics on much larger data sets in a much shorter amount of time.

References

Alpaydin E. 2015. *Introduction to Machine Learning*, 3rd ed. Delhi, India: Prentice Hall of India.

Anthony B, Boudnik K, Adams C, Shao B, Lee C, and Sasaki K. 2016. In-memory computing in Hadoop Stack, pp. 161–182. *Professional Hadoop*. Hoboken, NJ: John Wiley & Sons, Inc.

Balcan M-F, Liang Y, Gupta P. 2014. Robust hierarchical clustering. *Journal of Machine Learning Research* 15(1):3831–3871.

Borne K. 2017. Predictive and prescriptive power discovery from fast, wide, deep Big Data. https://www.brighttalk.com/webcast/9061/212377?utm_campaign=webcasts-search-results-feed&utm_content=prescriptive_analytics&utm_source=brighttalk-portal&utm_medium=web.

Caruana R, Niculescu-Mizil A. 2006. An empirical comparison of supervised learning algorithms, pp. 161–168. *Proceedings of the 23rd International Conference on Machine Learning.* New York: ACM.

Chen H, Chiang RHL, Storey VC. 2012. Business intelligence and analytics: From Big Data to big impact. *MIS Quarterly* 36(4):1165–1188.

Davidson I, Ravi SS. 2005. Agglomerative hierarchical clustering with constraints: Theoretical and empirical results, pp. 59–70. *Joint European Conference on Principles of Data Mining and Knowledge Discovery.* New York: Springer.

Gröger C, Schwarz H, Mitschang B. 2014. Prescriptive analytics for recommendation-based business process optimization, pp. 25–37. *International Conference on Business Information Systems.* New York: Springer.

Gubbi J, Buyya R, Marusic S, Palaniswami M. 2013. Internet of Things (IoT): A vision, architectural elements, and future directions. *Future Generation Computer Systems* 29(7):1645–1660.

Hamilton JD. 1994. *Time Series Analysis*, vol 2. Princeton, NJ: Princeton University Press.

Hastie T, Tibshirani R, Friedman J. 2009. Unsupervised learning, pp. 485–585. *The Elements of Statistical Learning.* New York: Springer.

Hunter JS. 1986. The exponentially weighted moving average. *Journal of Quality Technology* 18(4):203–210.

Karayiannis N, Venetsanopoulos AN. 2013. *Artificial Neural Networks: Learning Algorithms, Performance Evaluation, and Applications*, vol. 209. Berlin: Springer Science + Business Media.

Marr B. 2015. Big Data: 20 mind-boggling facts everyone must read. *Forbes*, 30 September 2015. http://www.forbes.com/sites/bernardmarr/2015/09/30/big-data-20-mind-boggling-facts-everyone-must-read/#314e0f326c1d.

Ranjan R. 2014. Streaming Big Data processing in data center clouds. *IEEE Cloud Computing* 1(1):78–83.

Rumelhart DE, Hinton GE, Williams RJ. 1985. *Learning Internal Representations by Error Propagation.* San Diego, CA: Institute for Cognitive Science, UCSD.

Shanahan JG, Dai L. 2015. Large scale distributed data science using Apache Spark, pp. 2323–2324. *Proceedings of the 21th ACM SIGKDD International Conference on Knowledge Discovery and Data Mining.* New York: ACM.

Soltanpoor R, Sellis T. 2016. Prescriptive analytics for Big Data, pp. 245–256. *Australasian Database Conference.* New York: Spinger.

Song S, Kim DJ, Hwang M, Kim J, Jeong D-H et al. 2013. Prescriptive analytics system for improving research power, pp. 1144–1145. *2013 IEEE Conference on Computational Science and Engineering.* New York: IEEE.

Sutton RS, Barto AG. 1998. *Reinforcement Learning: An Introduction*, vol 1. Cambridge, MA: MIT Press.

Werbos P. 1975. Beyond regression: New tools for prediction and analysis in the behavioral sciences. Ph.D. dissertation. Harvard University, Cambridge, MA.

Yegnanarayana B. 2009. *Artificial Neural Networks.* Delhi, India: Prentice Hall of India.

Zhang G, Patuwo BE, Hu MY. 1998. Forecasting with artificial neural networks: The state of the art. *International Journal of Forecasting* 14(1):35–62.

Zikopoulos P et al. 2011. *Understanding Big Data: Analytics for Enterprise Class Hadoop and Streaming Data.* New York: McGraw-Hill Osborne Media.

Online Sources

http://spotfire.tibco.com/solutions/technology/predictive-analytics
http://mahout.apache.org/

https://azure.microsoft.com/en-us/
http://www.philbrierley.com/main.html?code/bpproof.html&code/codeleft.html
https://home.cern/about/computing
https://en.wikipedia.org/wiki/Decision_tree
https://www.oracle.com/database/advanced-analytics/index.html
https://halobi.com/2016/01/halo-for-forecasting/
https://www-01.ibm.com/software/data/infosphere/
http://www.ibm.com/analytics/us/en/technology/spss/
http://home.cern/topics/large-hadron-collider
https://en.wikipedia.org/wiki/Linear_regression
http://xmpro.com/10-predictive-analytics-use-cases-by-industry/
https://www.palisade.com/risk/l
https://home.cern/scientists/updates/2015/09/big-data-takes-root
https://www.r-project.org/
https://www.wolfram.com/mathematica/

6

Big Data Predictive Modeling and Analytics

Mydhili K. Nair, Arjun Rao, and Mipsa Patel

CONTENTS

Introduction

This chapter aims to give insight into how Big Data predictive modeling and analytics can be used for effective planning of businesses. At the outset, we would like to note that this topic is a very niche upcoming area of research. There are numerous published works dealing with predictive modeling and analytics techniques, but they do not focus on the nuances and intricacies associated with Big Data and its four dimensions, namely, volume, variety, velocity, and veracity. Therefore, in this chapter, we strived to concentrate on the Big Data prediction aspects after giving a brief overview of the traditional predictive modeling and analytics techniques. We start the chapter by giving a glimpse to the user, with case study examples, on how precise predictions based on current and history data can help in effective business planning. After this brief introduction, we explain the predictive modeling process starting with the preprocessing step of selecting and preparing the data, followed by fitting a mathematical model to this prepared data and ending with estimating and validating the predictive model. Then in the next section we describe the various types of predictive models, starting with models for supervised learning, namely, linear and nonlinear regression, decision trees, random forests, and support vector machines. We end the section with cluster analysis, the only unsupervised learning predictive model covered in this chapter. Then we deal with measuring the accuracy of predictive models through target shuffling, lift charts, receiver operating characteristic (ROC) curves, and bootstrap sampling. Then we focus on the tools and techniques of predictive modeling and analytics. We cover the CRISP-DM technique here, which is used for data mining. We also describe implementation of predictive analytics using R, an open-source tool, by taking a sample case-study application. We wind up the chapter by giving insight into the research trends and upcoming initiatives by industry giants in this cutting-edge realm of research.

The Power of Business Planning with Precise Predictions

Elon Musk, the cofounder of PayPal, Tesla Motors, and creator of space foundation SpaceX said, "I've actually made a prediction that within 30 years a majority of new cars made in the United States will be electric. And I don't mean hybrid, I mean fully electric" ("Extended Interview" 2008). An engineer and innovator like Elon Musk did not say this out of the blue, but after pain-staking business data analytics and predictive modeling that helped him make this informed prediction. Companies like Netflix, Amazon, and Google have utilized predictive analytics for a number of years to predict consumer behavior and better target recommendations or advertisements.

Predictive Modeling for Effective Business Planning: A Case Study

Predictive modeling and analytics are being used by various companies to widen their customer base and to sell more products. It is also used in healthcare, customer relationship management, actuarial science, and many more fields. In this section, we take one such field where predictive models are used and examine the features that the model has and how it maximizes the results obtained.

In the field of e-commerce, millions of customers visit the site, but only a few of them buy products. Hence, retailers are using predictive modeling and analytics to make smarter decisions about the customer focus, marketing strategy, promotions, and so on, hence maximizing profit.

The model developed by companies focuses on improving the following:

- Targeting the right segment of customers—Retailers aim at developing a model that will target fewer customers but obtain better results during promotions. The model is created based on the user's browsing history, past purchases, demographics, and so forth. If the user looked up or purchased similar products in the past, he or she is more likely to be interested in them in the future. Also, regular visitors to the website are more likely to buy products from there.

- Personalized recommendations—Recommendations play an important role in attracting customers. One particular retailer called Stitch Fix has a unique sales model that asks users to take a style survey and then recommends clothes based on those choices.

- Optimal pricing—The price of a product is related to the number of customers buying the product, and the profit made by the company. Predictive models for pricing looks at customer interest, historical product pricing, competitor pricing, and so forth. A study shows that predictive pricing can deliver an additional net profit of about 20%.

- Predictive search—Companies focus on developing predictive models to optimize the search suggestions, as the search bar is the primary method in which the user interacts with the website. The predictive search model is based on the search history, products the user clicks on, purchase history, and so on. The model can anticipate what the user is looking for by typing just a couple of letters.

- Customer segmentation—Customers having similar characteristics are grouped together by using predictive modeling and analytics. This can help in targeting marketing of products.

Stitch Fix is a startup in the online retail sector. What makes the company stand out from other online retail companies is its unique sales model of delivering five highly curated pieces of clothing to its clients' homes monthly. Clients pay a $20 styling fee to get their set of five products, and if they decide to purchase any of the five items they received in their shipment, that $20 goes toward the purchase. Additionally, if a client buys all five items in their shipment, they receive a 25% discount off the entire purchase.

Each customer of Stitch Fix takes an extensive "Style Profile," which is a questionnaire about the customer's body type, height, weight, color preferences, zip code (to determine the type of weather), style preferences, and price range, among other topics. The customer is also asked to rate images of clothing to determine their style choices.

The gathered data is evaluated by data scientists and styling experts. The company has developed algorithms and predictive models that use a customer's data to evaluate how likely he or she is to keep a certain item based on parameters like style choices and occupation. Based on the results of the model, five most suited products are chosen and shipped to the customer. Each customer receives a personalized recommendation of products, reducing the number of choices to choose from, which can be a huge advantage. The company also uses the feedback provided and the products returned to better the algorithm and hence make more relevant recommendations to the customer the next time.

Stitch Fix does not provide exclusive clothes or fast shipping. But why it is such a huge hit in the market is because it is more relevant to the customers. The predictive models reduce complexity through relevant curation. With personalized recommendations and fewer, more relevant choices, customers are more likely to buy the products. Stitch Fix has thus utilized the power of predictive modeling and become a huge success in the e-retail field.

E-commerce is just one example where predictive modeling and analytics are used. Actuarial science, movie recommendations, and the banking sector are among the numerous applications. Each predictive model that is developed and tested is a step toward effective planning.

Effect of Big Data in Predictive Modeling

Big Data as cited in various research publications has four dimensions: volume, variety, veracity, and velocity. It is inherently voluminous, by being distributed across geographical regions, and has an exceedingly fast velocity of growth. Its type is varied in nature, with disparate forms such as structured, semistructured, and unstructured, available in a variety of formats such as documents, videos, audios, images, e-mails, and social-networking feeds. Due to this variety of sources of Big Data, as well as its velocity of growth and its veracity, the quality is unreliable and differs tremendously. This makes the task of creating an accurate and effective model for Big Data analytics, specifically predictive analytics, an uphill task indeed.

Predictive Modeling

Predictive modeling is the use of statistical or machine learning algorithms to make predictions about future or unknown outcomes based on historically collected data. Although predictive modeling techniques have been researched under the purview of data mining for several years, they have become increasingly prominent in real-world scenarios in recent times, impacting every facet of our lives. The nature of problems being solved or approached by using predictive modeling processes, range across a wide spectrum of fields from healthcare to climatology.

Exponential growth and adoption of e-commerce platforms, smarter devices, development of Internet of Things, and so on have led to tremendous amounts of data being generated every second. Collecting and processing such vast amounts of data and drawing meaningful insights from them are the objectives of predictive modeling of Big Data. Storage is a fundamental aspect when dealing with data on such scales, and it is now generally solved by using distributed databases and storage clusters. Bringing this data together and applying complex mathematical algorithms on it requires out-of-the-box thinking and innovative approaches. Techniques like MapReduce and harnessing the power of cloud computing have greatly helped in Big Data analytics.

In the following sections, we will briefly touch upon general stages of any predictive modeling task, and the nature of input and output of these said stages. Although each stage is in logical order of precedence, with direct flow of output from one stage to the next, the way any particular stage is to be interpreted and thus implemented greatly varies depending upon the problem being tackled. For example, the kinds of models used for something like weather data or market segmentation cannot be used for something like text classification or sentiment analysis of customer feedback data. As this chapter focuses on predictive modeling, we shall go over a few popular techniques for developing predictive models and their use cases for Big Data applications.

Predictive Modeling Process

For any given problem that requires the use of historical data of decision variables to predict the outcome when a new value for these decision variables is encountered, a predictive modeling approach is convenient. The process of predictive modeling starts by clearly understanding the objectives of the problem. Some of the questions we must ask at this juncture are

- What values do we have and what values do we need?
- What would be the kind of data available in this case for using a computer algorithm to raw insights?
- What are the kinds of insights we can get from using certain kinds of data?
- What algorithms are we going to use for processing data?

These questions are answered in various stages of the predictive modeling process. We shall discuss each step of the process in general, and then provide an example of that particular stage for a real-world use case. The actual implementations of each step using a particular framework or tool are discussed toward the end of the chapter. The general outline for a predictive modeling process begins with determination of the objectives, as stated earlier, following which is the data collection and preprocessing stage. Once prepared training data is available, a suitable model is selected that can be considered the best fit for the kind of data being used. The model is then trained on the large data set, and the results of the trained model are in essence parameters in the algorithm that ensure that the chosen mathematical model can accurately (at least to a large extent) map the input values to their outputs. The resulting model can be tested on a test data set for accuracy and validation, based on which the model is either revised or a superior model can be selected to improve the accuracy, or if the accuracy is reasonably good, it is used in production environments to analyze new data and gain insights for effective planning. Figure 6.1 illustrates the process from a high-level perspective.

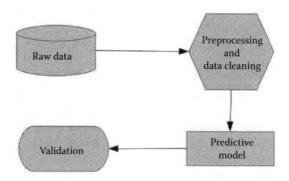

FIGURE 6.1
Predictive modeling process.

Selecting and Preparing Data

To begin with, we shall discuss the nature of data, in particular in the Big Data context. We would like to establish that the way we deal with Big Data requires additional processing steps than when the size of the data set is manageable. The primary source of any predictive modeling process is the data. Data here can be from multiple sources like sensors, customer click streams, Twitter data streams, and stock market statistics, depending on the nature of the problem being attempted. It is often the case that the obtained data is either inconsistent with the format expected by the model or is not clean. When we say data is not clean, it essentially means that there are records in the data set that are either corrupt (invalid in format or value) or missing fields. When we consider huge quantities of data, incorrect data can lead to wrong model outputs and effectively bad business decisions, which could lead to massive losses for companies that rely heavily on Big Data analysis. Some of the issues that arise with Big Data and potential reasons for inconsistencies are summarized as follows:

- Incomplete data validation—When we consider large amounts of data, in databases, especially when the data being collected is from outside the organization, there is a good chance that the data is not completely validated. For example, it could have data type inconsistencies or different formats for similar data (e.g., date formats could be inconsistent).

- Multiple data sources—When collecting data from different vendors or sources such as sensors, it can so happen that each source provides data in their own format. This is particularly common when dealing with data from different websites. For example, one website may supply data in a format like CSVs, whereas another may supply data as XML records.

- Contain superfluous information—Sometimes when dealing with large data sets, there can be superfluous information in the data, such as personal names or addresses that may not be useful for the modeling task at hand. Hence, such fields will need to be removed before the data can be used.

- Linguistic inconsistencies—When dealing with problems that use data from social media, a lot of users are bilingual in their posts or end up using unconventional vocabulary such as short forms like "ur" or emoticons. Such kinds of inconsistencies can severely affect the performance of predictive models.

Although this is not an exhaustive list of problems that can arise with data, it is illustrative of the need to perform data cleaning operations before the model training stage. Moving ahead with the discussion of preparing data, once the raw data is in a consistent format that can be used by a model, the question of handling Big Data still remains unaddressed. The general nature of Big Data is that it is stored across distributed databases and is so large in volume that it does not fit on a single machine. Predictive analysis uses mathematical computations that are generally probabilistic in nature and require a lot of memory to process. The difficulty with Big Data analytics is due to the demands on memory and processing capabilities. Thus it is important to address the optimization strategies to be considered when using predictive analysis techniques on Big Data, and look into techniques to process large amounts of data in limited memory scenarios. Although the exact discussions on handling big data is out of the scope of this chapter, we can highlight that technologies like Hadoop and Apache Mahout are considered some of the leading solutions that help in parallel processing. This involves writing machine-learning algorithms using a MapReduce paradigm in a manner that exploits Hadoop's distributed file system to handle Big Data. Alternatively, we can process the data set in batches, using manageable chunks of data in each iteration of the algorithm. This approach is much simpler than using MapReduce tasks, but the efficiency is reduced as it is time consuming and requires a large number of iterations to successfully process the entire data set.

When dealing with model fitting and prediction to evaluate the efficiency of the model, we need a certain amount of data for testing and validation. The general practice is to split the original data set into two distinct sets: the training set and the testing set. The ratio of samples in training versus test data is generally skewed toward training sets, as we require more historical data to fine-tune the parameters of a model than we need to test its accuracy. In the next section we discuss selection of models and using the preprocessed data for training a chosen model.

Fitting a Model

The logical step that follows data collection and processing is to fit a mathematical model that would map certain decision variables or features of a sample to some output performance or value that has a direct relation to the features being considered. For example, consider an online retailer that has data about customer purchases, value of purchase orders, shopping cart lists, ratios across product categories in shopping carts, time of purchase (such as during discounts or during certain seasons). This data will act as features for the retailer to segment its customer base into clusters of buyers whose purchase patterns are aligned. Using such a segmented customer base, the retailer can then take decisions to offer discounts or promotions targeted at specific segments of buyers to maximize chances of converting shopping carts to purchase orders. Here it must be noted that although variables like products in a shopping cart may seem like nonnumeric data, which may not lend themselves to a direct mathematical translation, it is always possible to associate such variables to numeric values.

Feature Vectors

When dealing with machine learning algorithms, we often need to represent objects of interest in numerical forms. By objects we mean real-world entities that are being modeled in the algorithm and involved in the decision-making process for predictive algorithms. In this context, we term such a representation as a feature vector. A feature vector in essence is a N-dimensional vector of numerical properties (measurable properties are called features). We illustrate the concept of a feature vector through the following example.

Consider the scenario of a retailer having six different product categories, with each category associated with a value, say 0 through 5. We can then model a user's shopping cart data as an array containing product quantities, with array indices mapping to a category. So a customer buying one product each in categories 2 and 3 and four products in category 5 can be represented by the array [0, 0, 1, 1, 0, 4]. So this would be the kind of feature vectors that is trained on an algorithm and is aimed at making certain predictions given a new user's shopping cart that is converted into a similar feature vector. The following is illustrated in the diagram in Figure 6.2.

Feature extraction is an important phase, as the quality of the features directly translate to the quality of a model's results. Once feature extraction is complete, a suitable mathematical model can be used to fit the training data set. The model is trained on the training set, and this generally implies that the algorithm on each successive iteration reads

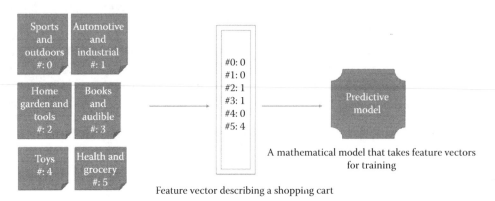

Categories and their array indices

FIGURE 6.2
Converting from textual data to numeric feature vectors.

a training sample and adjusts certain parameters to better match its output to the given output in the training set. This is the case with a class of algorithms called supervised learning algorithms dealing with data sets that have well-marked inputs and outputs. Some well-known supervised learning algorithms are regression algorithms (linear or logistic), support vector machines, decision trees, and random forests. Problems such as market segmentation are classified under the set of problems that are generally solved by what are called unsupervised learning algorithms or models, where the model is used to identify clusters or segments. In the case of unsupervised models, we will be providing extracted features from a data set as input and the model on each successive iteration identifies sample points that can come under a group or cluster, using algorithms like k-means. Thus the right model depends on the nature of the problem and the data set being used. In the upcoming section "Types of Predictive Models" we discuss a few different types of models and their merits, aimed at helping readers get an overview of the possible choices for model selection.

Estimating and Validating the Model

Once a model is selected and the training data set is used to train the model, the test data set is used to evaluate its performance. There are various methods that are used for model evaluation, including ROC curves, lift charts, and bootstrap sampling, which are discussed later. When the training stage is complete, we no longer depend on the training data set, and the trained model alone is sufficient for making predictions on new samples. This is because the trained model summarizes all the relationships between features and labels. At the same time, training models also make certain assumptions about data, regarding distribution of data, linearity of continuous variables, nature of effects of variables and correlations, and so on. Thus to ensure maximum accuracy of the trained model, it must be validated.

In a study by Steyerberg et al. (2001a), logistic regression models were developed to predict mortality of patients 30 days after undergoing surgical treatments for acute myocardial infraction. This is a binary classification problem that was evaluated by splitting the data set into train and test sets. The data set used for training the model was a subset of data collected during a large randomized trial of over 785 patients. The remaining data is provided for validation. Various evaluation techniques such as ROC curves and goodness-of-fit statistics were used in the validation stage.

As discussed by Steyerberg et al. (2001b), we can classify the nature of validation of a model based on the data set used for validation as apparent, internal, or external validation. They are discussed further next:

- Apparent validation—The apparent performance of a model is the result of validation using the same data set that was used to train the model. This is an obvious result that is generally better than validation on any other data set, even if the test set is from the same source population as the training set. However, this kind of validation is still necessary to ensure the model is developed correctly and is working with at least a baseline performance. Apparent validation is the simplest form of validation in terms of computational requirements and results in optimistic performance, as the same data set is used for defining the model, as well as determining performance.

- Internal validation—This type of validation is performed on the source population of the training data. Generally, an approach called the split-sample approach is used for internal validation, wherein the available data set is split into two parts: one for model development and the other for validation. Hence, the model is evaluated on independent data samples, which are not present in the training set, albeit similar in nature as they originate from the same root population. Internal validation is more difficult to perform than apparent validation. It generally gives an honest estimate of actual performance for a population that is similar to the training set. It is akin to an upper limit on the obtainable performance when using an external data set, as in the case of cross-validation techniques. Examples of internal validation techniques include bootstrap sampling and cross-validation.

- External validation—This is a more generalized form of validation that uses an independent validation population that is different from the population used for training or internal validation, but semantically related to it. It represents new samples that could arise in production settings for the model. External validation is dependent on the nature of available data sets for validation. The data set must ideally have similar features and output labels in order to be used for validation; otherwise some form of transformation must be applied to make it suitable for testing. Examples of external validation techniques include temporal validation, spatial validation, and fully external validation.

Types of Predictive Models

Now that we have discussed the process that is generally applicable to most predictive modeling scenarios, we are in a position to dive into the heart of predictive modeling, that is, the model itself. The task of identifying the right modeling technique is highly data dependent. Feature extraction operations for a given data set generally influence the type of model used for training. In this section we shall discuss a few popular modeling techniques that are to serve as an overview for the available options. They are by no means an exhaustive list of methods for predictive modeling; however, they are demonstrative of the variety of choices available to data scientists. We can broadly classify techniques under two categories: statistical modeling (such as linear regression and logistic regression) and machine learning techniques (such as support vector machines and neural networks). The difference between the two is in the amount of human involvement and the size of data being analyzed. The aim of the following sections is to illustrate the differences between different techniques and the kinds of problems they are best suited for. Much of the work by James et al. (2013) demonstrates the different techniques for statistical learning algorithms and their respective strengths and weaknesses in great detail. These algorithms are at the heart of predictive modeling processes.

Linear ar.d Nonlinear Regression

Regression in statistics is a measure of the relation between the mean value of one variable (output) and corresponding values of other variables (input). In the domain of predictive modeling, regression analysis is a method that obtains a relationship between independent variables called the predictors and a target variable whose value depends on the predictors. They generally solve problems that have cause-effect relationships or are used for forecasting events in a context given some determining factors.

In general, regression models not only help in identifying the associated output values for a given input, but they also help in measuring the degree of dependence of the output on different input parameters. They help determine the best set of input parameters that need to be optimized or given focus in order to get the desired output. For example, consider predicting the value of a house in the real-estate domain. Input variables in this case include number of rooms, year of construction, features of the neighborhood such as distance to nearest public transportation utility, and so on. However, to determine the price of the house, some features are more important than others such as number of rooms or carpet area of the house. Hence when a real-estate agent is deciding on what particular house to pitch to his customer, he would naturally focus on those variables that are more lucrative or important to a customer in making a decision. Similarly, in data science, when regression analysis is the chosen technique, we tend to focus on those input parameters that strongly influence the direction of output rather than include all the variables leading to more computationally intensive processes.

There are many different techniques that come under the umbrella of regression analysis. They are generally classified according to the shape of the line of regression, which is a mathematical function relating the input variables to the output variable. The most common of the techniques and also one of the simplest regression techniques is linear regression.

Types of Regression Algorithms

Figure 6.3 illustrates an overall perspective about the different types of regression algorithms that can be applied to Big Data. These are well-known algorithms available in literature. Descriptions of each of these algorithms are beyond the scope of this chapter. However, we do present details regarding linear and nonlinear regression algorithms here. Generally linear regression is considered one of the most basic of predictive models and is often considered too simple for most tasks. However, the real power of linear regression is seen when used in conjunction with neural networks, and deep neural networks in the domain of deep learning, which once again is beyond the scope of this chapter and is left for interested readers to research further.

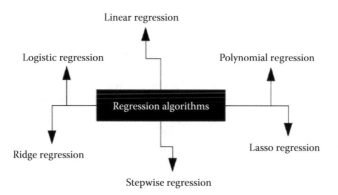

FIGURE 6.3
Types of regression algorithms.

Linear Regression

Linear regression is used to find the best straight line fit (called the line of regression) that establishes the relationship between a dependent variable (*Y*) and one or more independent variables (*X*) that influence the value of the dependent variable.

The line of regression is generally represented by the following equation:

$$Y = mX + c$$

In this equation, *Y* represents the output variable, *X* represents the input variable, *m* is a weight that is applied to the input variable, and *c* is the intercept of the line. Generally, *m* and *c* are determined by the method of least squares, which is a popular technique in statistics that aim to minimize the sum of squares of the difference between the expected output and the output predicted by the line of regression. It can be summarized by the following equation:

$$\sum [Y(i) - (m * x(i) + c)]^2$$

where *i* varies from 1 to *N* (being the number of data points). The data that is used in linear regression is generally of the form (*x,y*), where *x* is the input and *y* is the output corresponding to that input. This is the case when we are dealing with simple linear regression in just two dimensions. However, the technique is extensible to a higher number of input variables wherein we will have a higher dimensional vector as *X* and similarly a vector for *Y*. However, the equations and the method of least squares remains the same.

Computationally, to determine the values of *m* and *c*, a technique known as gradient descent (Ng 2000) is used. Gradient descent is an algorithm that aims to minimize a cost function by successively iterating over the data set and varying the parameters of the line of regression. The cost function takes (*m*, *c*) as the input and returns an error associated with the fit of the line to the data points. The aim of the gradient descent algorithm is to find the optimal values of *m* and *c* to fit the given data points. Although the mathematics behind the algorithm are fairly straightforward, involving the derivate of the error function with respect to *m* and *c*, we leave it as an exercise for interested readers.

Nonlinear Regression

Another popular technique when dealing with binary classification problems where the output of the predicted model is 0 or a 1, that is, a two-class classification problem, we can use the nonlinear regression technique known as logistic regression. It does not require that a linear relationship exists between dependent and independent variables. This technique is particularly powerful when using Big Data, as the large sample sizes ensure better maximum likelihood estimates that determine what class a given data point belongs to. Logistic regression generally relies on the sigmoid function, which is used to calculate the cost for gradient descent. Once again the details of the technique and the mathematics are more involved and beyond the scope of this chapter.

Although regression techniques are powerful and are often considered the base for any data analytics task, they are limited to smaller data sets where the relation between input variables is not very complicated. However, this is seldom the case when dealing with present-day predictive modeling problems where the data set is huge, and computing regression parameters is simply not efficient given the time-intensive nature of these algorithms. This leads to the widespread development and adoption of machine learning algorithms, which harness the power of computation to enable superior predictive modeling results by processing large amounts of training samples.

Decision Trees

In this section we discuss decision trees, a tree-based classifier, to set the foundation for the next section covering random forests, a specialized tree-based classifier. Decision trees (Kass 1980; Safavian and Langrebe 1991; Salzberg 1994) are also referred to as classifications trees or regression trees. The classification tree models are ordered in such a way that the root node and the internal nodes (called split nodes) have attribute test conditions that are used to classify records having different characteristics. The branches between nodes represent combinations of features that lead to the classifications. The leaf nodes represent the final class labels.

The tree-based classifier algorithm uses a divide-and-conquer approach to build the classifier model. After the classifier model is built, it can easily predict the class label of the data set freshly presented to it. For example, a decision tree classifier model can be used to predict if a new patient is prone to have a chronic kidney disease (CKD) by extracting the attributes of the patient such as the age, count of red blood cells, white blood cells, pus cells, levels of sodium, potassium, albumin, and sugar. The leaf nodes of this classification tree model would predict the class of a given data set by using predictor functions such as majority class or naive Bayes classifier. In this example, the leaf node could have two class-labels, CKD and NCKD, with N negating the possibility of having CKD.

Use of Decision Trees in Big Data Predictive Analytics

In the present context of Big Data, the traditional decision tree has to be modified to a distributed decision tree that aims to

- Parallelize the training process
- Perform the training process in a distributed environment

In this section we aim to give a glimpse of the various techniques used by researchers to apply decision trees in Big Data predictive analytics. The study of Big Data predictive analytics is closely linked with distributed machine learning frameworks, which should inherently be capable of handling large magnitudes of data in the order of terabytes or petabytes. Mahout (Apache Software Foundation n.d.) is a distributed machine learning framework deployed over Hadoop. It has built-in algorithms for pattern mining, classification, clustering, and recommendation. MLBase (Kraska et al. 2013), a component of Berkeley Data Analytics Stack, hides the complexity of the underlying distributed computation by giving a set of high-level operators to implement a scalable machine learning algorithm. There are many more distributed machine learning frameworks, a discussion of which is beyond the scope of this chapter. We, however, point to the work of Gillick, Faria, and DeNero (2006) in which the authors give a taxonomy of machine learning algorithms and catalog them based on their data processing patterns.

Panda, Herbach, Basu, and Bayardo (2009) were among the pioneers in developing classifier tree models for large data sets. They developed a framework called PLANET, which transforms steps in the learning process of the decision tree into MapReduce jobs that are executed in parallel. The work of Ye, Chow, Chen, and Zheng (2009) chronicles methods to distribute and parallelize gradient boosted decision trees (GBDT). GBDT is a commonly used technique to teach a classifier model to predict values by combining weak learners to a single strong learner in an iterative mode. This work discusses two techniques of Big Data partitioning:

- Horizontal—Here the data set was partitioned horizontally with all attributes appearing in each horizontal partition. The GBDT created is converted to a MapReduce model. The Hadoop Distributed File System (HDFS) is used for communication between nodes spread across machines in the distributed environment. To split a node of the classifier decision tree, HDFS has to write out multiple files for communicating between the nodes, as it currently does not have built-in support for internode communication.

- Vertical—Here Message Passing Interface (MPI) was used with Hadoop streaming. The data set was partitioned vertically based on its comma-separated attribute values. Thus, each machine operates on a subset of the attribute space and has only sufficient information to compute the best local split. The best gain among this subset of features is computed, and this information is sent to all machines using an MPI broadcast. Each machine then determines the global best split by aggregating the local splits from each machine and determining which split corresponds to the cut point that maximizes gain.

Inference

This work by Ye et al. (2009) gives a very important result. It proved that vertical partition helps reduce the communication overhead of computing a tree node. The time taken to train a GBDT was less than halved from 20 seconds to 9 seconds for their training data set comprising 1.2 million samples and 520 numeric features associated with it. This is a significant contribution to the researcher community as the idea is to build as quickly as possible; a distributed decision tree classifier model for the big training data set is to ensure that the model is ready to predict at any point in time. When the actual testing data arrives, the model should be able to accurately predict the class the data belongs to based on this previously processed training data.

Random Forests

In the preceding section, we discussed decision trees as a technique for predictive modeling. Random forests (see Genuer et al. 2015) are in essence the next step to decision trees. The technique is a combination of aggregation and bootstrapping, along with decision trees. It is a versatile learning algorithm that can be used to solve problems in regression analysis, as well as two or multiclass classification. They work by parallel construction of decision trees with extensive resampling. Hence, they are a natural solution to handling large continuous data streams, which is primarily what we deal with when we talk about Big Data. Apache Mahout is a learning framework that works using Apache Hadoop and HDFS, which has been effectively used for implementing predictive modeling algorithms using random forests for Big Data.

The details of the exact working of random forests is beyond the scope of this chapter, but we shall summarize their working and their primary advantages in the Big Data context as follows.

Random forest is derived from the classification and regression tree model, commonly known as CART (see Timofeev 2004). The algorithm takes a bootstrapping approach and builds multiple CART models with different samples from the original population. For instance, if the original sample had 10,000 observations, with 100 variables, the random forest model builds a random sample with 1,000 observations and 10 randomly chosen variables to build the initial decision tree. This process is repeated a number of times to cover a majority of the population, in order to make a final prediction on each observation. From each decision tree model, the predicted outputs are used to obtain a mean output that acts as the final prediction of the random forest.

By combining multiple decision trees, random forests give far superior accuracy when compared to a single CART model or regression models. Their strength, though lies, in dealing with massive data sets with large number of variables and samples.

Use of Random Forests for Big Data

In Genuer (2015), experiments conducted on massive data sets involving millions of observations of real-world airline data showed that random forests lead to reduced computational time with high accuracy. The experiments were aimed at predicting whether a flight would arrive on time, using as features metrics such as distance, time of day, and time of departure. The experiments involved three different implementations of random forests for evaluating their use and effectiveness on Big Data. The performance of these algorithms in terms of computational effort and accuracy were compared with that of the standard random forest implementation, wherein the training was done sequentially with 100 trees.

The three methods studied are summarized as follows:

- A sampling approach that used a subset of the original data set that was assumed to be representative in nature of the entire data set for training a forest
- Bag of little bootstrap method (Kleiner et al. 2014) for training a parallel random forest
- A MapReduce-based decomposition technique for training a random forest

The result of the experiments leads to the conclusion that scalability of random forests in particular when implemented using parallel programming techniques is one of its strongest selling points for predictive analytics of Big Data, as the methods reduce computational time with no loss in accuracy over sequential or traditional random forest approaches.

Support Vector Machines

Having discussed statistical modeling techniques, we now introduce a very popular modeling algorithm that comes under the class of supervised learning algorithms and is very popular in the domain of Big Data and machine learning, that is, support vector machines (Cortes and Vapnik 1995) or popularly known as SVMs. The strength of SVMs is in solving the problem of supervised binary classification. We briefly discussed the application of logistic regression to solve this problem. However, SVMs are considered to be far more superior techniques to solve binary classification.

The mathematics of SVMs is more involved than any regression technique discussed so far, and hence we shall try and discuss working of SVMs from a higher level perspective abstracting the complex mathematical derivations behind it.

SVMs primarily train a model that assigns categories to unseen values of the decision variable (independent variable). This is done by creating a linear partition on the feature space into the two binary categories. The partition is done using what is called a separating hyperplane, which is constructed in a high-dimensional vector space. The algorithm tries to classify the input by creating a feature space, which is a finite dimensional vector space, where each dimension is a feature of a particular object. For example, in classifying a particular customer feedback from a large data set of feedback collected by some retailer, as either positive or negative, a feature can be the prevalence of some characteristic word that is either considered positive or negative. Figure 6.4 illustrates the creation of a hyperplane.

The hyperplane constructed by the SVM is considered optimal when it provides a maximum distance to the nearest training samples (called the support vectors). This can be interpreted as the SVM's classification is optimal if the points are well separated by the constructed hyperplane, thus making the distinction between the two classes clearer. Thus SVMs are also called maximum margin classifiers.

It does happen that the feature space overlaps and is not linearly separable. When this occurs, the original feature space is mapped to a higher dimensional space, in which the separation of the two classes is more distinct. This is particularly the main reason for using

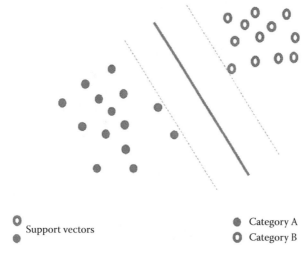

FIGURE 6.4
Hyperplane with maximum margin (dotted lines).

SVMs. The principal advantage of SVMs is their efficiency in handling high-dimensional data (such as textual data for sentiment analysis), and their versatility as they can be applied to a wide range of classification problems even when the class separation is not linear. One of the primary disadvantages of SVMs though is that they are nonprobabilistic. Thus effectiveness measurement of the classification is a concern when using SVMs.

Use of Support Vector Machines for Big Data Predictive Analytics

An interesting feature of SVMs is their application to Big Data using MapReduce (see Kiran et al. 2013). MapReduce is a popular parallel programming paradigm that can be used to implement a parallel SVM that can split the large training data set (Big Data) in to chunks that get mapped on to individual support vectors that are local to the space created by the corresponding data chunk. These output support vectors are used in the reduce phase to obtain the global weight vector by combining individual support vectors. The final global weight vector is then used to obtain the parameters of the model. Apache's Hadoop and HDFS can be used to implement a parallel SVM when the data set involved is huge. The process is illustrated in Figure 6.5.

Unsupervised Models: Cluster Analysis

The unsupervised classification model is a subdivision of machine learning that aims to find natural groupings, or clusters, in multidimensional data based on measured or observed resemblances among the input data sets, in this context "Big Data Sets" (Boinee, Angelis, and Foresti 2006). In the Big Data Sets context, one of the best examples of unsupervised classification that can be cited here to explain the use of cluster analysis is the work of Greene et al. (2014). Their source of the Big Data Set was The Cancer Genome Atlas (2012) and The Encyclopedia of DNA Elements (The ENCODE Project Consortium 2012). They addressed the task of discovering molecular subtypes causing different types of cancers. Their experimental result chronicled the molecular subtypes of serous and endometeroid ovarian cancer, which was divided into two different clusters. This was done based on measured differences between the various features extracted out of this data set, namely, somatic mutations, mRNA, and miRNA expressions. Thus, in unsupervised

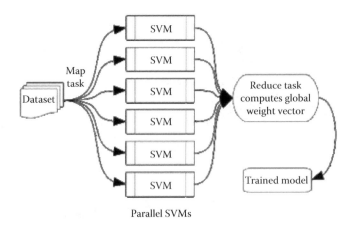

Parallel SVMs

FIGURE 6.5
Parallel SVM algorithm.

machine learning mode the learner algorithm is used to group the data set into clusters. These clusters are then examined by different cluster analysis techniques. A point to note here is that some specific unsupervised learning algorithms like self-organizing maps (SOMs) can be used for cluster visualization and data exploration. However, these are outside the scope of this chapter.

Cluster Analysis

The analysis of a cluster in the Big Data context begins with a large number of objects. Each object has many attributes (dimensions). Cluster analysis algorithms try to derive similarity among these objects based on these attributes. Related attributes are assigned into clusters so that attributes in the same cluster are similar in some sense. The aim is to derive patterns (clusters, anomalies, correlations, etc.) that depict the fundamental relations between the patterns in the data in human-understandable terms.

Algorithms for Cluster Analysis

Figure 6.6 illustrates an overall perspective about the different types of cluster analysis algorithms that can be applied to Big Data. These are well-known algorithms available in study materials. Descriptions of each of these algorithms are beyond the scope of this chapter. However, in the following we give a brief summary of the k-means algorithm because this appears to be the most popular among researchers who have used this as a base algorithm for predictive analytics of Big Data.

Lloyd's algorithm, commonly referred to as the k-means algorithm, is used to solve the k-means clustering problem. It works as depicted next:

- Step 1—First, decide the number of clusters, k.
- Step 2—Initialize the center of the clusters. μ_i = some value, $i = 1, ..., k$
- Step 3—Attribute the closest cluster to each data point.

$$c_i = \{j : d(x_j, \mu_i) \leq d(x_j, \mu_l), l \neq i, j = 1, ..., n\}$$

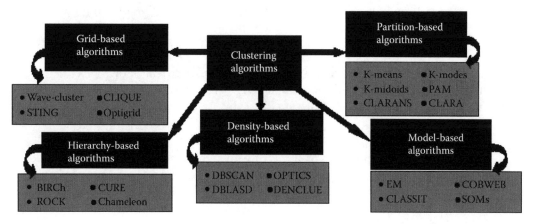

FIGURE 6.6
Taxonomy of cluster analysis algorithms.

- Step 4—Set the position of each cluster to the mean of all data points belonging to that cluster.

$$\mu_i = \frac{1}{|c_i|} \sum_{j \in c_i} x_j, \forall i$$

- Step 5—Repeat steps 3 and 4 until convergence.

Use of Cluster Analysis for Big Data Predictions

Clustering is generally used in data analytics as a preprocessing step for a variety of machine learning tasks. Some researchers are of the opinion that classification, a supervised machine learning approach with the end results known a priori, are a better fit for predictive analysis compared to clustering (Ahmad, Ismail, and Aziz 2015; Janecek and Gansterer 2009). While this may be true, in the realm of Big Data, it is highly impossible to be able to know in advance the classification bucket to which the input data set would fall under, making unsupervised learning and therefore clustering a natural preprocessing step.

In this section we examine how clustering can be used to obtain additional information about the data to get better prediction accuracy. Applying clustering for improving the prediction accuracy in the Big Data context is a very niche area of research and therefore there is a dearth of research publications with quantifiable analytical results. We hereby examine the work of Trivedi, Pardos, and Heffernan (2011), who try to find answers to the following two pertinent questions:

1. Can the prediction accuracy be improved by the fresh information obtained by combining the predictions received by changing the clustering parameters in the algorithm?
2. Can the idea of clustering as a surefire way of improving predictions be formalized?

The basic idea is to use a predictor algorithm in combination with a clustering algorithm such as k-means. Trivedi et al. (2011) run k-means at different scales on a number of data sets. For each scale, the predictor algorithm is trained. This will produce k sets of predictions. These predictions are then pooled together by a naïve ensemble to obtain the final prediction.

The approach of Trivedi et al. (2011) is fairly straightforward, consisting of two stages, as illustrated in Figure 6.7 and Figure 6.8, respectively. A succinct summary of the approach is given next:

Stage 1 (refer to Figure 6.7)

- Cluster the data set into k clusters using an algorithm such as k-means.
- Train each cluster by using predictive algorithms such as linear, stepwise linear, logistic regression, or random forests. The points inside each cluster are used as the training data set.

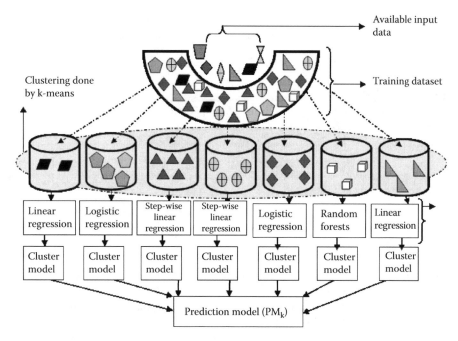

FIGURE 6.7
Stage 1: Create a prediction model (PM$_k$) for the entire data set.

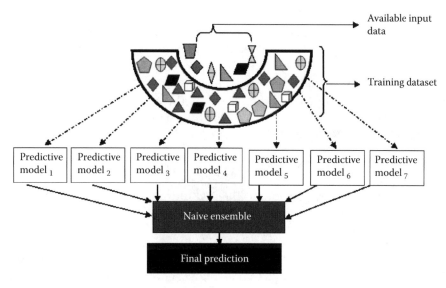

FIGURE 6.8
Stage 2: Using ensemble learning on different PMs to make the final prediction.

- The output is a set of cluster models for each of the k clusters.
- All the cluster models are combined to form a prediction model, represented in Figure 6.7 as PM_k, with the subscript indicating that there are k cluster models in it.

Stage 2 (refer to Figure 6.8)

- k is used as a free parameter to repeat the process described in stage 1, so that multiple prediction models (PMs) are generated for each iteration. A brief overview of how to use k as a free parameter is given next.
- Each of these prediction models will make a prediction on the test set. These predictions can then be grouped together by a naïve ensemble in order to obtain the final prediction.

Using k in k-Means as a Free Parameter

Multiple prediction models can be obtained by using k, the number of clusters, as a free parameter. This means k can be made to change over a scale or range of values, namely 1 to k, so that for each iteration a prediction model is obtained. As depicted in Figure 6.8, if there are seven clusters created by running k-means on a data set, there would be seven prediction models. They will be PM1 (predictor trained on the entire data set), PM2 (predictor trained on two clusters), and PM3 (predictor trained on three clusters) up to PM7 (predictor trained on all the seven clusters).

The k prediction models, in this case PM1 to PM7, are then engaged to make a set of k distinct predictions on the test data set. The prediction model employs three steps in order to make the predictions from the test data set. They are

1. Take the test data set points and spot the cluster to which they fit in.
2. Correlate the identified cluster with the cluster model associated with it. A point to note here is that the cluster models in different prediction models are different, as the prediction algorithm used is different, as shown in Figure 6.8.
3. Utilize this cluster model selected in order to formulate the prediction for that data point. Again, it should be noted that a predictive model (PM_i) generated during some iteration of choosing k as a free parameter may or may not yield a higher level of accuracy compared to PM_1 generated for the entire data set.

Reason for Two Stages to Make the Final Prediction

The work described here by Trivedi et al. (2011) did not stop at stage 1, but used two stages to make the final prediction after cluster analysis. The novelty of stage 2 is the use of a supervised method called "ensemble learning," in this case a naïve Bayes ensemble, on similar lines as proposed by Nikolić, Knežević, Ivančević, and Luković (2014). As indicated in Dietterich (2000), ensemble learning is a supervised learning method to collate predictions so that the generalization error of the final collated predictor is smaller when compared with that of each of the individual predictors. The inherent reason for the lesser error is that it injects diversity in each predictor. In the model represented in Figure 6.8, the diversity is caused by different predictive algorithms for creating the cluster models.

Inference

The results obtained by Trivedi et al. (2011) gave an affirmative answer to both the preceding questions put forth at the start of the section explaining the use of clustering for Big Data predictive analytics. It was observed that the prediction accuracy improved substantially and provided results better than a random forests predictor. It is, therefore, inferred that it is worth formalizing clustering as a surefire way of improving the predictive accuracy, as clustering exploits the structure in the multidimensional data and compresses it.

Measuring Accuracy of Predictive Models

In the previous sections, we explained the predictive modeling process for Big Data and the different types of predictive models that can be used to suit business needs. These predictive models can help businesses advance a great deal in terms of better decisions, cost reduction, customer segmentation, and so much more. However, developing a predictive model is a challenging task. Bad data sets, misunderstood relationships between data, and so on can lead to bad business decisions. It is worthless to have a model that does not provide value to the organization using it.

In such a scenario, it is imperative that the effectiveness of the predictive model be measured before it can be put into actual use. Tests that determine the accuracy of the predictive model need to be run on it. In the following sections, we go through four such tests: target shuffling, lift charts, bootstrap sampling (Garment 2014) and ROC curves to evaluate a predictive model. Although in the following sections we apply these four techniques to very small data sets for demonstration purposes, they can be easily extended to evaluate models created using Big Data.

Target Shuffling

We consider a sample scenario where a study shows that customers who are taller are more likely to buy products from online shopping portals. However, intuitively, we realize that there is no real relation between the two factors. Such relationships between variables are called spurious relationships, where the relation is merely a coincidence. If the company assumes this relationship to be true and creates a model to target customers who are taller to increase sales, the results obtained might be low. This can lead to unnecessary wastage of time, effort, and resources without giving significant results.

In predictive modeling, when many variables are used to determine the output of a model, there is a high probability of relationships between certain groups of variables being a spurious one. Target shuffling (Elder 2014) is a technique that can be used to fix this issue. It evaluates a predictive model by determining whether the input and output variables are actually related to each other or the relationship is merely coincidental.

In target shuffling, the values of the output variable are randomly shuffled with respect to the input variables to remove any possible relations. The model is then applied to this set of shuffled values and the most apparent relationships are noted. This process is repeated multiple times, randomly shuffling the output variable each time. A graph is plotted for the most apparent relationships. If the distribution value for the original result is high, then there is an actual relationship between the variables. Otherwise, the relationship is just a coincidence.

Let's take an example to simplify the understanding of the process of target shuffling. We collect personal details such as name, height, and age of customers who visit an e-shopping website. We will determine whether the height of the customer and the points given to him based on factors like past transactions and clicking patterns are actually related to each other.

Now we randomly shuffle the data so that the relationship between the heights and the points obtained is broken. After comparing the data, some new relationships might come up, for example, younger people are more likely to buy products online. These new relationships can also be true or false positives.

Let us say that out of 100 simulations or random shuffling, our original relationship (that taller customers are more likely to buy online products) performed better than the other results in just 20 of the cases. This means that the confidence level obtained is just 20%, which is not high enough to consider the relationship as true.

Target shuffling makes sense to a decision maker. Rather than giving complex equations and statistics, it gives an estimate of how likely or unlikely it is that the results obtained are by chance in a way that common people can understand. Target shuffling is also very easy to use, as it only requires randomly shuffling the data and running the predictive model on the new data.

Lift Charts

Lift charts are popular metrics in predictive modeling. They are used to calculate the performance of a predictive model by plotting the results obtained with and without the application of the predictive model. The results obtained by the predictive model are compared against random results.

Let's say an e-retail company wants to recommend products to customers. Each recommendation has a certain cost associated with it in terms of the time and resources used (Vuk and Curk 2006). Hence, the company needs to maximize the number of products sold, while minimizing the number of recommendations made.

Without a predictive model, we assume that out of 1,000 recommendations made to 1,000 customers, 100 are accepted and hence those many products sold. This means that by targeting 1,000 customers, the company sells 100 products. This implies a success ratio of 10%. Therefore, at each step, 10% of the recommended products are sold.

The company would like to develop a predictive model that can give the same success ratio by making fewer recommendations. Assuming the company has such a model, we must evaluate how much better the model is compared to having no model.

Table 6.1 gives us data about the number of recommendations made and the corresponding products sold. Using these values, we calculate the percentage of recommendations, the percentage of success, and the lift.

From Table 6.1, we observe that the best results are obtained by targeting the first set of 100 customers out of which 38 are likely to buy a product. Hence, recommendations can be made only to the first few groups of customers. This example is on a small scale; however, the same metric can be used in evaluating models that target a larger number of customers.

TABLE 6.1

Data Set for Number of Products Sold

Recommendations Made	Products Sold	% Recommendations	% Success	Lift
100	38	10	38	3.8
200	63	20	63	3.15
300	78	30	78	2.6
400	86	40	86	2.15
500	91	50	91	1.82
600	95	60	95	1.58
700	98	70	98	1.4
800	98	80	98	1.225
900	99	90	99	1.1
1000	100	100	100	1

A graph (Figure 6.9) of the percentage of products sold versus the percentage of recommendations made is plotted for both cases: without and with using a predictive model.

For each entry in Table 6.1, the ratio between the percentage of success by using a model and the percentage of success without a model is calculated. These values are called the lifts. For example, the first group has a lift of 3.8, which means that for this set of customers, the results obtained with the predictive model are 3.8 times better than the results obtained without any model. The lift values are plotted on a graph to obtain the lift chart in Figure 6.10.

From the lift chart, we know how much better the model will perform at each step compared to having no model. Hence, the company can target customers who are likely to give the best results. The company can also determine how effective their model is from the lift values.

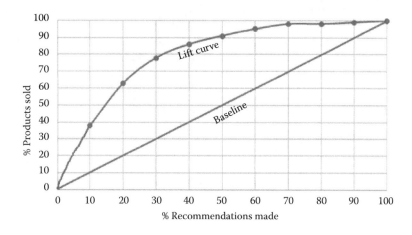

FIGURE 6.9

The baseline represents the positive responses without any model. The lift curve represents the positive responses with a predictive model.

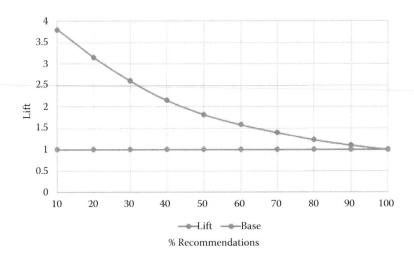

FIGURE 6.10
Lift chart.

ROC Curves

A receiver operating characteristic (ROC) curve (Fawcett 2006) is a common method to graphically represent the performance of classification models. It is a plot of the true positive rate against the false positive rate for different cutoff values that determine which output class the test case belongs to. The area under an ROC curve (AUC) (Bradley 1996) measures the accuracy of the test model. The greater the area, the higher the possibility of making a true positive classification. An area of 1 signifies a perfect model, whereas an area of 0.5 signifies a worthless model.

ROC curves can be very useful in effective planning, as they give information about how many correct classifications are made by the predictive model. If the accuracy is low, then the predictive model used to obtain results should be changed.

Let us consider the example of predicting whether a visitor on an e-commerce website will buy a product (Sismeiro and Bucklin 2004). A false positive occurs when it is predicted that the visitor will buy the product, but he actually does not. A false negative occurs when the prediction states that the visitor will not buy a product, but he actually does (Table 6.2). True positive and true negative can similarly be defined on the example set.

Taking a sample set of values, we will plot an ROC curve for evaluating the correctness of a predictive model that determines whether a visitor will get converted to a customer.

TABLE 6.2

Outcomes of a Test

Test	Present	n	Absent	n	Total
Positive	True Positive (TP)	a	False Positive (FP)	c	a + c
Negative	False Negative (FN)	b	True Negative (TN)	d	b + d
Total		a + b		c + d	
True positive rate = a/(a + b)					
False positive rate = c/(c + d)					

Source: MedCalc," ROC curve analysis," https://www.medcalc.org/manual/roc-curves.php.

Each visitor is given points based on his past purchase history, time spent viewing the product, and so on. Based on a threshold value, he is classified as a customer or not a customer.

Table 6.3 shows the points out of 100 received by a visitor, and whether he bought a product or not for 15 visitors.

Table 6.4 calculates the true positive rate and the false positive rate for different threshold values.

True positive if points ≥ Threshold and converted = Yes

True negative if points < Threshold and converted = No

False positive if points ≥ Threshold and converted = No

False negative if points < Threshold and converted = Yes

TABLE 6.3

Sample Data Set for Drawing a ROC Curve

Points	Converted to a Customer
12	No
23	No
45	No
50	No
61	No
76	No
85	No
56	Yes
67	Yes
72	Yes
78	Yes
86	Yes
89	Yes
91	Yes
95	Yes

TABLE 6.4

True Positive and False Positive Rates

Threshold	TP (a)	FN (b)	FP (c)	TN (d)	TPR	FPR
12	8	0	7	0	1	1
23	8	0	6	1	1	0.857
45	8	0	5	2	1	0.714
50	8	0	4	3	1	0.571
56	8	0	3	4	1	0.428
61	7	1	3	4	0.875	0.428
67	7	1	2	5	0.875	0.285
76	5	3	2	5	0.625	0.285
85	4	4	1	6	0.5	0.143
91	2	6	0	7	0.25	0
95	1	7	0	7	0.125	0

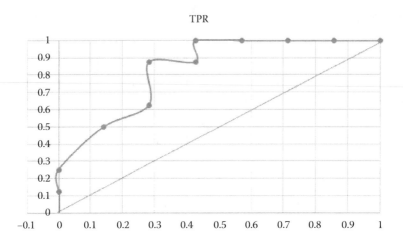

FIGURE 6.11
ROC curve for data in Table 1.4.

The ROC curve given in Figure 6.11 is a plot of the true positive rate against the false positive rate for the given data. The company can thus focus on visitors who are more likely to get converted to customers, making efficient use of resources.

A perfect predictive model would give an ROC curve that passes through the upper left corner, resulting in a 100% true positive rate and a 0% false positive rate. Using the area under an ROC curve, the people intending to use the model can test the accuracy of their model. If the area is less, it is better to discard the model and develop a new one because it will not give significant results.

Bootstrap Sampling

The concept of bootstrap was first invented by Bradley Efron (1979). Bootstrap sampling or bootstrapping refers to random sampling with replacement, that is, an element of the sample space can be picked more than once in creating a sample. This is especially useful when the size of the available data is not as large as required. The idea behind this technique is that by repeatedly picking samples from the same set of data, we can make estimates about the entire population of data.

Bootstrap sampling is different from cross-validation in the sense that in cross-validation, the data is divided into k subsets. k – 1 subsets are used for training the model, whereas one subset is used to test the model. This process is repeated k times, each time taking a different subset to test the model. As shown in Figure 6.12, in bootstrap sampling, we take random samples of data each time to train and test the model. The bootstrap data set is the same size as the original data set. It is also a more thorough procedure because many more subsamples can be created using this technique.

Bootstrap sampling is the preferred technique for internal validation. Fan and Wang (1996), through multiple simulations, found that the bootstrap technique is less biased and provides more consistent results than the various cross-validation techniques.

The data is divided into three subsets: training, testing, and validation. The model is built on the training data, and then tested on the testing data. If the model does not work well with this data, changes are made and the model is tested again. Continuous testing using the testing data can lead to overfitting. Hence, after testing, the model is evaluated on the validation data.

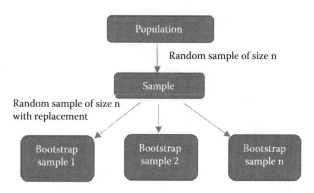

FIGURE 6.12
Sampling of data in bootstrap technique.

Consider the problem of determining whether a visitor will revisit an e-retail website within the next few days of the previous visit. If we have two models that do this, bootstrap sampling can help in finding out which model will win. We get an insight into how much better the model that wins is when used on real data. It also tells us how the accuracy of the model is bounded.

Tools and Techniques Used for Predictive Modeling and Analytics

Predictive analytics is a sought-after field in the market today. It is being applied everywhere to use past data to make accurate decisions about the future. Thus, many open-source and proprietary tools have been developed for predictive analytics and modeling. Tools like R, Weka, RapidMiner, Octave, and IBM SPSS are frequently used by data analysts. However, with each of these tools, it is a challenge to develop models when there is a large amount of data due to the excessive memory and computation speed required.

Data Mining Using CRISP-DM Technique

CRISP-DM, the Cross Industry Standard Process for Data Mining, is a structured approach for planning a data mining project. It is a compilation of the most common data mining approaches that experts use. It consists of the following six major phases, as mentioned by Shearer (2000). We will approach each phase with respect to an e-commerce company and the models employed by it to improve its business.

1. Business understanding—This phase focuses on setting the objectives and requirements of the data mining project. An e-retailer might want to attract more customers, increase the profit achieved by selling online products, or retain current customers by predicting when they might move to a competitor. The company should clearly set the goals they want to achieve and create a business model for it.

2. Data understanding—This phase includes collecting relevant data and identifying patterns, problems etc. in the data. On an online shopping portal, data can be gathered about the visitor's clicking patterns, products viewed, past transaction history, etc. Using this data, relationships between the various variables are figured out.

3. Data preparation—This phase focuses on cleaning and preparing the final data set that will be used in the predictive model task. Unnecessary data that is not relevant to the aim of the project might be collected. Such data is removed from the data set. Advanced techniques are also developed to predict missing data.

4. Modeling—For each problem or project, multiple predictive modeling techniques can be implemented, for example, regression, support vector machines, neural networks, or decision trees. All plausible techniques are applied and results are compiled for each technique. For example, to predict the probability of a user's return to the e-commerce website in the near future, a logistic regression model could be used based on criteria such as the number of visits to the page and the last visit to the page.

5. Evaluation—In this phase, evaluation of the effectiveness of the predictive model is done using the techniques mentioned in the previous section as well as other available techniques. The model is also evaluated based on whether it satisfies the business goals set up in the first phase and the degree to which they are satisfied. The model that performs the best is usually chosen for implementation.

6. Deployment—This phase includes implementation of the predictive model, producing final reports, and project reviews. Monitoring and maintenance of the model are important issues if the model is integrated in the day-to-day business of the company.

CRISP-DM Tool

The CRISP-DM tool is an extension of the standard IBM SPSS Modeler. It allows the user to develop a predictive model by following the aforementioned phases of data mining.

Predictive Analytics Using R Open-Source Tool

R is a programming language widely used by statisticians and data analysts. It contains a large number of built-in libraries and packages that make data analytics and production of good quality graphics very easy.

The amount of data available is increasing day by day. Conducting predictive analytics and modeling on Big Data can be a cumbersome process. Running a predictive model involves complex mathematical computation. The data needed to train the model also needs to be stored in memory. When the amount of data becomes larger, the computational speed and the amount of storage required also increase.

Therefore, while developing any predictive model, we face two challenges (Gondaliya 2014):

- Optimizing predictive model computation for Big Data with limited computation resources
- Processing a large amount of data with limited memory

To solve these two problems, a combination of R and MySQL can be used. The data set is divided into chunks and the model is fitted to each chunk of data. The entire data can be stored in a SQL database, which can then be queried to obtain a limited set of data in each iteration. This is repeated until all the data in the database is processed by the predictive model. Changes also need to be made to the predictive modeling algorithm (implemented in R) because only a part of the data is used each time, rather than the entire data set.

Using R, we will implement the algorithm of gradient descent with linear regression. Gradient descent is an iterative optimization algorithm to find the local minimum of a function.

In linear regression, we need to minimize the error function to obtain the best fit for the data.

The linear regression fit can be given by $h_\theta(x) = \theta_0 + \theta_1 x$ and the error function takes the values (θ_0, θ_1) to return the least squares error value based on how well the line fits the data.

Error function is given by

$$J(\theta_0, \theta_1) = \frac{1}{2m} \sum_{i=1}^{m} (h_\theta(x^{(i)}) - y^{(i)})^2$$

Gradient descent is used to minimize this error function by predicting values of θ_0 and θ_1 that will give the least error. The algorithm for gradient descent is as follows:

while not converged :

for all j :

$$tmp_j := \theta_j - \alpha \frac{\partial}{\partial \theta_j} J(\theta_0, \theta_1)$$

$$[\theta_0 \ \theta_1] := [tmp_0 \ tmp_1]$$

The data set taken for this example (Table 6.5) has random data in which y is a function of x. x and y can be replaced by anything, for example, the area of a house and its cost, or age of a person and probability of health issues.

The code snippet shown in Figure 6.13 returns the following value of theta:

```
[,1]
[1,]  3.0073306
[2,]  0.9712704
```

This implies that the gradient descent algorithm arrived at a local minimum for the example data set when the values of θ_0 and θ_1 are 3.0073306 and 0.9712704, respectively.

The first plot (Figure 6.14) shows the regression line that is obtained using lm(), a built-in R function to fit a line to the data. The second plot (Figure 6.15) shows the regression line obtained using the gradient descent algorithm. We notice that the slope and the intercept of both the fitted lines are almost the same.

Figure 6.16 shows how the cost function decreases with an increase in the number of iterations and then becomes constant after certain number of iterations.

TABLE 6.5

Few Rows of Sample Data Set for Gradient Descent

x	y
−4	−2
0.8	2.4
2	3

```
25  # error/cost function
26 ▾ cost <- function(x1, y, theta) {
27    sum( (x1 %*% theta - y)^2 ) / (2*length(y))
28  }
29
30  # learning rate
31  alpha <- 0.01
32
33  # number of iterations
34  num_iterations <- 1000
35
36  costValues <- double(num_iterations)
37
38  # intercept and slope initialized to 0
39  theta <- matrix(c(0,0), nrow=2)
40
41  X <- cbind(1, matrix(x))
42
43  # gradient descent
44 ▾ for (i in 1:num_iterations) {
45    error <- (X %*% theta - y)
46    delta <- t(X) %*% error / length(y)
47    theta <- theta - alpha * delta
48    costValues[i] <- cost(X, y, theta)
49    print(theta)
50  }
51
52  print(theta)
53
54  plot(x,y, col="Blue", main='Gradient Descent')
55  abline(a=theta[1], b=theta[2], col="red")
56
```

FIGURE 6.13
Snippet of gradient descent algorithm.

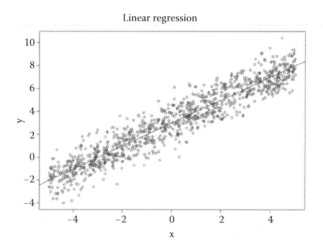

FIGURE 6.14
Regression line using lm().

In the example, we implemented the gradient descent algorithm on the data to calculate the most optimal values of the coefficients for a linear regression fit. This process can be applied to any data set that requires the calculation of parameters to minimize a function.

The data was not divided into chunks, as discussed in the beginning of the section, because of a small sample data set. However, when working with large data sets, it is a good method to train the model with chunks of the data and hence deal with low computation speed, using a simple tool like R.

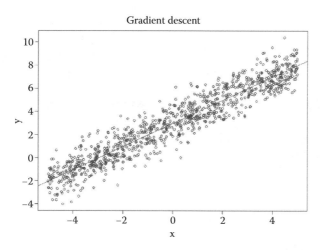

FIGURE 6.15
Regression line using gradient descent.

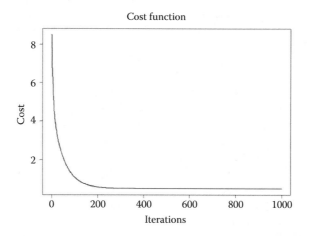

FIGURE 6.16
Effect on cost function with increase in iterations.

Research Trends and Conclusion

The idea of using Big Data for predictive analytics is fairly new and has gained momentum in the past few years. Most companies today have yet to start adopting processes that enable predictive analytics from business data in effective ways. It is generally seen that companies are either in the early stages of adoption or have started investing a fair amount of resources in this direction but have yet to achieve 100% efficiency in terms of relying on predictive analytics. Few companies can confidently admit to being power users of predictive analytics on Big Data. This trend is primarily due to some of the following factors:

- Specialist requirement—The number of available experts in the field is not enough to meet the demand as of now, and predictive modeling on Big Data is a fairly involved and complex task that most engineers in existing companies are not trained to handle. Data cleaning, preprocessing, and feature engineering are inherently tasks that require a specialist and cannot be directly automated.

- Resource requirement—Handling Big Data and predictive analytics from a resource perspective is demanding, in terms of both skilled workforce as well as capable hardware. Investments in dedicated hardware or in cloud-based solutions are still expensive and need to be examined carefully to make maximum utilization of resources.

- Financial requirement—Many small- or medium-sized enterprises may simply not have enough funds to invest in dedicated data analytics teams and provide them with adequate resources to get tangible results.

Thus the adoption of Big Data Analytics is still in its early stages in most companies, especially in the case of companies in emerging markets. As a result, the research scope is still fairly vast in this field. Although a lot of research has been done in the domain of mathematics for the development of mathematical models, similar research work in implementing these models in software is still in its growing stages. Advances in software are beginning to reduce the barrier for entry to newcomers in the field of Big Data and predictive analytics, via introduction of graphical interfaces for designing predictive workflows, like in IBM's SPSS Modeler. Hence there is a large scope for new researchers to pursue this field actively.

Lately a lot of companies are directing their attention to predictive analytics in cloud-based environments. This is the go-to solution for a majority of small- and medium-sized enterprises, as it allows them to reap the benefits of Big Data and predictive analytics while not having to worry about investments in infrastructure and maintenance, as they are handled by third-party cloud service providers. All the big players in the cloud computing space like Google, Amazon, Microsoft, and IBM offer a range of solutions targeting different levels of customers for predictive analytics and Big Data. These services come with a pay-per-use model that allows clients to pay for only the resources they use, thus allowing companies to easily incorporate Big Data analytics as part of their business practices and thus make better decisions.

To conclude, the models and techniques presented in this chapter are only demonstrative of the available options for data scientists to consider and are by no means exhaustive. The domain of predictive modeling is very large and warrants entire books to its discussion. However, within the purview of this chapter, it is hoped that the reader is able to get a fair overview of the entire process from a high-level perspective and some internal details regarding different types of predictive models and available validation techniques. This chapter was intended to serve as an introduction to predictive modeling with Big Data, hopefully empowering users to consider this approach to augment their business process and hence enable effective planning.

References

Ahmad F, Ismail NH, Aziz AA. 2015. The prediction of students' academic performance using classification data mining techniques. *Applied Mathematical Sciences* 9:6415–6426. doi:10.12988/ams.2015.53289.

Apache Software Foundation. n.d. What is Apache Mahout? Retrieved December 3, 2016, from http://mahout.apache.org/.

Boinee P, Angelis AD, Foresti GL. 2006. Insights into machine learning: Data clustering and classification algorithms for astrophysical experiments. Retrieved November 25, 2016, from http://inspirehep.net/record/923694/files/cer-002642933.pdf.

Bradley AP. 1996. The use of the area under the ROC curve in the evaluation of machine learning algorithms. The University of Queensland.

Cortes C, Vapnik, V. 1995. Support vector networks. *Machine Learning* 20(3):273.

Dietterich TG. 2000. Ensemble methods in machine learning, pp. 1–15. *First International Workshop on Multiple Classifier Systems*, J Kittler, F Roli (eds.). New York: Springer Verlag.

Elder J. 2014. Evaluate the validity of your discovery with target shuffling. Elder Research.

Extended interview: Tesla Motors Chairman Elon Musk. 2008. *PBS NewsHour*. Retrieved January 26, 2017, from http://www.pbs.org/newshour/bb/science-jan-june08-musk_06-25/.

Fan X, Wang L. 1996. Comparability of jackknife and bootstrap results: An investigation for a case of canonical correlation analysis. *The Journal of Experimental Education* 64(2):173–189.

Fawcett T. 2006. An introduction to ROC analysis. *Pattern Recognition Letters* 27:861–874.

Garment V. 2014. 3 ways to test the accuracy of your predictive models. Retrieved January 16, 2016, from http://www.plottingsuccess.com/3-predictive-model-accuracy-tests-0114/.

Genuer R, Poggi JM, Tuleau-Malot C, Villa-Vialaneix N. 2015. Random forests for Big Data. arXiv preprint arXiv:1511.08327.

Gillick D, Faria A, DeNero J. 2006, December 18. MapReduce: Distributed computing for machine learning. Technical report, Berkeley.

Gondaliya A. 2014. Build predictive model on Big Data: Using R and MySQL. Retrieved January 4, 2017, from http://pingax.com/build-predictive-model-on-big-data-using-r-and-mysql-part-1/.

Greene CS, Tan J, Ung M, Moore JH, Cheng C. 2014. Big Data bioinformatics. *Journal of Cellular Physiology* 229(12):1896–1900. doi:10.1002/jcp.24662.

James G, Witten D, Hastie T, Tibshiranie R. 2013. *An Introduction to Statistical Learning*. New York: Springer.

Janecek A, Gansterer W. 2009. Efficient feature reduction and classification methods: Applications in drug discovery and email categorization. Retrieved November 25, 2016, from https://homepage.univie.ac.at/andreas.janecek/stuff/dissertation-andreasjanecek.pdf.

Kass GV. 1980. An exploratory technique for investigating large quantities of categorical data. *Applied Statistics* 29(2):119. doi:10.2307/2986296.

Kiran M, Kumar A, Mukherjee S, Ravi Prakash G. 2013. Verification and validation of MapReduce program model for parallel support vector machine algorithm on Hadoop cluster. *International Journal of Computer Science Issues* 10(1):317–325.

Kleiner A, Talwalkar A, Sarkar P, Jordan M. 2014. A scalable bootstrap for massive data. *Journal of the Royal Statistical Society: Series B (Statistical Methodology)* 76(4):795–816.

Kraska T, Talwalkar A, Duchi J, Grith R, Franklin MJ, Jordan M. 2013. MLBase: A distributed machine-learning system. 6th Biennial Conference on Innovative Data Systems Research, January 6–9, Asilomar, California.

Ng A. 2000. CS229 lecture notes, pp. 1–3.

Nikolić S, Knežević M, Ivančević V, Luković I. 2014. Building an ensemble from a single naive Bayes classifier in the analysis of key risk factors for Polish State Fire Service, pp. 361–367. *2014 Federated Conference on Computer Science and Information Systems, Warsaw*. Retrieved January 2, 2017, from http://ieeexplore.ieee.org/abstract/document/6933038/.

Panda B, Herbach JS, Basu S, Bayardo RJ. 2009. Planet. *Proceedings of the VLDB Endowment* 2(2):1426–1437. doi:10.14778/1687553.1687569.

Safavian S, Landgrebe D. 1991. A survey of decision tree classifier methodology [Abstract]. *IEEE Transactions on Systems, Man, and Cybernetics* 21(3):660–674. doi:10.1109/21.97458.

Salzberg SL. 1994. Book review: *C4.5: Programs for Machine Learning* by J. Ross Quinlan. Morgan Kaufmann Publishers, Inc., 1993. *Machine Learning* 16(3):235–240. doi:10.1007/bf00993309.

Shearer C. 2000. The CRISP_DM model: The new blueprint for data mining. *Journal of Data Warehousing* 5(4):13–22.

Sismeiro C, Bucklin RE. 2004. Modeling purchase behavior at an e-commerce website: A task completion approach. *Journal of Marketing Research* 41(3):306–323.

Steyerber EW, Eijkemans MJC, Habbema JDF. 2001a. Application of shrinkage techniques in logistic regression analysis: A case study. *Statistica Neerlandica* 55(1):76–88.

Steyerberg EW, Harrell FE, Borsboom GJ, Eijkemans MJC, Vergouwe Y, Habbema JDF. 2001b. Internal validation of predictive models: Efficiency of some procedures for logistic regression analysis. *Journal of Clinical Epidemiology* 54(8):774–781.

The Cancer Genome Atlas (TCGA). 2012. Comprehensive molecular portraits of human breast tumors. *Nature* 490:61–70. Retrieved November 21, 2016, from http://cancergenome.nih.gov/.

The ENCODE Project Consortium. 2012. An integrated encyclopedia of DNA elements in the human genome. *Nature* 489:57–74. Retrieved November 16, 2016, from http://www.nature.com/nature/journal/v489/n7414/full/nature11247.html.

Timofeev R. 2004. Classification and regression trees (CART) theory and applications. Doctoral dissertation, Humboldt University, Berlin.

Trivedi S, Pardos ZA, Heffernan NT. 2011, September 5. The utility of clustering in prediction tasks. Retrieved December 11, 2016, from https://arxiv.org/ftp/arxiv/papers/1509/1509.06163.pdf.

Vuk M, Curk T. 2006. ROC curve, lift chart and calibration plot. *Metodoloski Zvezki* 3(1):89–108.

Ye J, Chow J-H, Chen J, Zheng Z. 2009. Stochastic gradient boosted distributed decision trees, pp. 2061–2064. *Proceedings of the 18th ACM Conference on Information and Knowledge Management, CIKM '09.* New York: ACM.

7

Deep Learning for Engineering Big Data Analytics

Kin Gwn Lore, Daniel Stoecklein, Michael Davies,
Baskar Ganapathysubramanian, and Soumik Sarkar

CONTENTS

Introduction

Most problems in engineering can be recast in the framework of inverse/design problems. The goal of inverse/design problems is to identify conditions, including the initial conditions, boundary conditions, or property and coefficient distribution conditions, that result in a desired behavior of the engineered system. Examples of these are everywhere in the engineering world. With the current focus on sustainable manufacturing, a good example is in the identification of tailored processing conditions that result in electronic devices with high-performance metrics. In most electronics manufacturing, it has been shown that various processing conditions can critically impact device properties, and the identification of optimal processing conditions is a key problem from financial and sustainability standpoints [1–5]. Another example is in identification of useful designs for biomedical diagnostic platforms [6,7]. In this chapter, we discuss how much rapid design iterations that result in a desired flow transformation (one that provides mixing for a rapid reaction, flow separation for disease diagnostics, etc.) are required. In both of these cases, considerable effort has been expended to construct excellent "forward" models of the engineering problem, i.e., models that map the set of input conditions, boundary conditions, and property distributions to the output quantity of interest ($\mathcal{F} : input \rightarrow property$). The design problem, however, calls for the reverse mapping ($\mathcal{G} = \mathcal{F}^{-1} : property \rightarrow input$) for a desired value of the output for a set of inputs.

Traditionally, the inverse/design problem has been solved by reformulating it as an optimization problem. That is, the forward model, $\mathcal{F}$, is solved multiple times within an optimization frameworks to identify those input conditions that minimize a cost function, with the minima representing the desired input values. Both gradient-based and meta-heuristic optimization methods can be used for solving these optimization problems. This approach, however, becomes more and more difficult to deploy as the complexity of the engineered systems increases and the design space becomes combinatorially large. Additionally, there is no robust or efficient way to assimilate the large amount of data that has been collected into the optimization framework.

It is in this context that Big Data analytics, especially deep learning approaches, provide a natural approach to construct fast surrogate models of the forward model and to learn the inverse mapping, as well as to extract insights via salient (hierarchical) feature extraction. The use of deep learning approaches for engineering design and optimization is a transformative approach that integrates the availability of forward models, with large data sets to create platforms that provide near-real-time design exploration of very complex engineering systems. In this chapter, we illustrate the application of deep learning for engineering design via a specific application involving the rapid design exploration of microfluidic platforms for biomedical lab-on-chip applications.

Overview of Deep Learning as a Hierarchical Feature Extractor

Deep learning is a set of machine learning algorithms that aim to learn multiple levels of abstraction from data in a hierarchical manner. In other words, the algorithms operate on high-dimensional data that arrive with a high volume, velocity, variety, veracity, and value, in order to generate low-dimensional, simpler representations that ease a decision-making process. Many domains, such as engineering, involve extensive collection and maintenance of large volumes of raw data for analysis and interpretation. As a data-driven approach, deep learning therefore has become an increasingly attractive option to enable automatic feature extraction without tedious handcrafting of features.

Deep learning has extensively been used in image processing due to its ability to learn a hierarchy of visual concepts. For example, the concept of a person's face can be represented in terms of simpler concepts, such as corners that are further defined by edges. Therefore, deep learning is of great interest for computer vision scientists to solve various problems ranging from object recognition and detection [8–14] to image generation and quality enhancement [15–18]. Apart from computer vision applications, deep learning has had a game-changing impact on speech processing [19–22] as well as on natural language processing [23–27]. With the advent of GPU computing, deep learning methods are also increasingly adopted by the engineering community to handle problems in complex dynamical systems. In particular, it is gaining rapid popularity in robotics [28–32], prognostics and health monitoring [33–35], engineering design [36–38], cyber-agricultural systems [39,40], and medical diagnostic systems [41–43].

In the context of engineering applications of deep learning, the primary technical challenges involve formulating the problem as a machine learning problem along with incorporation of appropriate domain knowledge. While characterizing the entire training data space is often intractable in traditional machine learning problems, engineering data sets, on the other hand, however large and high-dimensional they may be, can be well parameterized. Therefore, generating representative training data also becomes a key aspect in this context. This chapter illustrates a systematic deep learning approach to a thermomicrofluidic device design problem as a case study in solving engineering problems by using deep learning.

Flow Physics for Inertial Flow Sculpting

Problem Definition

We begin the discussion on microfluidic device design by introducing a recently developed method of fluid flow manipulation called flow sculpting. Flow sculpting uses sequences of bluff-body structures (pillars) in a microchannel to passively sculpt inertially flowing fluid (where $1 < Re < 100$ [Re is the Reynolds number; $Re = UD_H/\nu$, with fluid velocity U, viscosity ν, and channel hydraulic diameter D_H]). Specifically, fluid flowing in the inertial regimen past a pillar shows broken fore–aft symmetry in the pillar-induced deformation, which laterally displaces the cross-sectional shape of the fluid in some way, depending on the channel and pillar geometry and the fluid flow conditions [44]. By arranging pillars in a sequence within a microchannel, the fluid will experience individual deformations from each pillar, resulting in an overall net deformation at the end of the sequence (Figure 7.1). With sufficient spacing between each pillar in a sequence, the deformation from one pillar will saturate before the flow reaches the next pillar. Therefore, the deformation caused by a single pillar can be viewed as an independent operation on the fluid flow shape, enabling a library of precomputed deformations to predict the sculpted flow shape for a given pillar sequence. Work by Stoecklein et al. [45] demonstrated this forward model with a user-guided manual design in a freely available utility, uFlow (www.biomicrofluidics.com/software.php), to create a wide variety of useful flow shapes.

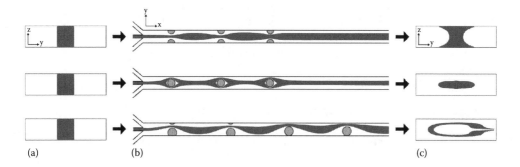

(a) (b) (c)

FIGURE 7.1
Illustration of inertial flow-sculpting devices for three pillar sequences. In each device, the same inlet flow pattern (a) (shown in a cross-sectional view) is passed through a different pillar sequence (b) (shown as a top-down view), which creates a distinct fluid flow shape at the device outlet (c).

Design Challenges and the State of the Art

Microfluidic device design via trial and error is tedious, and it requires user intuition with the design space. Choosing from many sizes and locations for individual pillars, in addition to their sequential arrangement in a microchannel, produces an enormous combinatorial space of fluid flow transformations. It has also been shown that the space is multimodal, with many micropillar sequences creating similar fluid flow shapes, making design optimization nontrivial. Thus, manual design of micropillar sequences is generally impractical for most of its intended users, including researchers developing applications in fields such as advanced manufacturing, biology, biosensing, health care, pharmaceuticals, and chemistry [46–48]. This drives the need for an automated solution to the inverse problem: designing a micropillar sequence that produces a desired fluid flow shape.

To date, two automated approaches have been described in the published literature: heuristic optimization via genetic algorithms (GAs) [49–50] and deep learning via trained convolutional neural networks (CNN) [51]. While the GA approach capably optimizes existing microfluidic devices and has explored novel flow shapes, there exist a few drawbacks to its use. GAs require well-crafted cost functions that are specific to the goals of the user. The GA approach also entails a stochastic method, with no guarantee of finding good optima when using a finite number of searches. For flow sculpting, this leads to an excessive run time (as much as 2 h), which makes swift design iterations difficult [50]. On the other hand, the application of deep learning, as described by Lore et al. [51] allows design with an extremely quick time-to-result of approximately 1 sec, but still lacks in accuracy, similarly to GA [51]. This disparity between speed and accuracy for deep learning approaches motivates the continued development for flow sculpting, in the hope that the gap can be closed.

Broad Implications

Since its formulation in 2013, flow sculpting by use of pillar sequences has been applied to problems in biological and advanced manufacturing fields. For example, polymer precursors can create shaped microfibers and particles [52–55], and a pillar sequence can shift fluid streams away from cells in a flow [56]. Although novel in their application, these use cases utilize simple micropillar sequence designs (e.g., forming an encapsulating stream, or shifting fluid to one side of a microchannel). More complex fluid flow shapes could lead to powerful new technologies in the aforementioned fields, for example, fabricated microparticles could be designed for optimal packing efficiency or to focus with a directed orientation to specific locations within a microchannel for improved on-chip cytometry [57]. Porous hydrogel could be designed to reduce wound healing time [58] or to study cell growth and chemotaxis [59]. These are perhaps more obvious applications of flow sculpting, but as more disciplines and industries are exposed to the technique, new possibilities are expected to abound.

Micropillar Sequence Design Using Deep Learning

Deep CNNs for Pillar Sequence Design

One way for sequence prediction with a given flow shape that is generated from an n_p pillar sequence is to perform a simultaneous multiclass classification (SMC) using a deep

CNN [51]. The CNN, depicted in Figure 7.1, extracts geometrical features from the flow shapes and simultaneously predicts the class for each of the n_p pillars to form a sequence of indices from which the positions and diameters for each pillar are retrieved. Essentially, instead of solving a single classification problem, as has been typically done with CNNs, the proposed CNN is designed to solve a multiclass, multilabel problem involving n_p pillars (i.e., n labels) and n_c classes for each pillar. Note that it is also possible to approach the problem as a regression problem, where the regressed values are the positions and diameters of each individual pillars. However, discretion of the design space reduces the design space into a finite set (albeit large) and is sufficient to aid designers in obtaining a viable design.

The number of possible pillar configurations (hence the size of the search space) increases exponentially with the number of pillars. With a constant training set size with increasing sequence length, the ratio of training samples versus the number of all possible pillar sequences shrinks very quickly. Figure 7.2b shows the capability of the deep learning framework under the curse-of-dimensionality challenge. While the coverage of the design space reduces exponentially, the pixel match rate, a similarity measure between the reconstructed flow shape and the target flow shape, only degrades linearly. Figure 7.3a shows the best flow shape reconstructed for pillar sequences with lengths of 5 to 10, given a target image.

The pure CNN framework is not without drawbacks. Simpler shapes typically achieve high similarity by favoring shorter sequences, as shown in Figure 7.2b. However, if it were forced to predict a long sequence for a simple shape, or conversely, forced to predict a short sequence for a complex flow shape, the performance of the framework would be severely degraded. The output sequence length is constrained because a new model needs to be trained specifically to generate a sequence with a different length. Furthermore, the sequence which deforms the flow into a target flow shape is predicted in a joint manner and does not provide sufficient insight on the interplay between pillars causing the

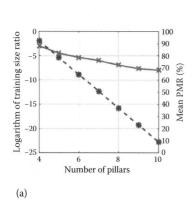

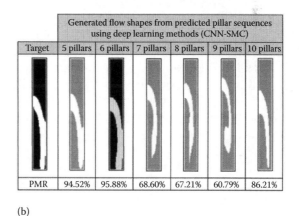

Generated flow shapes from predicted pillar sequences using deep learning methods (CNN-SMC)						
Target	5 pillars	6 pillars	7 pillars	8 pillars	9 pillars	10 pillars
PMR	94.52%	95.88%	68.60%	67.21%	60.79%	86.21%

(a)   (b)

FIGURE 7.2

(a) Variation of the average PMR and training size ratio (ratio of the number of training samples to the number of all possible pillar sequences on a logarithmic scale) with an increasing number of pillars in the sequence. PMR suffers only a gradual drop with increasing ratio, showing the generalizing capability of a deep learning framework. (b) Flow shapes reconstructed by CNN-SMC from the predicted fixed-length pillar sequences. Using the given example, one would consider using a 5-pillar sequence instead of the 6-pillar sequence to exchange accuracy for cost savings in manufacturing an additional pillar.

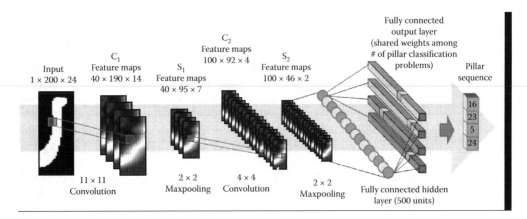

FIGURE 7.3
CNN with the SMC problem formulation. A classification problem is solved for each pillar in the sequence.

deformation. While it may produce satisfactory sequences which regenerate the desired shape, it is unclear how the successive pillars interact with one another. Therefore, we present an alternative sequential pillar prediction approach.

Action Sequence Learning for Flow Sculpting

It is important to learn the transformation function given the parameters (position and diameter) of the pillars. Using a deep learning architecture (proposed in reference 60), the intermediate shape between two images can be predicted and a sequence of causal actions contributing to desired shape transformation is learned. This architecture can be easily implemented in various engineering applications, such as:

- Learning to transform the belief space for robotic path planning. A robot may be chasing a mobile target while maintaining a posterior (that is transformed into a visual representation analogous to the flow shape) corresponding to the location of the target. If we would like to specifically maximize posteriorly in a certain region, the corresponding problem would be, "What is the best course of action to take by the robot in succession?"

- Learning the material processing pathways to obtain the desired microstructures. In materials processing, processing the materials, by altering the properties in succession, will alter the morphology (microstructures) of the material. The equivalent inverse problem would be, "If we want the material to achieve a specific morphology, what are the processing steps that should be taken?"

- Learning a sequence of manufacturing steps in additive manufacturing, with fast design being the main advantage.

To predict the sequence of pillars that results in the desired flow shape, we introduce the notion of transformation learning. Figure 7.4 shows the learning approach via supply of juxtaposed flow shapes, one before deformation and one after, into a CNN-based APN that extracts relevant features and predicts the class of the pillar causing the deformation. However, this formulation only works well for simpler target shapes. For more complex

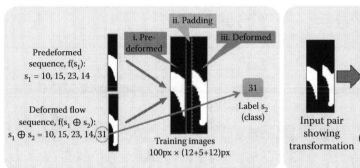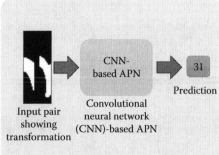

(a) Training data generation for the CNN-based APN

(b) Predicting a pillar given two flow shapes

FIGURE 7.4
The APN addresses the question, "Given a pair of pre- and postdeformed shapes, what is the identity of the pillar causing the deformation?" (a) Supervised learning scheme. $\oplus$ marks the concatenation operator. (b) Prediction of a pillar index given two flow shapes as input.

flow shapes characterized by many sharp angles, jagged edges, islands, swirls, or curls, the transformation path may be highly nonlinear; the current shape may never converge to the final desired shape. Furthermore, the training data cover a vanishingly small fraction of the design space, with coverage shrinking exponentially as the sequence length increases (i.e., an n_p sequence will result in $n_c^{n_p}$ different combinations), so it is necessary to learn the transformations in a meaningful way. To help alleviate this issue, we introduce Intermediate transformation networks (ITNs).

The ITN in Figure 7.5 attempts to construct a flow shape that bridges between two flow shapes in the nonlinear transformation path. We used a deep autoencoder to extract hierarchical features from the desired final shape as a pretraining procedure, then fine-tuned the model to approximate the bridging shape, or waypoint. The ITN evaluates the perimetric complexity C [61] of the target flow shape and generates a number of waypoints, depending on the computed complexity. Hence, we can have a smoother transformation pathway by setting these waypoints as temporary targets for pillar predictions. By combining both APN and ITN, we form a framework (Figure 7.6).

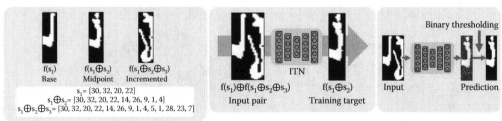

(a) Training data generation for the ITN

(b) Training scheme for the ITN

(c) Prediction of intermediate shape

FIGURE 7.5
The ITN addresses the question, "Given two flow shapes, what is the possible shape that lies in the middle of the nonlinear deformation pathway?" (a) The undeformed, bridging, and deformed shape, respectively. (b) The shapes are appropriately used for supervised learning of the ITN. (c) Prediction of the intermediate bridging shape, given two flow shapes.

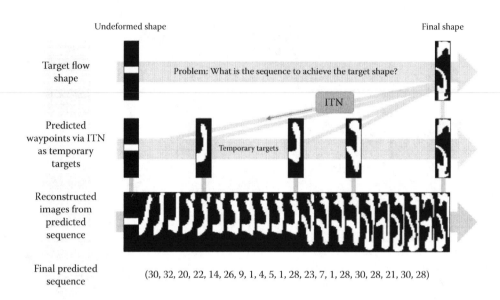

FIGURE 7.6
A higher-level overview of the framework, illustrated with a complex flow shape. The sequence can be postprocessed to remove redundant pillars that do not considerably deform the flow shape.

In all experiments, the target flow shape is generated from a random sequence to evaluate the model. In Figure 7.7, it is clear that by using the bridging shape as a temporary target, the prediction performance greatly improves. A comparison is performed on all previously discussed methods in Figure 7.7. A clear advantage of using APN and ITN together is that the model does not need to be retrained for variable sequence lengths, unlike the CNN+SMC model, where the number of pillars in the output sequence is constrained. This method is highly scalable and has enormous room for extension into sculpting highly complex flow shapes.

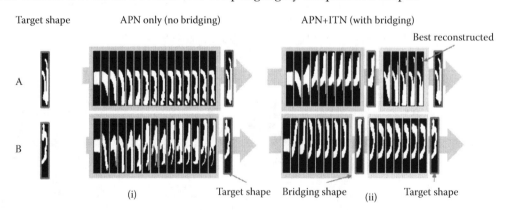

FIGURE 7.7
Two examples of sequence prediction on test shapes with C < 8.0 using (i) APN only, without bridging and (ii) APN+ITN with one waypoint. By predicting a bridging shape, the resulting predicted sequence is able to reconstruct flow shapes that are more similar to the target shape. Each frame shows the deformation on the flow shape with each additional predicted pillar added into the sequence.

Representative Training Data Generation

Appropriate selection of training data and an understanding of what constitutes "good" training remain open challenges in modern applications of machine learning [62]. However, unlike traditional problems in machine learning, e.g., image classification or speech and handwriting translation, where training data attempt to sample an unbounded and highly variable space, the domain of flow sculpting is finite (though extremely large). Furthermore, the space of sculpted flows presents a natural metric (i.e., binary images with sculpted flow and coflow) that enables efficient characterization of the data space. This offers a unique opportunity to explore how domain knowledge and the choice of sampling can influence high-level decision making in a deep learning model. Similar critical scientific optimization problems, such as robotic path planning, material processing, or design for manufacturing, can benefit from the insight on intelligent sampling gained here.

We speculate that an impediment to performance in deep learning techniques for design in flow sculpting is the many-to-one design space. (While our focus is clearly on the flow sculpting problem in this chapter, the issues raised would tend to appear in most inverse problems.) That is, there may be many solutions (pillar sequences) that produce a desired fluid flow shape. Consider the set of all possible pillar sequences s_i as the space S, and their corresponding fluid flow shapes o_i as the space O, with a forward model f that maps a specific realization $s \in$ S to $o \in$ O, i.e., f: S → O. A deep neural network attempts to construct an approximation to $g = f^{-1}$, with the inverse function g mapping g: O → S. During training, a deep neural network that has been shown a pillar sequence and fluid flow shape pair (s_1, o_1) may be trained on another flow shape, o_2, that is extremely similar to o_1 and thus occupies the same space in O. However, the pillar sequence s_2 that produces o_2 could be entirely different from s_1, and therefore very far apart in S. Hence, the many-to-one mapping, f: S → O, could make effective training quite difficult. We explore a sampling method for choosing training data, known as high-dimensional model representation (HDMR) [63].

Intuitively, an effective tool for design in fluid flow sculpting should have good coverage of the space O. However, knowledge of this space is difficult to come by, as the combinatorial possibilities are immense (for a pillar sequence size n_s, the number of possible combinations $n_c = A^{n_s}$, with A usually around 32). Additionally, the inlet fluid flow design, which dictates fluid flow shape as much as a pillar sequence, is entirely arbitrary, depending on the number of channels joining at the microchannel inlet and their respective flow rates. However, the current implementation of deep learning for the flow sculpting problem holds the inlet design constant and trains for pillar sequences of fixed length. Thus, while an ideal training set has completely uniform coverage of O, and despite the speed of the forward model, generating and making practical use of such a set for each length of pillar sequence and inlet configuration is computationally infeasible. And, as previously mentioned, the toolset in flow sculpting will likely grow to include curved channels, symmetry-breaking half-pillars and steps, and multifluid optimization [60]. Therefore, intelligent sampling on the space S is still a priority. Previous methods of sampling attempted uniform coverage of O via uniform sampling of S, through uniform-random and quasirandom Sobol sampling of n_s dimensional spaces in S for pillar sequences of length n_s [51].

Here, we apply a technique for multivariate representation, HDMR. In HDMR, a high-dimensional input variable $x = (x_1, x_2, \ldots, x_n)$ with a model output x is expressed as a finite hierarchical expansion:

$$h(x) = h_0 + \sum_i h_i(x_i) + \sum_{1 \le i < j \le n} h_{ij}(x_i, x_j)$$
$$+ \sum_{1 \le i < j < k \le n} h_{ijk}(x_i, x_j, x_k) + \cdots + \sum_{1 \le i_1 < \cdots < i_l \le n} h_{i_1 i_2 \ldots i_l}\left(x_{i_1}, x_{i_2}, \ldots, x_{i_l}\right)$$
$$+ h_{12 \ldots n}(x_1, x_2, \ldots, x_n)$$

Where the lth-order component functions $h_{i_1 i_2 \ldots i_l}(x_{i_1}, x_{i_2}, \ldots, x_{il})$ give outputs of h evaluated for contributions by l-order sampling of x. That is, h_0 is a scalar value as the mean response to $h(x)$, $h_i(x_i)$ represents each variable x_i independently (holding all other variables constant), and so on. $h_{12 \ldots n}(x_1, x_2, \ldots, x_n)$ contains residual contributions for permutations of all variables x_n. In many cases, a high-dimensional system can be well described using up to second-order terms [65]:

$$h(x) \approx h_0 + \sum_i h_i(x_i) + \sum_{1 \le i < j \le n} h_{ij}(x_i, x_j)$$

We use this expression to hierarchically sample S, choosing k points along each chosen dimension of x such that we limit the training set size to be comparable to the pseudorandom and quasirandom sampling used by Lore et al. [51], which is 150,000 $(s, o) \in (S,O)$. The pseudorandom, uniformly distributed sampling is accomplished via *mt19937ar* Mersenne twister in MATLAB [66], while the quasirandom sampling was accomplished via Sobol sequences [67], which seek to maximally separate the sampled points in a deterministic manner to prevent clustering or gaps. We neglect the mean response term in the HDMR expansion, as there is no effective mean pillar. Since the first- and second-order terms sample a limited number of points in each dimension (choosing 1 of 32 pillar configurations at each point), there is a choice as to what pillars will be chosen as constant for the rest of the sequence. We desire statistical metrics on the use of HDMR for a fixed k, so we randomly pick k points in the ith dimension.

For each pillar sequence that is predicted during testing, we use the forward model to create a corresponding flow shape o and then compare that to the target image o_t from the testing set (Figure 7.8). Thus, while the classification error during training is based on label

$C_1 = 8.2427$ $C_2 = 9.2144$ $C_3 = 8.0268$ $C_4 = 8.6141$

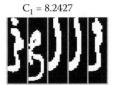  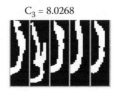 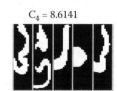

FIGURE 7.8
Four sample test shapes with reconstructed flow shapes generated from sequences predicted using different methods. From left to right, the first subcolumn is the desired flow shape (ground truth). The second subcolumn is the flow shape reconstructed from the predicted sequence using CNN+SMC; the third with APN, the fourth with a variant of APN (using depth-concatenated inputs) [56], and the fifth with APN+ITN. C denotes the perimetric complexity of the test shapes, which have values of >8.0.

error (that is, correct prediction of the pillar sequence), we judge model performance on whether the trained neural network effectively solves the inverse problem. The metric for performance is a per-pixel norm, the pixel match rate (PMR). (The PMR can vary from 0 (no pixels in common between prediction and target) to 1.0 (a perfect match), but a threshold for a successful result is up to the microfluidic practitioner. For example, if the goal is to simply displace bulk fluid without care for the overall shape, a PMR greater than 0.8 may be suitable. However, if the user requires fine details in the prediction to match the target, a PMR of 0.9 and above is an appropriate threshold.) More generally, a PMR of 0.85 is a good result, which is defined for a target image o_t and a predicted image $\hat{o}$ as:

$$\text{PMR} = 1 - \frac{\left\| o_t - \hat{o} \right\|_1}{o_t}$$

In testing, we observe an increased capacity for performance with HDMR sampling compared to random and quasirandom sampling of training data [9]. In considering the methods of sampling at equal training set size (Figure 7.9a), HDMR sampling improves the high-end of CNN-SMC performance with a more favorably skewed distribution of PMR values in testing. The use of HDMR sampling also allows for larger data sets to meaningfully contribute to more effective training, unlike random sampling, which shows worsening performance with larger data sets (Figure 7.10b). This trend is if special interest for engineering problems such as flow sculpting, where significant computational effort is embedded in a lightweight utility. For deep learning in particular, where the end user runtime is extremely low, an increase in training set size can improve accuracy without

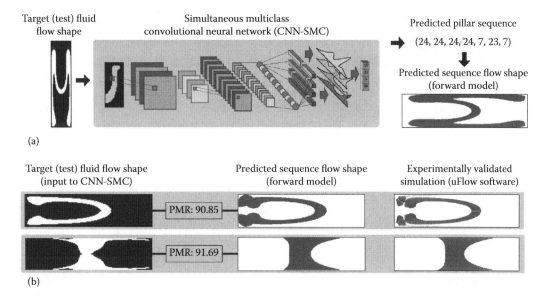

(a)

(b)

FIGURE 7.9
(a) Process of testing the trained CNN, whereby a target fluid flow shape is the input for the tool and a predicted pillar sequence is the output. The pillar sequence is then used with the forward model, which creates a corresponding fluid flow shape. This shape is compared to the target fluid flow shape by using the PMR. (b) Several examples of target flow shape, predicted sequence flow shape (with PMR), and a flow shape from the experimentally validated software uFlow, derived from the same predicted sequence flow shape.

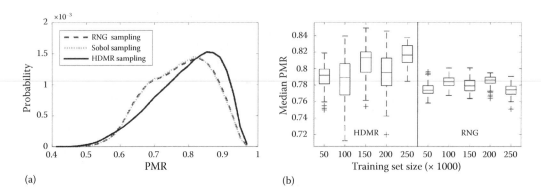

FIGURE 7.10
(a) Performance of HDMR, quasirandom (Sobol), and pseudorandom (RNG) sampling of 150,000 fluid flow shapes for training data. The median PMR value shifts by 2.5% from 0.79 (RNG/Sobol) to 0.81 (HDMR). (b) Training size study of HDMR vs. pseudorandom sampling of training data. Note that in both panels a and b, intelligent sampling raises the ceiling of performance and shifts the PMR distribution in a positive direction.

being detrimental to utility runtime. In this work, we have seen that intelligent sampling can motivate the use of larger training data to great effect.

Summary, Conclusions, and Research Directions

This chapter discussed a case study of solving an engineering design problem by using deep neural networks. In this age of Big Data, a large variety of engineering problems are generating large volumes of data that can be leveraged to significantly improve state-of-the-art designs, operation, and performance monitoring of such systems. In particular, we showed that microfluidic device design can be dramatically expedited via a deep convolutional neural network. To generate more complex flow shapes, a sequential approach was shown that enabled causal shape transformation. Such a method has a potentially high impact on the innovation of manufacturing processes, material sciences, biomedical applications, decision planning, and many other arenas. We also note that generating a properly representative training data set is critical for the data-driven learning of engineering systems. In this regard, it may be very expensive to generate data (especially labeled data) from real-life engineering systems. Other than appropriate sampling of the data space, incorporation of domain knowledge in problem formulation, model learning, inference, and interpretation of decisions remains one of the most difficult challenges in data-driven modeling of engineering systems.

References

1. Zhao K et al. 2016. Vertical phase separation in small molecule: Polymer blend organic thin film transistors can be dynamically controlled. *Advanced Functional Materials*.
2. Wodo O, Ganapathysubramanian B. 2012. Modeling morphology evolution during solvent-based fabrication of organic solar cells. *Computational Materials Science* 55:113–126.

3. Gu KL et al. 2017. Tuning domain size and crystallinity in isoindigo/PCBM organic solar cells via solution shearing. *Organic Electronics* 40:79–87.

4. Ganapathysubramanian B, Zabaras N. 2005. Control of solidification of non-conducting materials using tailored magnetic fields. *Journal of Crystal Growth* 276(1):299–316.

5. Ganapathysubramanian B, Zabaras N. 2004. Using magnetic field gradients to control the directional solidification of alloys and the growth of single crystals. *Journal of Crystal Growth* 270(1):255–272.

6. Stoecklein D et al. 2014. Micropillar sequence designs for fundamental inertial flow transformations. *Lab on a Chip* 14(21):4197–4204.

7. Stoecklein D et al. 2016. Optimization of micropillar sequences for fluid flow sculpting. *Physics of Fluids* 28(1):012003.

8. Krizhevsky A, Sutskever I, Hinton GE. 2012. ImageNet classification with deep convolutional neural networks. *Advances in Neural Information Processing Systems*.

9. He K et al. 2016. Deep residual learning for image recognition. *Proceedings of the IEEE Conference on Computer Vision and Pattern Recognition*.

10. Simonyan K, Zisserman A. 2014. Very deep convolutional networks for large-scale image recognition. arXiv:1409.1556.

11. Sermanet P et al. 2013. Overfeat: Integrated recognition, localization and detection using convolutional networks. arXiv:1312.6229.

12. Redmon J et al. 2016. You only look once: Unified, real-time object detection. *Proceedings of the IEEE Conference on Computer Vision and Pattern Recognition*.

13. Long J, Shelhamer E, Darrell T. 2015. Fully convolutional networks for semantic segmentation. *Proceedings of the IEEE Conference on Computer Vision and Pattern Recognition*.

14. Ren S et al. 2015. Faster r-cnn: Towards real-time object detection with region proposal networks. *Advances in Neural Information Processing Systems*.

15. Dong C et al. 2016. Image super-resolution using deep convolutional networks. *IEEE Transactions on Pattern Analysis and Machine Intelligence* 38(2):295–307.

16. Zhu J-Y et al. 2016. Generative visual manipulation on the natural image manifold. *European Conference on Computer Vision*. Berlin: Springer International Publishing.

17. Gregor K et al. 2015. DRAW: A recurrent neural network for image generation. arXiv:1502.04623.

18. Lore KG, Akintayo A, Sarkar S. 2017. Llnet: A deep autoencoder approach to natural low-light image enhancement. *Pattern Recognition* 61:650–662.

19. Deng L et al. 2013. Recent advances in deep learning for speech research at Microsoft. *2013 IEEE International Conference on Acoustics Speech and Signal Processing*. New York: IEEE.

20. Yu D, Deng L. 2014. *Automatic speech recognition: A deep learning approach*. New York: Springer.

21. Hinton G et al. 2012. Deep neural networks for acoustic modeling in speech recognition: The shared views of four research groups. *IEEE Signal Processing Magazine* 29(6):82–97.

22. Deng L, Hinton G, Kingsbury B. 2013. New types of deep neural network learning for speech recognition and related applications: An overview. *2013 IEEE Conference on Acoustics Speech and Signal Processing*. New York: IEEE.

23. Hermann KM et al. 2015. Teaching machines to read and comprehend. *Advances in Neural Information Processing Systems*.

24. Chung J, Cho K, Bengio Y. 2016. A character-level decoder without explicit segmentation for neural machine translation. arXiv:1603.06147.

25. Jozefowicz R et al. 2016. Exploring the limits of language modeling. arXiv:1602.02410.

26. Luong M-T, Pham H, Manning CD. 2015. Effective approaches to attention-based neural machine translation. arXiv:1508.04025.

27. Sutskever H, Vinyals O, Le QV. 2014. Sequence to sequence learning with neural networks. *Advances in Neural Information Processing Systems*.

28. Levine S et al. 2016a. End-to-end training of deep visuomotor policies. *Journal of Machine Learning Research* 17(39):1–40.

29. Levine S et al. 2016b. Learning hand-eye coordination for robotic grasping with deep learning and large-scale data collection. arXiv:1603.02199.

30. Mnih V et al. 2015. Human-level control through deep reinforcement learning. *Nature* 518(7540):529–533.
31. Mnih V et al. 2013. Playing Atari with deep reinforcement learning. arXiv:1312.5602.
32. Lore KG et al. 2015. Deep value of information estimators for collaborative human-machine information gathering. *2016 ACM/IEEE 7th International Conference on Cyber-Physical Systems.*
33. Liang Y et al. 2016. Big data-enabled multiscale serviceability analysis for aging bridges. *Digital Communications and Networks* 2(3):97–107.
34. Sarkar S et al. 2015. Early detection of combustion instability from hi-speed flame images via deep learning and symbolic time series analysis. *Annual Conference of Prognostics and Health Management.*
35. Akintayo A et al. 2016. Early detection of combustion instabilities using deep convolutional selective autoencoders on hi-speed flame video. arXiv:1603.07839.
36. Suryanita R. 2016. The application of artificial neural networks in predicting structural response of multistory building in the region of Sumatra Island. *KnE Engineering* 1(1).
37. Szabó JZ, Bakucz P. 2016. Identification of nonlinearity in knocking vibration signals of large gas engine by deep learning. *2016 IEEE 20th Jubilee Internationa Conference on Intelligent Engineering Systems.* New York: IEEE.
38. Guo X, Li W, Iorio F. 2016. Convolutional neural networks for steady flow approximation. *Proceedings of the 22nd ACM SIGKDD International Conference on Knowledge Discovery and Data Mining.* New York: ACM.
39. Singh A et al. 2016. Machine learning for high-throughput stress phenotyping in plants. *Trends in Plant Science* 21(2)110–124.
40. Akintayo A et al. 2016. An end-to-end convolutional selective autoencoder approach to soybean cyst nematode eggs detection. *Proceedings of the 22nd ACM SIGKDD Workshop on Data Science for Food Energy and Water.* New York: ACM.
41. Cruz-Roa AA et al. 2013. A deep learning architecture for image representation, visual interpretability and automated basal-cell carcinoma cancer detection. *International Conference on Medical Image Computing and Computer-Assisted Intervention.* Berlin: Springer.
42. Fakoor R et al. 2013. Using deep learning to enhance cancer diagnosis and classification. *Proceedings of the International Conference on Machine Learning.*
43. Cireşan DC et al. 2013. Mitosis detection in breast cancer histology images with deep neural networks. *International Conference on Medical Image Computing and Computer-Assisted Intervention.* Berlin: Springer.
44. Amini H et al. 2013. Engineering fluid flow using sequenced microstructures. *Nature Communications* 4:1826.
45. Stoecklein D et al. 2014. Micropillar sequence designs for fundamental inertial flow transformations. *Lab on a Chip* 14(21):4197–4204.
46. Amini H, Lee W, Di Carlo D. 2014. Inertial microfluidic physics. *Lab on a Chip* 14(15):2739–2761.
47. Zhang J et al. 2016. Fundamentals and applications of inertial microfluidics: A review. *Lab on a Chip* 16(1):10–34.
48. Lu M et al. 2016. Microfluidic hydrodynamic focusing for synthesis of nanomaterials. *Nano Today.*
49. Stoecklein D et al. 2016. Optimization of micropillar sequences for fluid flow sculpting. *Physics of Fluids* 28(1):012003.
50. Stoecklein D et al. 2017. Automated design for microfluid flow sculpting: Multiresolution approaches, efficient encoding, and CUDA implementation. *ASME Journal of Fluids Engineering* 139(3):031402-11.
51. Lore KG et al. 2015. Hierarchical feature extraction for efficient design of microfluidic flow patterns. *Proceedings of the 1st International Workshop on Feature Extraction: Modern Questions and Challenges.*
52. Nunes JK et al. 2014. Fabricating shaped microfibers with inertial microfluidics. *Advanced Materials* 26(22):3712–3717.

53. Paulsen KS, Di Carlo D, Chung AJ. 2015. Optofluidic fabrication for 3D-shaped particles. *Nature Communications* 6.

54. Paulsen KS, Chung AJ. 2016. Non-spherical particle generation from 4D optofluidic fabrication. *Lab on a Chip* 16(16):2987–2995.

55. Wu C-Y, Owsley K, Di Carlo D. 2015. Rapid software-based design and optical transient liquid molding of microparticles. *Advanced Materials* 27(48):7970–7978.

56. Sollier E et al. 2015. Inertial microfluidic programming of microparticle-laden flows for solution transfer around cells and particles. *Microfluidics and Nanofluidics* 19(1):53–65.

57. Uspal WE, Eral HB, Doyle PS. 2013. Engineering particle trajectories in microfluidic flows using particle shape. *Nature Communications* 4.

58. Griffin DR et al. 2015. Accelerated wound healing by injectable microporous gel scaffolds assembled from annealed building blocks. *Nature Materials* 14(7):737–744.

59. Fiorini F et al. 2016. Nanocomposite hydrogels as platform for cell growth, proliferation, and chemotaxis. *Small* 12(35):4881–4893.

60. Lore KG et al. 2016. Deep action sequence learning for causal shape transformation. arXiv:1605.05368.

61. Watson AB. 2011. Perimetric complexity of binary digital images: Notes on calculation and relation to visual complexity.

62. Zeiler MD, Fergus R. 2014. Visualizing and understanding convolutional networks. *European Conference on Computer Vision*. Springer International Publishing.

63. Rabitz H, Aliş OF. 1999. General foundations of high-dimensional model representations. *Journal of Mathematical Chemistry* 25(2–3):197–233.

64. Xie Y, Olga W, Ganapathysubramanian B. 2016. Incompressible two-phase flow: Diffuse interface approach for large density ratios, grid resolution study, and 3D patterned substrate wetting problem. *Computers and Fluids* 141:223–234.

65. Rabitz H, Aliş OF. 1999. General foundations of high-dimensional model representations. *Journal of Mathematical Chemistry* 25(2–3):197–233.

66. Matsumoto M, Nishimura T. 1998. Mersenne twister: A 623-dimensionally equidistributed uniform pseudo-random number generator. *ACM Transactions on Modeling and Computer Simulation* 8(1):3–30.

67. Sobol IM et al. 2011. Construction and comparison of high-dimensional sobol generators. *Wilmott* 56:64–79.

8

A Framework for Minimizing Data Leakage from Nonproduction Systems

Jacqueline Cope, Leandros A. Maglaras, Francois Siewe, Feng Chen, and Helge Janicke

CONTENTS

Introduction

Organizations copy tens of millions of sensitive customer and consumer data to nonproduction environments and very few companies do anything to protect this data, even when sharing with outsourcers and third parties (Oracle Corporation 2013). Corporate business systems have for many years become centralized in the pursuit of improved efficiency and cost savings. The support of these systems is affected by legal, business, and human factors. Existing frameworks and guidelines are reviewed for their benefits and limitations. Original research has been undertaken for both an organization's use of data and an individual's opinions on data usage and protection. The proposed model and framework describes the integration of and interaction between elements affecting an organization. A hypothetical case study has been devised and performed as a tabletop exercise to ascertain the practical use of the framework. In this book chapter we review the factors affecting nonproduction systems and propose a simplified business model and framework to understand the practical application. The technology/technical terms used in the book chapter are explained wherever they appear or in the "Glossary" section.

Nonproduction Environments

Nonproduction environments may be used within the software development life cycle (SDLC) during maintenance and testing. Data within nonproduction environments are subject to data protection laws, business requirements, and human factors. Several frameworks and sets of guidelines exist, and review different aspects of the SDLC. These, however, do not consider minimizing data leakage from nonproduction environments holistically within the legal, business, or human context. The following sections thoroughly describe these aspects.

Legal, Business, and Human Factors

Data is a business asset (Mohanty et al. 2013). The business should know where its assets are and how they are being used. In this respect, data is no different from any other asset; it has value, not only to the individual and the organization but also to those with unlawful intentions. This section provides an overview of the legal and business reasons for protecting data, and introduces the complexity of legal and industry standards, with some dependencies on the nationality of the organization, the business sector of the organization, the country in which the data resides, and ongoing legal challenges. The impact of the human factor is investigated with a brief analysis of the types of threat from employees and other insiders.

There is currently no global legal standard for protecting data. The legal requirements differ between the United States and the European Union (EU), and additionally between individual EU countries. The General Data Protection Regulation (GDPR) is expected to bring consistent regulation and improved data protection within the EU (European Union Court of Justice 2015). The United States has a similar legal organization with a number of national data security and privacy laws, which are subject to additional state law. The Federal Trade Commission (FTC) enforces regulation (DLA Piper 2016). The current U.K. legislation is the Data Protection Act 1988 (DPA), which enacts the EU Data Protection Directive, formally known as Directive 95/46/EC (Reouse 2008), and is expected to change to incorporate GDPR. Privacy Shield, the EU–US information sharing agreement was introduced in February 2016 (European Commission 2016) to support transatlantic commerce.

Organizations dealing with financial transactions by credit or debit card are recommended to comply with the global industry standard guidance of the Payment Card Industry Security Standards Council (PCI SSC), founded to improve financial transaction security, prevent the theft of payment card data, and avoid security breaches (PCI Security Standards Council n.d.). PCI DSS v3.1 is a framework for data security, risk reduction, and incident response (PCI 2015). There are standards for software, hardware vendors, and resellers in the Payment Application Data Security Standard (PA DSS) (PCI 2014). Business reasons for protecting data are based on the risk and impact of loss. Data breaches may lead to a direct financial loss to the business, disruption (U.K. Department for Business, Innovation and Skills 2015b), consequential financial costs (Stempel and Bose 2015), fines (European Union Court of Justice 2015; Information Commissioner's Office [ICO] 2015), criminal prosecutions (ICO n.d.), and loss of market position through loss of intellectual property or loss of reputation (Fiveash 2015). The impact on the customer, patient, or data subject may be distress, financial loss, or identity theft (Verizon 2014).

Business requirements are greater than that covered legally. Business confidential information can cover intellectual property, new product details, purchase or sales details, and analytics in data warehouses. In addition to legal, regulatory and business reasons for protecting data, human factors also affect data security. Staff-related data breaches rose in 2015 (U.K. Department for Business, Innovation and Skills 2015a), with half of the worst breaches being caused by inadvertent human error. Deliberate misuse of a system contributes to the number and size of data breaches. There is no indication of whether the source of the data breach was from production or nonproduction environments or unstructured data; however, a data breach from whatever source is still a data breach. The number of health care data breaches resulting from insider theft almost doubled (Symantec 2015), with unintentional breaches as the most common. In the 2016 report, health care remained at the top. Fewer companies declined to publish details of breaches unless legally required, leading to an increase in breaches where the full extent was not revealed (Symantec 2016).

Hurran (2014) categorizes the insider actions as following.

- Nonmalicious and unintentional—A substantial part of the problem. Employees have no intention of doing wrong, but process failure such as in recruitment or training leads to mistakes such as being socially engineered. If blame has to be attributed, it is the fault of the organization not the employee.

- Nonmalicious and intentional—A bigger problem, often caused by employees circumventing processes in place, such as copying data or sharing passwords, attributing the fault to the organization as a business process failure.

- Malicious and intentional—Can occur because factors within an organization enable the action to take place. If the factors had been addressed, the risk of the event would have been lowered.

Silowash et al. (2012) outlines a number of U.S.-based case studies to develop best practices relevant to an organization. The following are particularly relevant to the protection of production data in a nonproduction environment:

- Consider threats from insiders and business partners, protecting information both from internal and external threats
- Know the types of data that are processed, devices used to process and/or store data and their geographical locations
- Prevention of unauthorized data exfiltration is also applicable to nonproduction data if it has not been de-identified

The Software Engineering Institute's (Carnegie Mellon University 2013) unintentional insider threat concurs with Hurran's intentional and unintentional nonmalicious insiders, with accidental disclosure examples given as sensitive information being mishandled or sent to the wrong party. In the case of nonproduction environments, live examples may be unintentionally sent out or recorded in quality assurance (QA) documents, issue logs, and test scripts.

Evans et al. (2016) questions the effectiveness and suitability of existing assurance methods and the treatment of sensitive data being a compliance exercise rather than an ethical consideration.

Existing Frameworks, Solutions, Products, and Guidelines

The identification and analysis of frameworks and guidelines is done with the intention of finding an adaptable practical solution for the selection and preparation of a nonproduction environment, which reduces the possibility of data leakage, while providing a fit-for-purpose implementation. Existing proprietary and vendor independent frameworks and guidelines have provided commentary from different viewpoints looking for specific points applicable to nonproduction environments. The conclusion drawn is that the most practical points of each form an adaptable solution for an organization to select and prepare a suitable nonproduction environment. Free and/or open-source products and guidelines were researched. Some, however, were suitable for small organizations only or have not been maintained.

Data classification is the starting point for each of the frameworks, with data identification as the first step (National Institute of Standards and Technology [NIST] 2010; Oracle Corporation 2013). Without identification, classification cannot take place. Consider whether all the data identified is required for business purposes. If it is not required, then it should not be collected. Minimizing the collection of sensitive data reduces the data to be protected.

The classification process includes understanding which legal requirements and industry standards apply to which business areas. Initially it would appear straightforward to align the business area with the requirements, for example, health care information is covered by Caldicott principles. Taking a holistic approach to the business may uncover unexpected complexity; for example, provisions of adult social care services may involve Caldicott principles for adult social care data, PCI DSS for the payments made by credit and debit card, and also be subject to DPA. Therefore, it does not necessarily appear beneficial to separate business areas by function when applying legal and regulatory requirements.

The classification of individual data items without the context will not provide sufficient information. For example, a postcode is publicly available information used to identify one or more addresses, and is used for delivery, satellite navigation, and a factor in the calculation of some charges such as home insurance. However, when combined with other information, such as age and gender, it may identify an individual. The initial data classification may take into account the context in which the data is held and also any newer data considerations, for example, fitness data trackers will give a person's location, route, and times and could be used to establish a travel pattern. Smart heating controllers such as Hive learn heating patterns and the data could be used to identify when properties are empty. Other information such as images and video should be considered. Data classification schemes or policy, for example, the NIST PII Confidentiality Impact Levels (NIST 2010) of low, medium, or high to indicate a level of harm resulting from leaked data; or Informatica's (2011) public, internal, and confidential; or London School of Economics's (2013) extended version of public, internal, restricted, and confidential to describe the data will be of benefit to align the use of data in a nonproduction environment with the organization's information security standards.

Following classification of data, an analysis of the nonproduction system requirements is the next area for consideration. Understanding the use of the nonproduction system is a key factor in achieving a balance of security and usability. It is likely that different instances of a system will have different requirements (Oracle Corporation 2013). For example, a live support system may require a full data set with de-identification of particularly sensitive data, but an interface development system will fulfill requirements by using a subset of data with all sensitive data de-identified, or even containing a representative synthesized test data set. If the level of de-identification is light, then further protection such as access control and audit procedures are required. Once the nonproduction system requirements have been assessed, the specific techniques for de-identification can be investigated.

The Open Data Center Alliance's (2013) levels of de-identification appear useful. Each nonproduction system requirement would be categorized as follows.

- Synthesized or generated data, where no original data is required, may be used for unit testing, or training databases.
- Anonymization, the application of de-identification techniques following optional subsetting.
- Pseudonymization, the application of tokenization techniques with optional subsetting.
- No de-identification, where alternative methods of protection are required.

Data treatment requirements refer to the techniques available and to investigating the products appropriate for the architecture of the system. Capgemini (2015) and Securosis (2012) offer advice on principles that the data resulting from de-identification techniques should balance usability and security. The de-identification, where possible, should be managed, nonreversible, and repeatable, resulting in data that is representative of the source data, with integrity maintained. In the cases where light or no de-identification takes place, supplementary security and documentary evidence for audit purposes are required.

Limitations

The term *de-identified* has been used as the generic term because other terminology, such as de-identified (U.K. Department of Health 2013), anonymization (U.K. Department of

Health 2013), data sanitizing (NIST 2010), masking (Muralidhar and Sarathy 2006), obfuscation (NIST 2010), obscured (NIST 2010), and pseudonymization (U.K. Department of Health 2013), is used to describe both different and multiple techniques and, at times, becomes confusing (Duncan and Stokes 2009). De-identification techniques such as adding noise (Wilson and Rosen 2003), shuffling and swapping (National Institute of Statistical Sciences [NISS] n.d.), and permutation (Cormode and Srivastava 2009) have limited use because of the amount of original data remaining. Techniques including gibberish generation, nulling out (Raghunathan 2013), redaction, and suppression (Sweeney 2002) remove sensitive data, but reduce data quality by producing unrealistic data sets, so may suit free text fields such as memos and notes. Generated or synthetic data (Machanavajjhala et al. 2008) is realistic-looking data that contains no original data, limiting potential disclosure, but is time-consuming to construct.

The proposed framework demonstrates a practical way to evaluate the legal, business, and system constraints on a nonproduction environment. There is a balance to be found between the security of sensitive data, and the requirements of developers and support personnel and the organization's business principles. There is also a balance to be found between data de-identification and other protection methods such as access controls. The framework also allows for the provision of evidence to demonstrate compliance.

Research for Framework Development

This research project investigates the prevalence of the use of production data in nonproduction systems; the reasons for using production data; the alternatives to or treatment of production data; methods for assessing the risk; and the frameworks available to guide an organization to an appropriate choice of protection for the nonproduction system data.

Research the Use and Protection of Data in Nonproduction Systems

In order to conduct our research, requests were made under the Freedom of Information Act (FOIA) to obtain an organizational view of data protection. A questionnaire was used to obtain the individual professional's view. The former is helping the qualitative analysis but since it is a rather small sample, the latter research method, the questionnaires, was used in order to be able to perform quantitative analysis.

Freedom of Information: An Organizational View

FOIA requests were made to ten public bodies that by the nature of their business were expected to hold some sensitive information as part of the research into the organizations' stance on the prevalence of using production data in nonproduction environments and the desensitization, if any, of that data. It is acknowledged that such a small sample cannot be used to extrapolate expectations or to make any deductions from the results. The results from a convenience sample (Walliman 2011) may indicate whether a larger study would be beneficial. Of the organizations responding, there was an even split between those that copied production environments and those that did not. This provided some information to support the idea that organizations were using copies of production data but would benefit from a greater number of FOI requests over a wider range of public bodies. This is represented in Figure 8.1.

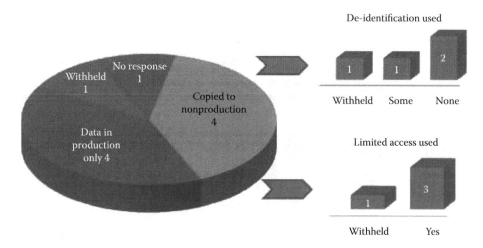

FIGURE 8.1
FOI requests.

In conclusion, the sample size is too small to be anything other than a pilot exercise, but it highlights that some organizations copy production data to nonproduction environments, with some de-identifying sensitive data and others relying upon user access restrictions to protect the data.

Questionnaire: Opinion

The questionnaire was undertaken to collect the opinions and experiences of professional people with access to potentially sensitive data especially in nonproduction environments (Hoffer 2013). Respondents within business areas such as user acceptance testers, and in information technology (IT) roles including applications, database, hardware, and network potentially have valuable experience that informs their opinions. A target of 50 responses is considered small for qualitative research (Malhotra 2016) but is an appropriate convenience sample (Walliman 2011) for initial research before developing a process for further research. There are polarized opinions about the appropriate use of data within development and test systems (Fanadka 2015; Howard 2013), this survey provides a selection of current opinion, with the benefit of additional details of the reasoning behind the choices and ways of addressing concerns. It is acknowledged that results may be skewed within a comparatively small sample by respondents working in the same area, such as operational support. Nine questions were formulated to gauge opinion.

Question 1 ascertains the areas of the software development life cycle (SDLC) in which the respondent is involved. The categories suggested and the percentage of responses for each is in Figure 8.2. The category of other included architecture, assurance, configuration, consultancy, data administration, data migration, project management, and systems administration. The respondent's role is a possible indicator of a relationship between their role and their opinion. For example, a support analyst may perceive a need for live data across all environments because their work is resolving live issues, whereas a developer may only require generated data because they have to meet the application specifications. This can only be treated as speculation because of the small size of the convenience sample (Boulmetis and Dutwin 2014).

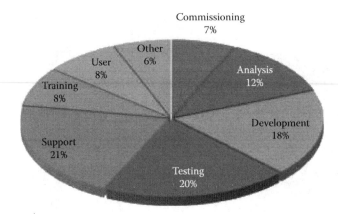

FIGURE 8.2
Question 1: Role within SDLC.

Analysis of the respondents working in multiple roles showed that 33% of respondents performed a single role, with the remaining performing multiple roles (Figure 8.3). The most common combination of multiple roles was within development, test, and support. The performance of multiple roles could indicate that good practice of separation of duties (Zurko and Simon 2011) may not necessarily be applied within the software development life cycle. However, this cannot be taken as anything more than an indication for an area of further research because this is a comparatively small sample with broad interpretative categories.

Question 2 indicates types of sensitive data available to the respondent. The respondents may select multiple options from the list of No sensitive data; Personally identifiable information (PII); Financial; Health; Intellectual property (IP); Trade secrets; Vulnerable people; or select Other and include a description. The category of Vulnerable People covers information that becomes more sensitive because of the data subject rather than the data itself and includes both adults (U.K. Department of Health n.d.) and children (Her Majesty's Government 2015). Figure 8.4 shows the range of sensitive data identified by the respondents. The category of Other contained only Government classification (Cabinet Office 2014). An interesting point is the low number of respondents with no access to sensitive data.

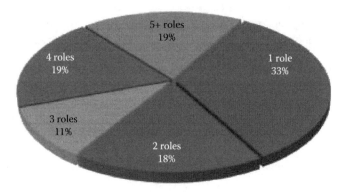

FIGURE 8.3
Question 1: Respondents in multiple roles.

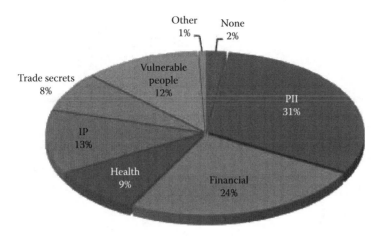

FIGURE 8.4
Question 2: Use of sensitive data types.

Question 3 finds the environments to which respondents have access, and is expected to indicate any additional data exposure from nonproduction systems. A single option was selected from Production only; Nonproduction only; Both production and nonproduction environments with the same rights; Both production and nonproduction with different rights; and Other, which must be specified. The assumption has been made that where respondents have access to production and nonproduction environments with differing rights, the nonproduction rights will be the same or greater than their production rights. Figure 8.5 shows the access to environments, with over half of the respondents having access to data through the nonproduction environment. Those respondents selecting the option of Other had access rights defined by each task or contract.

Question 4 aims to find the respondents access levels. When considering data leakage, it is not just whether data can be altered that increases the risk, but also the visibility of data. The responses of Other described access as depending on the task or contract. Figure 8.6 shows the respondents' access levels.

Question 5 looks at the de-identification used. The respondent may select multiple options from the list of Complete copy of production data; Copy of production data

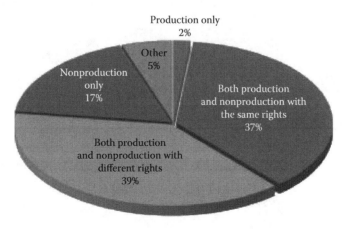

FIGURE 8.5
Question 3: Access to environments.

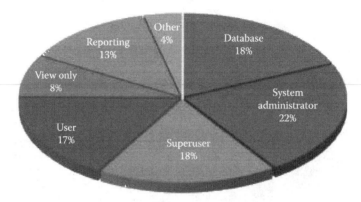

FIGURE 8.6
Question 4: Access levels.

with some sensitive data de-identified; Copy of production data with all sensitive data de-identified; Generated data containing no real data; and Other defining a description. Figure 8.7 shows the usage of generated data and levels of de-identification. Those categorized as other include subsets of production data, hybrid versions including production data (with and without desensitized data) combined with generated data, and different de-identification depending on the task or contract. The progression through phases of SDLC using different data sets is also mentioned.

Question 6 seeks to understand the respondent's knowledge of data de-identification methods using free text that was classified and fed into Wordle (Feinberg 2014). The responses are presented giving greater prominence to frequently used words, showing that masking is the most commonly mentioned technique (Figure 8.8), and SQL is most popular of tools and software (Figure 8.9).

Question 7 checks for an understanding of terminology. The results in Figure 8.10 show that masking is the most used and recognized technique, supported by the unprompted request for techniques in question 6. There appears to be a reasonable understanding of a number of common de-identification techniques. It would be interesting if a larger survey was available to cross-reference the use of techniques with the levels of de-identification in question 5 to see if knowledge of techniques had any correlation with the level of de-identification used,

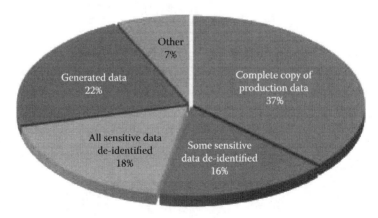

FIGURE 8.7
Question 5: Levels of de-identification used in nonproduction environment.

FIGURE 8.8
Question 6: De-identification techniques.

FIGURE 8.9
Question 6: De-identification tools and software.

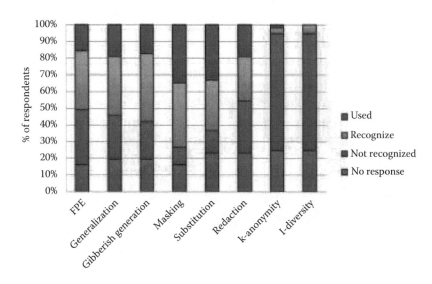

FIGURE 8.10
Question 7: Understanding techniques.

then to further consider if the respondent's knowledge had any impact on the quality of de-identification. The outcome of this could lead to a further study to consider whether an improved understanding of techniques, through awareness and education, would lead to increased or improved levels of de-identification in nonproduction environments.

Question 8 is a four-part question to find the perceived benefits and drawbacks of using live and de-identified data. Themes were extracted from the free text format, and categorized (Walliman 2011). The respondent's opinions on the benefits of using live data (Figure 8.11) showed that the major benefit perceived was that issues could be replicated. Inspecting the raw data showed comments related to issues in production environment being replicated in a test environment, as well as issues found in a test environment such as user acceptance testing (UAT) also being replicated in a development environment. The disadvantages (Figure 8.12) were an increased risk of sensitive data being exposed, followed by unacceptable access, and extra security required for sensitive data.

The benefits of de-identification were the reduced risk of sensitive data exposure, followed by improved data security, and fewer issues with third parties (Figure 8.13). Respondents' opinions on the disadvantages of using de-identified data (Figure 8.14) were the inability to replicate issues, followed by unrealistic, unrecognizable, or unfamiliar data, and reduced test data quality.

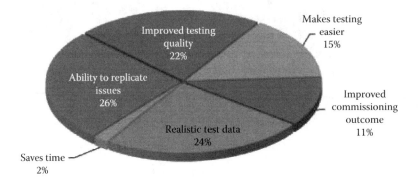

FIGURE 8.11
Question 8a: Benefits of using live data.

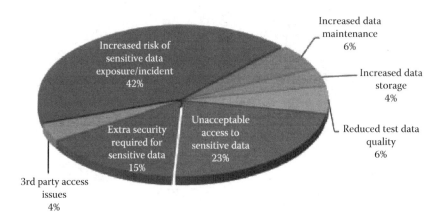

FIGURE 8.12
Question 8b: Disadvantages of using live data.

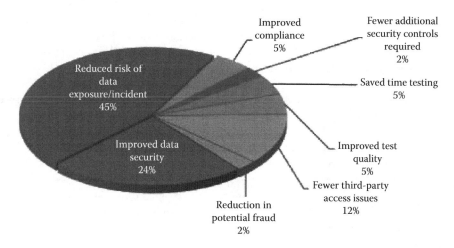

FIGURE 8.13
Question 8c: Benefits of using data de-identification.

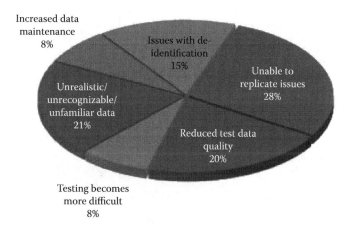

FIGURE 8.14
Question 8d: Disadvantages of using data de-identification.

The benefits of using live data (Figure 8.11) and disadvantages of using data de-identification (Figure 8.14) showed similarity in some indicating a similar perceived benefit and opposing disadvantage responses (see Table 8.1). When comparing the responses, four categories showed similar sizes of response. For example, 22% of responses identified live data improving test data quality and 20% showed de-identification as reducing test data quality.

TABLE 8.1

Comparison of Benefits of Live Data and Disadvantages of De-Identification

8a. Benefits of Using Live Data		8d. Disadvantages of Using Data De-Identification	
Improved testing quality	22%	Reduced test data quality	20%
Makes testing easier	15%	Testing becomes more difficult	8%
Realistic test data	24%	Unrealistic/unrecognizable/unfamiliar data	21%
Ability to replicate issues	26%	Unable to replicate issues	28%

The individual responses in the raw data showed some respondents identified both the benefit and disadvantage, but others had identified either one or the other. This area would benefit from more in-depth scrutiny.

A similar comparison between responses to disadvantages of using live data (Figure 8.12) and benefits of using data de-identification (Figure 8.13) again shows similarities in some responses (see Table 8.2). This highlighted issues of test data requirements, risk of data exposure, third-party data access, and de-identification techniques as requiring consideration when using live or de-identified data.

Question 9 analyzes respondents' concerns in using data in nonproduction environments and possible solutions. Ten areas of concern are shown in Figure 8.15 with data security incidents and compliance being the most prominent. Data security incident responses include examples of deliberate misuse of data such as theft; unintentional data loss, including misdirected test invoices and copies of sensitive data in test scripts; application demonstrations using real data; and a misconfiguration resulting in a production web front end being connected to test backend database. Regulatory and compliance concerns include DPA, PCI, and Financial Conduct Authority (FCA). Additional concerns of poorly managed environments, burden of trust placed on staff, poor security practice, testing strategies, and staff training may be seen as contributing factors to data security incidents and compliance concerns. An interesting point is that both a loss of realistic test data and insufficient de-identification are equally mentioned, as opinions expressed earlier (see Table 8.1). Solutions suggested (Figure 8.16) were to desensitize data, enforce policy, and

TABLE 8.2

Comparison of Disadvantages of Using Live Data and Benefits of Using Data De-Identification

8b. Disadvantages of Using Live Data		8c. Benefits of Using De-Identification	
Increased risk of data exposure	42%	Reduced risk of data exposure	45%
Third-party access issues	4%	Fewer third-party access issues	12%
Extra security required for sensitive data	15%		
Unacceptable access to sensitive data	23%	Improved data security	24%

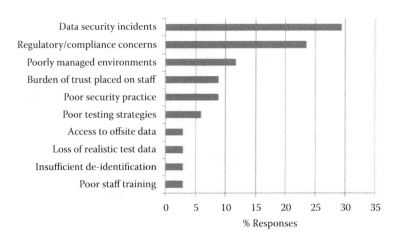

FIGURE 8.15
Question 9a: Concerns over nonproduction environments.

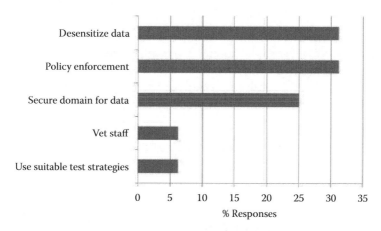

FIGURE 8.16
Question 9b: Suggested solutions to concerns over nonproduction environments.

adhere to guidelines; provide a secure domain for sensitive data; vet staff; and use suitable test strategies. These results may be interpreted as there is a place for de-identification, but that which cannot conveniently be de-identified should be protected in a secure domain, and subject to suitable policy and guidance.

Some suggested solutions appear to contradict previous areas of the survey. Desensitizing data is supported by the benefits identified (see Figure 8.13) but also has perceived disadvantages (see Figure 8.14). The most common disadvantage identified is the inability to replicate issues (28%). Replication difficulties are anticipated between production and production support environments, and between a UAT environment using production data and previous test environments using de-identified data.

In conclusion, there may be a case for a production support environment to use a copy of production data to assist the replication of issues before attempted resolution; however, the environment should be secured to the same level as the production environment. This leads to the primary use of the nonproduction environment being an influence on data treatment. It may provide justification for copying production data and using production-level security controls. It also indicates that nonproduction environments have different purposes and require different levels of de-identification or protection. The roles of the respondents may affect the perception of advantages and disadvantages. The mixture of roles may predispose the respondent's perception of data requirements. For example, if the respondent fulfills roles of production support and development testing, they may consider that the same production support environment is required for both roles. However, analyzing the requirements of each role may lead to a different decision for each nonproduction environment. Production support can be argued to require a copy of production data, but development testing does not require the same level of sensitive data especially when test plans are scripted in advance. It also highlights a possible deficiency in testing behavior, of whether the tests are covering a number of scenarios or simply not failing. The suggestion of policy enforcement is interesting because it could imply that policies are made and either not communicated or not followed up causing a possible disconnection between policy, procedure, and actual practice.

The results may only be used as an indication and a possible basis for further research. The sample size and propagation is insufficient to draw anything other than tenuous suggestions rather than conclusions. The overall view suggested that de-identification reduced the risk of data exposure and data incidents by reducing access to sensitive data. However, it highlighted possible disadvantages in replicating production support issues and providing recognizable test data. It has also highlighted possible conflicts of interest in the reduction of quality in an attempt to complete tasks quickly, sometimes confusing the requirements of speed with economy and the different attitudes toward testing.

Simplified Business Model

The simplified business model (Cope et al. forthcoming) shows the integration of legal and regulatory requirements, human interactions, business requirements, business systems, and nonproduction environments (Figure 8.17). Business systems are simplified as comprising data, software, and infrastructure to support administrative and commercial purposes. Human interaction occurs with each area.

Nonproduction environments may be perceived as separate from the business systems, but remains subject to the same legal and regulatory requirements. Environments serve different purposes, requiring a practical aid to identify influencing factors and to guide the decision makers through a process of providing nonproduction environments with adequate security (NIST 2013).

Six Stages of the Framework, Detailing from Organization to Compliance

The framework describes a process flow from the legal and regulatory requirements to data treatment and protection; gained through understanding the organization's business, the production system, the purpose, and requirements of the nonproduction environment. Each stage builds on earlier stages of the process and provides appropriate feedback with demonstrable knowledge provided by governance, compliance, audit, policy, and procedure. Figure 8.18 (Cope et al. forthcoming) shows the framework diagrammatically. This framework is not prescriptive and ideally would be used in the order described, but allows the position and knowledge required to be assessed from any stage before moving on.

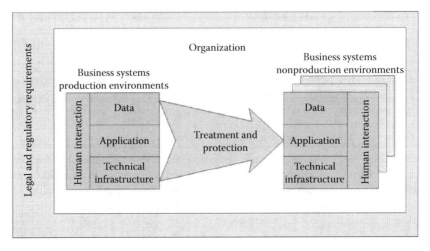

FIGURE 8.17
Simplified business model showing the interaction of elements affecting the organization.

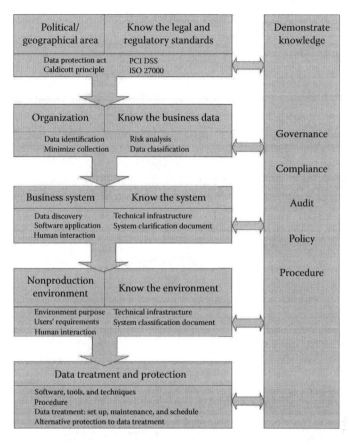

FIGURE 8.18
Framework for minimizing data leakage from nonproduction systems.

Know the Legal and Regulatory Standard

Knowledge of legal and regulatory standards relating to the business is necessary, specifically those relating to the use, transmission, and storage of data across business, political, and geographical areas.

Know the Business Data

Organization-level risk assessments are required to consider threats to data security from insiders and business partners as well as outsiders (Silowash et al. 2012). The information management function may advise on details of information management, governance, or policy relating to specific privacy aspects. Business data should be identified and described using business terminology and a suitable classification scheme. Know what is held, for what purpose, where, and its classification (Hutchinson and Warren 2001). Sensitive data should be identified because it is only possible to effectively protect what is known (NIST 2010). The collection and retention of data without sound business reason should be challenged. Regular scheduled reviews of data retention policy and conformity to that policy with the planned removal of unnecessary sensitive information lowers the risk of data leakage. Retention schedules that meet legal requirements, industry practice, sector specific needs, and business requirements should be communicated to data controllers.

The documentation should include the sensitivity rating, applicable law or regulation, and the reasons for the benefit of future compliance checks or when dealing with regulatory or legal changes.

Know the System

Organizations use a number of business systems, which may be hosted internally, cloud based, outsourced, or a combination. The responsibility for data held must be known, whether it is complete responsibility for systems hosted internally, shared responsibility for cloud security, or assurance from third-party suppliers. Knowing the system is about the data that the business actually holds within its systems as compared with the organizational-level knowledge of what it expects to hold. Differences between expected data and data actually held should be analyzed and, if necessary, fed back to the earlier stage. System-level data may be cataloged against the business use. A holistic approach to data identification and classification is recommended because data at a system level may not be considered sensitive, but becomes sensitive when combined with data from another system.

Know the Environment

Environments, in addition to the production environment, may be required for development, support, and maintenance, and may be controlled by the business area, another business area such as IT, or an external organization. The environment's purpose and the users' needs must be understood. The software application, technical infrastructure, or human interactions may differ from those of the production system, necessitating an investigation of how the data should differ from the production system to maintain the required level of protection (Graham et al. 2008). The nonproduction environment users' needs and data security needs should be the basis for the nonproduction system. Cost, ease of use, and data security may conflict because of the perceptions of need rather than the actual need.

It is expected that the data owner has responsibility for its use, following consultation with those responsible for nonproduction environment users to give the best compromise in the conflicting triangle of security, usability, and cost (Sherwood et al. 2015). The agreed format of each environment with reasons should be documented for future reference. The output of this process is the environment classification document that describes the system, and the requirements for the data in this environment and its expected use. Further detail of the degree of de-identification required may also be documented.

Data Treatment and Protection

Neither data treatment nor protection can be considered an easy option. There is no simple one-size-fits-all solution. The level of data treatment and protection should be agreed before defining the method. Generated data should not require further treatment or additional protection, but requires assurances that it contains no real data. "As-live" data

FIGURE 8.19
Plan–do–check–act.

requires "as-live" protection. The treatment and protection must be documented to meet compliance standards. Plan–do–check–act (PDCA) (Deming 1982) may be used to define the process (Figure 8.19).

- Plan—Identify and analyze the problem. Use the requirements in the system classification document during the "know the environment" stage, and ensure it meets the security needs and the needs of the users. Keep de-identification to a minimum; do not de- identify data unless classified as sensitive. Identify tools and techniques to meet the requirements of the environment.

- Do—Develop and test potential solutions. Consider data subsetting, generate a series of potential solutions, and perform a pilot exercise of the best solution.

- Check—Measure the effectiveness of the proposed solution, and improve as necessary. Check that de-identification provides the expected results. If the de-identified data is suitable to be passed on to the environment users, then it is possible to progress to the act stage, otherwise the do and check phases may be performed until a satisfactory outcome is found.

- Act—Implement the de-identification routine, include automation for maximum efficiency. The de-identification process should be repeatable.

As the quantity of sensitive data increases or the sensitivity of data increases in the nonproduction environment, the need for additional security from the application software, infrastructure, or control over human factors also increases.

Demonstrate Knowledge

Assurance expects to give confidence that intended security controls are effective (NIST 2013), but confirmation that controls have been applied correctly or as intended is also required (Evans et al. 2016). Demonstrate knowledge explicitly provides that assurance at each stage of the process, which may be tailored to each organization's specific requirements.

Tabletop Case Study

The tabletop case study is used as a worked example to demonstrate how the use of the simplified business model and framework for minimizing data leakage from nonproduction Systems will practically aid discussion, the collection of information required, and the decision-making process regarding the use of data and protection of nonproduction environments. It also validates the stages proposed in the framework.

Hypothetical Case Study Scenario

The subject of the hypothetical scenario is a large U.K.-based service sector organization employing in the region of 4,000 staff members across the business, having 30,000 service users and a turnover of £150 million. The organization is consolidating its business systems and moving to enterprise resource planning (ERP) to manage service delivery of sales, purchasing, central accounting functions, human resource management, and payroll functions. The consolidation has also been taken as an opportunity to rationalize the contents and use of nonproduction environments.

The postimplementation nonproduction environments initially identified are

- A training environment, for scheduled in-person training sessions for each of the functional areas as they are implemented, and eventually for ongoing staff training
- A production support environment, to be used for the replication and possible resolution of live issues
- Development, test, and user acceptance environments to be used for the release of customizations

The details for the case study are that the organization has documented the legal and regulatory requirements as applicable to its existing systems. In summary the Data Protection Act is the legal basis for privacy. The organization accepts a minimal number of card payments using a third-party provider, which reduces the requirement for PCI DSS compliance. However, the ERP implementation will improve the ability to accept card payment, and PCI DSS compliance will be a future requirement and should be considered at this point. All data is currently held in data centers within the United Kingdom, and no change is expected.

Information security policies exist for both public and internal publication, and are the responsibility of the organization's information security function. The data categorization in use is based upon the popular (Cabinet Office 2014) classification of confidential, internal, and public, with the confidential category subdivided as business confidential and personal confidential.

- Public—Information that is publicly available and does not contain either personally identifiable or commercially sensitive information. No impact in the event of data loss.
- Internal—Personal information that is not considered to be sensitive under DPA and contains no financial information. Inappropriate disclosure could result in

personal distress. Commercial information that is not considered commercially sensitive but may have minor adverse impact on the business.

- Personal confidential—Sensitive personal information, as defined by DPA, is personal information associated with financial data such as account numbers. Loss of data likely to cause significant distress, harm, or adverse financial impact on individuals or organizations.

- Business confidential—Intellectual property and financial information, the loss of which would have a major impact on the commercial viability of the organization.

The data has been classified within the existing systems, and classification and data retention will be reviewed with the procurement and implementation of ERP.

The current systems are separate software applications, residing on the organization's own on-site servers, with no direct access available outside of the organization. Access is controlled using a combination of network and application access; single sign on is not used. ERP will be hosted on a multitenant cloud provided and managed by a third party, to be confirmed during the procurement process. Nonproduction environments, with the exception of production support, expect to be hosted on the organization's own servers, but the decision will be confirmed when the transition is complete.

Discussions Using the Simplified Business Model and Framework

The tabletop exercise discussions review and possibly challenge decisions made in the scenario, and consider the treatment and protection of the nonproduction environments. This is a reflection of the process expected to take place within an organization, and would highlight gaps in knowledge and challenge assumptions made.

Know the Legal and Regulatory Standards

Using the framework, "know the legal and regulatory standards" is partially covered by the current adherence to DPA, but must take account of GDPR and demonstrate compliance to meet the accountability principle (ICO 2016) and the compliance aspect of "demonstrate knowledge." The organization's security policy has been devised within the information security role, and is communicated throughout the organization by regular mandatory online training sessions, and by inclusion within the normal working practice.

Know the Business Data

GDPR prioritizes the data retention policy, and requires evidence of data-retention reviews. This may be accomplished using scheduled regular reviews of data retention policies and evidence of conformity. Consider how long data should be held, assessing legal, regulatory, and business requirements. Verifiable records of affirmative consent of data subjects' information being held are required under GDPR (ICO 2016). The classification of existing data has been devised and agreed between the information security function and the corporate finance function. The data classification will be extended to include current manually administered data that will be included in ERP, such as absence recording and workforce and service user diversity records.

Know the System

In this case, the production system is an organization's ERP covering sales, purchasing, central accounting functions, human resource management, and payroll functions. This is a wide remit, and may be better approached looking at the systems' modules and identifying core data, and module-specific data. A system classification highlights system areas applicable to the data classification in "know the business." For example, DPA defines sensitive personal data as relating to a person's ethnic origin, political opinions, religious belief, trade union membership, physical or mental health, sexual life, and criminal or alleged behavior (Data Protection Act 1998) because it could be used in a discriminatory way and so should be treated with greater care. This information, including ethnicity, religion, disability, and sexuality, are part of employee equality monitoring, and union subscriptions are taken as payroll deductions, and so should be recorded in the system classification and additionally in data classification using the "personal confidential" classification. The system classification should be communicated to relevant employees and sufficient training given.

Human interaction covers access to the data using either the software application or through the technical infrastructure. Controls on user access include applying least privilege for application access, which complements separation of duties to minimize both inadvertent error and deliberate or malicious misuse. Concerning the technical infrastructure, GDPR Article 26 is expected to affect the regulation of cloud provision requiring the client to ensure the cloud provider meets the processing and security requirements (Voss 2013).

Know the Environment

Business systems require development, support, and maintenance throughout the software development life cycle. Nonproduction environment requirements may be affected by users' perceptions based on job role. For example, a developer performing production support perceives a need for a live data set during development because he "knows the data" rather than using a generated data set based on good data analysis. The environments discussed in the tabletop exercise are for training, production support, development, test, and user acceptance testing.

The requirements of the training environment were dealt with first. In-person training sessions were a requirement in the scenario, but both the in-person and e-learning training provisions were considered in the tabletop exercise. It was decided that no real personal or sensitive information should be used. Data sets should contain standard configuration items and realistic-looking information to be reloaded as required. For example, payroll training sessions required the departmental structure of posts, grades, and cost codes along with standard payments and deductions be available, but employee-related data should be created to meet the particular needs of the training, and to allow the trainers to become familiar with the data sets. In-person training data sets could also form the basis of e-learning provision to provide continuity. The training data would be available to trainees during in-person supervised sessions and to any employee as e-learning, so care must be taken to ensure the personal or sensitive data is realistic but unconnected to real data. As some nonproduction environments are to be hosted on-site, a process for refreshing the environments is required. The issues raised included the technical aspects of the separation of application software, configuration and data, and the secure transportation of sensitive data between sites.

The production support environment was considered next, as it was thought to be at the opposite end of the spectrum from the training environment. It differs by being hosted on the multitenant cloud environment rather than on the organization's own servers. The purpose of the production support environment is to allow support analysts to recreate and, where possible, provide solutions without using the production environment. Discussions centered on the persons having access to the environment, the data required, and how access to that data should be managed. Access to both the environment and the roles within the environment should be limited. Support analysts should be the only employees who would have greater access to the sensitive data in the support environment using both the application and interrogating the database using other software tools. It was considered that de-identification of the most sensitive or potentially high profile data would be appropriate. Particularly sensitive information, such as equality monitoring information, health-related data, and financial details such as bank accounts, should be de-identified. E-mail addresses were thought to be potentially high profile because of the risk of unintentionally sending documentation from the production support environment.

Access to the multitenant environment was also considered, and assurances were required from the cloud provider that security of the nonproduction environment would be as stringent as that of the production environment. This area was considered to be poorly understood and needed expert assistance. The term "cloud supply chain" (Lindner 2010) describes the supply chain of cloud services. The provenance of cloud storage was discussed, and concerns raised about business continuity and data leakage risks. It was acknowledged that this area required further understanding.

Development, test, and user acceptance environments were considered. The environments are hosted on the organization's servers, so it would also be administered by the organization's technical staff. They would be accessible to a range of analysts, developers, and testers including third party and contract staff. The discussion of usability versus security followed, showing a similar set of ideas to those highlighted in the research questionnaire. Time to construct test cases was considered an overhead, but possibly more efficient when viewed in the longer term. The perception of usability appeared to be the greatest hurdle with assurances being required that any generated or de-identified data would be suitably representative of the live data. In a hypothetical scenario it was agreed that generated or de-identified data would be the most appropriate, but with the caveat that there would be occasions where developers and testers may be unable to recreate suitable data to replicate production support issues. The basis of the software development life cycle was discussed, and agreed that different ways of working would impact the use of the development environments. The traditional progress of development, test, and UAT was considered to be too slow for some development schedules. More agile methodologies (Griffiths and Griffiths 2016) would require a more dynamic data set. It was agreed that whatever methodology was used, continuity between the data sets would be required.

Data Treatment and Protection

The definition between the stages of "know the environment" and "data treatment and protection" became blurred at times, with questions being raised over how the data treatment was to be performed and the range of software tools and services available. The constraints of both the software and cloud providers were broached, and must be resolved before purchase and implementation of any de-identification products. Concerns over the de-identification process included assurance that sufficient de-identification had taken place, whether data transfer from the cloud to internal server was secure, and whether de-identification should be performed on the cloud or internal server. Creating and uploading generated data was not an issue, as the ERP software included a "bulk upload" facility; however, there was little knowledge of application programming interfaces (APIs), so methods for de-identification needed more investigation. Concerns were expressed that using third-party products or services would invalidate vendor support. The future maintenance of any data generation and/or de-identification was also considered. Upgrades or patching cycles would require data generation and de-identification routines to be checked and the impact of any changes addressed. The knowledge of existing in-house systems was much greater than that of the ERP software, leading to lower confidence in the stability of de-identified data sets.

Maintaining integrity between interfaced systems needed further investigation. Using development, test, and UAT as standalone environments was not considered to be detrimental to productivity, but using de-identification for two or more connected systems, where interfaces relied on common details such as National Insurance number to match records and details, caused some concern.

Demonstrate Knowledge

To meet GDPR Article 5(2), a data retention policy and review schedule is required with details of how it is applied to the business data. Evidence of the data retention reviews and data archiving or removal that has taken place in "know the system" should be recorded. Document the data used and protection afforded to non-production environments, including justification for using as-live data. GDPR also requires organizations with over 250 employees to maintain additional internal records of processing activities, including verifiable records of affirmative consent from data subjects (ICO 2016).

Summary of the Impact of the Framework on the Case Study

The case study, as a hypothetical scenario, demonstrated that protecting sensitive data is not an easy or straightforward task. The simplified business model allowed the requirements to be visualized, which enabled requirements to be discussed more thoroughly, and concepts needing further explanation to be noted for follow up. It encouraged any assumptions made to be stated and challenged as necessary. Using the framework showed the significance of information policy for direction, and the importance of communication and understanding between business areas to support decision making. Larger and more complex organizations require good communication channels between the support areas, such as legal, information security, policy, IT, and business, to be able to work together rather than as separate entities.

There are areas during a transition, as described in the case study, where decisions are made because of a lack of information or understanding, or due to the speed and degree of change, and should be revisited and confirmed. The documented basis for the decisions allows those decisions to be either validated or improved as required. The interdependency of data, infrastructure, and human interaction emerged where the change in infrastructure led to a change in the user base, and to a possible need for the data change or protection.

Overall the perception of the simplified business model and framework was seen as useful to focus on the requirements of each stage, and the interaction between those stages. Concerns were raised about the time taken, and the possible costs of data treatment and protection. This could be countered with the understanding of the personal, business and financial impact of the loss or leakage of data.

Conclusions

Data loss and data leakage continues, with high-profile cases regularly reaching the news. Legal requirements are expected to change with the introduction of GDPR; responsibility for data security and demonstration of compliance will be required. Data classification according to risk of loss is not new and is the basis for many existing information security policies. However, the ability for organizations to collect, store, and retain increasing amounts of data may be leading to what could be perceived as an overwhelming administrative burden of data classification and protection. The practice of reusing production data in nonproduction environments was the subject of a small research exercise. FOI requests provided an organizational response, and the questionnaire provided a sample of employee opinion.

The sample sizes were small and would benefit from further work to increase the sample size, which may change the statistical outcomes discovered. The FOI research showed that half of the organizations that provided a response, copied production data to their nonproduction environments, and half of those relied on access restriction to protect the data. The questionnaire showed over a third of responses with access to a complete copy of production data, and a similar number with access to production data with some or all sensitive data de-identified. Practical reasons for using production data were put forward in the responses to the questionnaire, highlighting the need for treatment and protection of nonproduction environments to be assessed on their primary use rather than as a whole. Human factors affect data security, with several high-profile data breaches being attributed to inadvertent human error. Exposing sensitive data in nonproduction environments increases the risk of data breach simply by the additional availability. The questionnaire showed some examples of potentially sensitive data from nonproduction environments being recorded in documents available to a wider audience.

It is possible that the role performed by an employee leads to a perceived need for a certain type of data, and that a combination of roles such as support and development leads to a perceived need for using one data set for all roles. Having access to sensitive data on a regular basis may lead to an increased risk of data leakage due to the action of employees circumventing procedures in an attempt to get the job done.

The simplified business model shows that elements affecting an organization are then translated into the framework for minimizing data leakage from nonproduction systems. The framework allows the five stages to be considered both independently and in conjunction with other stages. Using the sixth stage of "demonstrate knowledge" is a check that compliance can be evidenced effectively.

Glossary

data leakage: unauthorized transfer of personal and/or sensitive data from a computer, system, or data center to the outside world.

nonproduction environment: any system, hardware or software combination that is not the production environment.

production environment: also known as a live or operational environment.

References

Boulmetis J, Dutwin P. 2014. *ABCs of Evaluation: Timeless Techniques for Program and Project Managers.* San Francisco: Jossey-Bass. Accessed April 24, 2016. ProQuest ebrary.

Cabinet Office. 2014. Government security classifications. Accessed April 25, 2016. https://www.gov.uk/government/uploads/system/uploads/attachment_data/file/251480/Government-Security-Classifications-April-2014.pdf.

Capgemini. 2015. *Data masking with Capgemini using Informatica.* Accessed March 9, 2016. https//:www.uk.capgemini.com/resource-file-access/resource/pdf/data_masking_with_capgemini_using_informatica_5_0.pdf.

Carnegie Mellon University. 2013. Unintentional insider threats: A foundational study. Software Engineering Institute Technical Note CMU/SEI-2013-TN-022.

Cope J, Maglaras LA, Siewe F, Chen F, Janicke H. Forthcoming. Data leakage from non-production systems: A review. *Information and Computer Security.*

Cormode G, Srivastava D. 2009. Anonymized data: Generation, models, usage, pp. 1015–1018. In *Proceedings of the 2009 ACM SIGMOD International Conference on Management of Data.* New York: ACM.

Data Protection Act. 1998. (c. 29).

Deming WE. 1982. *Quality, Productivity and Competitive Position*, vol. 183. Cambridge, MA: Massachusetts Institute of Technology, Centre for Advanced Engineering Study.

DLA Piper. 2016. Data protection laws of the world. Accessed September 9, 2016. https://www.dlapiperdataprotection.com/index.html#handbook/law-section/c1_US.

Duncan G, Stokes L. 2009. Data masking for disclosure limitation. *WIREs Comp Stat* 1:83–92. doi:10.1002/wics.3.

European Commission. 2016. Press Release IP/16/216. EU Commission and United States agree on new framework for transatlantic data flows: EU-US Privacy Shield.

European Union Court of Justice. 2015. Press Release Memo/15/3802. Data Protection Day 2015: Concluding the EU Data Protection Reform essential for the Digital Single Market.

Evans M, Maglaras LA, He Y, Janicke H. 2016. Human behaviour as an aspect of cyber security assurance. arXiv preprint arXiv:1601.03921.

Fanadka K. 2015. 3 steps to building test databases for the real world. TechBeacon. Accessed November 25, 2015. http://techbeacon.com/3-steps-building-test-databases-real-world.

Feinberg J. 2014. *Wordle* [software] build #1458. Accessed April 2, 2016. http://www.wordle.net/.

Fiveash K. 2015. TalkTalk claims 157,000 customers were victims of security breach. *The Register.* Accessed March 9, 2016. http://www.theregister.co.uk/2015/11/06/talktalk_claims_157000_customers_data_stolen/.

Graham D, van Veenendaal E, Evans I. 2008. *Foundations of Software Testing: ISTQB Certification.* London: Cengage Learning EMEA.

Griffiths D, Griffiths D. 2016. *The Agile Sketchpad: Understanding Agile's Core Concepts and Methods* [DVD]. O'Reilly Media/.

Her Majesty's Government. 2015. Working together to safeguard children: A guide to inter-agency working to safeguard and promote the welfare of children. Accessed April 25, 2016. https://www.gov.uk/government/uploads/system/uploads/attachment_data/file/419595/Working_Together_to_Safeguard_Children.pdf.

Hoffer JA. 2013. *Modern Systems Analysis and Design.* 7th ed. Boston: Pearson.

Howard V. 2013. Using copies of "live" data in development and testing? Accessed November 24, 2015. https://www.grid-tools.com/using-copies-of-live-data-in-development-and-testing/.

Hurran C. 2014. Cyber insiders: A board issue. cybersecurity-review.com. Accessed March 9, 2016. http://swiftinstitute.org/wp-content/uploads/2014/11/2014-Cyber-Insiders-A-Board-Issue-Hurran.pdf.

Hutchinson W, Warren M. 2001. *Information Warfare: Corporate Attack and Defence in a Digital World.* London: Butterworth-Heinemann.

Informatica. 2011. Best practices for ensuring data privacy in production and nonproduction systems. Accessed March 9, 2016. https://www.informatica.com/downloads/6993_Data_Privacy_BestPractices_wp.pdf.

Information Commissioner's Office (ICO). 2015. Notice of Intent [PECR]. Accessed March 9, 2016. https://ico.org.uk/media/action-weve-taken/mpns/1432017/vodafone-mpn.pdf.

Information Commissioner's Office (ICO). 2016. Overview of the General Data Protection Regulation (GDPR): 12 steps to take now. Accessed November 30, 2016. https://ico.org.uk/media/for-organisations/data-protection-reform/overview-of-the-gdpr-1-1.pdf.

Information Commissioner's Office (ICO). n.d. Taking action—Data protection. Accessed March 9, 2016. https://ico.org.uk/about-the-ico/what-we-do/taking-action-data-protection/.

Lindner M, Galán F, Chapman C, Clayman S, Henriksson D, Elmroth E. 2010. The cloud supply chain: A framework for information, monitoring, accounting and billing. 2nd International ICST Conference on Cloud Computing (CloudComp 2010).

London School of Economics. 2013. Data classification policy. Accessed March 5, 2016. http://www.lse.ac.uk/intranet/LSEServices/policies/pdfs/school/infSecStaIT.pdf.

Machanavajjhala, Kifer D, Abowd J, Gehrke J, Vilhuber L. 2008. Privacy: Theory meets practice on the map, pp. 277–286. *IEEE 24th International Conference on Data Engineering*, Cancun, April.

Malhotra R. 2016. *Empirical Research in Software Engineering: Concepts, Analysis, and Applications.* Boca Raton, FL: CRC Press.

Mohanty S, Jagadeesh M, Srivatsa H. 2013. Extracting value from big data: In-memory solutions, real time analytics, and recommendation systems, pp. 221–250. In *Big Data Imperatives.* New York: Apress.

Muralidhar K, Sarathy R. 2006. Data shuffling: A new masking approach for numerical data. *Management Science* 52(5):658–670.

National Institute of Standards and Technology (NIST). 2010. Guide to Protecting the confidentiality of personally identifiable information (PII). Special Publication 800-122. Accessed March 9, 2016. http://csrc.nist.gov/publications/nistpubs/800-122/sp800-122.pdf.

National Institute of Standards and Technology (NIST). 2013. Glossary of key information terms, NISTIR-7298rev2.

National Institute of Statistical Sciences (NISS). n.d. Confidentiality: Data swapping. Accessed March 9, 2016. http://www.niss.org/research/confidentiality-data-swapping.

Open Data Center Alliance. 2013. Data security framework rev 1.0. Accessed March 9, 2016. http://www.opendatacenteralliance.org/docs/Data_Security_Framework_Rev1.0.pdf.

Oracle Corporation. 2013. Data masking best practice. Accessed March 9, 2016. http://www.oracle.com/us/products/database/data-masking-best-practices-161213.pdf.

PCI. 2014. PIN security requirements. Accessed March 9, 2016. https://www.pcisecuritystandards.org/documents/PCI_PIN_Security_Requirements_v2 Dec2014_b.pdf.

PCI. 2015. Payment Application Data Security Standard v3.1. Accessed March 9, 2016. https://www.pcisecuritystandards.org/documents/PA-DSS_v3-1.pdf.

PCI Security Standards Council. n.d. *PCI Security.* Accessed March 9, 2016. https://www.pcisecuritystandards.org/security_standards.

Raghunathan B. 2013. *The Complete Book of Data Anonymization: From Planning to Implementation.* Boca Raton, FL: CRC Press.

Reouse M. 2008. EU Data Protection Directive (Directive 95/46/EC). Accessed March 9, 2016. http://searchsecurity.techtarget.co.uk/definition/EU-Data-Protection-Directive.

Securosis. 2012. Understanding and selecting data masking solutions: Creating secure and useful data. Accessed March 9, 2016. https://securosis.com/assets/library/reports/Understanding DataMasking_WhitepaperV2.pdf.

Sherwood J, Clark A, Lynas D. 2015. *Enterprise Security Architecture: A Business-Driven Approach.* Boca Raton, FL: CRC Press.

Silowash GJ, Cappelli DM, Moore AP, Trzeciak RF, Shimeall T, Flynn L. 2012. Common sense guide to mitigating insider threats. 4th ed. Technical Report CMU/SEI-2012-TR-012.

Stempel J, Bose N. 2015. Target in $39.4 million settlement with banks over data breach. Reuters. Accessed March 9, 2016. http://uk.reuters.com/article/us-target-breach-settlement-idUKK BN0TL20Y20151203.

Sweeney L. 2002. k-anonymity: A model for protecting privacy. *International Journal on Uncertainty, Fuzziness and Knowledge-Based Systems* 10(5):557–570.

Symantec. 2015. Internet security threat report, vol. 20. Accessed March 9, 2016. https://www4 .symantec.com/mktginfo/whitepaper/ISTR/21347932_GA-internet-security-threat-report -volume-20-2015-social_v2.pdf.

Symantec. 2016. Internet security threat report, vol. 21. Accessed September 9, 2016. https://www .symantec.com/content/dam/symantec/docs/reports/istr-21-2016-en.pdf.

U.K. Department for Business, Innovation and Skills. 2015a. 2015 Information Security Breaches Survey. Ref: BIS/15/302.

U.K. Department for Business, Innovation and Skills. 2015b. Small businesses: What you need to know about cyber security. URN BIS/15/147.

U.K. Department of Health. 2013. The information governance review.

U.K. Department of Health. n.d. No secrets: Guidance on developing and implementing multi-agency policies and procedures to protect vulnerable adults from abuse. Accessed April 25, 2016. https://www.gov.uk/government/uploads/system/uploads/attachment_data/file/194272/No _secrets guidance_on_developing_and_implementing_multi-agency_policies_and_procedures _to_protect_vulnerable_adults_from_abuse.pdf.

Verizon. 2014. 2014 Data breach investigations report: Executive summary. Accessed March 9, 2016. http://www.verizonenterprise.com/DBIR/2014/reports/rp_dbir-2014-executive-summary_en _xg.pdf.

Voss WG. 2013. One year and loads of data later, where are we? An update on the proposed European Union General Data Protection Regulation. *Journal of Internet Law* 16(10).

Walliman N. 2011. *Research Methods: The Basics*. Abingdon, UK: Routledge. Accessed April 27, 2016. http://www.myilibrary.com?ID=304249.

Wilson RL, Rosen PA. 2003. Protecting data through "perturbation" techniques: The impact on knowledge discovery in databases. *Journal of Database Management* 14(2):14–26.

Zurko ME, Simon RT. 2011. Separation of duties, pp. 1182–1185. *Encyclopedia of Cryptography and Security*. HCA van Tilberg, S Jajodia (eds.). New York: Springer.

9

Big Data Acquisition, Preparation, and Analysis Using Apache Software Foundation Tools

Gouri Ginde, Rahul Aedula, Snehanshu Saha, Archana Mathur, Sudeepa Roy Dey, Gambhire Swati Sampatrao, and BS Daya Sagar

CONTENTS

Introduction

Challenges in Big Data analysis include data inconsistency, incompleteness, scalability, timeliness, and data security. The fundamental challenge is the existing computer architecture. For several decades, the latency gap between multicore CPUs and mechanical hard disks has increased each year, making the challenges of data-intensive computing harder to overcome (Hey et al. 2009). A systematic and general approach to these problems with a scalable architecture is required. Most of the Big Data is unstructured or of a complex structure, which is hard to represent in rows and columns. A good candidate for a large design space can efficiently solve the Big Data problem in different disciplines. This chapter highlights two specific objectives:

1. To introduce an efficient model, termed singular value decomposition (SVD), for complex computer experiments arising from Big Data which can be used across different scientific disciplines; and

2. To introduce optimization techniques and tools for handling Big Data problems.

Modern data-mining applications (Leskovec et al. 2011), often called Big Data analyses, require us to manage and analyze immense amounts of data quickly. Some examples work with "irregular" structures, and efficient solutions have been proposed using crowdsourcing (Agarwal et al. 2016a,b). However, many of these applications are endowed with extremely regular data, and there is ample opportunity to exploit parallelism. Here are a few examples:

- The ranking of Web pages by importance, which involves an iterated matrix-vector multiplication where the dimension is many billions.

- Searches in "friends" networks at social networking sites, which involve graphs with hundreds of millions of nodes and many billions of edges.

- The search for life on planets outside the solar System, which involves data analytics on massive data volumes generated from next-generation telescopes (Bora 2016).

To deal with such applications, a new software stack has evolved. These programming systems are designed to inherit their parallelism not from a supercomputer, but from "computing clusters," which are defined as large collections of commodity hardware, including conventional processors (computer nodes) connected by ethernet cables or inexpensive switches. The software stack begins with a new form of a file system, called a distributed file system, which features much larger units than the disk blocks in a conventional operating system. Distributed file systems also provide replication of data or redundancy, to protect against the frequent media failures that occur when data are distributed over thousands of low-cost computer nodes. On top of these file systems, many different higher-level programming systems have been developed. Central to the new software stack system is a programming system called MapReduce. Implementations of MapReduce and many other projects from Apache Software Foundation (ASF) provide path-breaking software programs for data-intensive problem solving. ASF projects enable large-scale data operations using computing clusters efficiently in a manner that is tolerant of hardware failures during the computation.

Apache has been a powerful contributor to the open source ecosystem. ASF has been home to numerous important open source software projects from its inception in 1999 (Web API 2017), as an all-volunteer international foundation with more than 350 leading open source projects, including the Apache HTTP server, the world's most popular Web server software. Through the ASF meritocratic process, known as The Apache Way, more than 620 individual members and 5,500 committee members successfully collaborate to develop freely available enterprise-grade software that benefits millions of users worldwide; thousands of software solutions are distributed under the Apache license, and the community actively participates in ASF mailing lists, mentoring initiatives, and ApacheCon, the foundation's official user conference, training, and exposition. The ASF is a U.S. 501(c)(3) charitable organization, funded by individual donations and corporate sponsors, including Alibaba Cloud Computing, ARM, Bloomberg, Budget Direct, Cerner, Cloudera, Comcast, Confluent, Facebook, Google, Hortonworks, Hewlett-Packard, Huawei, IBM, InMotion Hosting, iSigma, LeaseWeb, Microsoft, OPDi, PhoenixNAP, Pivotal, Private Internet Access, Produban, Red Hat, Serenata Flowers, WANdisco, and Yahoo. There are currently 300+ open source initiatives at the ASF. Of these initiatives, 225 projects use Java. Thirty-six are Big Data-related projects, and 12 are Cloud-related projects. The success story of ASF ranges from Geronimo and Tomcat to Hadoop, the distributed computing system that now serves as a lynchpin of the Big Data realm.

The Hadoop project is all the rage these days and is synonymous with Big Data, in which enterprises and Web properties sift through reams of data to reveal insights about customers and users. Hadoop provides an operating system for distributed computing. "If you want to run computations on hundreds of thousands of computers instead of just on one, Hadoop lets you do that," says Doug Cutting, a primary contributor to Hadoop for several years. Hadoop originated from the Nutch Web software project in 2006. Companies like Cloudera and HortonWorks are building businesses around Hadoop.

This chapter provides a description of basic methods of Big Data gathering, curation, and analysis with an example. Figure 9.1 shows the overall flow of the chapter. We discuss the data acquisition methods and various methodologies of data gathering, and we explore the data-curing and preprocessing methods in the Big Data paradigm. Finally, the last section will focus on data analysis. We will briefly introduce data visualization and Apache Foundation projects which may help in processing and representing Big Data.

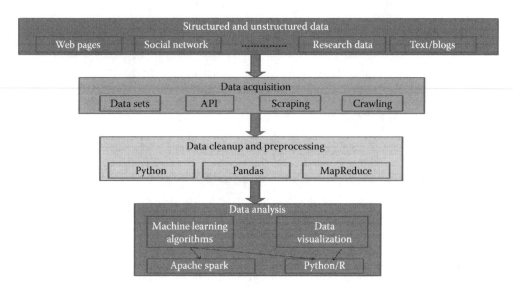

FIGURE 9.1
Overall flow of the chapter.

Data Acquisition

For any data-related project, the critical step is to chart the blueprint of the expected end result and the stages of reaching those goals through a data tunnel. Data accumulation is the first milestone in that direction. Data collection (Shukla 2014) is arguably as important as the data analysis step to extrapolate results and form valid claims which may be generalized. It is a scientific pursuit; therefore, great care must be taken to ensure unbiased and representative sampling. There isn't much to analyze without data, and the data collection step demands careful observation of the techniques laid out to build a formidable corpus. There are various ways to harness data once the problem to be solved has been decided. Information can be described as structured, unstructured, or sometimes a mix of the two, i.e., semistructured. In a very general sense, structured data are anything that can be parsed by an algorithm. Common examples include JSON, CSV, and XML. Provided any structured data, we may design a piece of code to dissect the underlying format and easily produce useful results. As mining structured data is a deterministic process, it allows us to automate the parsing. This, in effect, lets us gather more input to feed to data analysis algorithms. Unstructured data comprise everything else and are defined in a specified manner. Written languages such as English are often regarded as unstructured because of the difficulty in parsing a data model out of a natural sentence. In our search for good data, we often find a mix of structured and unstructured text. This is called semistructured text. This recipe will primarily focus on obtaining structured and semistructured data from the following sources. However, this list is not at all exhaustive.

Freely Available Sources of Data Sets

There are a number of nonprofit or nongovernmental organizations, government websites, and other places which host data sets available for download for free. Some examples are the following websites.

- http://pesitsouthscibase.org/datacenter provides scholarly article data sets that are mined from authentic websites, such as those of ACM, IEEE, Springer, etc., and organized and fed into scientific computing exercises.
- https://aws.amazon.com/datasets/, the Amazon public data sets on AWS, provide a centralized repository of public data sets that can be seamlessly integrated into AWS Cloud-based applications. AWS hosts the public data sets at no charge for the community, and like all AWS services, users pay only for the computing and storage they use for their own applications.
- https://www.kaggle.com/datasets, Kaggle releases data sets and provides a platform for predictive modeling and analytics competitions. On this website, companies and researchers post their data in the form of data sets that are available for free to all statisticians and data miners from all over the world to compete and produce the best models.
- http://data.worldbank.org/, this is a World Bank data repository which is the source of data regarding poverty and world development. It is a free source that enables open access to data about development in countries around the globe.

Data Collection through Application Programming Interfaces

Many governments collect a lot of data, and some are now offering access to these data. The interfaces through which these data are typically made accessible are Web application programming interfaces (APIs). Web APIs allow access to data, such as budget, public works, crime, legal, and other agency data, by any developer in a convenient manner. The United States is one of the pioneers in allowing government data be open for public use through the portal Data.gov, the central site for U.S. Government data (Wang et al. 2015). Following are a few more examples of websites that provide API-based data access.

- https://developers.facebook.com/docs/graph-api
- https://dev.twitter.com/
- http://api.altmetric.com/

Web Scraping

Web scraping is a website-specific data acquisition method, where a program is written to read the website's HTML page and decode the HTML tags of a web page to extract the data of interest. Web scraping represents a very superficial mode of web crawling, and the data source can be anything for the scraping task.

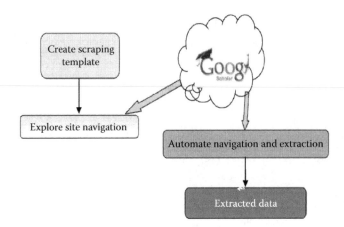

FIGURE 9.2
Web scraping for data acquisition from the Google Scholar website.

Figure 9.2 demonstrates the essential components of the web-scraping methodology (Ginde et al. 2015, 2016). DOM parsing is the philosophy which assists the system with retrieving element content created by client-side scripts by utilizing undeniable Web program controls, for example, the Internet Explorer browser or the Mozilla browser control. These programs control similar parsed Web pages into a DOM tree, in light of which program can recover parts of the pages.

Create the Scraping Template

Inspect Element is a developer's tool that allows views of the HTML, CSS, and JavaScript that is currently on a Web page. One may right click and select "inspect element" on practically every Web page. This will pull up the developers console to view the HTML and CSS of the Web page.

Explore Site Navigation

In order to explore and understand the website's navigation for dynamic URL formulation and data extraction, the Beautiful Soup parser library package developed in Python can be used. The Beautiful Soup parser is also called an elixir, and Tonic is the screen-scraper's friend. It uses a pluggable XML or HTML parser to analyze a possibly invalid document into a tree representation. It also provides methods and pythonic idioms that make it easy to navigate, search, and modify the parse tree.

Automate Navigation and Extraction

Python is a scripting language which is easy to learn and equipped with powerful programming interfaces. Python interpreter library is freely available in source and binary forms for all major platforms.

Web Crawling

The internet is the only data source for Web crawling, and this task is similar to what Google performs. Web crawling is essentially what search engines do. It's all about viewing a page as a whole and indexing it. When a bot crawls a website, it goes through every page and every link, to the last line of the website, looking for any information. Web crawling is mostly harmless. Crawling usually refers to dealing with large data sets where one develops crawlers (or bots) which crawl to the deepest of a Web page. Nutch crawler is one such open source crawler which is widely used. One can use one or a combination of various data accumulation methods to gather useful data. These accumulated data need to be tidied up for any further processing, which necessitates data preprocessing and cleanup.

Data Preprocessing and Cleanup

Data can be structured, unstructured, or semistructured. Structured database management is accomplished in two stages. In the first stage, data are stored in a schema-based manner; this storage is known as a relational database. The stored data are queried via query-based data retrieval in the second stage. In order to manage large-scale structured data sets, data warehouses and data marts are widely used approaches. A data mart handles data that belong to a unit or operation of an organization. Conversely, a data warehouse is not limited to a particular department; it represents the database of a complete organization. Unstructured data are generally nonrelational. NoSQL databases are widely used in storing massive-scale unstructured data. NoSQL databases focus on the scalability of data storage with high performance. They are also schemaless, which enables applications to quickly modify the structure of data without any need to write operation queries on multiple tables, as opposed to relational schema-based databases.

Irrespective of the type of data, preprocessing of the data is necessary before they are stored. Data in the raw form, called raw data, might not always be lucid for interpretation. It is not always possible to directly start analyzing data in its native construct. Data curation and preprocessing are aimed at data discovery and retrieval, data quality assurance, value addition, reuse, and preservation over time (Chen and Zhang 2014). Raw data may contain a lot of inconsistencies, duplicate entries, and redundancies. Data preprocessing and cleanup is performed to eliminate all of these and make the data more palpable for analysis and transformation. Data preparation is not just a first step; it also must be repeated many times over the course of analysis as new problems come to light or new data are collected. It is an iterative process. In case of ready data sets, there might be inconsistencies, such as incomplete fields or parameter values or special characters, etc. In the case of scraped data sets, the data might be in pure text format, a comma-separated values format, or JSON format. Such data might contain just long strings, which need further text processing, computation of parameters based on the various numerical values, a mere sorting of the data, or all of these, to extract the meaningful information for further analysis.

Preprocessing steps might vary from one data set to another data set. The complexity of any such data preprocessing operation increases with an added volume of raw data. Generally, massive-scale data in the crude form are voluminous and can be very messy to work with. It is essential to use the right kind of data tools to perform such preprocessing operations on a massive scale. The most challenging of these problems is the magnitude of the data. Most conventional methods use a higher specification system to contain all of the data in a single computing system. The drawback with this approach is the exponential increase in cost and complexity. Alternatively, we can resort to cluster computation, which provides a foolproof solution for massive-scale computations. Cluster-based frameworks, like Apache Hadoop MapReduce, are the next biggest step to achieve such high efficiency. The use of clusters significantly improves the ease of processing voluminous data, reduces the overhead of preprocessing on a single system, and instead utilizes a collective set of machines to perform cleanup in a comparatively short time. Voluminous tasks are divided into several smaller tasks, which are then assigned to machines of the cluster to produce the collective final output at the end. Python and R are the other preferred tools used to perform cleanup. These tools don't have a significant use of clusters for load reduction, but their use of in-memory computation and an eclectic collection of libraries makes them very favorable to handle the data at a reasonable velocity. Tools like Apache Spark try to integrate scalability and in-memory computation features into a single framework to maximize efficiency. Appendix 1 of this chapter provides additional information related to Apache Spark's architecture.

The next concern is the removal of noise in the data. Noise removal refers to the deletion of any unwanted part of the data to prepare the data set for further analysis and decision making. Almost all languages discussed in this chapter are capable of performing data preprocessing tasks.

Need for Hadoop MapReduce and Other Languages for Big Data Preprocessing

Data in the raw form do not provide any value. As shown in Figure 9.3, raw data need to be processed and transformed into a readable structure which can be further processed. Accomplishing this by using some algorithms to draw inferences is a daunting task. Preparing a volume of data to run through algorithms is the most time-consuming task of the complete data processing tunnel. For preprocessing tasks, we can use batch processing frameworks and languages to ease the work.

When to Choose Hadoop over Python or R

Data processing methods need close scrutiny of various aspects, such as the size of the data, size of RAM, language of choice, etc. If a data set ranges in the few gigabytes

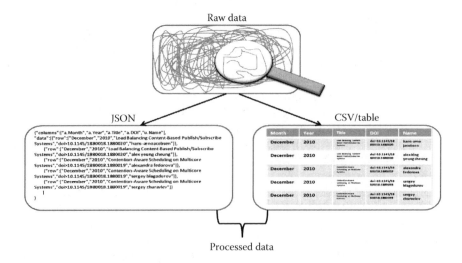

FIGURE 9.3
Transformation from raw data to processed data.

(GB; medium scale) with a RAM size 4 or 8 GB, preference should be given to use of scripting languages, such as R and Python. Moreover, if these data are structured, i.e., in CSV format, tabular format, or any format that can be converted to CSV, then R, Python, or even Java can be agreeably used. For advanced data analytics of medium-scale data, one can use Python's machine-learning library, Scikit-learn, or R. For data visualization, online tools such as Tableu and Plotly can give quick visual results for medium-scale data.

Conversely, when data are unstructured and range from a few hundred GBs to tera-bytes, hexabytes, or a few petabytes, a distributed computing methodology, such as Hadoop MapReduce or PIG can be used, as this volume of data cannot be contained in standard RAM size for processing. Hadoop uses a distributed computing methodology with a clustered and fault-tolerant storage mechanism. This provides a robust solution for the batch mode of data processing. It is important to understand the advantages and disadvantages of various languages for efficient processing of medium-scale and massive-scale data.

Comparison of Hadoop MapReduce, Python, and R

Hadoop MapReduce is a programming mechanism which is used for batch processing of large data sets, where the data are split into blocks and distributed to all the available nodes for parallel computation. This has proven to be an effective model in solving the Big Data problem, because of its ability to utilize the Hadoop Distributed File System (HDFS). The Hadoop file system is a distributed file system which stores data in data nodes that are scattered across a cluster. The metadata are maintained by the name node, which is also a master node. To increase fault tolerance, a single data block is replicated three times by default. This feature provides robust fault tolerance, as data loss is immediately handled by one of the replicas. MapReduce splits the tasks into mapper and reducer functions. The mapper first maps all the similar elements of the data set and sends the results to a temporary data file; the reducer reads from this file and performs the computations on these separated data sets. This use of parallelization makes Hadoop MapReduce more effective than most other tools in terms of how the data are handled and also shows efficiency on large volumes of data.

Python is a general purpose programming language created for easy readability. Python's biggest strength lies in its eclectic collection of libraries to perform various tasks, such as data extraction, text processing, and machine learning algorithms. It is a widely supported programming language today. In the context of data analysis, Python provides a lot of built-in packages and frameworks, such as Pandas, Scipy, Scikit-learn, and Numpy. These make data preprocessing and analysis an easy task, but scalability poses a serious issue. Python's performance for large batch processing doesn't make it a favorable tool. Since most of the analysis tasks and computations take place in-memory, its performance drastically degrades data compared to a distributed system, when data are massively scaled.

R language was designed from a statistical point of view. Its primary focus is to bolster mathematical modeling and to help create analytical prototypes. R provides a less convoluted route to access many machine learning and mathematical functions. However, from the data analysis and data processing prospective, R is comparatively slow in performance versus its rival Python and also the aforementioned Apache Hadoop. The use of a cluster to achieve parallelization in Hadoop and the faster in-memory computation of Python make them much more dominant for such data-related tasks.

Cleansing Methods and Routines

Data cleansing is a highly iterative process which completely depends on the type of data at hand. In this section, we focus on text data, which is in the JSON structure. We will first provide the generic cleansing operations on a test data set and then provide an example of a Hadoop MapReduce-based solution for the same data set. This exercise will help readers understand how the data cleansing prototype, developed for a small data set, scales up for batch processing of voluminous data.

Table 9.1 shows sample data scraped using Web-scraping methodology. This sample contains the affiliations of the authors of the various scholastic articles which belong to a journal. Some authors have multiple affiliations. The data cleansing on this data set involves the following operations:

- Elimination of extra spaces, such as tab, newline, etc.
- Strip or truncate the unwanted characters suffixed and postfixed, such as #, ;, etc.
- Encode the text using UTF-8 encoder just to be careful about the unicode characters, if any.
- Process the affiliation string (the address string) and disintegrate into university and country names. All these operations can be performed iteratively or in a single iteration. Table 9.2 shows the output after processing.

TABLE 9.1

Sample Data Obtained Using Web-Scraping Methodology

Author: Beth A. Reid Affiliation: Institute of Space Sciences (CSIC-IEEC), UAB, Barcelona 08193, Spain
Author: Daniel J. Eisenstein Affiliation: Steward Observatory, University of Arizona, 933 N. Cherry Ave., Tucson, AZ 85121, USA
Author: David N. Spergel Affiliation: Department of Astrophysical Sciences, Princeton University, Princeton, NJ 08544, USA
Author: Ramin A. Skibba Affiliation: Max-Planck-Institute for Astronomy, Knigstuhl 17, D-69117 Heidelberg, Germany

TABLE 9.2

Output of Content of Table 9.1 after Processing

Author: Beth A. Reid University: Institute of Space Sciences Country: Spain
Author: Daniel J. Eisenstein University: University of Arizona Country: USA
Author: David N. Spergel University: Princeton University Country: USA
Author: Ramin A. Skibba Institute: Max-Planck-Institute for Astronomy Country: Germany

TABLE 9.3

Sample MapReduce Pseudo Code for Massive Scale Processing

```
map(String key, String value)
//key: Journal name
//value: Journal contents; All the article's authors and affiliation information
 for each sentence S in value
  EmitIntermediate(key, S)

reduce(String key, String values):
//key: some random number
//values: Author or Affiliation information
 if values contain 'Author' :
 result += TextOperation(values);
 else:
     result += TextOperation and UniversityInfo(v);
 Emit(AsString(result));
```

Cleansing operations like these can be easily translated into MapReduce jobs or PIG scripts. The operations explained above are mutually exclusive operations; hence, massively scaled data can be easily run through these algorithms in batches.

Table 9.3 is the MapReduce pseudo code to get the above output for massive scale data.

Note that in-depth source code, instructions to load the data to HDFS, and aggregation commands to demonstrate the final output are beyond the scope of this chapter. These can be looked up easily in the book, *Hadoop: The Definitive Guide* by Tom White.

When data are in the form of flat files or compressed files or in different formats, one has to give more effort to bring the data into a format or structure that can be understood by a programming and/or scripting language for further processing. Next, we elaborate on these challenges and the solutions offered by contenders of Big Data processing.

Loading Data from Flat Files

Loading data with these respective tools differs significantly, as Hadoop and Python interpret and analyze data in different ways. As mentioned earlier, Hadoop uses a cluster-based approach, and Python uses an in-memory approach to process data. The corresponding input formats are accordingly tailored to suit the processing methodology.

Hadoop in Java provides various categories of input format for structured data. It can process the data or files only when they are mounted on the HDFS. HDFS is a specialized system designed to exploit cluster computing. Hadoop can process only flat files as of now. Apache POI and HSSF Java libraries can be used to read and write to Excel files. JDHF5 can be used to read and write to HDF5 format files. Official Hadoop supports for Excel and HDF5 are yet to be provided.

Reading and writing to a database by using Hadoop MapReduce can be tedious and cumbersome. Data warehousing also becomes difficult due to similar problems. Solutions for these probelms are to use Apache community-developed Sqoop and Hive. Sqoop is a tool built for Hadoop and is used to transfer contents from a traditional relational database (RDBMS), such as MySQL (Oracle) to a NoSQL-type database, such as HBase, Hive, etc. Sqoop works by spawning tasks on multiple data nodes to download various portions of the data in parallel. Each piece of data is replicated to ensure reliability and fault tolerance for parallel processing on a cluster. This can be easily accomplished by specifying a JDBC connection between RDBMS.

TABLE 9.4

Sqoop Commands to Import Data from RDBMS

```
sqoop import-all-tables \
  -m 1 \
  --connect jdbc:mysql://quickstart:3306/mydata_db \
  --username=ABC \
  --password=ABC123 \
  --compression-codec=snappy \
  --as-parquetfile \
  --warehouse-dir=/user/hive/warehouse \
  --hive-import
```

The Sqoop import command can be used to read data from an RDBMS and an export command to transfer data from Hadoop to an RDBMS. The parallel execution feature of Sqoop boosts the processing performance when a database is voluminous. For example, Table 9.4 shows the commands to import data from an RDBMS:

To export data, we would use the corresponding export command. This helps to integrate the data into a SQL-free format.

Python, on the other hand, is built from an eclectic collection of libraries, so it has a lot of native support for almost all the data formats. Depending on the type of operation, one can use a wide variety of ways to load the different formats of data. For example, if Numpy is used for matrix manipulations, then the built-in commands, like loadtxt(), can be utilized to load the flat files. If a library like Pandas is used, the file can be read using pd.read_csv (). Similarly, to write corresponding save operations, savetxt () and to_csv () can be used. For data formats like Excel files and HDF5, Python provides a number of libraries, such as xlrd, openpyxl for Excel, and h5py for HDF5.

Loading data from databases can be done using the MYSQLdb API. It supports a wide variety of databases, such as MySQL, Oracle, and Sybase. This API can be used to run queries and extract the required data if necessary. Python also provides other libraries, such as pymysql and oursql, to perform similar tasks.

Merging and Joining Data Sets

Merging data refers to concatenation of the two different data sets composed of either the same or different structures. It is generally done to eliminate redundancy and to effectively store similar data in one data set. The methods of merging data sets vary based on the type and structure of the data. Hadoop stores all data in the HDFS, so the data can be accessed and manipulated by various Apache Foundation software, such as Hive and Pig. Data sets can be directly modified by using the Hadoop built-in framework MapReduce. However, performing such tasks can be tedious and convoluted when MapReduce alone is used. Hive is integrated with SQL and helps in simplifying this task, because SQL not only makes it easy to use but also utilizes MapReduce in the background, thus making it much more efficient. In order to reap the benefits of Hive and MapReduce, data should be voluminous and the number of nodes in the cluster should be proportional to handle the massive data efficiently. So, usage of Hive to perform merging and joining of data sets is the ideal choice.

This can be done by using the UNION ALL command, a simplified syntax to join two tables from the Hive warehouse into one single resultant table, as shown in Table 9.5.

TABLE 9.5

The UNION ALL Command To Merge Data Sets

```
SELECT *
FROM (
select_statement // Select condition 1 from the first table
UNION ALL
select_statement // Select condition 2 from the second table
) unionResult
```

The command spawns a set of MapReduce tasks in the background which collectively query the data, gather the necessary result, and join the end result into one single table. The command can also utilize various other clauses, like order by, sort by, cluster by, etc. These clauses will refine the results and aid quality merge by reducing any type of redundancy. Figure 9.4 shows one such sample-merging operation.

Python can also achieve the same results by using its abundant libraries. If data merging is to be done at the database level, then MySQLdb can be used. The query is similar to a Hive query, where UNION query can be made using the previously mentioned API and then the tables can be merged and updated. To perform even more intricate operations, join commands like inner join, left join, and right outer join can also be utilized, which will yield more refined results.

Pandas, a Python package, uses a different merging technique. The data are stored in files and, based on requirements, data are retrieved into memory and required actions are performed. Interestingly, data are not stored in a conventional database but rather within the files themselves. The data are retrieved subsequently into memory, and required analysis tasks are performed.

For example, in Pandas, let us assume that there are two data frames which are similar to the tables in Figure 9.4. The instructions from Table 9.6 have be executed to merge these two tables.

Pandas has been the leading package used in Python for data analysis because of its ease of use and its flexibility in handling the data. Although not suitable for large voluminous data, Python utilizes its in-memory capacity for analyzing data with high efficiency, making Python suitable to handle small- or mid-sized data sets.

X	Y	Z
X0	Y0	Z0
X1	Y1	Z1

X	Y	Z
X2	Y2	Z2
X3	Y3	Z3

X	Y	Z
X0	Y0	Z0
X1	Y1	Z1
X2	Y2	Z2
X3	Y3	Z3

FIGURE 9.4
Sample-merging operation.

TABLE 9.6

Pandas Code Snippet to Merge Data Frames

```
df1 = pd.DataFrame({'X': ['x0', 'x1'],
'Y': ['Y0', 'Y1'],
'Z': ['Z0', 'Z1']}
index=[0, 1, 2])
df2 = pd.DataFrame({'X': ['x2', 'x3'],
'Y': ['Y2', 'Y3'],
'Z': ['Z2', 'Z3']}
index= [0, 1, 2])
merge1 = [df1, df2]
result = pd.concat(merge1)
```

Query the Data

Querying data usually refers to extraction of results, which are computed based on several operations on the data set. Generally, querying the data operations range from displaying information to making charts for visualization. Python and Hadoop operate very similarly in terms of implementation when display of information is concerned. Hadoop's output is stored in a directory of HDFS and it can be shifted to the local file system when required. Hadoop can utilize Hive's service for a better-quality query result. Hive. as mentioned earlier, typically works in the same fashion as a standard database, so the query results can be obtained just by running the Select command in Hive. One can specify the parameters and the required query conditions (such as Where, Order by Cluster by) and can obtain a result appropriately. Other queries include insertion and deletion of records from a database, and they too can be executed by using the appropriate commands. like Insert, etc. Hive is usually preferred when handling data in Hadoop because it maintains data in a readable format.

Other tools, such as PIG, can also be used to achieve these results. In juxtaposition, Python can query from databases similarly by utilizing the MYSQLdb API and furnish the same results. It is important to note that query capabilities of Python are highly dependent on the memory at its disposal. Functions such as fetchall () yield good results to retrieve the data present in rows. Similarly, one can interact with the database with other queries as well. For example, insertion and updating the database also can be done by first using the regular SQL query and executing the API query function. However, when using packages like Pandas in Python, we can improvise a number of ways to query the data. Similarly, for an insert operation, Pandas has a pd.DataFrame.insert () function, which helps in inserting a certain value to a specified position. Similarly, for all other operation it has its respective functions. Depending on the choice of package, there are different functions for different query operations. Nevertheless, Python provides versatility compared to Hadoop, because it is tightly coupled with the data, rendering some flexibility for easier manipulations compared to Hadoop. Selecting one of the various methods or a combination of methods provides a near-perfect solution for efficient preprocessing, which paves the crucial foundation for a solid analysis.

Data Analysis

Once data are accumulated and cured to a desired level, we may proceed to perform analysis, which is the most interesting stage of the complete process. Data analysis refers to the meticulous examination of data to determine any useful results or changes. The analysis process on the data could be operations such as estimation, reductions, etc. Each process trying to extract a specific result can help in making informed decisions and give other important inferences of significant value concurrently. The tools which perform data analysis have to keep up with the variety and volume of the data. The quality of the results of analysis depends on the type of methods used and the effective use of the tools. These various analysis operations could be as simple as counting occurrences to as intensive as machine learning algorithms, such as regression and forest ensemble (Mitchell 1997). The characteristic to efficiently obtain results within the given finite resources makes it the superior form of data analysis. It is said that 2.5 quintillion bytes of data are created every day, and most of the data generated are subjected to different forms of analysis. It is absolutely imperative to optimize the resource consumption while analyzing such heavy loads of data of so much variety and velocity. But the ultimate goal is to obtain results which give us a decision theoretic advantage over another scenario. Apache Foundation projects have consistently evolved on this front and have shown promising results so far.

Big Data Analysis Using Apache Foundation Tools

Big Data analysis using machine learning is often misunderstood in a convoluted sense. It simply refers to the use of various algorithms that make prudent choices to ensure a more accurate result. The nature of the data at hand and the expected results from data analytics are the primary driving factors for selection of a machine learning algorithm. The structure of data can be explained using factors such as format, variance in the data, accuracy, and volume. Also, it is important to find out if the data are linearly separable. For example, if the expected result is to effectively store a large matrix, then one would prefer using dimensionality reduction, such as principal component analysis (PCA), and the knowledge discovery paradigm, such as singular value decomposition.

Machine learning is slowly taking over the data analysis platform as data, when examined for results, are no longer dependent on the old, trivial ways for solutions. The present state of data is much more complex, which not only refers to the volume but also the finer details that it contains. It is imperative to use more refined algorithms to not only analyze the current state of data but also have a prudent approach to the upcoming data. This gives an edge over traditional analysis methods and boosts the effort in the search for the ideal estimation methods to give the best results.

Various Language Support via Apache Hadoop

Hadoop MapReduce is conventionally written in Java. This has forced data analysts, who are trying to use Hadoop, to learn Java. However, in order to eliminate this inconvenience, Apache developers introduced Hadoop streaming, a feature of Apache Hadoop which supports MapReduce code in any language, provided that the language has a model to handle standard input (stdin) and standard output (stdout). This support allows use of an array of scripting languages, such as Python, Scala, etc., to perform MapReduce tasks. The biggest advantage of Hadoop streaming is not just the eclectic languages, which can be used, but also the libraries and packages that are associated with them. For example, Python is filled with diverse libraries, such as Numpy and Scipy, etc., which can be used along with MapReduce to give better choices in terms of the task execution. Reading from different formats, which are not supported by Hadoop, is also temporarily solved as one can use the corresponding libraries of those languages to extract from those formats.

Although this results in a proportional increase in time with the increase in the data size, it presents a temporary fix for the problem.

Apache Spark for Big Data Analytics

Apache Spark is the latest addition to the cluster computation family (Ryza et al. 2015, Apache Spark™—Lightning-fast cluster computing n.d.). It not only claims lightning-fast computation but also shows prudent promise in efficient RAM utilization compared to any other previously discussed frameworks. Apache Spark originated at the UC Berkeley AMPLab. It is an open source framework. Spark combines an engine for distributing programs across clusters of machines with an elegant model for writing programs atop it. Spark has been contributed to the Apache Software Foundation, which is arguably the first open source software that makes distributed programming truly accessible to data scientists. Spark (Ryza et al. 2015, Spark 2015) maintains MapReduce linear scalability and fault tolerance but extends it in three important ways.

1. Unlike MapReduce, which writes intermediate results to the distributed file system, Spark can pass them directly to the next step in the pipeline, i.e., Spark's engine can execute a more general directed acyclic graph of operators, rather than relying on a rigid map-then-reduce format.

2. It supplements this ability with rich transformations that empower developers to express computations all the more actually. It has a solid engineer center and streamlined API that can speak to complex pipelines in a couple of lines of code.

3. Spark extends MapReduce with in-memory processing. This ability opens up use cases that distributed processing engines could not previously approach. Spark is well suited for algorithms that require multiple passes over a data set, such as profoundly iterative or linear algorithms, as well as interactive applications that require scanning of large in-memory data sets in order to quickly respond to user queries.

Hence, machine learning algorithms that make multiple passes over their training set can cache it in memory. Data scientists can keep data set in memory while exploring and getting a feel for it; they can run queries and easily cache transformed versions of it without suffering a trip to disk. Spark supports a variety of tools that already exist in the Hadoop ecosystem. It can read and write data in all of the data formats supported by MapReduce. This allows Spark to interact with the formats commonly used to store data on Hadoop, such as Avro and Parquet (and good old CSV). It can also read from and write to NoSQL databases, like HBase and Cassandra.

1. *Spark programming model*

   As shown in the Figure 9.5, Spark programming starts with a data set which resides in some form of distributed and persistent storage, like HDFS (Maniyam 2015). A typical Spark program consists of the following steps:
   - Specify the transformations on the provided data
   - Call the functions to generate outputs and return the results to the local memory or persistent storage
   - Execute the local operations on the results generated by distributed computing; based on these results, the next set of actions are determined.

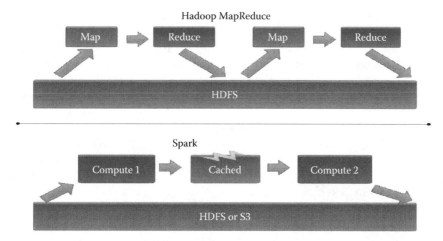

FIGURE 9.5
Comparison of Hadoop and Spark data-processing pipelines. *Source*: White, T., *Hadoop: The Definitive Guide*, 3rd ed., 2012.

Understanding Spark means understanding the intersection between the two sets of abstractions of the framework: storage and execution. Spark pairs these abstractions in an elegant way that essentially allows any intermediate step in a data processing pipeline to be cached in memory for later use.

2. *Resilient distributed data set*

Spark uses a resilient distributed data set (RDD) to achieve full performance efficiency. An RDD is nothing but partitioned data, a chunk of data which is fault tolerant, easily parallelizable, and immutable. Apache Spark has been the leading software to perform much more efficiently in juxtaposition with the other software that were mentioned above. Its use of the RDD makes very high utilization of RAM and the cache, such that it is able to tackle Big Data with a much more efficient approach. The fast access of the data stored in the cache and the use of RDD in coalition with the involvement of a cluster makes this the most relevant Big Data framework for data analysis. In addition, Apache Spark has a collection of a wide variety of machine learning algorithms which take advantage of the RDD mechanism and the cluster to provide better results than with any other tool in this genre.

Case Study: Dimensionality Reduction Using Apache Spark, an Illustrative Example from Scientometric Big Data

Scientometrics is the study of measuring and analyzing science, technology, and innovation. It is a method for differentiating quality from quantity. Scientometrics deals with the measurement of the impacts of journals and institutes, understanding of scientific citations, mapping of scientific fields, and production of indicators for use in policy and management contexts. The implosion of journals and conference proceedings in the science and technology domain, coupled with the insistence of different rating agencies and academic institutions for use of journal metrics for evaluation of scholarly contributions, present a Big Data accumulation and analysis problem. The motivation of this project proposal originated from the paradox that the research community faces today, which is "need versus greed." The otherwise-noble insight to build and maintain citation-based indices and to endorse all scientists and researchers who have made major contributions in the advancement of research and development, attributed in impact factors, is being abused of late. The H-index, another highly known metric, is often misused and manipulated by the research community through practices like extensive self-citation, copious citation, and at the journal level, coercive citation, is no longer beyond doubt. There have been instances of misuse, where Editors-in-Chief of two high-impact factor journals were found to be publishing extensively not only in their own journals but also in each other's journals. The journals continue to demonstrate such a practice, undermining the dignity and integrity of the structure of scholarly publications. Another notable trend, followed opportunistically by editors of low-ranked journals, is to persuade authors to cite their journal articles with the ulterior motive of pushing impact factors. If one journal coerces authors to improve its rank, others gravitate to this action, and it becomes a trend that contaminates the whole publication process.

One possible solution could be penalizing the usage of self-citations, which might reduce, if not deter, the coercive motivation. Although a journal's prestige is reflected in its impact factor, the overall framework of measuring prestige and for that matter a journal's internationality demands a clear understanding and usage of deep-rooted parameters. Chooosing a set of smart indicators and, alternatively, defining new and unbiased ones is inevitable for measuring internationality. There exist several vague and unreliable indicators for the term internationality, and these are based on attributes such as like ISSN number, editorial board members, reviewers, authors, editors, publishers, and other associated entities within the publishing community. Authors refute such definitions and claim that internationality should be defined as a quantifiable metric, a measure of international spread and influence which is devoid of any kind of misuse or manipulation. It must remain unbiased towards the origin of the journal, author, or article and must calibrate journals on the basis of the quality of research output they publish. This case study intends to build and validate such models.

Why SVD? The Solution May Be the Problem

A section of academia is not very pleased with the use of scientometric indicators as the primary yardstick for faculty evaluations. There are theories that discredit the entire methodology, and they blame the "Publish or Perish" doctrine. The authors have been to discourses where Eugene Garfield, the father of Impact Factors, has been criticized, unfairly and relentlessly. There is some element of truth in the claims that the evaluation scheme is not fair; however, the premise that the field of scientometric analysis should not be taken seriously is a bit far-fetched. Scientometric indicators have become tools for survival and a weapon to attain glory. It is not the metric or the study of metrics; rather, it is a survival instinct and human greed that are responsible for importing uncertainty. So, incremental improvements and sophisticated modeling and evaluation methods are required in scientometric analysis, not the extremist recommendation of ignoring it altogether. The solutions presented by several scholastic investigations have proposed new metrics, such as NLIQ (a nonlocal influence quotient), OCQ (other citation quotient), internationality, cognizant citations, copious citations, diversity score, NGCR (nongenealogy citation score), NGCN (nongenealogy citation network), etc. (Ginde et al. 2015, 2016, Ginde 2016). However, given the huge corpus of articles published in several issues of a journal, published over a period of years, it is a daunting task of rating the articles. The task of scholarly value characterization by using a single metric is therefore a pragmatic way to address the issue of identifying article impact rather than exploring and computing several different metrics. SVD could thus turn out to be an effective way of achieving such a goal. After mining the massively scaled scholarly data via the Web-scraping methodology, we constructed a matrix where the rows represented the number of articles in a journal, published over a period of years and columns represented the different metrics proposed by experts and agencies wthin scientometrics. Clearly, the matrix is rectangular and computaion of eigenvalues, reliable indicators of the characteristics of an information matrix, is not possible. This justifies the motivation for exploiting SVD. This is a classic Big Data problem, with scientometric implications.

Need for SVD

The huge rectangular matrix, which represents the complete scholarly data set gathered using Web scraping, is the source of this case study. We have described the SVD method for visualization and representation of article data sets using a smaller number of variables. SVD also yields detection of patterns in an article information matrix. Since the matrix is humongous, we performed exploratory research and evaluated SVD computations by using MapReduce, Apache Mahout, and Apache Spark. Dimensionality reduction played a significant role in helping us ascertain results of analysis for this voluminous data set. The propensity to employ such methods is evident, because of the phenomenal growth of data and the velocity at which it is generated. Dimensionality reduction, such as singular value decomposition and PCA, solve such Big Data problems by means of extracting more prominent features and obtaining a better representational version of the data. The representative data set tends to be much smaller for storage and significantly easier to handle for further analysis. These dimensionality reduction methods are often found in the tools for handling large data sets, and are used to performing rigorous data analyses. These tools include Apache Mahout, Hadoop, Spark, R, and Python, to name a few. The ease of employing these tools is directly dependent on the performance of each one of these tools to compute, assess, and store the results efficiently, with optimal use of resources. SVD is a convoluted dimensionality reduction technique. It requires multiple steps that need to be performed in order to extract singular values and the following right and left singular vectors. Therefore, the capacity of a Big Data tool to perform such computations efficiently is a necessity.

SVD is a very useful tool, and it is used for almost every scientific discipline. For example, it can be used for efficiently simulating high-dimensional partial differential equations by taking all the data generated from the simulations, reducing the data dimensionality by throwing away some of the singular values, and then simulating the lower-dimensional system. SVD gives us an optimal low-rank representation. This fact guarantees that a previously explained sort of simulation preserves most of the details in a system, because getting rid of the extra modes (singular values) in the system is guaranteed to get rid of the least important modes. With a little variation, SVD is used everywhere from physics to machine learning for dimensionality reduction. In fact, the algorithm commonly known as PCA, for instance, is just a simple application of the singular value decomposition.

Relationship between Singular Values and the Input Matrix

The singular value decomposition (Kalman 1996, Golub and Van Loan 2012) takes an $m \times n$ matrix and returns three matrices that approximately equal it when multiplied together.

$$A \approx U\,DV^T$$

1. U is an $m \times k$ matrix whose columns form an orthonormal basis for the articles space.
2. D is a $k \times k$ diagonal matrix, each of whose entries correspond to the strength of one of the concepts. The values on the diagonal of D are called the singular values.
3. V is a $k \times n$ matrix whose columns form an orthonormal basis for the features parameters space.

The m-dimensional vectors making up the columns of U are called left singular vectors, whereas the n-dimensional vectors making up the columns of V are called right singular vectors. The set of left and set of right singular vectors are orthonormal (that is, both orthogonal and normal). Normality means that each singular vector is of unit length (length 1). A set of vectors is said to be orthogonal if any pair of vectors in the set is orthogonal; recall that vectors are orthogonal if and only if their product (equivalent to cosine) is 0.

For large matrices, usually we don't need the complete factorization but only the top singular values and associated singular vectors. This can save storage, and denoise and recover the low-rank structure of the matrix.

Suppose $D = \text{diag}\{\sigma_1, \sigma_2, \ldots, \sigma_n\}$; by convention, it is assumed that $\sigma_1 \geq \sigma_2 \geq \sigma_3 \geq \sigma_n \geq 0$. The values $\sigma_1, \sigma_2, \sigma_3,$ and σ_n are called the singular values of A. In other words, singular values are unique to a particular column in A, and they can be used to associate a relation, even if they are not arranged in descending order they can be used to obtain the A matrix back. This transformation itself doesn't solve dimensionality reduction; to completely be able to reduce dimensions, we must be able to decide the least significant singular values of the Σ matrix. Here, least significant values most often refer to the lowest values of the Σ matrix and then these equate to 0. In doing, so we retain the most prominent values and discard the least significant values that form the original matrix. When we put back the decomposed matrix to derive a new matrix, it will have reduced dimensions. To demonstrate this, we could assume the following:

$$\Sigma = \begin{bmatrix} \sigma1 & 0 & \ldots & 0 \\ 0 & \sigma2 & \ldots & \vdots \\ 0 & 0 & \ddots & 0 \\ 0 & 0 & \ldots & \sigma n \end{bmatrix}$$

So, on removing p least significant values or the lowest values of the singular values and equating them to 0, we have Σ':

$$\Sigma' = \begin{bmatrix} \sigma1 & 0 & \ldots & 0 \\ 0 & \sigma2 & \ldots & \vdots \\ 0 & 0 & \sigma(n-p) & 0 \\ 0 & 0 & \ldots & 0 \end{bmatrix}$$

Now, on recomposing the matrix using the newly formed Σ', we obtain a dimensionality reduced matrix. So,

$$U \; \Sigma' \; V^T = A'$$

where A' is the dimensional reduced matrix which has an order lesser than $m \times n$ ideally. In this manner, we can observe how SVD achieves dimensionality reduction and how we can manually set the least significant values or the lowest values of the Singular Values. For example, less values of p are used to ensure minimal information loss for a more precise and reduced matrix. Higher values of p are needed for a resultant matrix with relatively higher information loss and a greater degree of dimensionality reduced matrix, depending upon the use case.

SVD Using Hadoop Streaming with Numpy

The aforementioned use of various languages in Hadoop is termed Hadoop streaming. This feature showcases the flexibility of using different languages to achieve certain tasks more effectively. It uses API such that it interacts with the Unix standard streams as input and output, hence making it very suitable for large text batch processing (White 2012). First, in a MapReduce job the input is passed to the mapper as a standard input file. Hence, using the Numpy loadtxt function, we get the initialized array, which is fed to HDFS when the program is initialized. Next, we use a self-improvised method to pass the values from the mapper and reducer. Conventionally, Reduce works in a shuffle-and-sort fashion in order to segregate the data and process it line by line. Since we are using an array, sorting this could prove fatal, as the values of the matrix get interchanged. Thus, after the array is read from standard input, we initialize the key to 1.

For every row, the first column element is the key.

$$\text{Key} = \text{key} + 1$$

We fill the entire first column with the key values. Sorting the array doesn't change the orders of the original values. This provides an extra row of an arbitrary key value for solving the sort problem on MapReduce with arrays. Newly keyed values are sent to the reducer through standard output. Next, matrix sorting is stopped to enable the reducer to directly work on the dense matrix. Just like the mapper, the reducer also reads input from the standard input file written by the mapper. The reducer has essentially only one task before it starts to compute the singular values, which is to first dekey the array passed by the mapper, as it initially has a column of key elements in the first column. This is done in the first nested loop, where x[i][j] = a[i][j + 1]. Next, we shift the actual array within the key values to a new array which is going to be used for computing the values of the SVD. API provided by the Numpy library is used to compute the individual matrices of the SVD. The reason for using Numpy is its speed and accuracy in matrix manipulations. The corresponding data sets can be easily imported for other ML algorithms, as Numpy extensively supports ML on data sets. After finding the singular values, we observe that the following singular values appear in a single row and it does not retain its diagonal matrix form. However, since we need the singular values in their original form, we will transfer all the values to the diagonals of another arbitrary matrix so as to associate the following relationship later with the input matrix. We now print the following individual matrices of the singular valued decomposition: $A = U \Sigma V^T$.

Complexity of Using MapReduce

The following equations represent complexity of the mapper and reducer functions used for these computations. These complexity polynomials are derived from the code snippets sourced from github. The gist of the mapper and reducer codes outlines a few operations, such as reading the values line by line, keying the array, and then performing the SVD with the reducer.

For mapper: $6n^2 + 14n + 9$

For reducer: $7n^2 + 9n + 12 + A(n)$

$A(n)$ is the complexity polynomial of Numpy SVD function.

The following MapReduce operations take place sequentially, because the reduce function cannot start until we have the complete dense matrix. This implies that we have to wait for the mapper to pass the complete matrix to the reducer. The complexity will be the summation of the mapper and reducer results. Calculations yield $n \geq 23$.

By definition, $f(n) \leq c * O(n^2)$ and $13n^2 + 23n \in O(n^2) + A(n)$.

As mentioned above, $A(n)$ is the complexity polynomial of the Numpy SVD function. Figure 9.6 shows the complexity plot of these two functions. The results show that using MapReduce alongside Python might be easy, but the complexity of performing this task is not ideal. We note that after a certain cardinality of dimensions, this method is known to fail for much larger matrices (Ding et al. 2011).

SVD Using Apache Mahout

Apache Mahout is an open source project that is primarily used in producing scalable machine learning algorithms and also to perform complex matrix operations given a large

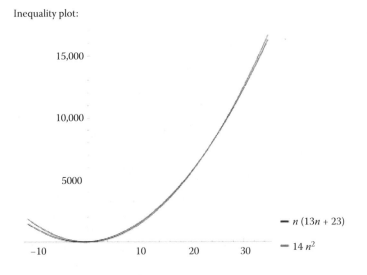

FIGURE 9.6
Complexity plot.

data set (Owen 2012). Apache Mahout depends heavily on the use of HDFS and the Hadoop ecosystem in general, as its main focus is on performing intensive distributed machine learning on commodity hardware. This is considered an advantage, as most other tool kits require highly configured hardware to perform similar operations. Mahout allows for these computations in a distributed environment. It enables performance of such tasks in spite of the greater complexity of the computations involving Big Data. The next section showcases the performance and accuracy of Apache Mahout's singular value decomposition function over a voluminous data set.

Generating Sequence Files for Mahout

Apache Mahout requires a very specific type of input in order to process any operation. Apache Mahout utilizes sequence files. A sequence file is essentially a binary file which contains data in a key–value pair formation. Usually, Hadoop uses sequence files as a part of its intermediate operations in MapReduce, which occurs during the shuffle and sort operation of the MapReduce phase. However, for our requirements we needed to associate the sequence files into vectors so as to run it through Mahout. The primary reason for this approach was that a vectorized sequence file can be easily parallelized within the Hadoop ecosystem. This can be performed using code snippet, as shown in Table 9.7, in Java.

Further processing completely relies on this sequence file. The writer code in Table 9.7 accepts any text file and converts it into a sequence file accordingly. The code in Table 9.8 is used to convert sequence file format into a vectored state for further computations.

Lanczo's Algorithm

Lanczo's algorithm has a neat design to extract eigenvalue decomposition of a matrix. This algorithm also tries to achieve parallelization in order to utilize Hadoop to its best potential. To understand this algorithm better, let us look at the necessary computations and transformations that are required to perform SVD using Lanczo's algorithm. In this case, to extract singular vectors, they are essentially taken from the eigenvectors of $X^T * X$, where X is the matrix which has to be decomposed (Wilkinson and Wilkinson 1965). This operation utilizes a seed vector (v) which is obtained from the cardinality equal to that of the number of columns that are found in the matrix. The seed vector is repeatedly multiplied with X to obtain v'=X times (v). Syntactically, we use "times (v)" instead of just multiplying it v times, because this ensures that Mahout runs the whole operation in a single iteration or pass, hence maintaining efficiency, and then after that the previous v" part is removed

TABLE 9.7

Source Code to Generate Sequence Files

```
Writer matrixWriter = new SequenceFile.Writer(fs, configuration, new
 Path(matrixSeqFileName),
IntWritable.class, VectorWritable.class);
```

TABLE 9.8

Code to Convert Sequence File to Vector Format

```
IntWritable key = new IntWritable();
VectorWritable value = new VectorWritable();
```

(here, X is assumed to be symmetric). If the matrix is not symmetric, then the following seed vector is multiplied with the product of $X * X^T$. After a certain number of iterations, let us assume it to be k. Thus, there is now a formation of a new auxiliary matrix of the order $k \times k$. This matrix provides the best estimation of the singular values that are needed for the extraction. Most times, the estimated values are very near to the expected values, but there is a small chance that the following singular values might not be the same. Therefore, to ensure better accuracy, the largest singular values around $3k$ and the smallest singular values are maintained; the rest are usually discarded for practical purposes. A given spectrum is maintained to ensure accuracy.

Reading the Mahout-Generated Vectors

On running the Mahout job using CLI, we obtain our results in a vector format. The small snippet of code in Table 9.9, which was written in Java, can be used to help us convert these vector files into a readable format. Similar to writing a file, we have to also read a file; this can be done using the code in Table 9.9.

The code in Table 9.10 refers to the Hadoop sequence file reader, use of which ensures that the configuration is met. We then used the vector package to perform read operations on the so-called given sequence file. This can be done using the code in Table 9.10.

And we then place the values into a temporary matrix and print it back into a text file for readable format. This is pretty much the inverse of the writer function. Upon running the Java program to convert these sequence files back to text files, we then get the orthonormal matrix V from the SVD, which can be used for further applications.

SVD Using Apache Spark

MLlib is Spark's scalable machine learning library and consists of common learning algorithms and utilities, including classification, regression, clustering, collaborative filtering, and dimensionality reduction, as well as underlying optimization primitives (Meng et al. 2016). The Spark machine learning library is the primary source of packages for all the machine learning algorithms. Here, we utilized the spark.mllib.linalg package for the purpose of computing SVD and any other linear algebra operations. We also utilized spark.mllib.linalg.distributed.RowMatrix. This is one of the most efficient ways to perform operations on large, dense, or sparse matrices that use distributed row matrices. This utilizes the RDD element in Spark to perform faster operations on matrices. MLlib has other packages as well, such as regression, recommendation, etc., but we used only the linalg package for demonstration of the working principle. The MLlib library, as mentioned before,

TABLE 9.9

Code to Convert a Vector File into Readable Format

```
Reader matrixReader = new SequenceFile.Reader(fs, new Path(fileName),
 configuration);
```

TABLE 9.10

Sequence File Reader

```
Vector vector = value.get();
```

was built on Spark, so that it can use the Spark RDD framework more efficiently, but more importantly we can take advantage of the parallelization potential offered by Spark.

We utilize the distributed matrix component of Spark to meet this objective. A distributed matrix has both row and column indices. It is stored in a distributed manner in one or multiple RDDs. This is an effective tool to handle large scale matrix operations in an in-memory approach of computation. There are four categories of distributed matrices provided by Spark, but we emphasize only the row matrix. To demonstrate SVD or any eigenvalue decomposition, the best implementation can be done only by using row matrix. A row matrix is a row-oriented matrix. The indices are labeled for each row of the matrix. Each row is maintained inside an RDD as a local vector, hence making the row matrix a collective set of local vectors. However, the column size is kept as small as possible to ensure better efficiency while storing the matrix in an RDD. As shown in the code snippet in Table 9.11, we can determine the singular values and the right singular vectors from the eigenvalues and the eigenvectors of the matrix X^TX, where X is the input matrix. The left singular vectors, on the other hand, are calculated if specifically requested by the user by setting the parameter as true. Depending on the size of n and k, we can calculate the eigenvalues and vectors, respectively. If n is <100 or if k is >$n/2$, then we can calculate the following values of greatest and smallest eigenvalues locally, or else we can use ARPACK to compute these values in a more distributive manner and compute the following results on the driver.

Execution of the Scala code in the Spark Scala shell can provide different computation times for different sizes of the matrices. Figure 9.7 shows how well Spark maintains its scalability over different sizes of data. The Spark Scala code utilizes the complete potential of the distributed row matrix synchronously with the use of RDD to provide a much more efficient use of resources involved in computation. Following is a simple code for the SVD computation in Apache Spark, along with the starting and completion time for the operation.

TABLE 9.11

Simple Code for SVD Computation in Apache Spark

```
import org.apache.spark.mllib.linalg.Vectors
import org.apache.spark.mllib.linalg.Matrix
import org.apache.spark.mllib.linalg.Vector
import org.apache.spark.mllib.linalg.distributed.RowMatrix
import org.apache.spark.mllib.linalg.SingularValueDecomposition
import java.util.Calendar
 // Load and parse the data file.
 val rows = sc.textFile("file:///home/cloudera/test.txt").map { line =>
  val values = line.split(' ').map(_.toDouble)
  Vectors.dense(values)
}
//Show Starting Time
 val mat = new RowMatrix(rows)
val currentHour = Calendar.getInstance().get(Calendar.HOUR)
val currentMinute = Calendar.getInstance().get(Calendar.MINUTE)
{
 // Compute SVD
 val svd = mat.computeSVD(mat.numCols().toInt, computeU = true)
 }
//Show Ending Time
val currentHour = Calendar.getInstance().get(Calendar.HOUR)
val currentMinute = Calendar.getInstance().get(Calendar.MINUTE)
```

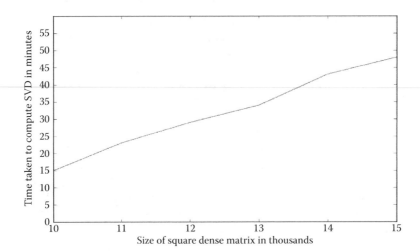

FIGURE 9.7
Time versus size of matrix for SVD, determined using Apache Spark.

Of the three tests, Apache Sparks wins with flying colors and proves to be the best solution for Big Data analytics based on problem solving among all the Apache Foundation Projects for machine learning-based analysis.

Data Analysis through Visualization

Data visualization can be termed as a form of data analysis. It provides the visual representation of patterns in data (Ginde 2016). Effective visualization can help to understand and relate to the data, communicate and represent data intuitively to others. As author, data journalist and information designer David McCandless said in his TED talk: "By visualizing information, we turn it into a landscape that you can explore with your eyes, a sort of information map. And when you're lost in information, an information map is kind of useful."

Data visualization can be as trivial as a simple table, elaborate as a map of geographic data depicting an additional layer in Google Earth or complex as a representation of Facebook's social relationships data. Visualization can be applied to qualitative as well as quantitative data. Visualization has turned into an inexorably well-known methodology as the volume and complexity of information available to research scholars has increased. Also, the visual forms of representation have become more credible in scholarly communication. As a result, increasingly more tools are available to support data visualization. High impact visualization is like a picture speaking a thousand words. Selecting good visual technique to display the data holds key to a good impact. Fancy bubble charts, Time domain based motion graphs are possible now because of the languages such as python and R.

Why Big Data Visualization Is Challenging and Different from Traditional Data Visualization

Visualization approaches are used to create tables, diagrams, images, and other intuitive display ways to represent data. Big Data visualization is not as easy as traditional small data sets visualization. The extension of traditional visualization approaches have already been emerged, but far from good enough. As Wang (Wang, Wang, and Alexander 2015) says, Visualization can be thought of as the "front end" of Big Data. Traditional data visualization tools are often inadequate to handle Big Data, scalability and dynamics are two major challenges in visual analytics of it. In large-scale data visualization, many researchers use feature extraction and geometric modeling to greatly reduce data size before actual data rendering. Choosing proper data representation is also very important when visualizing Big Data (Wang et al. 2015). There is plenty of visual analytics solutions available online. SAS Visual analytics, Plotly and Tableau are the most popular. Tableau is a business intelligence (BI) software tool that supports interactive and visual analysis of data. It has an in-memory data engine to accelerate visualization. Tableau has three main products to process large-scale data sets, including Tableau Desktop, Tableau Server, and Tableau Public. Tableau Desktop is free for students and academicians. It embeds Hadoop infrastructure and uses Hive to structure queries and cache information for in-memory analytics. Caching helps reduce the latency of a Hadoop cluster. Therefore, it can provide an interactive mechanism between users and Big Data applications (Wang et al. 2015). Plotly is built with 100% web technology. This makes our Plotly is Free for hosting public data (like Tableau Public). It is an online analytics and data visualization tool which provides online graphing, analytics and statistics tools for individuals and collaboration, as well as scientific graphing libraries for Python, R, MATLAB, Perl, Julia, Arduino, and REST. However, all these visualization tools lack advanced visual analytics capabilities. Hence, scripting languages such as R and Python need to be used to provide adept visualizations utilizing the complex data sets. Following are a few visualizations for the scholarly articles data set, acquired through web scraping and cured using various data cleansing operations in Plotly.

Figure 9.8 shows one such graph, which plots over 40 journals and 4,000 thousand articles spanning over the last 30 years.

Figure 9.9 shows the visualization of the total citations versus total articles, where each bubble size corresponds to the journal's internationality score.

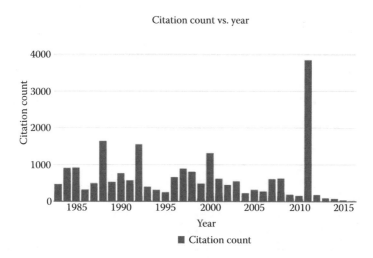

FIGURE 9.8
Simple bar chart of citation count versus year.

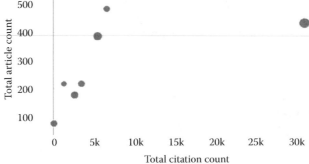

FIGURE 9.9
Bubble chart with multiple dimensions.

Conclusions

This era of Big Data, which is the next frontier for innovation, competition, and productivity, has begun a new scientific revolution. This revolution is here to stay for a very long time. Fortunately, we will witness the upcoming technological leapfrogging. Today's Big Data problem will become a small data set problem in the near future, due to steady growth in technology and improved computer architecture. The gap the computation and performance is steadily decreasing. Any Big Data problem has to be solved in various stages. First is data accumulation. There are four basic methods of data accumulation, and the toughest ones are Web scraping and Web crawling. Second is data curation. This stage is the most time-consuming and most crucial stage of Big Data problem solving. Data curing can be done using various languages and methodologies based on the requirements. Python, R, and Apache Foundation Project's Hive and PIG are the most preferred language and platforms for this. We have explained how a simple Python cleansing operation can be scaled to the MapReduce program with legible and apt adaptations in source code. The third stage is data analysis. This stage provides solutions and answers to all the complex questions. The answers are acquired using desired machine learning algorithms on the cured data. Data visualization, which is also a form of effective data analysis, can be used based on the project requirements. Tableau is a most widely used solution of data visualization so far. As a case study, we elaborated on architectural changes of Apache Spark, such as RDD, which boost the overall performance of Spark in Big Data computations. Apache Foundation projects are the place to find solution for all the Big Data relation computational solutions.

It should not be lost in translation that the role of computing in Big Data is beyond storage and high performance. Rich discovery from data is imperative and extremely useful. With advances in technologies in the past decade, the amount of data generated and recorded has grown enormously in every field of science. This extraordinary amount of data provides unprecedented opportunities for data-driven decision making and knowledge discovery. However, the task of analyzing such large-scale data sets poses significant challenges and calls for innovative analytical and statistical methods specifically designed for faster speed and higher efficiency. In this chapter, we have elaborated on a few methods and tools used to tackle the Big Data problem for complex computer modeling, analysis, and discovery of knowledge.

While developing methodologies for Big Data and exploiting the existing ones for discovery of knowledge, we foresee a number of applied research problems to be addressed in the next decade or so. These include (1) the problem of sustainable computing in data centers (e.g., those provided by Amazon, Google, Microsoft, and IBM) and particularly a host of small- and medium-scale players; (2) the problem of flood forecasting based on complex computer modeling and Big Data methods; (3) prediction of pest infestations in agriculture, so as to measure reductions in crop quality or quantity; (4) identification of the optimal number of control factors and parameters in the context of designing products in the industry, with applications in the pharmaceutical industry, nanoengineering, and bioplastic production; and (5) use of methods like SVD to identify single-valued and most critical aspects from multidimensional and voluminous data.

References

Agarwal B, Ravikumar A, Saha S. 2016a. Big Data Analytics—A Novel Approach to Big Data Veracity using Crowdsourcing Techniques. Unpublished manuscript.

Agarwal B, Ravikumar A, Saha S. 2016b. A novel approach to big data veracity using crowdsourcing techniques and Bayesian predictors, pp. 153–160. *Proceedings of the 9th Annual ACM India Conference*. New York: ACM.

Apache Spark™—Lightning-fast cluster computing (n.d.). Retrieved February and March 2017, from https://spark.apache.org.

Bora K, Saha S, Agrawal S, Safonova M, Routh S, Narasimhamurthy AM. 2016. CD-HPF: New habitability score via data analytic modeling. *Journal of Astronomy and Computing* arxiv:1604.01722v1.

Chen LP, Zhang C. 2014. Data-intensive applications, challenges, techniques and technologies: A survey on Big Data. *Information Sciences* 275:314–347.

Ding M, Zheng L, Lu Y, Li L, Guo S, Guo M. 2011. More convenient more overhead: The performance evaluation of Hadoop streaming, pp. 307–313. *Proceedings of the 2011 ACM Symposium on Research in Applied Computation: ACM*.

Ginde G, Saha S, Balasubramaniam Chitra RS, Harsha A, Mathur A, Daya Sagar BS, Narsimhamurthy A. 2015. Mining massive databases for computation of scholastic indices: Model and quantify internationality and influence diffusion of peer-reviewed journals. *Proceedings of the Fourth National Conference of Institute of Scientometrics*.

Ginde G. 2016. Visualisation of massive data from scholarly Article and Journal Database A Novel Scheme. CoRR abs/1611.01152

Golub GH, Van Loan CF. 2012. *Matrix Computations*, 3rd ed. Baltimore: John Hopkins University Press.

Gouri G, Saha S, Mathur A, Venkatagiri S, Vadakkepat S, Narasimhamurthy A, Daya Sagar BS. 2016. ScientoBASE: A framework and model for computing scholastic indicators of non local influence of journals via native data acquisition algorithms. *Journal of Scientometric* 1–51.

Hey T, Tansley S, Tolle KM. 2009. *The Fourth Paradigm: Data-Intensive Scientific Discovery*, vol. 1. Redmond, WA: Microsoft Research.

Kalman D. 1996. A singularly valuable decomposition: The SVD of a matrix. *College Mathematics Journal* 27:2–23.

Leskovec J, Rajaraman A, Ullman JD. 2011. *Mining Massive Data Sets*. Cambridge University Press.

Maniyam S. (2015, February 23). Moving From Hadoop to Spark—SF Bay Area ACM. Retrieved February 12, 2017, from http://www.sfbayacm.org/sites/default/files/hadoop_to_spark-v2.pdf

Manyika J, Chui M, Brown B, Bughin J, Dobbs R, Roxburgh C, Byers AH. 2011. Big Data: The next frontier for innovation, competition, and productivity. McKinsey Global Institute.

Meng X, Bradley J, Yavuz B, Sparks E, Venkataraman S, Liu D, Freeman J, Tsai DB, Amde M, Owen S, Xin D, Xin R, Franklin MJ, Zade R, Zaharia M, Talwalkar A. 2016. Mllib: Machine learning in Apache Spark. *Journal of Machine Learning Research* 17(34):1–7.

Mitchell TM. 1997. *Machine Learning*. McGraw-Hill.

Owen S. 2012. Mahout in action. Manning Publication.

Ryza S, Laserson U, Owen S, Wills J. 2015. Advanced Analytics with Spark. O'Rielly Publications.

Shukla N. 2014. *Haskell Data Analysis Cookbook*. Packt Publishing.

Wang L, Wang G, Alexander CA. 2015. Big data and visualization: Methods, challenges and technology progress. *Digital Technologies* 1(1):33–38.

White T. 2012. *Hadoop: The Definitive Guide*, 3rd ed. O'Rielly Publications.

Wilkinson JH, Wilkinson JH. 1965. *The Algebraic Eigenvalue Problem*, vol. 87. Oxford, United Kingdom: Clarendon Press.

Zicari R. 2012. Big Data: Challenges and Opportunities, 1st ed.

Appendix 1

Spark Implementation and Configuration

We have already discussed the architecture and features of Apache Spark. Let us now in detail see the practical implementation of Spark on a cluster, along with its respective configuration.

Building Apache Spark Using Maven

As we mentioned in the main text, building Apache Spark is very crucial and using a prebuilt version of Spark is not advised for our purpose. This is mainly because the prebuilt version of Spark doesn't come with the necessary BLAS and ARPACK libraries, which are required. This causes Spark's MLlib library to use a built-in F2J implementation of most of the machine learning algorithms, and this can seriously affect the performance of the task at hand as we deal with Big Data. Building from source also ensures that it perfectly integrates Scala with Spark. First, download the Spark source code from the Spark official website and extract the tar file.

Apache Maven

The Maven-based build is the build of reference for Apache Spark. Building Spark using Maven requires Maven 3.3.9 or newer and Java 7+.

Setting Up Maven's Memory Usage

You'll need to configure Maven to use more memory than usual by setting MAVEN_OPTS:

```
export MAVEN_OPTS="-Xmx2g -XX:ReservedCodeCacheSize=512m".
```

To add the BLAS AND ARPACK dependencies, OpenBLAS is an optimized BLAS library. First, install the openblas library to your system using the following command:

```
sudo apt-get install libopenblas-dev.
```

This will install the Fortran libraries for the basic linear algebra subprograms packages which are required for the best performance of some of the machine learning algorithms which will be used, such as eigenvalue decomposition, etc. ARPACK, the ARnoldi PACKage, is a numerical software library written in Fortran 77 for solving large-scale eigenvalue problems. This can be done by including a few of the dependencies to the pom file in the respective mllib and mllib-local directories. The following snippets of code are to be added to the dependencies in those pom files.

```
<dependency>
<groupId>com.github.fommil.netlib</groupId>
<artifactId>all</artifactId>
<version>1.1.2</version>
<type>pom</type>
</dependency>

<dependency>
<groupId>net.sourceforge.f2j</groupId>
<artifactId>arpak   combined   all</artifactId>
<version>0.1</version>
</dependency>

<dependency>
<groupId>com.github.fommil.netlib</groupId>
<artifactId>netlib-native_ref-linux-x86_64</artifactId>
<version>1.1</version>
<classifier>natives</classifier>
</dependency>

<dependency>
<groupId>com.github.fommil.netlib</groupId>
<artifactId>netlib-native_system-linux-x86_64</artifactId>
<version>1.1</version>
<classifier>natives</classifier>
</dependency>
```

These dependencies ensure that while building it extracts the necessary libraries from the sources specified. This will ensure that we won't get implementation errors when Spark is trying to run the SVD operation on Big Data and also keeps the performance optimal. Now navigate to the Spark folder and follow the build instructions given below.

build/mvn

Building Spark using Maven or sbt is preferred because it gives you the additional customization options which can help you choose specific libraries and packages that can be used for any specific task, by changing and adding those specific dependencies to the pom file. Spark comes with an easy default build for Maven; we could also use sbt to get the same results to help in building it. This will automatically set up the required environment, such as the Scala version and more elements that Spark utilizes. You can build Spark using the following command:

```
/build/mvn -Pyarn -Phadoop-2.7 -Dhadoop.version=2.7.0 -DskipTests clean
package.
```

This should be executed in the Spark directory wherever it was extracted.

Required Cluster Configurations for Spark

Let us now discuss the configuration of the cluster for the Spark job using the Spark shell. We first have to set the required options to the Scala shell to give the cluster settings in order for it to run. Let's first discuss the hardware settings of each of the working parts but also let's see the required changes to make in the configuration file before running.

NOTE: Due to hardware limitations, we are using a 48-Gb server so that all the worker nodes will be launched on the server itself in a cluster mode. First, make sure that there is a copy of each of the given files:

```
slaves.template to slaves
spark-env.sh.template to spark-env.sh
spark-defaults.conf.template to spark-defaults.conf
Now, add the following lines to the following corresponding files:
In slaves add #. A Spark worker will be started on each of the machines
listed below.
master
In spark-env.sh, add
export SPARK_MASTER_MEMORY="8g"
export SPARK_DRIVER_MEMORY="48g"
export SPARK_WORKER_INSTANCES="6"
export SPARK_EXECUTOR_INSTANCES="6"
export SPARK_WORKER_MEMORY="8g"
export SPARK_EXECUTOR_MEMORY="8g"
export SPARK_WORKER_CORES="16"
export SPARK_EXECUTOR_CORES="16"
In spark-default.conf add
spark.master              spark://master:7077
```

NOTE: We are assuming the named IP address of the system to be the maste. Please do change the name if you're using any other name in the/etc/hosts file for your respective IP address accordingly Starting your cluster.

In our demonstration case of hardware constraints, we are using only one system to launch all our worker nodes and master node alike, so we will be using the following command:

```
/<sparkdirectory>/sbin/start-all.sh.
```

In case you have other workers in other slave computers, then make sure you start them from other computers by using the following command:

```
/<sparkdirectory>/sbin/start-slaves.sh <master-IPaddress>
```

Then, check master:8080 in any Web browser to see if your worker nodes have successfully started.

For the code used, check it out on GitHub (https://github.com/rahul-aedula95/Mahout-spark_SVD).

```
https://github.com/rahul-aedula95/singval
```

Key Terminology and Definitions

Apache Software Foundation Projects: Apache provides support for the Apache community of open source software projects. There are over 140 different Apache project communities that provide free software for the public benefit. About 35 open source Apache projects are dedicated to Big Data, including, Hadoop, Spark, Pig, Mahout, Hive, Sqoop, Storm, etc.

CLUSTER BY: this is a Hive command used as CLUSTER BY x which ensures that each of the N reducers get nonoverlapping ranges. Then, it sorts those ranges at the reducers.

CSV: comma-separated values (CSV) is a file format primarily used in storing data in a tabular format. Each line of a CSV file indicates an entry in the record, and the different fields of the record are separated by using delimited values in this specific format, which is a comma.

Data Analysis: this is a process of inspecting, cleaning, transforming, and modeling data with the goal of discovering useful information, suggesting conclusions, and supporting decision making.

Data Cleansing: this is the process of detecting and correcting (or removing) corrupt or inaccurate records from a record set, table, or database.

Data Collection and Acquisition: data collection is the process of gathering and measuring information on targeted variables in an established systematic fashion, which then enables one to answer relevant questions and evaluate outcomes. Data collection is a primary component of research and is common to all fields of study, including the physical and social sciences, humanities, and business.

Data Visualization: this is a general term that describes any effort to help people understand the significance of data by placing it in a visual context. Patterns, trends, and correlations that might go undetected in text-based data can be exposed and recognized more easily with data visualization software.

HDF5: hierarchical data format (HDF) is a file format extensively used in storing data which involve metadata. Most of these formats are popularly used in instrumentation data storage.

Hive: Hive is a tool provided by the Apache Foundation which can be used in the Hadoop environment. This tool allows important elements such as data warehousing and SQL to act synchronously with Hadoop MapReduce.

HSSF: this is an API provided by the Apache POI project. This provides the pure implementation of Java regarding Excel sheets. It provides functions to create, modify, write, and read into Excel documents.

JHDF5: also known as HDF5 for Java, this is a package which provides a high-level interface that works over other packages and includes functionality and support mechanisms for handling and manipulating the HDF5 file format.

JSON: Java Script Object Notation (JSON) is a data interchange format. It is extensively used for denoting data with various fields and it is very easy to work with, as there are many packages and API which support it.

Machine Learning: this is a type of artificial intelligence that provides computers with the ability to learn without being explicitly programmed. Machine learning focuses on the development of computer programs that can teach themselves to grow and change when exposed to new data.

Mahout: Mahout is a tool provided by the Apache Software Foundation which integrates machine learning and its relevant algorithms to work in a Hadoop environment. It tries to utilize the potential of the distributed computation of a Hadoop cluster.

MySQLdb: this is a package which provides APIs in Python to communicate with the MYSQL database. We can perform various database manipulations with this tool, such as querying and inserting records, etc.

NoSQL: traditionally termed non-SQL, this tool is used to associate a data-storing mechanism that holds data without involving tables and other relational database concepts.

NUMPY: this is a package or library provided by Python and includes several matrix and array manipulation functions, which make it much simpler to use. It is widely used by the data science community for high-end matrix operations.

ORDER BY: this is a Hive command which is derived from SQL; it basically performs data sorting in ascending or descending order. In Hive, it guarantees the total ordering of data.

Pandas: this is a high-performance library provided by Python for easy-to-use functions which help in data analysis and data structuring.

PCA: principal component analysis (PCA) is a statistical method used to obtain a number of uncorrelated data sets. The main purpose of PCA is to identify maximum variance by using a smaller number of prominent components to represent it.

POI: this is an Apache project which was developed for the primary purpose of modifying Microsoft Office files. It provides a set of functions and APIs which can interact with various different file formats for modifications, including HSSF, which is used to handle Excel files in Java.

RDD: resilient distributed data (RDD) sets can be defined as data structures widely used in Spark. The main characteristics are its fault tolerance; it can be parallelized easily, and it is an immutable collection of objects.

Scikit-Learn: this is a machine learning library made for Python and was built using NUMPY, SCIPY, and MATPLOTLIB. It favors easy implementation of machine learning algorithms, such as classification, regression, and dimensionality reduction, without any cumbersome code.

Spark: Apache Spark is an open source project built as a framework for data processing, specifically, for Big Data. It was designed in a manner to enhance clustering capabilities to perform more complex algorithms much faster and with greater resource efficiency than other frameworks.

Sqoop: Sqoop is a tool created by the Apache Software Foundation. Its main purpose is to transfer data from a relational database to a NoSQL database. It is effectively used in the Hadoop ecosystem to transfer data from MYSQL and other such databases to Hive and PIG.

UNION ALL: this is a command used in Hive that can combine all results of select statements into one result.

10

Storing and Analyzing Streaming Data: A Big Data Challenge

Devang Swami, Sampa Sahoo, and Bibhudatta Sahoo

CONTENTS

Introduction

The availability of distributed computing and storage systems has made Big Data processing a reality. The term Big Data refers to data which cannot be processed by a traditional system, owing to the limited amount of resources available from traditional systems. Of the many problems encountered and solved by Big Data systems, a set of problems classified under streaming data has brought unparalleled challenges and opportunities for industries and research institutes. "Streaming data" (or data pipelines) as we use the term refers to a long sequence of unbounded data that arrives continuously at varying rates for a very long duration. Although stream processing had its origins in the 1970s, most of the work in this field has been done in the last decade. Applications such as IoT, WSN, RAN, and GSM systems (3G and 4G LTE technologies) and others have allowed use of stream processing for Big Data environments, owing to the velocity and variety of data processing possible, as well as the quality of service (QoS) demanded by such applications. Moreover, these data pipelines also generate massive amounts of data over periodic intervals, making them candidates for the Big Data domain.

Systems for big data processing may be available on premises, but extending such systems or modifying an existing architecture for stream processing may be a very costly solution, owing to the requirements of skilled administrators and developers, as well as the costly hardware and software solutions. Hence, a majority of research work now focuses on bringing stream processing on a scale-out architecture, such as the Cloud, to take advantage of scalability and utility computing. Examples of current streaming service providers include Amazon AWS and Microsoft Azure. To deploy the stream processing services over these platforms, modification of existing algorithms to the divide and conquer (DAC) paradigm is required to be able to process them on the multiple systems (discussed below).

Although many resources are available on Cloud systems for data pipelines, the potentially long sequences of unbounded data make it necessary for architects and designers to develop and use algorithms that make very few loops over the data and use much less space than the input size of the stream. Hence, the terms one-pass algorithms and sublinear space algorithms are designated for stream processing algorithms that achieve the goals of processing the stream by reading the data only once and storing only a portion of the streaming data in the main memory, respectively.

In the next section, we introduce the basics of distributed systems and the challenges that streaming data brings for processing in a distributed environment. In subsequent sections, we explore more deeply the mathematical models for streaming data. Thereafter, we provide a brief discussion on probabilistic data structures, along with a computational model that has been utilized. We then focus on data models for storage of streaming data classified as cold data on secondary storage devices. Finally, we provide a brief note on industrial and research challenges that streaming problems bring.

Streaming Algorithms

There are two alternatives for designing an algorithm (Sanders 2014):

1. Design data structures and storage first, then design an efficient algorithm; or

2. Design an algorithm first, then design a good data structure or storage

It is intuitive that an intelligent storage structure needs a brilliant process for extracting and processing data. Consider the case of using a B+ tree for creating an index on an important column for some data stored on the hard disk drive. This data structure would require an intelligent algorithm that understands the query and utilizes indexes wherever possible to reduce overall time consumption. However, the choices of data structures and models depend highly on the level of memory hierarchy.

Most work on data pipelines has focused on the processing of the latest data, which resides in the main memory. Now, technologies such as MapReduce (on Apache Hadoop) cannot be used, since MapReduce will be able to process the data only if it is stored on an Hadoop distributed file system. Thus, an algorithm's inherent dependency on storage structures is explained. In addition, once a storage structure is devised to store data, it limits the type of operations as well as the number of concurrent operations that may be carried out on the data. For example, you cannot carry out range queries on data stored by using a hash-based index. Thus, both the storage structure as well as algorithms are important, and a choice of one of them limits the choices available for the other. Usually, design of systems is an iterative process wherein at each iteration we edit either the algorithm or the storage structure to arrive at the best solution.

A major problem when it comes to designing most streaming data systems is that a large portion of data is on secondary storage, while the latest piece of data would always be in the main memory. Both of these are at different levels of the memory hierarchy, as shown in Figure 10.1. Now, the size of streaming data is such that storing a complete stream in the main memory is not feasible. Hence, an algorithm that fits the stated problem is required to process ad hoc query requests by the operator. The best way of dealing with algorithms today lies in converting algorithms from different paradigms, such as greedy or dynamic programming and others, to a DAC approach, thus exploring parallelism and enabling higher latency for operations. However, data have to be brought into the main memory for processing. If algorithms in the DAC paradigm are modified to execute on multiple systems and still maintain

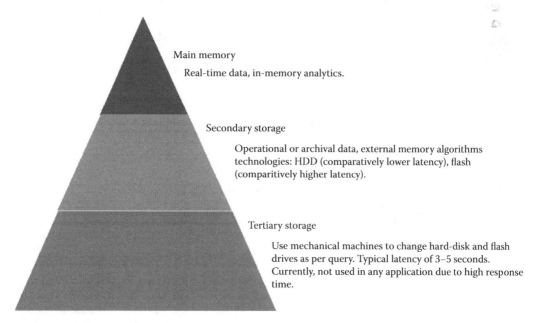

FIGURE 10.1
Memory hierarchy.

consistency in results, then the problem is solved. Only two types of conceptual data structures are available in the literature for maintaining consistency, namely, Semaphores and Monitors. Although, initially designed for use in interprocess communication, these can also be modified for use in distributed environments. Another design problem that may be utilized to solve the concurrency problem in stream processing is the Drinking Philosopher problem, which is a modification of the Dining Philosopher problem. A Drinking Philosopher problem addresses the demand by using shared resources and is mostly used for modeling and solving problems in distributed systems. With a Drinking Philosopher problem, a set of bottles are available that provide the drink, and philosophers can use a bottle to get a drink one at a time (Chandy and Misra 1984). Herein, the bottles are resources, i.e., data for streaming applications and multiple systems (or philosophers) may require a piece of data from the stream. There may be multiple bottles and, hence, multiple philosophers may be able to use them at the same time. The problem is to design a method such that no philosopher remains thirsty forever. The conflict resolution devised should be such that one process be favored against another and that it guarantee fairness (the same process should not be favored every time) (Chandy and Misra 1984). The above discussion clearly suggests that distributed stream processing involves solving mutual exclusion, concurrency, and synchronization problems.

Modeling Data Pipeline Problems

Development of a solution to big data streaming problems begins with modeling the requirements of the application into one of the available streaming models or by proposing a new streaming model. Most streaming models available in the literature are based on one or more of the following three factors:

1. One pass over the data
2. Unbounded data
3. Fast processing time per element

The first characteristic, one pass over the data, simply means that data are processed only once, so that the system can complete in the time frame required. One pass over data may be easily achieved for aggregate operations, like Min, Max, Average, Sum, and others, while problems such as sorting are very difficult to achieve by only one pass over the data. Some literature has also used the term fast processing group of algorithms for these one-pass algorithms. The fast processing of data property may also allow some randomness, since most applications of this branch require approximate answers rather than accurate results.

A streaming model is a computational model that represents how data would be organized (in the main memory) and processed. From the perspective of design, there are four streaming models, namely, the Vanilla, Sliding Window, Turnstile, and Cash Register models; these are of prime importance and cover most application domains in this field (Babcock et al. 2002b, Che-Qing et al. 2004).

Vanilla Model

Vanilla, is the simplest model and is based on the assumption that a data stream A is composed of discrete units called tokens $\{A_1, A_2, A_3, ..., A_m\}$; where each element A_i is drawn from the universe $U[n] = \{1, 2, 3, ..., n\}$ and both m and n are very large and represent the stream length and universe size, respectively. The main aim of this model is to process a stream in much less space, s, of main memory in a short time, usually the deadline for task completion. Based on the deadline of a task, a designer may estimate the number of tokens that can be processed during that interval, which can give an approximate size of the main memory s required for processing. This model allows estimation of main memory, CPU clock rate, and network bandwidth, which can be used as system requirements during the deployment phase. As we mentioned above, the main objective in stream processing is to process the data in a very small space. However, both m and n are very large. Hence, s must be sublinear in both of these parameters. The space complexity of s can be represented by Equation 10.1.

$$s = O[\min(m, n)] \tag{10.1}$$

However, an optimal algorithm would always take a constant number of tokens and constant number of counters to determine the length of the stream; hence, it would be able to achieve a constant space complexity, as shown in Equation 10.2. Until now, most works have been able to achieve space complexity as shown in Equation 10.3. Equation 10.3 denotes that an algorithm makes p passes over the data. If $p = 1$, then Equation 10.3 and Equation 10.2 would be the same.

$$s = O[\log(m) + \log(n)] \tag{10.2}$$

$$s = polylog[\min(m, n)] \tag{10.3}$$

This model has been widely used for aggregate operations in various industries. Any algorithm in this model can be easily converted into a DAC paradigm by using concepts such as semaphores and monitors for concurrency, making it a candidate for Big Data applications.

Sliding Window Model

The Sliding Window model computes operations on a set of instances, as opposed to a single instance as with the Vanilla model. The advantage of using Sliding Window in video surveillance is that it can be used for motion detection. Most industrial applications find only an excerpt of the data pipeline to be useful at any given time, and hence these applications find the Sliding Window model a candidate solution. The Window model for streaming applications can be categorized based on the following three parameters (Babcock et al. 2002b):

1. Direction of Movement: Based on the direction of movement there are three possible scenarios: If both the endpoints are fixed it is known as a fixed window. If window has one sliding point and a fixed point it is called a landmark window and for both the points being sliding, we call it a sliding window.
2. Physical versus Logical: Physical or time-based windows use a time interval as a parameter, while logical or frequency-based windows uses counts of an object in

the window as a parameter. The choice of physical versus logical is always application specific; however, physical is preferred when designers want to limit the amount of main memory available to the program. Logical Sliding Window algorithms use dynamic memory allocation and are prone to segmentation fault if a sufficient amount of main memory is not provided.

3. Update Interval: A window that processes as soon as a new data item arrives is called eager reevaluation, while one which waits for a batch of new items is called lazy reevaluation or jumping window. Babcock et al. (2002b) also argued that the result of a window with a larger update interval than the window size would create a series of nonoverlapping tumbling windows.

Turnstile Model

The Turnstile model of data streams uses a vector presented as a long sequence of positive and negative integer updates to its coordinates. The vector X is always said to be in the following range: $\{-m, -m + 1, \ldots, m - 1, m\}n$, where $m > 2n$. Updates for this model follow the types of equations in Equation 10.4 or Equation 10.5, were e_i is the ith standard unit vector.

$$X = X + e_i \tag{10.4}$$

$$X = X - e_i \tag{10.5}$$

The objective of this model is to make a single pass over the data by using limited memory to compute functions of X, such as the frequency moments, the number of distinct elements, the empirical entropy, the heavy hitters, treatment of x as a matrix, and various quantities in numerical linear algebra, such as a low rank approximation (Leavitt 2010). This model was for Count-Min sketch data structure used for aggregating data streams.

Cash Register Model

The Cash Register model is a modification of the Turnstile model wherein only positive updates are allowed (Muthukrishnan 2005). It is used for signal rendering. Another model, namely, the aggregate model, is also used for signal rendering and has a small difference in that it aggregates the value instead of updating a single value. For the purpose of this chapter, we have focused only on the Cash Register model, since the Unordered Cash Register model is the most general model and poses more challenges in data processing. The items that arrive over time in the Unordered Cash Register model are domain values in no particular order, and the function is represented by implicitly aggregating the number of items with a particular domain value (Gilbert et al. 2001). Real-life examples of this model include telephone calls. The Cash Register model allows updates of the form <i, c>, where c is a positive integer and i denotes the ith element. A special case for the Cash Register model is when $c = 1$. The Cash Register model becomes very complicated and difficult when it comes to modeling graph problems, such as shortest path and connectivity.

The Misra-Gries algorithm for finding repeated elements also utilizes the Cash Register model. Misra-Gries is a comparison-based algorithm and has achieved time complexity of $O[n \times \log(n)]$, which is the best case for any comparison-based algorithm. However, it requires extra space proportional to k, where k is a parameter used for governing the quality of the solution. The algorithm stores stream tokens and their counter in an array. At the end of each pass, if the element exists in the list, the counter is increased incrementally. If not, then the element is added to the array list and the counter is set to 1. Also, the Misra-Gries algorithm is a deterministic algorithm used in stream processing, while most of the other data structures and algorithms are probabilistic in nature and do not give accurate results.

Probablistic Data Structures and Algorithms

Once we have decided on a computation model fit for an application, it becomes increasingly necessary to design an efficient data structure and data model for the same to produce a solution that is optimal for real world application. In this section, we focus on data structures only.

Use of deterministic data structures, like hash tables and hash sets, is quite common for most applications with frequent items and unique items. While almost all deterministic data structures require loading completely in main memory, this cannot be achieved for Big Data applications. This is where another class, namely, probabilistic data structures, comes into play. Probabilistic data structures usually use hash functions to randomize and compactly present the data. However, one must note that use of these data structures should be encouraged given that application may result in approximate results rather than precise answers. As stated earlier, most probabilistic data structures use hash functions to randomize the data; collisions are unavoidable keeping the size of hash constant. There are three benefits of using probabilistic data structures:

1. Requires a very small amount of main memory in comparison with deterministic data structures

2. Easily made parallel

3. Have a constant query time

Most probabilistic data structures allow type 1 errors (false positives) but not type 2 errors (false negatives). Examples of probabilistic data structures include Bloom Filter, Count-Min Sketch, T-Digest, HyperLogLog, and Filtered Space Saving (FSS).

Bloom Filter

Bloom Filter is one of the simplest probabilistic data structures; it was discovered in 1998 (Fan et al. 2000). It is used to determine whether an element exists in the input data with a high degree of likelihood. Bloom Filter is basically an m-bit array which is initialized to 0 and has k different hash functions. The elements to be compared are fed to all the k hash functions, which yields k different positions of the bit to be changed from 0 to 1 (Figure 10.2, after using k hash functions on elements A and B, we changed bits 0, 3, 4, 5, and 7 to 1). The input data were then fed to k hash functions, which yielded k positions, and we verified that all the k positions were 1 (Figure 10.2, compare positions for input data I after getting k positions from the set of hash functions.). If all positions are a 1, then Bloom

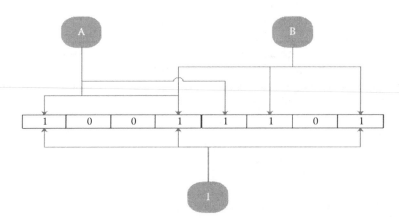

FIGURE 10.2
Probabilistic data structures: Bloom filters.

Filter returns that element might be in the set, or else the element is definitely not in the set. From Figure 10.2, it is also clear that type 1 error is possible, because input I checks for positions 0, 3, and 7, which are not covered by elements A and B, but then all three bits were changed by both of them to 1. Thus, false positives are possible in Bloom Filter results but a false negative is not, since if an element has been in the list then it must have flipped the bits. There are two major disadvantages of Bloom Filter:

1. We can add an element into the set for comparison, but we cannot remove an added element from the comparison set
2. The rate of false-positive errors increases with the number of elements used for the comparison

Bloom Filter can be replaced by the Mirsa-Gries algorithm if the user needs 100% accurate results. Then, cost of storage space, which is relatively high for use of the Mirsa-Gries, algorithm, cannot be ignored. Hence, a tradeoff must be designed before choosing a particular solution. Akamai Technologies uses Bloom Filter for their content delivery network and Cloud services to prevent one-hit wonders (i.e., data objects that users request just once), which helped in utilizing cache memory properly (Maggs and Ramesh 2015).

Count-Min Sketch

Count-Min Sketch is an extension of Bloom Filter that records the frequency of occurrence of an element apart from checking the existence of an element in the list. It was invented in 2003. Count-Min Sketch is also quite space optimized and uses a two-dimensional array for storing information. Although it uses hash function, it is different from hash table in the sense that it uses sublinear space for storing the details. However, it may produce over-counting, since collisions are possible. It finds applications in summarizing data streams like points, ranges, and inner product queries, approximately. The Count Sketch algorithm from which Count-Min sketch was devised was based on the Turnstile Model, while the Count-Min sketch algorithm is based on the Cash Register model. Either Count-Min sketch can have only positive updates, and a value of 1 specifically for counting frequency. Thus, Count-Min sketch uses the special case of the Cash Register model, where $c = 1$.

HyperLogLog

The HyperLogLog data structure and algorithm are used for cardinality estimation problems. It only supports adding elements and estimating the cardinality. HyperLogLog is very much similar to Bloom Filter but uses much less memory space than Bloom Filter and does not support membership check, like Bloom Filter does. HyperLogLog works by subdividing its input stream of added elements and storing the maximum number of leading zeros that have been observed within each subdivision. Since elements are uniformly hashed before checking for the number of leading zeros, the general idea is that the greater the number of leading zeros observed, the higher the probability that many unique elements have been added. It is used mostly for finding unique elements and for continuous views over streaming data. PipelineDB's HyperLogLog implementation has a margin of error of only about 0.81%. The performance of HyperLogLog decreases in the presence of large variances, since hash functions will use only fixed lengths of data to create buckets. If the variance is high, few buckets will get very few values from the stream and other buckets will face many collisions. Thus, HyperLogLog should be discouraged if data tend to have a very high range of variance.

T Digest

T Digest finds its usage in measuring rank statistics such as quantiles and medians by using a fixed amount of storage space. This space efficiency comes at the cost of marginal errors, making T Digest a candidate for streaming problems. T Digest is essentially an adaptive histogram that intelligently adjusts its buckets and frequencies as more elements are added to it. T Digest begins with initializing m empty centroids, each of which contains a mean and a count. As a new element arrives, it is checked for distance from the mean value of the centroid. If it is close enough, then the count of the centroid is increased incrementally and the mean is updated based on the weight. Weight is a term introduced in this algorithm to control the accuracy of quantiles. Open source implementation of T Digest is already being used with modifications in Apache Mahout and stream-lib projects.

Filtered Space Saving

The Filtered Space Saving (FSS) data structure and algorithm are used for finding the most frequent items. Now, maintaining a list of all items occurring in the list is not feasible for streaming data; hence, FSS uses a hash function for computation, just like Count-Min Sketch. However, it differs by putting constraints on what items are kept for comparison. Either FSS would remove an element from the list of comparison at any time when it does not fulfill a given criteria, e.g., likelihood of occurrence of a specific item is below a threshold. FSS, like Count-Min Sketch, is also based on a Turnstile model and uses the concept of filtering atop a space-saving algorithm. The FSS mechanism is to hash an incoming value into buckets, where each bucket has a collection of values already added. If the incoming element already exists in a given bucket, its frequency is incremented. If the element doesn't exist, it will be added as long as certain properties are met.

Suitability of Data Models for Storing Stream Data

Streaming data needs to be stored on some persistent device so as to be able to retrieve it after a long duration or after turning off the system. Storing the streaming data on secondary storage devices is in itself a challenge, since latency of random reads is very low for spinning disks and an efficient organization is required. A data model is an abstract model providing a view of how data would be organized on a secondary storage device. A major limitation of traditional data models (relational) has been that it entails no predefined notion of time (unless a time stamp has been explicitly defined), predefined schema, an inability to handle data partitions, and costly join operations. Hence, choice of a data model should be done wisely. Data streams differ from conventional data sources in the following ways (Babcock et al. 2002a):

1. Data arrives online

2. System has no control over the order in which data elements arrive to be processed

3. Streaming data are potentially unbounded in size

4. Once processed, a data element may be discarded or archived

Emerging systems such as sensor networks, internet traffic management systems, Web usage logs, internet-based auctions, and others, have demanded support for streaming data storage. The major plot in streaming data is that initially when produced it is utilized the most (referred to as hot data), but as time increases the usage decreases exponentially (referred to as cold data), as shown in Figure 10.3.

Initially, when data are produced, they are consumed repeatedly many times, but as time passes consumption decreases and data become archival. A simple example is be that of stock exchange data of a company, which by virtue of production are of a streaming nature. Initially, they are utilized by many customers, and then their usage decreases gradually and is only used for aggregation of weekly or monthly or bimonthly trends. Such trends require a storage structure that gives access to hot data at a very high latency in comparison to cold data. The traditional relational data model fails to provide such services, as the normalization process destroys preaggregation and prejoins and encourages

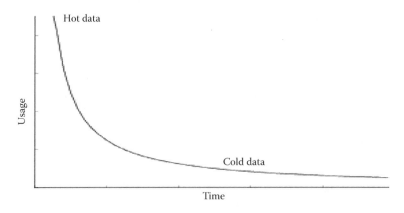

FIGURE 10.3
Data usage versus time.

costly operation, like joins. NEWSQL (Grolinger et al. 2013) is an exception in this case. Preaggregation and prejoin design techniques use a reasonable design for storing intraday, intraweek, or intramonth data. Such a design facilitates deriving the best from cold data in only a few rows, allowing archiving of cold data in a very early stage and thus reducing the overall size of operational data. The same cannot be done in a relational model, because normalization, especially the third normal form, of the normalization process in a relational database design does not allow decomposition, and if queries require frequent join operations then such an archive could be very costly. Prejoining the data doubtlessly increases data duplication, but it has many advantages. Above all, streaming data once stored is largely not updated but only read; hence, data duplication is affordable.

From the literature, it was found that streaming data storage requires data models with the following properties to address the above-mentioned needs and fulfil the voids of the relational model:

1. Implicit or explicit support of a time stamp (Babcock et al. 2002b)
2. Allow time-based or sequence-based query operations (Chandrasekaran and Franklin 2002)
3. Queries should be allowed to run continuously over a period of time, incrementally (Chandrasekaran and Franklin 2002)
4. Support for shared execution of multiple queries (Khalilian et al. 2016)
5. Scalability over large and unstructured data (Khalilian et al. 2016)

There are more than 10 data models available on the market for Big Data applications, of which the following models are of great interest for streaming data storage:

Key Value Stores Model

The key value stores model is the simplest data model and includes a key and its corresponding value. For streaming applications, the key could be a time stamp and the value could be an object or a variable of the object. It should be used only if the schema remain constant for a long duration and operations involved are simple (Chandra 2015). Key value stores are very good at handling large data volumes. Tokyo Cabinet and Tokyo Tyrant are examples of key value stores. Another example is Flare, but this supports only memcached protocols (Chandra 2015). It is best suited to applications that require processing of a constant stream with a small number of reads and writes.

Document Stores Model

In the document stores model, if schema of the stream change very frequently, then the document data model is a candidate solution because of its flexibility to handle schema variation easily. It has an advantage in supporting complex operations, which the key value stores model lacks. It uses a JSON-like structure as the physical data model. Document stores usually find themselves in the CA part of the famous CAP theorem (Chandra 2015). (The CAP theorem: In the presence of a network partition [P], one has to choose between consistency [C] and availability [A].) Databases which have an implemented document model are MongoDB, Cloudant, Cache, BaseX, CouchDB, and others. Of these, MongoDB is more successful and has been used widely in IoT systems, financial logs, system logs, social networks, and regulatory reporting systems. However, it requires the use of a time stamp explicitly while storing data.

Wide-Column Stores Model

The wide-column stores model, also known as the column-family model, is a data model that allows a dynamic number of rows or columns or both. It can also be realized as a two-dimensional key-value pair. Most wide-column stores utilize the concept of block chains and are thus mostly applied for write-intensive workloads (Abramova and Bernardino 2013). Column-family databases are candidates for streaming problems, since they have overcome the deficiency of document databases by introducing an implicit time stamp for every data row. Databases which have implemented this data model include Apache Cassandra, Apache HBase, Google Big Table, Sqrrl, and others (Chandra 2015). Use cases of this data model include social networks, IoT, monitoring systems, and more. Also, Apache Cassandra has a built-in support for streaming queries based on a sliding window model in its CQL/STREAM, allowing both physical and logical sliding windows. It also has support for custom or user-defined operations on streams. Above all, support for massive write loads and MapReduce are like extra cheese on the burger for a developer.

Other Models

Many novel models also support stream processing, like Redis (Leavitt 2010), a database which uses a data structure with the concept of key-value pairs and finds its application in click tracking. Click tracking deals with storing location of a user who visited a page or used a service. Another exploratory model-gaining pace is NEWSQL (Grolinger et al. 2013), which improves the relational data model for Big Data and also finds its application in data pipelining. PipelineDB is another database solution which has been developed only to cater to the needs of streaming applications. It utilizes a window model and provides SQL query language for operations, making it one of the very few of its type. Most of the queries in PipelineDB are processed using probabilistic data structures and approximate algorithms (http://docs.piplinedb.com/introduction.html); hence, if you require an accurate solution, then PipelineDB may not be a candidate solution for your application. A unique feature of PipelineDB is Continuous Joins. However, CROSS-JOIN and FULL-JOIN are not supported as of the writing of this chapter.

The Holy Grail of research interest in stream processing is Apache Spark (a framework for real-time data analytics that sits on top of the Hadoop distributed file system), a proprietary solution. However, the required skilled developers and administrators have moved a fraction of customers to using SQLStream, which is a better choice since it is a complete enterprise platform for streaming analytics that can be deployed quickly without a large development effort (Wayne 2014). While Spark and other open source frameworks like Storm may be free, they require a lot of development talent and time.

Challenges and Open Research Problems

Industrial Challenges

1. Beating the CAP Theorem

   The CAP theorem states that, "Consistency and high availability cannot be guaranteed in presence of large number of partitions" (Brewer 2012).

2. Lambda Architecture

Lambda architecture relies on the concept of using two different systems to process data, combine results from these systems, and produce results. Lambda architecture was developed to beat the famous CAP theorem. It finds application in stream data processing. It is a data processing architecture that processes persistent data by using batch processing programming models (e.g., MapReduce), and real-time processing models. Then, a glue code is used to combine results from both of the systems and is presented to the users. Lambda architecture consists of three layers, namely, the batch layer, stream layer, and serving layer.

a. *Batch layer*

The batch layer processes persistent data stored on secondary storage devices, such as hard disk drives, flash drives, and others. One of the candidate solutions, namely, Apache Hadoop, has become a de facto tool for batch processing, as this software provides high scalability and distributed data storage with redundant copies of each datum for fault tolerance. Output is usually stored in databases and then combined later with the output of speed layers. ElephantDB and Cloudera Impala are candidate databases for storing output of batch layers. ElephantDB is a database solution which specializes in exporting key-value pair data from Hadoop (https://github.com/nathanmarz/elephantdb).

b. *Speed layer*

The speed layer focuses on processing real-time or online data. This layer sacrifices throughput as it aims to minimize latency by providing real-time views into the most recent data. The main task of this layer is to process the data when it resides in main memory and fill the gap introduced by the lag of the batch-processing layer in storing the most recent data.

c. *Service layer*

The service layer uses the results from the above layers and combines them before producing output to the user. It uses views of data already processed and combines different views to produce output of a user query. This layer implements the glue code necessary to combine results from both the batch and speed layers.

The Netflix Suro project and the advertisement data warehouse processing system of Yahoo loosely use the Lambda architecture. Disadvantages of Lambda architecture include writing a single code twice (once for the batch layer and the other for the speed layer), transformation logic implementation, and writing a glue code for combining results. Finally, management of two different systems is very difficult.

3. Kappa Architecture

Kappa architecture is a simplification of Lambda architecture. It overcomes the limitation of maintaining a glue code in Lambda architecture, which produces the same results in more than one distributed system. Overall, running and maintaining two different distributed systems is costly and complex. Kappa architecture overcomes this limitation by adopting a strategy of using append-only immutable (write-only) data stores. Note that Kappa architecture is an extension of Lambda architecture and not its replacement. As of the writing of this chapter, Kappa architecture is still in the initial phase. However, most efforts have concentrated on the tools for stream processing systems (e.g., Apache Samza, Apache Storm, Amazon Kinesis, Apache Spark, and others) and log stores (e.g., Apache Kafka and DistributedLog). Kappa architecture also has three layers:

    a. Log data stores are used in Kappa architecture to store results of batch jobs by the job ID and output. Apache Kafka and DistirbutedLog are candidate stores for this layer.

    b. Streaming computation systems process data from log data stores and produce the result.

    c. Serving layer stores are responsible for optimized responses to queries.

4. BDAS Architecture

    BDAS (Berkeley Data Analytics Stack) architecture is an open source software stack which has integrated software components developed by AMPLab at the University of California, Berkeley, for Big Data analytics. This group has also released a RESTful Web service for sending tasks to human workers, such as Amazon Mechanical Turk.

5. SQL or SQL-like query languages for stream processing

    The popularity and simplicity of SQL has attracted many customers. There are many works, such as AQuery, Aurora, CQL/STREAM, StreaQuel/TelegraphCQ, Tribeca, Spark SQL, HiveQL, SQLstream, PipelineDB Streaming SQL, and others that are already providing SQL or SQL-like language for processing streaming data. Most of these require only minor changes in codes so that software can be compatible with them. Oracle Big Data SQL, Azure, and Amazon are players in this field; they provide these facilities that are using probabilistic data with structures, as discussed elsewhere in this chapter.

6. Giascope

    Giascope is a distributed network monitoring architecture and one of the only of its type. It proposes pushing some of the query operations near the source (e.g. routers).

7. Feasibility study, design, and implementation of Cross-joins

    Feasibility study, design, and implementation of Cross-joins and Full-joins for the Continuous Join feature on PipelineDB (http://docs.pipelinedb.com/introduction .html) and other database solutions.

Open Research Problems

1. In-memory joins for streaming queries is a requirement for many sliding window algorithms.

2. Distributed optimization strategies aim at decreasing communication costs by reordering query operators, so that results remain the same. (Note that decreasing communication cost of data flying between systems is also studied under the paradigm termed "small data aside Big Data.")

3. Exploring the space of materialized views over infinite streams under the resource constraints (Chandrasekaran and Franklin 2002).

4. Determining lower bounds of storage space required by algorithms using the Turnstile model is also a huge challenge and includes complex terms owing to the nature of the model. Use of communication complexity to find the lower bounds in space for the Turnstile model is one of the candidate methods (Li et al. 2014).

5. Replacing distributed systems with multicore servers with a very large main memory for streaming data. "With the advent of multi-core servers that today can pack upwards of 48 cores in a single CPU, the traditional SMP approach is worth a second look for processing big data analytics jobs" (Wayne 2011). For instance, DataRush by Pervasive Software uses multiple core and performs better than the Hadoop program for data of sizes between 500 GB and 10 TB; above this limit, Hadoop outperforms the DataRush program. In addition, an octa-core system will definitely consume less energy than four dual-core systems. Commercial systems with more than 50 cores are available on the market. Multithreaded implementation models, such as OpenMP, OpenACC, and others, may be utilized for the processing of streams on multiple cores.

6. Adaptive query implementations. Can we design a querying system that will change a query algorithm based on the schema of the stream that arrived recently or that can figure out which algorithm to use from a set of algorithms of the same class?

Conclusions

In conclusion, it can be said that streaming data storage and processing is a Big Data challenge, as it fits all the three Vs of Big Data: volume, velocity, and variety. Streaming problems are more challenging in a distributed environment, owing to the requirement of synchronization between different stream data distributed among the nodes for many applications. We have already listed computation models, data structures, and data models that have been created as solutions for these problems. It is conclusive that the nature of streaming application is a predominant factor in determining the type of model at the levels of processing, main memory, and secondary storage devices. Market scenarios indicate two major requirements: (i) to provide tools that enable users to harness the best from streaming data by using SQL or SQL-like programming languages, and (ii) to solve the famous CAP theorem by using Lambda and Kappa architectures. Beating the CAP theorem is the most significant research challenge, and such work will revolutionize the field of streaming data.

References

Abramova V, Bernardino J. 2013. NoSQL databases: MongoDB vs Cassandra, pp. 14–22. *Proceedings of the International Conference on Computer Science and Software Engineering.* New York: Association for Computing Machinery.

Aggarwal CC. 2007. *Data Streams: Models and Algorithms.* New York: Springer Science & Business Media.

Babcock B, Babu S, Datar M, Motwani R, Widom J. 2002a. *Models and Issues in Data Stream Systems*. New York: Association for Computing Machinery.

Babcock B, Datar M, Motwani R. 2002b. Sampling from a moving window over streaming data. *Proceedings of the Thirteenth Annual ACM-SIAM Symposium on Discrete Algorithms*. Philadelphia, PA: Society for Industrial and Applied Mathematics.

Bockermann C. 2015. Mining Big Data streams for multiple concepts. Ph.D. dissertation. Technischen Universitat Dortmund an der Fakultat fur Informatik, Dortmund, Germany.

Brewer E. 2012. Pushing the CAP: Strategies for consistency and availability. *Computer* 45:23–29.

Chandra DG. 2015. BASE analysis of NoSQL database. *Future Generation Computer Systems* 52:13–21.

Chandrasekaran S, Franklin MJ. 2002. Streaming queries over streaming data, pp. 203–214. *Proceedings of the 28th International Conference on Very Large Data Bases*. Very Large Data Bases Endowment.

Chandy KM, Misra J. 1984. The Drinking Philosophers problem. *ACM Transactions on Programming Languages and Systems* 6(4):632–646.

Che-Qing J, Wei-Ning Q, Ao-Ying Z. 2004. Analysis and management of streaming data: A survey. *Journal of Software*.

Dmitry N. 2015. On big data stream processing. *International Journal of Open Information Technologies* 48–51.

Fan L, Cao P, Almeida J, Broder AZ. 2000. Summary cache: A scalable wide-area web cache sharing protocol. *IEEE ACM Transactions on Networking* 281–293.

Gartner. 2016. *Gartner Survey Report 2016*. http://www.gartner.com/technology/research/.

Gibbons PB, Tirthapura S. 2002. Distributed streams algorithms for Sliding Windows. *Proceedings of the Fourteenth Annual ACM symposium on Parallel Algorithms and Architectures*. New York: Association for Computing Machinery.

Gilbert AC, Kotidis Y, Muthukrishnan S, Strauss M. 2001. Surfing wavelets on streams: One-pass summaries for approximate aggregate queries. *VLDB* 79–88.

Golab L, Ozsu MT. 2003. Issues in data stream management. *ACM Sigmod Record*.

Grolinger K, Higashino WA, Tiwari A, Capretz MA. 2013. Data management in Cloud environments: NoSQL and NewSQL data stores. *Journal of Cloud Computing: Advances Systems and Applications*.

Khalilian M, Sul N, Norwati M. 2016. Data stream clustering by divide and conquer approach based on vector model. *Journal of Big Data*.

Leavitt N. 2010. Will NoSQL databases live up to their promise? *Computer* 12–14.

Li Y, Huy LN, David PW. 2014. Turnstile streaming algorithms might as well be linear sketches. *Proceedings of the 46th annual ACM Symposium on Theory of Computing*. New York: Association for Computing Machinery.

Maggs BM, Ramesh KS. 2015. Algorithmic nuggets in content delivery. *ACM SIGCOMM Computer Communication Review* 52–66.

Misra J, Gries D. 1982. Finding repeated elements. *Science of Computer Programming* 143–152.

Morales D, Bifet G, Khan A, Gam L. 2016. IoT Big Data stream mining, pp. 2119–2120. *Proceedings of the 22nd ACM SIGKDD International Conference on Knowledge Discovery and Data Mining*. New York: Association for Computing Machinery.

Muthukrishnan S. 2005. Data streams: Algorithms and applications. *Foundations and Trends in Theoretical Computer Science* 117–236.

Samet H. 2006. *Foundations of Multidimensional and Metric Data Structures*. Burlington, MA: Morgan Kaufmann.

Sanders P. 2014. Algorithm engineering for Big Data. *GI Jahrestagung*.

Schulte HC, Dustdar SS, Lecue F. 2015. Elastic stream processing for distributed environments. *IEEE Internet Computing* 54–59.

Wayne E. 2011. *The Next Wave in Big Data Analytics: Exploiting Multi-core Chips and SMP Machines*. http://www.b-eye-network.com/blogs/eckerson/archives/2011/01/the_next_wave_i.php.

Wayne E. 2014. *SQLstream Bets on the Internet of Things*. http://www.b-eye-network.com/blogs/eckerson /archives/2014/09/sqlstream_bets.php.

Further Readings

A comprehensive list of works on streaming problems can be found on the git repository: https://gist.github.com/debasishg/8172796.

For the repository of Kappa architecture, see http://milinda.pathirage.org/kappa-architecture.com.

Pantos R, May W. 2016. HTTP live streaming, see https://tools.ietf.org/html/draft-pantos-http-live-streaming-23.

11

Big Data Cluster Analysis: A Study of Existing Techniques and Future Directions

Piyush Lakhawat and Arun K. Somani

CONTENTS

Introduction

Cluster analysis (clustering) is a fundamental problem in an unsupervised machine learning domain. It has a huge range of applications in various fields, including bioinformatics, gene sequencing, market basket research, medicine, social network analysis, and recommender systems. The main idea in clustering is to arrange similar data objects from a given data set in clusters (groups). Clusters usually represent some type of real world entities or a meaningful abstraction. The knowledge of the abstraction acts as a stepping stone to further analysis and is therefore a fundamental requirement for data analysis problems. With the growing capabilities in data collection, transmission, storage, and computing, there has been a steady increase in cluster analysis-based research.

The realm of Big Data has affected almost all machine learning techniques. The existing data mining techniques have had to adapt to the three primary facets of Big Data: volume, velocity, and variety (Laney 2001). These are referred to as the three Vs of Big Data, and they are depicted in Figure 11.1. Volume refers to the big size of data being collected every day and used for analysis. Velocity refers to the continuous data collection pipelines active in various fields. Variety refers to the heterogeneous nature of data, ranging from text, image, numerical, etc., in unstructured, semistructured, and structured forms. The ways in which these three Vs affect any machine learning technique can be very different based on the technique's functioning.

In this chapter, we first provide an overview of cluster analysis along with a broad categorization of clustering techniques. Following this, we discuss each category of clustering techniques along with a detailed study of one prominent method in each category. While studying these techniques, we also focus on aspects which are likely to be affected by the three Vs of Big Data. Finally, we discuss important future directions for Big Data cluster analysis and research and provide our perspective on them.

Overview of Cluster Analysis

Any data considered for cluster analysis are implicitly expected to contain a set of clusters. A cluster can be imagined as a group of data objects which are similar to each other based on a specified criterion. Individual clusters are expected to possess different qualities

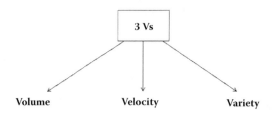

FIGURE 11.1
The three primary Vs of Big Data.

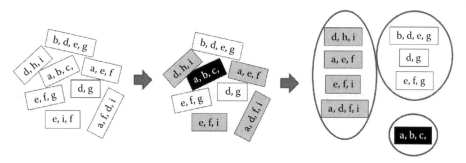

FIGURE 11.2
Visualization of clustering.

(usually judged by a specific metric) that distinguish them from one another. Such a scheme of clusters is found in many real-life applications, and knowledge of such schemes helps directly or indirectly when extracting useful information from the data. The varied nature of data and the types of similarity desired in clusters have led to the development of various clustering techniques. The eventual goal always is to obtain a suitable condensed representation of the data. Figure 11.2 gives a visual illustration of the clustering process.

The clusters obtained from the given data are sometimes the desired final information. For example, with a clustering analysis of bioinformatics data, researchers are able to identify useful associations among many data sets. Such information helps in designing future experiments. On other occasions, the knowledge of clusters can help quickly associate a new object to a cluster type and make a corresponding decision for it. For example, based on a customer's shopping basket, an online retailer can immediately try to predict which type of a customer he or she is (i.e., they are most similar to which cluster) and recommend suitable products. Attributes like the type of data (numerical, categorical, multimedia, etc.), the expected properties of the data (correlation, skewness, mean, etc.), size, and speed of the data all play important roles in deciding the type of cluster analysis to be performed. We use a small example scenario to explain the intuition behind the clustering problem.

An Illustrative Example

Let us consider a log kept of all items bought by each customer from an online retail store. Table 11.1 is an illustration of one such log of a short period on the store's database.

By observing the contents of Table 11.1 we notice that customers 2, 3, and 4 bought similar items and customers 5 and 6 bought similar items that were different from those

TABLE 11.1

Illustration of Transactions during Five Minutes at a Retail Store Website

Customer ID	Time of Purchase	Items Bought
1	3:00 PM	Printing paper, printer cartridge
2	3:02 PM	Detergent, cooking oil, bread, a novel "abc"
3	3:02 PM	Coffee beans, sugar, bread, a novel "abc"
4	3:03 PM	Bread, coffee beans, soap
5	3:03 PM	T-shirt, shorts, socks
6	3:05 PM	T-shirt, shoes

for customers 2, 3, and 4. Items bought by customer 1 were not similar to any other customer. This observation points to an attribute of the data set that there are types of customers who buy similar items. But how should we formally analyze and report such an attribute? This is one of the primary questions that needs to be answered by cluster analysis.

Let us try to identify the important factors behind developing such a cluster analysis technique. First, we need to identify a metric to compare the similarities of various customers. Let us use the number of common items bought by two customers as a metric in this case. So, based on this metric, we can state that customer 2 and customer 3 have two common items and therefore are more similar than customer 5 and customer 6, who only had one common item. Second, we also need to identify a metric of similarity for clusters (groups of customers in the example). A possible metric could be the ratio of the number of common items between the two clusters versus the mean sizes of the two clusters.

Similarity

If we consider a cluster of {customer 2, customer 3} and a singleton cluster of {customer 4}, then the similarity between them would be 2/1.5, or 1.3. Note that the definitions of similarity for clusters of customers and single customers become equivalent for singleton clusters. This can be a flawed similarity metric, because once the cluster sizes become varied, the effects of averaging will distort the similarity values. However, for the sake of simplicity, let us continue with this definition. We also need a clustering criterion based on this definition on similarity. In each incremental step, we can merge a pair of clusters with the highest similarity. This idea is actually the skeleton of an important class of clustering techniques called hierarchical agglomerative clustering.

Termination

One final step that we now need to perform is a criterion to terminate the clustering process. A simple way in this case can be a predefined number of clusters to be obtained before stopping. Many existing clustering techniques do follow such a criterion. However, the state-of-the-art techniques try to identify such a criterion based on the data set and how the clustering process is proceeding. That is, whether the formation of new clusters is yielding new information or is oversimplifying the data set. In this example, let us assume that we find three clusters and terminate the process.

Following the clustering technique steps identified above, we first merge customers 2 and 3 or 3 and 4 into a cluster. Following that, we form a cluster of customers 2, 3, and 4. Next, we form a cluster of customers 5 and 6. At this point, we have formed three clusters: {customer 1}, {customer 2, customer 3, customer 4}, and {customer 5, customer 6}. We can name them clusters A, B, and C, respectively. This gives us a formal way to analyze and report any clusters present in a data set of the type present in Table 11.1. A more sophisticated version of such a process leads to the development of various cluster analysis techniques. The knowledge of clusters in any data set acts as a final or intermediate step in further analysis for various scientific and business applications. For example, in our illustrative example, assume a new customer 7 adds the following to her cart: bread, coffee beans, and sugar. Then, we can immediately associate this customer with cluster B and suggest the novel "abc" item for her to buy. With this understanding, let us now discuss a broad categorization of clustering techniques.

Types of Clustering Techniques

Clustering techniques are developed and chosen based on the prior understanding of the data. Since these belong to the unsupervised machine learning category, making a right choice of clustering technique is very important. Based on the wide variety of data types, many corresponding clustering techniques have been developed, as depicted in Figure 11.3. Most of the clustering techniques can be categorized based on the cluster-building methodology. The four broad categorizations (Berkhin 2006) are: hierarchical clustering, density-based clustering, partitioning-based clustering, and grid-based clustering. There are few other techniques which do not fall under any of the above categories; these can be categorized under a fifth category, termed miscellaneous clustering techniques. In the following sections, we briefly discuss all of these techniques and provide one specific example from each category in more detail.

Hierarchical Clustering

Overview

As the name suggests, these techniques follow a hierarchy (ranking) criterion to perform the clustering. This ranking is typically based on some metric of similarity among clusters, and a top-down or bottom-up approach is used based on the choice of clustering.

The top-down and the bottom-up hierarchical clustering approaches are also commonly known as divisive and agglomerative hierarchical clustering, respectively. Figure 11.4 aids in visualizing the two types of hierarchical clustering. The key benefits of hierarchical clustering are:

1. Ability to define data-specific merging and dividing criterion, making it widely applicable
2. Option to achieve cluster structures of various shapes and sizes based on the termination criterion

However, the same reasons can also lead to inaccurate clusters sometimes due to:

- Lack of knowledge of how the merging and dividing criterion will influence the clustering process
- Not knowing the best level at which to stop the clustering, as this can cause information loss as well

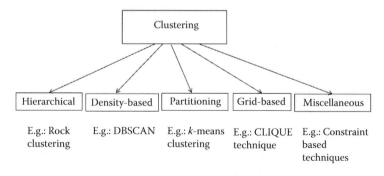

FIGURE 11.3
Categorization of clustering types.

Agglomerative hierarchical clustering

Divisive hierarchical clustering

FIGURE 11.4
Two types of hierarchical clustering.

A key concept in hierarchical clustering is a dendrogram. It is a tree type structure made of clusters based on the hierarchical relationships among them. Since it is a tree type structure, there is a natural concept of child, sibling, and parent. Children of a cluster divide the data into subclusters. Therefore, it is very convenient with hierarchical clustering to achieve any desired level of coarseness or fineness. As shown in Figure 11.4, bottom–up clustering starts by defining each data point as a single cluster and keeps merging clusters based on similarity. Top-down clustering follows the exact opposite criterion by defining the entire data set as a single cluster and dividing it into subclusters based on dissimilarity. Both the processes continue until a termination criterion (frequently, a requested number [*k*] of clusters) is achieved.

Agglomerative Hierarchical Clustering

For agglomerative hierarchical clustering, there can be numerous choices for merging techniques with different pros and cons among them based on complexity, convergence, speed, etc. A popular choice is to calculate the average distance between all possible pairs of data points in the two clusters to be used as the final distance between them. Other techniques recommend using the difference between some version of the mean of the data in the two clusters to evaluate their distance. Techniques like using the shortest distance between any two data points for use as the cluster distances are not recommended, as these lead to big clusters getting bigger over time. In case of large clusters, it is not uncommon to use variety of sampling techniques to reduce the computational complexity while still achieving reasonable accuracy.

Divisive Clustering

As shown in Figure 11.4, divisive clustering techniques are initiated with the entire data set defined as a single cluster. The final goal is to achieve a dendrogram of desired qualities with all leaf nodes as the final set of clusters. In certain situations, divisive clustering can be favored over agglomerative clustering, especially when clusters of varying granularity are expected or more than one type of clustering criterion is required. Due to it being a type of hierarchical clustering, there is an option of evaluating the clusters formed at each step. Therefore, if it is expected that the current data arrangement already consists of fewer clusters, then divisive clustering can save a lot of computation by partitioning those clusters in just one step.

A suitable similarity (or dissimilarity) index is very important in all hierarchical clustering techniques. The reason for this is that these indexes drive the entire clustering process, and therefore inaccuracy in them will propagate throughout the whole analysis. Therefore, the state-of-the-art techniques of this category justify their choice of such a metric very succinctly; and this step should be followed by verifying the validity of the clusters found in applicable data sets. Such metrics are also required to have good scalability, because of their repeated usage in their respective clustering algorithm and the possibility of large clusters in the data. Let us now study in further detail one of the most popular hierarchical clustering techniques, called ROCK clustering.

ROCK Clustering Technique

For an algorithm-specific understanding of the hierarchical clustering technique, we shall analyze the popular ROCK clustering algorithm (Guha et al. 2000). The main strength of this algorithm is that it provides very intuitive clustering logic for categorical data. Ideas like using averages or other numerical operations are not applicable to categorical data. To overcome this, ROCK clustering entails production of a similarity graph, with links connecting objects based on similarities among them. The core concept is that the higher the number of links between objects, the greater the implied similarity. Such a methodology allows an application to numerical, Boolean, and categorical data or their combinations. Zaïane et al. (2002) mentioned that since this algorithm uses global parameters, it inhibits the clustering process to generate naturally present clusters of uneven sizes.

The idea of links is very important in this clustering technique. The authors define a link(a,b) to be the number of common neighbors to a and b. Therefore, higher values of link(a,b) lead to a higher chance for a and b to be in the same cluster. The objective is for each cluster to have its highest possible degree of connectivity. Hence, the sum of link(a,b) for the data point pairs (a,b) should be maximized for each cluster as well minimized for each pair (a,b) from different clusters. This rationale led the authors to include the following criterion function for k clusters, which they try to maximize:

$$E_l = \sum_{i=1}^{k} n_i * \sum_{a,b \in C_i} \frac{link(a,b)}{n_i^{1+2f(\theta)}}$$

They defined $f(\theta)$ as a function which depends on the data and the clusters of interest. The function $f(\theta)$ is designed to have the following property: each data point in cluster C_i should have approximately $n_i^{f(\theta)}$ neighbors. Besides ensuring strong connectivity, $f(\theta)$ also allows clusters to be unique. Guha et al. (2000) explained this in further detail: with the goal of maximizing this function, the ROCK algorithm follows an agglomerative approach to incrementally merge clusters until a predefined number of clusters is achieved.

Expected Effects of the Three Vs on the ROCK Clustering Technique

The computation of links is one of the more expensive steps in the ROCK technique, achieving a complexity of $O(n^{2.37})$ with matrix multiplication techniques. However, this is not the biggest challenge among the three Vs of Big Data, as there is potential to achieve distributed versions of this technique. Overall algorithmic complexity is described by Guha and Shim (2000) to be $O[n^2 + nm_m m_a + n^2 \log(n)]$ in the worst case, where m_a is the average number of neighbors and m_m is the maximum number of neighbors at a point. Since this overall nature of the algorithms is agglomerative in nature, many steps in the algorithm can be distributed.

The velocity of data can be a bottleneck if it is above a certain limit, but we believe the biggest challenge to adopting ROCK clustering (and most other hierarchical clustering techniques) would be due to the variety of data. The link-based connectivity definitions will be too simplistic for rich variety and unstructured data sets. The knowledge of the number of clusters that need to be formed will also be almost impossible to obtain *a priori* in most cases. Therefore, in future versions of such algorithms, it is imperative to develop clustering progress monitoring techniques, so that each cluster analysis can be tailored for specific data sets.

Density-Based Clustering

Overview

If we interpret a data set as a density distribution in some Euclidean space, then the connected components of such a space can be interpreted as the clusters present in the data set. The central idea in density-based clustering is to do such mapping as accurately as possible and then through iterative steps it improves the connectivity strength of clusters.

Every density-based clustering algorithm starts with the strongly connected parts of the data set as individual clusters and then keeps expanding these clusters by searching for points which enhance the density function. A combination of two reasons makes this category of techniques unique. First, the initial cluster assignment captures the global picture of the data set and ensures that the analysis doesn't strongly deviate from that. The second reason is that the iterations to improve the connectivity capture the local information related to each cluster and therefore improve the overall accuracy. This allows the density-based techniques to detect clusters of varied shapes and sizes along with the freedom to rearrange data in any order necessary.

The clusters eventually found are dense sections from the data set, after information has been filtered out, leaving behind sparse sections. There is a risk in these techniques that sometimes two dense sections will be fused together due to inaccurate parameter settings. Such oversimplifications need to be avoided. Figure 11.5 visually illustrates this drawback.

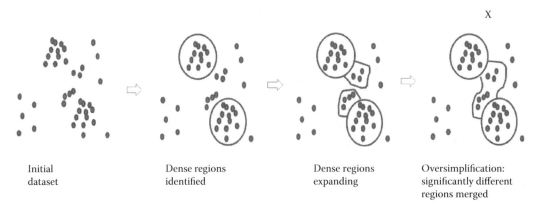

| Initial dataset | Dense regions identified | Dense regions expanding | Oversimplification: significantly different regions merged |

FIGURE 11.5
Potential drawbacks of density-based clustering.

Due to a lack of visual interpretation of data density in some cases, visualization can be challenging for density-based clustering. It is not uncommon to find clusters of seemingly arbitrary shapes.

The implicit assumption in density-based clustering is that the outliers and noise in the data don't have enough density to significantly affect other clusters or form a cluster themselves. Therefore, at the end of density clustering, any section of data which is declared sparse should be assumed not useful in the clustering analysis (Aggarwal and Reddy 2013). Key ideas to focus on when working with a density-based algorithm are density estimations and the definition of connectivity.

Next, we study and present details of one of the most popular density-based algorithms, called DBSCAN.

DBSCAN Clustering Technique

DBSCAN (Ester et al. 1996) builds up the clusters by finding densely connected data points in a data set. Its starts by finding any "core point." A data point is called a core point if it has more than a minimum number of data points near it. By "near it," we imply that the distance metric of the algorithm should be less than a predefined value (usually referred to as Eps). The minimum number of points required to call a data point a core point are referred to as MinPts. Any point which is in the range of Eps for a given point is said to be directly reachable from that point. While any point which can be reached by hopping on successive directly reachable points is called a reachable point. Therefore, points not reachable from any other data point are considered sparse and ignored from the analysis.

DBSCAN starts with an arbitrary point and checks all other points in its surrounding "Eps" space. If no point is found, then this point is ignored and some other arbitrary point is selected. If a point(s) is found in the Eps space, then points in their Eps are searched for. This goes on until each point in the cluster has no other reachable point from it. Once this is done, another arbitrary point from outside this cluster is selected and the process is repeated. The algorithm terminates when each point either belongs to some cluster or is a completely isolated point (not reachable from anywhere).

It should be noted that even though the initial core point selection is arbitrary, every point in its associated cluster will eventually be found. And the same cluster would have been found even if any other point in that cluster had been the initial selection in the process. However, this is true when the value of Eps and MinPts are fixed. The accurate estimation of these two parameters has always been a challenge when using the DBSCAN algorithm.

Expected Effects of the Three Vs on the DBSCAN Clustering Technique

While the DBSCAN algorithm has many strong points, it still needs to adapt to the nature of Big Data. In its native form, DBSCAN requires an entire data set to perform clustering. This approach is infeasible, even for moderate-sized data sets in today's times. However, to cater to the large volume, parallel versions of DBSCAN have already been proposed (Januzaj et al. 2004).

While the big volume of the data is a problem, another problem is the velocity of the data. This translates into a need for faster approximate versions of the algorithm. Certain sampling-based versions of DBSCAN have been introduced (Borah and Bhattacharyya 2004). The goal of these techniques is to obtain a near-accurate cluster structure while not having to process the entire data set.

The variety aspect of Big Data is also an important factor, and addressing that in a density-based algorithm like DBSCAN can be especially challenging. The key challenge comes with suitable definitions for connectivity and density functions.

Partitioning-Based Clustering

Overview

As the name suggests, partitioning-based clustering relies on achieving the final clusters through successive partitioning and refinement steps. There is always either a clustering quality measurement criterion or an indicator function which decides the conclusion of the algorithm. The intrinsic benefit of partitioning-based clustering methods is that they can exploit any existing data partitioning, in which the data are provided, and start building up the clusters from there. Some other techniques, like hierarchical clustering, will always start the clustering process from the same state irrespective of the formatting of data provided. The design of partitioning-based algorithms also facilitates generation of distributed and parallel solutions.

The idea of iteratively improving the search space has been very effective in various domains, like linear programming (Luenberger 1973) or advanced sorting techniques (Mehlhorn 2013), to name a few. Therefore, it is not surprising that it yields strong results in cluster analysis as well. Classical partitioning techniques, like the *k*-means algorithm, is still highly used and is very effective for a variety of applications. A disadvantage of that type of clustering is that getting a rough idea of cluster structure can be difficult for the initial iterations.

k-Means Clustering Technique

If we were to develop a list of the most-used clustering algorithms, most would agree that the *k*-means algorithm deserves a place on that list. The simple yet powerful clustering logic of this technique along with its applicability to most numerical data applications are the reasons for it.

The key idea in *k*-means clustering is to identify the "*k*" means from the data set that are representative of most data points around them, while each of these *k*-means is sufficiently different from each other. The choice of a suitable number *k* is a challenge, and there are ways to estimate the best *k* for a given data set in order to avoid overfitting. The main function to be minimized in this technique is the distance between the mean (also referred to as a centroid) and the points associated with each mean. Vector-based distance, like the following, is a common distance function used.

$$Obj.\ Func. = \sum_{j=1}^{k} \sum_{x_i \in C_j} \left\| x_i - C_j \right\|^2$$

In the above function, k represents the number of clusters, C_j represents the mean, and x_i represents a point associated with that mean. Such an objective function is applicable when data are numerical in nature and also each data point has the same dimensions. For other cases, like categorical data, techniques with similar logic have been developed (Huang 1998) which use the mode as the central idea instead of the mean.

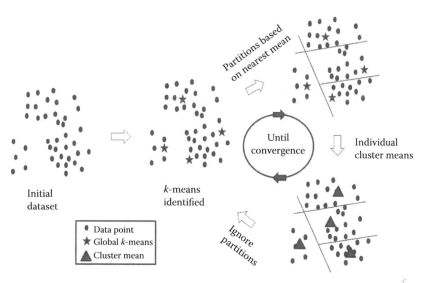

FIGURE 11.6
Key concepts of *k*-means clustering.

The basic version of the *k*-means algorithm (Hartigan and Wong 1979) initializes the clustering process by defining the first set of *k*-means and then assigning the points to each mean based on minimizing the total distances as per the objective function. This assignment is called partitioning the data. Following this step, new means (centroids) are computed for each data partition individually. These individual means from each partition are now considered the new *k*-means and are used to create new partitions based on minimizing the objective function. This process is ideally repeated until the new partitions are not changing. That is, all the *k*-means coincide with the individual partition means. Figure 11.6 provides a visualization of *k*-means clustering.

Finally, the initialization of the clusters also has an effect on the clustering performance. Milligan (1981) suggested the use of a dendrogram (via hierarchical agglomerative clustering) to identify the initial cluster assignment, while Hartigan and Wong (1979) used the nearest-neighbor density to develop an initial clustering. A random sampling-based approach is described by Bradley and Fayyad (1998).

Expected Effects of 3 Vs on the k-Means Clustering Technique

k-means will probably continue to be one of the more popular clustering techniques in the times of Big Data. Many variants of the *k*-means technique have been developed over time. Because the core premise of the technique is simple and effective, various types of numerical data respond well to this analysis. Since there is scope for both parallelization and addition of machine learning components to the *k*-means technique, it will continue to be effective in terms of handling the volume and velocity components of Big Data.

However, further sophistication is needed in terms of handling the variety aspects of Big Data (e.g., images, texts, etc.). Combination of other machine learning techniques (or even some other clustering techniques) with *k*-means to achieve more versatility in terms of data interpretation will be required.

Grid-Based Clustering

Overview

It can be argued that most grid-based clustering techniques can be classified as density, partitioning, or hierarchical clustering techniques, or at least be called a combination of them. However, a true classification of a clustering technique should be based on its core clustering strategy. The key concept in grid-based clustering is that of projecting the data set (or more specifically the data space) to a more appropriate space which can be easier to manipulate and identify the clusters within. This makes grid-based clustering unique and separates it into its own category of techniques. High-dimensional data sets found in current applications make this type of clustering especially relevant.

Reducing the computation complexity is one of the main goals of using grid-based techniques. Once data are transformed into the desired grid space, the rest of the process is to find clusters by using the grids. The grids can have attributes like means or densities associated with them. The success of grid-based clustering techniques depends upon the accuracy of such transformations in capturing the essential data attributes required for clustering. Let us now discuss in further detail the popular grid-based CLIQUE clustering technique.

CLIQUE Clustering Technique

Agrawal et al. (1998) proposed the CLIQUE clustering algorithm. It is a grid-based clustering algorithm which uses the concept of data density to locate clusters. Like all grid clustering techniques, the goal is to find clusters in the subspace of high-dimensional data sets. A strong feature of CLIQUE clustering is that it presents the final cluster description as a disjunctive normal form expression. This is the minimal description of the clustering aids in understanding and interpretability of the cluster structure.

Agrawal et al. (1998) claimed that it is important to use a subset of real dimensions of data instead of creating new dimensions by mathematical operations, the reasoning being that real dimensions represent some factual information while created dimension might be difficult to interpret. Since this is a density-based clustering approach, a cluster is interpreted as a region with data points present in high density compared to other regions. Therefore, the CLIQUE clustering algorithm proceeds to identify simplifying transformations of a data set which make high-density areas either visible or easier to locate.

The CLIQUE algorithm transformation begins with mapping its data set points onto the units of the grid structure. A data point will be mapped onto a particular unit (grid) if the value of all the dimensions of the data point lie within the specified range of this unit. Once the transformation process (also called taking projections step) is over, all the units are observed and the units with more than a certain number of data points in them are considered dense. The remaining units are ignored. Different choices of dimensions to transform will result in different projections of the data set. The goal is to find the most suitable projection for clustering.

Algorithmically, the clustering process can be divided into three components: identifying the subspaces (a bottom-up technique is used to achieve this), identifying clusters in the subspaces (a graphical representation is used followed by a depth-first search), and finally generation of a minimum description of clusters. Agrawal et al. (1998) showed that an optimal solution is NP hard and developed a greedy approach to achieve these components.

Expected Effects of the Three Vs on the CLIQUE Clustering Technique

While the worst-case behavior of the subspace discovery process has been shown to be exponential in the highest dimension, in most practical cases it can be controlled by pre-defining the number of passes over the data set. This criterion will need to be studied in further detail, given the increasing variety in data sets in recent times.

One strength of the CLIQUE clustering technique is that once the subspaces are identified, the cluster discovery and the minimum description generation can be done in a distributed fashion. This helps subdue the effects of the volume and velocity aspects of the data.

Overall, such grid-based techniques have the important feature of simplifying a complex data set. This makes such techniques very promising as we look ahead. We expect aspects of these techniques to be present in most future Big Data clustering techniques.

Miscellaneous Clustering Techniques

Certain clustering techniques do not fit in any of the above categories. Often these techniques are an amalgamation of a clustering technique and other application-specific technique. Berkhin (2006) discussed these in much detail. In this section we provide an overview of these methods.

In recent years, a new class of clustering has emerged from a practical point of view; it is called constraint-based clustering (Tung et al. 2001). The need for constraint-based clustering is understandable, as it is hard to imagine any real world applications without specific constraints associated with them. While traditional clustering techniques typically aim to maximize (or minimize) certain clustering criterion, constraint-based clustering tries to do the same, along with maintaining the specified constraints for validity. If constraint-based clustering was an optimization problem, then traditional clustering would be a problem of just maximizing the objective function. Tung et al. (2001) specified a few ways in which constraints are imposed in clustering algorithms: a constraint on certain objects to be clustered together, a constraint on objects not to be clustered together, bounds on certain algorithm parameters, specific constraints on individual clusters, etc.

There have been certain modifications to the partitioning clustering methods as well. For example, supervised learning techniques are used to train classifiers specific to clustering decisions (Liu et al. 2000). These classifiers then influence the future decisions for partitioning. Swarm optimization techniques have also been used in conjunction with k-means clustering to accelerate the centroid discovery process (Van der Merwe and Engelbrecht 2003).

Recent works have also used evolutionary techniques in clustering algorithms. The SINICC (simulation of near-optima for internal clustering criteria) (Brown and Huntley 1992) algorithm uses simulated annealing in a framework of partitioning-based clustering. Genetic algorithms are also being applied for cluster analysis. The GGA (genetically guided algorithm) (Hall et al. 1999) applies fuzzy and hard means logic in finding the k-means clustering. Those authors found that the use of genetic algorithms especially helped in the initialization aspect of k-means clustering.

Our discussion here is far from an exhaustive discussion of clustering techniques, i.e., merging with other data mining techniques to provide improved application-specific results. However, we have shed light on such a need in data mining research. With the data being richer and more detailed in the future (increased variety), the need for multiple data mining techniques in combination is going to increase.

Future Directions for Big Data Cluster Analysis Research

An understanding of the effects of the nature of Big Data on existing powerful clustering techniques helps in adapting to the new developments. However, it is also very important to understand the qualities that are desirable for future clustering algorithms which will seamlessly fit in the Big Data realm. In this section, we discuss three future directions for Big Data cluster analysis research. Independent as well as a collaborative pursuit in these areas will be required to manage the three Vs of Big Data.

Distributed Techniques

With data being collected globally and stored in geographically distributed data centers, the need for distributed clustering techniques will be inevitable. Clustering by nature is not a distributed operation, so innovative techniques are required to bridge that gap. According to Aggarwal and Reddy (2013), the general framework for all distributed clustering techniques can be described using the following four steps.

1. Divide and distribute the data
2. Local clusters are found at each node
3. Global clusters are found by gathering all the distributed information
4. Cluster refinement takes place in each of the local nodes, based on the knowledge of global clusters

While distributed techniques have the benefits of parallel performance speedup and distributed memory utilization, the communication costs have to be managed. Especially in recent times with the data sets being massive, moving data from one node to another can be very expensive. Therefore, a key challenge for distributed clustering algorithms is to find data representations for local clusters which require the least memory bandwidth for communication while still maintaining a high degree of useful information. Data space projections used in grid-based clustering techniques can be used here towards this end. Network architects will also need to keep the demand for such applications in consideration when designing the next generation of data center networks.

Figure 11.7 depicts a distributed clustering flow of data in such a class of algorithms. In the following, we discuss further details of three recent distributed clustering algorithms: DBDC (a density-based distributed clustering technique), ParMETIS (a graph partitioning-based clustering technique), and PKMeans (a MapReduce-based *k*-means-type clustering technique). Aggarwal and Reddy (2013) described these and addtional algorithms in further detail.

Density-Based Distributed Clustering

DBDC, as the name suggests, uses density-based clustering (more specifically, the DBSCAN algorithm) as its key concept (Januzaj et al. 2004). This turns out to be a good choice, because data densities are naturally good for superimposition. Therefore, obtaining the global clustering is very straightforward. Another benefit of using density-based clustering in a distributed framework is that it allows for very sparse local clustering (and hence lower communication costs) by slight parameter adjustments when needed.

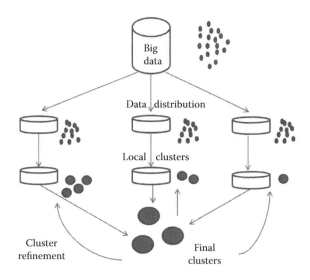

FIGURE 11.7
Distributed clustering flow.

Graph Partitioning-Based Clustering

Permits are built as a distributed version of the graph partitioning METIS algorith (Karypis and Kumar 1998, 1999). METIS is one of the popular graph partitioning algorithms. Graph partitioning aims to divide the nodes of a graph into subgraphs with nearly equal sums of node weights, while minimizing the sums of edge weights of boundary edges. METIS achieves this by first using matching techniques to gather strongly connected nodes in groups, followed by partitioning these groups into k subgraphs. This is followed by some final refinements. ParMETIS (Karypis and Kumar 1999) performs the matching techniques in a distributed fashion and then incrementally achieves a global matching, which is then transmitted to every node. The refinements are then done locally for ParMETIS.

MapReduce-Based k-Means-Type Clustering

PKMeans (Zhao et al. 2009) is a MapReduce-based version of the popular k-means algorithm. Parallel performance is achieved by dividing the two steps of k-means between the mapper and the reducer part. The first step of k-means clustering (partitioning), where each data point needs to be associated with the mean, is done by the mapper. The second iterative step, where the individual cluster means are computed, is done by the reducer. Since k-means is a partitioning-based clustering, it gels well with the MapReduce framework.

Robust Techniques

More data also means more noise. Therefore, future clustering techniques will need to be more adept in dealing with noisy and inaccurate data. While the need for robustness in clustering techniques has already been identified, it has become more relevant in the times of Big Data. The lack of robustness in one of the most famous clustering algorithms, k-means, led to the development of its variant, called trimmed k-means (Cuesta-Albertos et al. 1997). García-Escudero et al. established that the k-means method has a breakdown point of 0.

This implies a single outlier data element placed randomly far away can completely disturb the *k*-means clustering (Garcia-Escudero and Gordaliza 1999, García-Escudero et al. 2010).

Trimming is a useful concept to achieve robustness. A simple trimmed mean cuts out a particular ratio of the largest and the smallest observations before finding the mean of the data. However, for used in clustering, we cannot simply trim data from the top and bottom. A self-trimming method, like the following, should allow less useful parts of data (outliers) to be removed so that they do not influence the clustering (Garcia-Escudero and Gordaliza 1999, García-Escudero et al. 2010):

$$\arg \underset{Y}{\min} \; \underset{m_1,\ldots,m_k}{\min} \sum_{X_i \in Y} \underset{j=1\ldots k}{\min} \left\| X_i - m_j \right\|^2$$

This is a double minimization problem to find *k* centers $\{m_1, \ldots, m_k\}$. The range of Y will be a subset of the entire sample $\{X_1, \ldots, X_n\}$. Such conditions add robustness for finding *k*-means clusters and make it is less susceptible to extreme outliers.

Similar robustness while using the knowledge of data distributions and the ideas from sampling theory will need to be adopted into more clustering techniques in the future. This will ensure the maximum extraction of useful information from data while minimizing the effects of outliers.

Clustering Engines

Fundamental machine learning tasks like clustering can be generalized, and there can be generic techniques which cluster a variety of data. A sizeable amount of being heterogeneity in nature calls for development of such clustering engines.

While this research area is in a relatively nascent state, there have been certain interesting contributions. Ferragina and Gulli (2004) investigates the Web snippet hierarchical clustering problem from a software-based perspective and developed an algorithmic solution. They drew snippets from 16 different Web engines and built clusters on the fly without any knowledge of any predefined clusters. They labeled the clusters based on sentence structures and content, while using two knowledge bases built during preprocessing for selecting sentences and assigning clusters. Their technique arranges clusters into a hierarchy and then allocates them to appropriate nodes based on relevant sentences in them. Their technique also allows overlapping of clusters across various levels of the hierarchy in order to be flexible in assignments.

Carpineto et al. (2009) provided a detailed discussion on Web clustering engines. They claimed that clustering engines successfully overcome many of the challenges of present-day search engines by generating clusters of search results as an extra feature. They strongly emphasized that clustering engines are complementary to search engines. They mentioned that benefits like subtopic search of a group of search results and fast information summarization make clustering engines highly useful. With the huge variety of data available through Web searches these days, any tool which helps in arranging and visualizing this information does seem very useful. The views presented by Carpineto et al. (2009) reenforced our belief that, moving forward in the Big Data age, clustering engines will play an important role in the industry.

Conclusions

We have presented the needs, the processes currently utilized for analysis, and future directions for cluster analysis. We discussed the intuition behind clustering methods and the various types of cluster analysis techniques based on their clustering criterion. We analyzed the strengths and weaknesses of various clustering techniques and discussed in detail one popular technique in each category. We also discussed the possible effects of the three Vs of Big Data on each of these techniques. We also described a few additional clustering techniques which do not fall into any particular category. Finally, three important future research directions for cluster analysis in the Big Data age were discussed, namely, distributed clustering, robust clustering techniques, and clustering engines.

References

Aggarwal CC, Reddy CK (eds.). 2013. *Data Clustering: Algorithms and Applications*. Boca Raton, FL: CRC Press.

Agrawal R, Gehrke J, Gunopulos D, Raghavan P. 1998. Automatic subspace clustering of high dimensional data for data mining applications, pp. 94–105. *SIGMOD '98 Proceedings of the 1998 SIGMOD International Conference on the Management of Data*. New York: ACM.

Berkhin P. 2006. A survey of clustering data mining techniques, pp. 25–71. *Grouping Multidimensional Data*. Berlin: Springer.

Borah B, Bhattacharyya DK. 2004. An improved sampling-based DBSCAN for large spatial databases, pp. 92–96. *Proceedings of the 2004 Conference on Intelligent Sensing and Information Processing*. New York: IEEE.

Bradley PS, Fayyad UM. 1998. Refining initial points for k-means clustering, pp. 91–99. *ICML Proceedings of the Fifteenth International Conference on Machine Learning*. New York: ACM.

Brown DE, Huntley CL. 1992. A practical application of simulated annealing to clustering. *Pattern Recognition* 25(4):401–412.

Carpineto C, Osiński S, Romano G, Weiss D. 2009. A survey of web clustering engines. *ACM Computing Surveys* 41(3):17.

Cuesta-Albertos JA, Gordaliza A, Matrán C. 1997. Trimmed k-means: An attempt to robustify quantizers. *Annals of Statistics* 25(2):553–576.

Ester M, Kriegel HP, Sander J, Xu X. 1996. A density-based algorithm for discovering clusters in large spatial databases with noise. *Kdd* 96(34):226–231.

Ferragina P, Gulli A. 2004. The anatomy of a hierarchical clustering engine for Web-page, news and book snippets, pp. 395–398. *Fourth IEEE International Conference on Data Mining*. New York: IEEE.

Garcia-Escudero LA, Gordaliza A. 1999. Robustness properties of k means and trimmed k means. *Journal of the American Statistical Association* 94(447):956–969.

García-Escudero LA, Gordaliza A, Matrán C, Mayo-Iscar A. 2010. A review of robust clustering methods. *Advances in Data Analysis and Classification* 4(2–3):89–109.

Guha S, Rastogi R, Shim K. 2000. ROCK: A robust clustering algorithm for categorical attributes. *Information Systems* 25(5):345–366.

Hall LO, Ozyurt IB, Bezdek JC. 1999. Clustering with a genetically optimized approach. *IEEE Transactions on Evolutionary Computation* 3(2):103–112.

Hartigan JA, Wong MA. 1979. Algorithm AS 136: A k-means clustering algorithm. *Journal of the Royal Statistical Society C Applied Statistics* 28(1):100–108.

Huang Z. 1998. Extensions to the k-means algorithm for clustering large data sets with categorical values. *Data Mining and Knowledge Discovery* 2(3):283–304.

Januzaj E, Kriegel HP, Pfeifle M. 2004. DBDC: Density based distributed clustering, pp. 88–105. *International Conference on Extending Database Technology*. Berlin: Springer.

Karypis G, Kumar V. 1998. Multilevel k-way partitioning scheme for irregular graphs. *Journal of Parallel and Distributed Computing* 48(1):96–129.

Karypis G, Kumar V. 1999. Parallel multilevel series k-way partitioning scheme for irregular graphs. *Siam Review* 41(2):278–300.

Laney D. 2001. 3D data management: Controlling data volume, velocity and variety. *META Group Research Note* 6:70.

Liu B, Xia Y, Yu PS. 2000. Clustering through decision tree construction, pp. 20–29. *Proceedings of the Ninth International Conference on Information and Knowledge Management*. New York: ACM.

Luenberger DG. 1973. *Introduction to Linear and Nonlinear Programming*, vol 28. Reading, MA: Addison-Wesley.

Mehlhorn K. 2013. *Data Structures and Algorithms. 1: Sorting and Searching*, vol. 1. Springer Science & Business Media.

Milligan GW. 1981. A Monte Carlo study of thirty internal criterion measures for cluster analysis. *Psychometrika* 46(2):187–199.

Tung AK, Han J, Lakshmanan LV, Ng RT. 2001. Constraint-based clustering in large databases, pp. 405–419. *International Conference on Database Theory*. Berlin: Springer.

Van der Merwe DW, Engelbrecht AP. 2003. Data clustering using particle swarm optimization, pp. 215–220. *2003 IEE Conference on Evolutionary Computation*. New York: IEEE.

Zaïane OR, Foss A, Lee CH, Wang W. 2002. On data clustering analysis: Scalability, constraints, and validation, pp. 28–39. *Pacific-Asia Conference on Knowledge Discovery and Data Mining*. Berlin: Springer.

Zhao W, Ma H, He Q. 2009. Parallel k-means clustering based on MapReduce, pp. 674–679. *IEEE International Conference on Cloud Computing*. Berlin: Springer.

Key Terminology and Definitions

Big Data: it has a moving definition in time. It typically means the amount of data which requires high-performance machines for analysis.

Cluster Analysis: a class of unsupervised learning problems where the goal is to obtain a set of clusters (a group of similar objects) for a given data set. The clusters themselves are expected to be unique among each other.

Clustering Engines: a relatively new concept. These are software systems which continuously perform incremental cluster analysis on streaming data.

Distributed Clustering: a special class of clustering analysis where data are explicitly divided into separate chunks, analyzed, and then summarized globally. It is done to achieve computation speedup and to manage large data sets.

Noisy Data: data which contain inaccuracies with respect to the expected ideal properties of the data. All real data are expected to be noisy. However, with huge amounts of data being collected these days, it is even more difficult to understand the nature of data and, hence, the additional noise.

Three Vs: volume (the generally big size of data), velocity (the fast speed of data arrival), and variety (the heterogeneous nature of data). These are used to describe the nature of Big Data as a result of modern data collection, transmission, storage, and computing capabilities.

Unsupervised Machine Learning: class of machine learning problems where no data labels are available to supervise the learning process. In contrast, supervised machine learning entails correct outputs that are known and it can help in guiding the learning process.

12

Nonlinear Feature Extraction for Big Data Analytics

Adil Omari, Juan José Choquehuanca Zevallos, and Roberto Díaz Morales

CONTENTS

Introduction

In recent years, there has been a noticeable incremental increase in the number of available Big Data infrastructures. This increase has promoted the adaptation of traditional machine learning techniques in order to be able to address large-scale problems and to adapt solutions to be launched in distributed environments. These platforms provide scalability, fault tolerance, and highly intuitive programming languages to develop software, but they need to train algorithms that are efficient in terms of computational time and communication. For these reasons, linear models are among the most common predictive modeling techniques in working with Big Data. However, these methods show poor performance when there is a nonlinear relationship between the features and the variables being predicted. To solve this limitation, one alternative is to extract features based on the original ones in order to solve problems that are nonlinear in the original feature space. In this chapter, we explain some feature extraction techniques capable of working in distributed Big Data platforms.

Traditional Methods: Feature Extraction with PCA

Principal component analysis (PCA) (Jolliffe 2002) is a procedure that highlights similarities and differences in data by transforming the original set of correlated variables into a new set of uncorrelated variables; these new variables are called principal components. PCA also allows a reduction in the number of variables and renders the information less redundant. The other main advantage of PCA is that it can identify patterns in data, which is difficult with high-dimensional data, where the luxury of graphical representation is not available. PCA is possibly the most frequently used method for dimensionality reduction.

Algorithm

Given the data matrix $X \in \mathbb{R}^{N \times D}$, where each of N rows represents a single sample and every column a feature, we can follow a sequence of steps to perform a PCA.

1. Subtract the mean. We create a new matrix, X^*, by removing the mean from the original data set from each of D features:

$$x_d^{*(n)} = x_d^{(n)} - \sum_{i=1}^{N} x_d^{(i)} \tag{12.1}$$

2. After that, we calculate the covariance matrix, $C \in \mathbb{R}^{D \times D}$

$$C = \frac{1}{N} X^{*T} X^*$$ (12.2)

3. Calculate the eigenvectors and eigenvalues of the covariance matrix. Since the covariance matrix is square, we can compute the eigenvectors $v^{(1)}, \dots, v^{(D)}$ and eigenvalues $\lambda^{(1)}, \dots, \lambda^{(D)}$ for this matrix. These are very important, as they tell us useful information about our data.

4. Choose components. The next step is to sort the eigenvectors in descending order, looking at the value of their corresponding eigenvalue. The eigenvectors with the highest eigenvalues are the principal components of the data. To reduce the number of features from D to D', one simply must choose D' eigenvectors with higher eigenvalues and ignore the less significant ones. (We will possibly lose some information, but if the eigenvalues are small, we will not lose too much.)

   There is a common criterion called the explained variance that is used to choose the new number of features. With this criterion, we select eigenvectors until the sum of the eigenvalues represents between 70% and 90% of the total sum of eigenvalues.

5. Create the new data set. Once we have chosen the components (eigenvectors), we can proceed to transform the original feature space into the new one by multiplying the zero mean training set, X^*, by a matrix V that contains in every column every one of the eigenvectors that we have selected.

$$X_{PCA} = X^* V$$ (12.3)

PCA for Big Data

The formulation is easy to apply when the size of data is limited, and every linear algebra software package has functions to perform PCA. The main problem comes when we need to apply PCA to a data set that does not fit into a memory.

When we have too many observations in our data set, the covariance matrix itself can be located in the memory, and the limitation is in calculation of the covariance matrix when our data set has been split into smaller data sets, stored into Q workers, in a network:

$$X^{(1)} \in \mathbb{R}^{N_1 \times D}, \dots, X^{(Q)} \in \mathbb{R}^{N_Q \times D} \text{ and } X = \bigcup_{q=1}^{Q} X^{(q)}$$

The most expensive computational cost, in this case, is step 2 of the algorithm (the covariance matrix calculation). This step can be computed using a MapReduce scheme, where every node computes the product of its data set, and the Transpose and a Master node receive all the results and the sum of the individual matrices:

$$C = \frac{1}{N} \sum_{q=1}^{Q} X^{*(q)} X^{*T(q)}$$ (12.4)

This is the schema that libraries such as Spark MLlib (Meng 2016) use to perform PCA.

Kernel Methods

Kernel methods (Scholkopf 2001) are a very popular family of machine learning algorithms. The main reason for their success is their ability to very easily create nonlinear solutions by transforming the input data space onto a highly dimensional one by using a kernel function. They have proved their effectiveness in practice through highly competitive results in many different tasks.

As an example of kernel methods, we can consider support vector machines (SVMs) (Vapnik 2013), which are commonly used in classification problems, or Gaussian processes (GPs) (Rasmussen 2006), a Bayesian nonparametric algorithm that is very useful in regression problems.

After training these algorithms, we obtain a model for classification or regression problems whose associated function to process new data, x, has the following form:

$$f(x) = \sum_{m=1}^{M} w^{(m)} K(x, c^{(m)}) \qquad (12.5)$$

Where the set $\{c^{(1)}, \ldots, c^{(m)}\}$ is a set of centroids and the function K is the kernel function and represents a similarity measure between the two data sets.

The kernel function can model the nonlinearity of a problem, because we can operate very easily in a high-dimensional space rather than in the original one. We can see this family of algorithms as instance-based learning, instead of fixing parameters on the original features. The algorithm learns a representative set of training data and processes future data using information about the similarity of the new data with the memorized samples; it learns a set of different weights based on these similarities.

Problems Associated with Kernel Methods

The original formulation of kernel methods has two main limitations that reduce their practical application in Big Data problems:

- The first one is the run time associated with their training procedure. The original formulation of the SVM is a quadratic programming problem, and in the case of GPs we have to solve a least-squares problem of size n (n is the size of the training set). This means that the cost of the training procedure is on the order $O(n^3)$, resulting in a very long training time and a totally unaffordable task for Big Data problems.

- The second problem is associated with the nonparametric nature of kernel methods. The complexity of the models is not limited, since the classifier size depends on the training set size. This means that N can take any value between 1 and n. The ability to self-adjust their architecture made these methods very popular in the past, but the resulting classifiers can become very large and could, therefore, lead to very slow processing of new samples.

Fortunately, new lines of research, such as parallel computing or semiparametric approximations, have emerged to help us cope with these problems.

To deal with the excessive classifier size in large-scale problems and to obtain a solution capable of processing new samples within a reasonable time, semiparametric solutions are approximations that fix the complexity of the resulting model in advance. Some works (Schölkopf 1997) have proposed to reduce the machine size *a posterior*, i.e., they reduce the classifier size by solving a preimage problem (Kwok 2004) after the SVM training step, to avoid the calculation of a full SVM. There are several alternatives that we will discuss in this chapter.

In distributed computing (Díaz-Morales 2011), multiple processing resources work simultaneously following the principle that problems can be divided into smaller subtasks that can be solved at the same time. With Big Data clusters, different systems in a network work independently and communicate results periodically. The scope of Big Data computing is focused on large-scale problems where a single machine cannot store the full data set and communication times are negligible compared with the run time of every iteration.

Kernel Functions as New Features

To illustrate the usefulness of kernel functions as new features, we prepared Figure 12.1, which contains an example of a nonlinear classification task. The left side represents a linear classifier, which is a line in the original feature space; this method cannot attain good classification accuracy.

When we replaced the original features with a single new feature, x_3, which is a distance with a point in the original space, we correctly classified all the samples; the new classifier is nonlinear when we look back at the original feature space (the right side of the figure).

With that idea in mind, the more kernel functions we add to our data set, the more complex will be the classification functions we can create in the original space. Figure 12.2 shows a classification region in the original space, where we used a linear classifier and several kernel functions.

Many machine learning algorithms, like SVMs, can be expressed in terms of dot products of samples. To obtain nonlinear solutions, we replace those products by using kernel functions, so they represent the dot product in another high-dimensional feature space (Mercer's theorem).

A kernel function must represent similarity between two samples. Although automatic kernel selection is possible and has been discussed in the work of Howley (2005), when using generic kernel functions to obtain good results within a reasonable period of time it

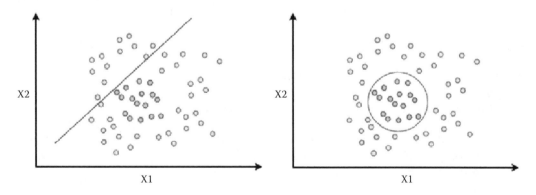

FIGURE 12.1
Linear classification versus nonlinear classification.

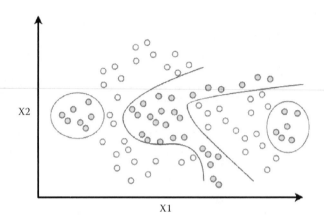

FIGURE 12.2
A complex classification task.

is necessary to use the knowledge of a domain expert, because choosing the most appropriate kernel depends highly on the problem at hand, and fine-tuning the kernel parameters using generic kernel functions can become a tedious task.

Kernel Properties

Usually, it is better to work with positive definite kernels, because that ensures that the optimization problem will be convex with a unique solution. That means that the kernel matrix of every combination of elements of the data set contains positive semidefinite and only nonnegative eigenvalues. Kernel functions must be symmetric, continuous, and preferably have a positive semidefinite Gram matrix. Some kernel functions which are not strictly positive definite have been shown to perform very well in practice. The sigmoid kernel is not positive semidefinite for certain values of its parameters. Boughorbel (2005) showed how some kernel functions that are only conditionally positive definite are better than traditional kernels in some applications. Another division is scale invariant and scale variant; this is also an interesting property, because a classifier built using scale-invariant kernels is not affected by changes in the scale of the data. Kernel functions can be classified in many different ways: compactly supported, anisotropic stationary, isotropic stationary, locally stationary, nonstationary, or separable nonstationary.

The Most Common Kernel Functions

The most common kernel functions reported in the literature are as follows:

- **Linear kernel.** This is the simplest kernel function. It is obtained from the inner product plus an optional constant. This is still a linear combination of features; the classifiers obtained with this kernel are still linear, but this can be useful to perform a dimensionality reduction that replaces the original features space by a reduced number of linear kernel functions.

$$K(x, y) = x^T y + c \qquad (12.6)$$

- **Polynomial kernel.** The polynomial kernel is a nonstationary kernel that is well suited for problems where all the training data have been normalized. Adjustable parameters are the degree, d, the slope, α, and the constant term, c.

$$K(x,y) = (\alpha x^T y + c)^d \tag{12.7}$$

- **Radial basis function.** This function is also called a Gaussian kernel.

$$K(x,y) = e^{-\frac{\|x-y\|^2}{2\sigma^2}} \tag{12.8}$$

The parameter σ plays a major role in the performance of this function and should be carefully tuned to the problem at hand. A too-high value will behave linearly, and the high-dimensional projection will lose its nonlinear power. A too-low value will be highly sensitive to noise in the training data.

Alternatively, this function can also be implemented as follows:

$$K(x,y) = e^{-\gamma\|x-y\|^2} \tag{12.9}$$

- **Laplacian kernel.** This is similar to the radial basis function, with only L_1 norm and a less sensitive effect from changes in σ.

$$K(x,y) = e^{-\frac{\|x-y\|}{\sigma}} \tag{12.10}$$

- **Hyperbolic tangent kernel.** This kernel type comes from the artificial neural networks field, where the function is often used as activation for neurons.

$$K(x,y) = \tanh(\alpha x^T y + c) \tag{12.11}$$

An SVM using this kernel function is equivalent to a two-layer, perceptron neural network. This kernel was quite popular for support vector machines due to its origin from artificial neural network theory. Despite being only conditionally positive definite, it has been found to perform well in practice.

There are two adjustable parameters in the sigmoid kernel: the slope α and the constant c. A more detailed study on sigmoid kernels can be found in the works of Lin (e.g., Lin 2003).

Selecting Basis Elements

Once we have selected the correct kernel function, we need good criteria to select a good set of centroids $\{c^{(1)}, \ldots, c^{(m)}\}$.

In Big Data architectures, where data are distributed among different nodes, once the centroids have been selected we can broadcast them so that they are available on every computing node, and we can transform our original feature space to a new one composed by the kernels function $\{K(x, c^{(1)}),\ldots, K(x, c^{(m)})\}$ or merge the new features with the original ones by using a map function on the distributed data set. There are several techniques that can be applied to Big Data problems to select the set of centroids; depending on the number of centroids we want to obtain, we can choose a different technique.

Random Sampling

A random selection of samples among the training data elements is extremely simple but also very fast. This method is less accurate than other techniques but is recommended when we want to obtain a large number of elements. Most of the Big Data frameworks provide this functionality; for example, Apache Spark implements the functions Take and Sample on the resilient distributed data sets (RDDs) to sample a random number of data points or to sample data with a probability from the original data set. The sampling can be with or without replacement, depending on whether you want to avoid the possibility of repeating the same data or not.

k-Means

k-Means is a clustering method of vector quantization that aims to partition n observations into k clusters, in which each observation belongs to the cluster with the nearest mean, serving as a prototype of the cluster.

Given a set of observations $\{x^{(1)},\ldots, x^{(N)}\}$, k-means clustering aims to partition the n observations into $k (\leq n)$ sets, $S = \{S^{(1)},\ldots, S^{(K)}\}$, so as to minimize the within-cluster sum of squares (sum of distance functions of each point in the cluster to the cluster center). In other words, its objective is to find:

$$\arg \min_{S} \sum_{k=1}^{K} \sum_{x \in S^{(k)}} \left\| x - \mu^{(k)} \right\|^{2} \tag{12.12}$$

where $\mu^{(k)}$ is the mean of points in $S^{(k)}$; this means $\mu^{(k)}$ can be used as our basis elements.

This results in a partitioning of the data space into cells. The problem is computationally difficult (NP-hard); however, there are efficient heuristic algorithms that are commonly employed, and they converge quickly to a local optimum.

The most common algorithm uses an iterative refinement technique; it is called Lloyd's algorithm. The algorithm proceeds by alternating between two steps:

- **Assignment step.** Assign each observation to the cluster whose mean yields the least within-cluster sum of squares (WCSS). Since the sum of squares is the squared Euclidean distance, this is intuitively the "nearest" mean.
- **Update step.** Calculate the new means, which are the centroids of the observations in the new clusters.

The algorithm has converged when the assignments no longer change. The algorithm may converge to a (local) optimum. There is no guarantee that the global optimum will be found using this algorithm.

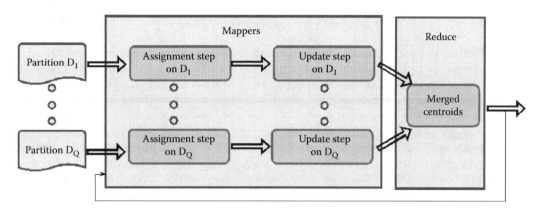

FIGURE 12.3
Distributed Big Data k-means.

We can find distributed implementation of k-means in most of the Big Data frameworks, like Spark MLlib (Meng 2016) and Apache Mahout (Owen 2011). It is easy to adapt the formulation for a distributed environment by using a MapReduce scheme in every iteration (Figure 12.3).

The set of means $\{\mu^{(1)},...,\mu^{(K)}\}$ obtained via k-means will be our set of centroids.

Sparse Greedy Matrix Approximation

The sparse greedy matrix approximation (SGMA) method (Scholkopf 2001, Smola 2001) is a common unsupervised machine learning technique to approximate the kernel matrix and, therefore, it is suitable to select the basis elements of semiparametric models. It is a greedy technique that works by iteratively selecting a group of candidates among the training set and growing the set of basis with the candidate that obtains the highest decrease in the approximation error.

As shown by Scholkopf (2001), with a set of basis elements $\{c^{(1)},..., c^{(m)}\}$, we can approximate the kernel functions as a linear combination of other kernels. This approximation involves an approximation error. When we add a new basis element $c^{(m+1)}$, the error can be expressed as a function of the previous error:

$$Err(\{c^{(1)},...,c^{(m)}\}) = Err(\{c^{(1)},...,c^{(m)},c^{(m+1)}\}) - \underbrace{\eta^{-1}\left\|K_{n,m}z - k_{m+1,n}\right\|^2}_{Error\ Decrease} \qquad (12.13)$$

where:

$$
\begin{aligned}
(k_{m+1,n})_i &= K(c^{(m+1)}, x^{(i)}) & \forall i = 1,...,n \\
(k_{nc})_i &= K(x^{(i)}, c^{(m+1)}) & \forall i = 1,...,m \\
(k_{mc})_i &= K(c^{(i)}, x^{(m+1)}) & \forall i = 1,...,m \\
z &= K_c^{-1}k_{mc} \\
\eta &= 1 - z^T k_{mc} \\
(K_{nm})_{ij} &= K(x^{(i)}, c^{(j)}) & \forall i = 1,...,n, \forall j = 1,...,m
\end{aligned}
\qquad (12.14)
$$

The last part of the formula is called error decrease (ED), because it measures the error difference with that of the previous set of basis. The goal of SGMA is to find a good set of basis elements by making use of the ED information. To do that, in every iteration it selects a group of new candidates and grows the set of basis elements with the element that obtains the highest ED.

Modern Big Data platforms provide functionalities to easily sample data from distributed data sets and to broadcast variables to be used for every worker (with read-only access). Making use of these features, in every iteration the algorithm takes some candidate samples to grow the semiparametric model and shares them among every worker in the cluster. To obtain the ED of every candidate, the workers in the distributed cluster calculate the partial error associated with their data set partition. This approach allows us to evaluate the ED in parallel. This evaluation of the ED does not require communication between workers until the end. This is a good schema for MapReduce architectures.

The computational cost of evaluating the ED on a candidate element using the whole data set becomes a critical limiting factor when working with Big Data problems. In order to be capable of handling large amounts of data, it is possible to use a stochastic version of the algorithm. Instead of computing the ED exactly, each iteration estimates the ED of every candidate by using a data subset randomly picked from the full data set. The main advantage of this approximation is that the amount of time required is independent of the number of examples in the data set when the number of elements in the data subset is fixed. This approximation represents a great advantage in terms of run time in experiments; below, we discuss the validity of this approximation and provide empirical results as a function of the subset size.

Example of Semiparametric SVMs

The primal optimization problem in solving an SVM using kernel functions is the following (Cortes 1995):

$$\min_{w,b} \frac{1}{2}\|w\|^2 + C\sum_{i=1}^{n} \xi^{(i)}$$

$$\xi^{(i)} = \max\left(0, 1 - y^{(i)}\left(\sum_{j=1}^{n} y^{(j)}\alpha^{(j)}K(x^{(j)}, x^{(i)}) + b\right)\right), \forall i = 1, \ldots, n \qquad (12.15)$$

$$w = \sum_{i=1}^{n} y^{(i)}\alpha^{(i)}\phi(x^{(i)})$$

where C is a penalty parameter to trade off the misclassification error, $\phi(\cdot)$ is a nonlinear transformation (usually unknown) where inner products can be computed using a kernel function $\phi(x^{(i)})\phi(x^{(j)}) = K(x^{(i)}, x^{(j)})$, and $\alpha^{(i)}$ is the Lagrange multiplier associated with the constraint of the sample $x^{(i)}$. This optimization problem is equivalent to solving an n-dimensional convex quadratic programming (QP) problem.

The solution of the SVM is nonparametric, and so the size of the classification function (that is, the number of support vectors) is not predetermined and is modeled based on the training samples. To keep the complexity and the run time under control, semiparametric models (Burges 1997) can be adopted.

Once the A set of m basis elements $\{c^{(1)}, \ldots, c^{(m)}\}$ is selected using one of the techniques described in the previous section, w is approximated by $w \simeq \sum_{j=1}^{m} \beta^{(j)} \phi(c^{(j)})$, giving rise to a classifier of size m:

$$f(x^{(i)}) = \boldsymbol{\beta}^T k_i + b$$
$$(k_i)_j = K(x^{(i)} c^{(j)}), \forall j = 1, \ldots, m \tag{12.16}$$

The weights, β, are obtained by solving the following optimization procedure:

$$\min_{\beta} \frac{1}{2} \boldsymbol{\beta}^T K_C \boldsymbol{\beta} + C \sum_{i=1}^{n} \xi^{(i)} \tag{12.17}$$

where:

$$\xi^{(i)} = \max(0, 1 - y^{(i)}(\boldsymbol{\beta}^T k_i + b)), \forall i = 1, \ldots, n$$
$$(K_C)_{i,j} = K(c^{(i)}, c^{(j)}) \tag{12.18}$$

There are two different approaches that are commonly used in Big Data problems to solve this task: stochastic gradient descent and iterative reweighted least squares.

Stochastic Gradient Descent

Even though stochastic gradient descent (SGD) has been around in the machine learning community for a long time, it has received a considerable amount of attention just recently in the context of Big Data learning.

The SGD algorithm updates the parameters θ of the objective function $L(\theta)$ as follows:

$$\theta = \theta - \eta \left\langle \frac{\partial L(\theta)}{\partial \theta} \right\rangle \tag{12.19}$$

where the expectation in the above equation is approximated by evaluating the cost gradient over the full training set. SGD simply does away with the expectation in the update and computes the gradient of the parameters using only a single or a few training examples.

Gradient descent algorithms are very easily implemented in distributed Big Data platforms (Rect 2011) because it is possible to use a MapReduce schema (Dean 2008) to implement them.

When we apply the SGD to the semiparametric SVM formulation, we must take into account that the hinge function $\max(0, 1 - y^{(i)}(\boldsymbol{\beta}^T k_i + b))$ is not differentiable at $y^{(i)}(\boldsymbol{\beta}^T k_i + b) = 1$. We can use the following expression:

$$\frac{\partial \xi^{(i)}}{\partial \beta} = \begin{cases} -y^{(i)} k_i & \text{if } y^{(i)}(\boldsymbol{\beta}^T k_i + b) \leq 1 \\ 0 & \text{if } y^{(i)}(\boldsymbol{\beta}^T k_i + b) > 1 \end{cases} \tag{12.20}$$

Iterative Reweighted Least Squares

An IRWLS schema has been successfully used to train semiparametric SVMs by rearranging the cost function (Parrado-Hernández 2003):

$$
\min_\beta \frac{1}{2}\beta^T K_C \beta + C\sum_{i=1}^{n} a^{(i)}(e^{(i)})^2
$$

$$
e^{(i)} = y^{(i)} - (\beta k_i + b)
$$

$$
a^{(i)} = \begin{cases} 0, & y^{(i)}e^{(i)} \leq 0 \\ \dfrac{C}{y^{(i)}e^{(i)}} & y^{(i)}e^{(i)} > 0 \end{cases}
$$

(12.21)

These procedures can be solved iteratively. The weights (β) are then obtained, considering that $a^{(i)}$ does not depend on β, and solving a least squares problem. Then, the value of $a^{(i)}$ is recalculated for every sample by using the new β, and the procedure is repeated until convergence.

This procedure can be implemented in parallel for Big Data problems, as described by Díaz-Morales (2016a, 2016b). When the data set is distributed in a Big Data platform, the matrices of the least squares problem can be computed in parallel by using a MapReduce schema.

Deep Feature Learning

An important point in Big Data analytics is that in many cases it is desirable to get an overcomplete set of features that allows attaining higher performance on certain tasks, and such features cannot be obtained by methods described in previous sections (Hinton 2007).

Deep learning methods are receiving a lot of attention, given their impressive results in several tasks, such as image restoration (Xie et al. 2012), classification (Ciregan et al. 2012, Walid et al. 2014), audio recognition tasks (Dahl et al. 2012), etc.

We can say that deep learning techniques are a pooled set of algorithms that allow building structures of many hidden layers, with the ability to form complex nonlinear transformations that can disentangle factors that describe input data (Bengio 2009). Even more, in many tasks, these methods are capable of being exploited directly from raw data and allow understanding of the factors that explain variations in the data set.

Recent studies have also investigated the good generative capacities of these methods (Vincent et al. 2008). If a machine is able to understand variations inside the structure of data, then it is possible for it to generate new samples from the learned distribution, as well as to better distinguish among samples of different classes.

Under this scenario, it is important to highlight the impulse that Big Data gives to these techniques. Mainly, these methods usually suffer from overfitting, since the number of free parameters is huge. So, having data sets of millions of samples directly helps to reduce this bad effect due to the scarcity of samples. However, a large amount of available data also imposes other problems (memory, multimodality, a fast-growing number of samples, etc.). It is undeniable that we could gain benefits from deep learning methods.

Since the introduction of the work on this topic by Hinton (2002), followed by that of Vincent et al. (2008), several approaches have been introduced to construct such deep models. In the following sections, we analyze these approaches and explain their usefulness and the versatility of such methods in Big Data scenarios. Also, we note that these methods serve as essential building blocks of deep nets that can benefit from parallel and distributed learning to train large-scale deep models.

Auto-Encoders

An auto-encoder (AE) is a machine that tries to learn features from a given data set with the primary intention of reconstructing samples by means of reducing a loss function that measures the difference between the true value and the reconstruction obtained by AE. In general terms, this equation represents the loss to be minimized during training.

$$L = \frac{1}{N} \sum_{n=1}^{N} l(\mathbf{x}^{(n)}, \hat{\mathbf{x}}^{(n)})$$

(12.22)

where N represents the number of samples and l is any function that measures a discrepancy between a given sample, $\mathbf{x}^{(n)}$, and its reconstruction, $\hat{\mathbf{x}}^{(n)}$.

Measuring Discrepancies in AE

Regarding the reconstruction error criterion, we can consider different forms that will depend mostly on the type of data we manage. There exists a wide availability of loss functions. The most common ones are the followings:

- Mean squared error (MSE): This is the most common function to measure the reconstruction error. The benefit of this measure is that there is no limitation in the range of values of samples or, more precisely, in the values in any dimension.

$$l(\mathbf{x}^{(n)}, \hat{\mathbf{x}}^{(n)}) = \left\| \mathbf{x}^{(n)} - \hat{\mathbf{x}}^{(n)} \right\|^2$$

(12.23)

- Log likelihood: This is a general setting that can be used to measure discrepancies among samples and reconstructions. It is first defined as a measure of discrepancy between distributions. Under certain conditions, values of samples can be considered probability values, for instance, pixels in a gray scale picture are in the range of [0; 1] and can be taken to represent the probability that a given pixel is 1, i.e., $P(x_d = 1)$. In this case, the distribution of all pixels will follow a Bernoulli distribution that results in Equation 1.24, also known as cross-entropy.

$$l(\mathbf{x}^{(n)}, \hat{\mathbf{x}}^{(n)}) = -\sum_{d=1}^{D} (x_d \log(\hat{x}_d) + (1 - x_d) \log(1 - \hat{x}_d))$$

(12.24)

A usual simplification that has shown good results in many applications is the semi-cross-entropy function, defined as follows:

$$l(\mathbf{x}^{(n)}, \hat{\mathbf{x}}^{(n)}) = -\sum_{d=1}^{D}(x_d \log(\hat{x}_d)) \qquad (12.25)$$

Architecture of AEs

Among AEs, we recognize three types of units: sensory or input units (x), hidden units (h^1; possibly distributed across more than one hidden layer [l] and each of them connected to lower and bottom layers), and output units. In essence, an AE can be divided into two parts: an encoder function, $h = f_c(x)$, and a decoder function, $\hat{x} = f_d(h)$. The encoding layer performs feature extraction from data and the encoder layer gives an estimate of the data. The nonlinearity due to the activation functions at the output of each hidden layer provides the net to obtain complex functions.

Despite the fact that AEs can be formed by several hidden layers, in advance we focus our discussions on the machines of one hidden layer, given that they have been shown to be essential when trying to build complex models.

In its most basic setting, an AE is a neural net with one hidden layer (Figure 12.4), and so under this structure, the label is the sample itself.

$$h = f_c(\mathbf{W}^T x + b) \qquad (12.26)$$

$$\hat{x} = f_d(\mathbf{U}^T h + c) \qquad (12.27)$$

where W and U represent synaptic connections between input x data and hidden variables h and between the hidden and the output variables $\hat{x}$; b and c are biases. f_c and f_d are activation functions (for instance, the hyperbolic tangent or the sigmoid function).

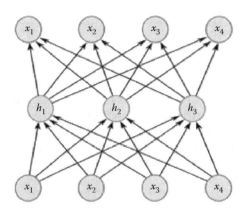

FIGURE 12.4
Architecture of an AE with one hidden layer. The encoder is represented by the hidden variable, $h = f_c(x)$, and the decoder, $\hat{x} = f_d(h)$, tries to generate a reconstruction of the input.

In early stages, the AE was restricted to only have a number of hidden units less than the number of characteristics of the data set, because otherwise it will learn just the identity matrix. By making the number of hidden units limited by the input dimension, the net compresses the data, avoiding in this way of learning such identity function. Also, for dimensionality reduction, it can be shown that the effect is the same as performing a simple PCA operation. These reasons were forgotten until the breakthrough of Vincent et al. (2008), who introduced the sparse denoising AE (SDA) concept.

Let's say that we have a corrupted sample $\tilde{x}$, for instance, obtained by just simply adding additive Gaussian noise; then, an AE should be able to bring that sample to the manifold where data live. In other words, an AE should reconstruct that sample from its noisy version by taking advantage of the learned features.

Regularizing AEs

The simple procedure that consists of adding noise to the data acts as a Tikhonov regularization (Bishop 1995), allowing inclusion of more hidden units, since the learned function will be different than the trivial identity function. This overcomplete feature set helps to better reconstruct a sample.

Learning

As stated above, optimization of SDAs needs a corruption procedure, e.g., addition of noise, applied to the input data and an estimated sample at the output of the net. As when training neural nets (Bottou 1991), AEs are trained to minimize the loss function L by gradient descend (GD) and back-propagation (BP) procedures (LeCun et al. 2012).

Constructing Deep Structures

The hidden layer contains a first representation capable of assimilating basic structures in the data. We can use this first representation of the data and enable classification over this new set of features. However, as this new representation can offer better performance on a given task; we can continue to obtain a second and more abstract representation level by performing the same procedure but contaminating the data with noise in these hidden representations. The same operation can be repeated several times.

Regarding the contamination-by-noise procedure, one can simply add Gaussian noise at the input of the AE; however, the kind of noise should be data dependent, and so we should employ all prior information available in advance. For instance, when input data are gray-scale images, then a salt-and-pepper noise could be added, or to perform operations such as rotations, we can zoom in (out), use occlusion, etc. Utilization of such mechanisms also has the effect of a data augmentation procedure, which also helps to avoid overfitting.

Benefits for Big Data

Given the amount of available data, the procedure to train SDAs to take a "plunge" at the data, perform a step (or few steps) of learning (BP), and discard those samples. Then, take another plunge at the data and perform the same operation. Also, given that neural networks are unstable machines, we can use such characteristics to play in favor of and train several AEs in parallel, so that all joint outputs will help in learning different faces of the problem, or even more if different machines are trained with independent distortion procedures.

At the same time, we can extract an overcomplete set of features or, on the contrary, reduce the dimensionality of input data, by simple augmenting or reducing the size of the hidden layers.

Probabilistic Models

This section presents a kind of probabilistic models, known as energy models, which are another set of algorithms that have been used to discover features in data and are good building blocks for constructing deep models. More precisely, we will focus on a subgroup called Boltzmann machines (Bengio 2009). In these machines, an energy term defines the interactions among variables. For instance, given a sample x and latent variable h, we can define the energy function $E(x, h, \theta)$, where $\theta = \{a, b, W, C, D\}$ are free parameters to be learned:

$$E(x,h,\theta) = a^T x + b^T h + x^T W h + x^T C x + h^T D h \tag{12.28}$$

This energy function defines a graph where all units from the input data x (visible units) and latent variable h (hidden units) are connected, as shown in Figure 12.5. Parameters in W relate relationships among visible and hidden units, parameters in C (D) define relationships among visible (hidden) units, and parameters a and b represent biases.

This kind of configuration is almost intractable and hard to use in training a business machine. In turns, we can reduce the complexity of this model, making $C = 0$ and $D = 0$; this reduced form is known as RBM (Figure 12.6) and the posterior distribution $[h \sim p(h|x)]$ can be interpreted as a representation (or set of extracted features) of the input data.

Equation 12.28 is suitable for applications where the input data are binary (or on a scale that falls in the [0;1] interval, as in gray-scale images). Also, we can use other energy functions when variables follow, for instance, Gaussian distributions, as shown in Equation 12.29. For this case, the machine is a Gaussian-Gaussian-RBM, or GGRBM. We consider

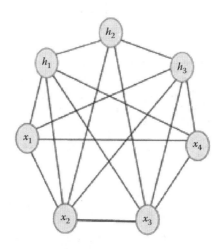

FIGURE 12.5
A fully connected network containing four visible units and three hidden units.

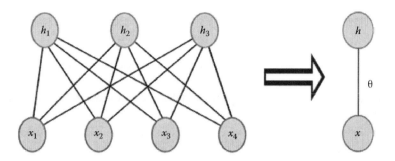

FIGURE 12.6
A restricted Boltzmann machine. The graph is undirected, and there are no connections between units belonging to the same layer. (Left) All connections between visible and hidden units. (Right) Simple representation of the graphical model. θ represents the parameters of the model.

different distributions for input and hidden variables; for example, Equation 12.30 shows an RBM where the input variable is real Gaussian valued and the hidden variable is a binomial distribution.

$$E(\mathbf{x}, \mathbf{h}) = \sum_i \frac{(x_i - a_i)^2}{2\sigma_i^2} + \sum_j \frac{(h_i - b_i)^2}{2\sigma_j^2} + \sum_i \sum_j \frac{x_i}{\sigma_i} \frac{h_j}{\sigma_j} w_{ij} \tag{12.29}$$

$$E(\mathbf{x}, \mathbf{h}) = \sum_i \frac{(x_i - a_i)^2}{2\sigma_i^2} + \sum_j b_j h_j + \sum_i \sum_j \frac{x_i}{\sigma_i} h_j w_{ij} \tag{12.30}$$

Learning

The learning of an RBM follows a gradient descent procedure over the maximum-likelihood (ML), to optimize parameters. We define the likelihood function:

$$L(\chi, \theta) = \frac{1}{N} \sum_{n=1}^{N} \log \frac{1}{Z} e^{-E(x,\theta)} \tag{12.31}$$

Learning by gradient descent optimizes parameters following the negative gradient:

$$\theta^{\tau+1} = \theta^\tau - \eta \frac{\partial L(\chi, \theta)}{\partial \theta} \tag{12.32}$$

In general, this procedure leads to

$$\frac{\partial L(\chi, \theta)}{\partial \theta} = -\left\langle \frac{\partial E(x, \theta)}{\partial \theta} \right\rangle_{p_0(\chi)} + \left\langle \frac{\partial E(x, \theta)}{\partial \theta} \right\rangle_{p_\infty(\chi, \theta)} \tag{12.33}$$

where $\langle \ \rangle_{p()}$ is an expectation over distribution $p_{()}$.

The difficulties in computing the second term in Equation 12.33 are well known, i.e., the expectation over the true–unknown model distribution $p_{\infty\,(\chi,\theta)}$. A common approach is to set up a Markov chain that reaches equilibrium. Unfortunately, a Markov chain Monte Carlo (MCMC) simulation has a huge drawback, which is the slowness of its convergence. In addition, there is not a foolproof method to determine whether equilibrium has been reached (a sufficient condition, the so-called detailed balance condition). Besides, it presents large variance in its estimated gradient.

Contrastive Divergence

Contrast divergence (CD), unlike ML learning, minimizes the difference of two Kullback-Leibler divergences (KL) (Hinton 2002, Carreira-Perpinan and Hinton 2005, Bengio 2009), as stated in Equation 12.34:

$$CD_k = KL\left(p_0 \,\|\, p_\infty\right) - KL\left(p_k \,\|\, p_\infty\right) \tag{12.34}$$

where $KL\left(p(x)\,\|\,q(x)\right) = \int p(x)\log\left(\dfrac{p(x)}{q(x)}\right)dx$, $p_k = p_k\,(\chi,\theta)$ is the probability density function obtained by running an MCMC, k steps in advance. A Gibbs sampler is widely used here, because of its simplicity and good convergence; nevertheless, it is possible to use another sampling method.

For updating parameters, we can follow a GD procedure to minimize CD_k, which leads to:

$$\frac{\partial CD_k(\chi,\theta)}{\partial \theta} = -\left\langle\frac{\partial E(x,\theta)}{\partial \theta}\right\rangle_{p_0(\chi)} + \left\langle\frac{\partial E(x,\theta)}{\partial \theta}\right\rangle_{p_k(\chi,\theta)} \tag{12.35}$$

As said before, Equation 12.35 implies that to obtain expectations over distribution, $p_k = p_k\,(\chi,\theta)$ can be approximated following the next procedure:

1. Get $p_0\,(h|x,\theta)$
2. Get a sample $h \sim p_0\,(h|x,\theta)$
3. For $k = 1,2,\ldots$
   a. Get a sample $x \sim p_k\,(x|h,\theta)$
   b. Get a sample $h \sim p_k\,(h|x,\theta)$

Once we are able to perform sampling on an RBM, then the gradients can be easily calculated. Equations 12.36 to 12.38 are gradient updates for the energy function in Equation 12.28, where the parameters are $\theta = \{a, b, W\}$. Δ represents the change in the parameter.

$$\frac{\partial CD_k(\chi,\theta)}{\partial w_{ij}} = \left\langle x_i h_j \right\rangle_{p_0(\chi)} - \left\langle x_i h_j \right\rangle_{p_k(\chi,\theta)} \tag{12.36}$$

$$\frac{\partial CD_k(\chi, \theta)}{\partial a_i} = \left\langle x_i \right\rangle_{p_0(\chi)} - \left\langle x_i \right\rangle_{p_k(\chi, \theta)} \tag{12.37}$$

$$\frac{\partial CD_k(\chi, \theta)}{\partial b_j} = \left\langle h_j \right\rangle_{p_0(\chi)} - \left\langle h_j \right\rangle_{p_k(\chi, \theta)} \tag{12.38}$$

Constructing Deep Structures

Regarding the construction of complex deep models to obtain higher levels of abstractions, the simplest way to build such machines is by stacking several layers of more basic (but usually difficult to train) machines which previously were pretrained in an unsupervised way (e.g., AEs and RBMs). Then, each layer is added once it has been pretrained.

After successive RBMs have been trained and stacked, we obtain a structure that can represent highly nonlinear functions (Hinton 2009), and the name for this is a deep belief net (DBN) (Figure 12.7).

However, we can perform classification tasks by adding a classifier at the top (e.g., an SVM), and more significant results can be obtained by adding a logistic repressor. This is because the final structure is similar to a common neural net and can be fine-tuned by simply running a BP procedure for some steps.

Deep Distributed Learning

Deep structures with several hidden layers can pose millions of free parameters (Ciresan et al. 2010), and to prevent overfitting we need a large amount of data. This brings more difficulties when training deep models, since constraints come from two sides: the size of the model and the size of the data set (Dean et al. 2012). We can consider two strategies to satisfy both requirements: data parallelism and model parallelism.

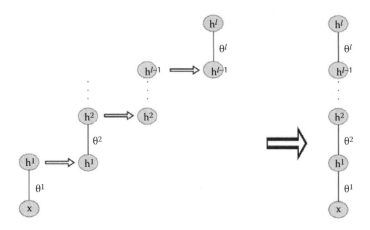

FIGURE 12.7
Graphical model of a deep belief net (left). Parameters of each hidden layer are independently trained in a layer-wise manner (right).

Data Parallelism

In certain applications, we can consider a parallel training approach in case a data set is too big to be saved in a single machine. In such a case, we divide the data set into several subsets, $Q\left(X = \bigcup\limits_{q=1}^{Q} X_q\right)$, and make replicas of the model for each worker (Figure 12.8). Then, we proceed to obtain gradient estimates, and once they are obtained, a parameter server uses them to arrive at a better estimate of true gradients (e.g., by simply averaging gradients coming from workers) and update the model's parameters (Agarwal et al. 2011). Then, these new updated parameters are returned back to each worker to continue with the process until convergence.

Model Parallelism

In cases where a model is so big that it is impossible to fit into the memory for a given worker, we can split the parameters across multiple workers and parallelize the training of the model (Figure 12.9). Several problems can arise, because the merge of individual computations of the pieces of the gradient is not trivial. First of all, all workers should maintain communication with each other so that all workers have enough information to adequately obtain gradient updates (Agarwal et al. 2011, Ngiam et al. 2011, Le 2013). This communication is a bottleneck that restrings the training time.

Data and Model Parallelism

With data and model parallelism, the parameter server not only collects information related to the gradient but also manages relations between individual workers.

Updating Parameters in Large-Scale Networks

So far, we have analyzed mechanisms to extract highly nonlinear features from data and strategies to allow training of large-scale networks. In addition, a crucial decision is how each worker will communicate the gradient information to the server node (for instance, a step in the SGD). In both data and model parallelism scenarios, we can consider updating

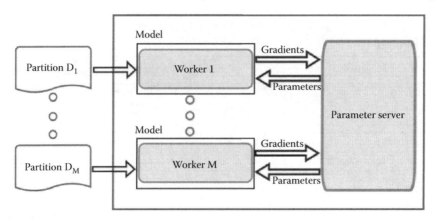

FIGURE 12.8
Data parallelism: the parameter server collects the gradient calculations from each worker and, after an update parameter step, returns the new parameters to each worker.

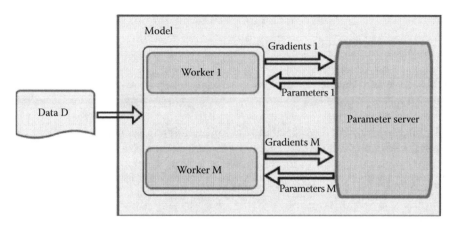

FIGURE 12.9
Model parallelism: the server collects pieces of information of gradients from each worker, updates the final model, and returns to each worker a piece of the model.

the necessary variables using synchronous and asynchronous modes of communication between workers or workers and servers (Ooi et al. 2015).

Synchronous Mode

In order to update the model parameters, the server node has to wait until all operations of the workers have been finished. Naturally, this incurs high communication times because the bandwidth of the bus limits communication between workers and between workers and servers. Also, there are the need for waiting until the last worker has finished its calculations and the necessity of queuing gradient information coming from workers. So, we should be sure that there is enough memory space to save all such information.

Asynchronous Mode

In asynchronous mode, we can reduce the time for updating parameters based on the fact that gradients should not be changing dramatically (Zinkevich et al. 2010, Le 2013). For instance, we can communicate when operations have been finished by a worker, and a master merges this information to the previous one or drives to update parameters for each worker whose waits are affected by such changes, i.e., the server does not wait until all calculations have been completed.

Ensemble Methods

Ensemble methods train multiple learners with the intention of combing their outputs to solve a problem. One of the most popular families of ensemble methods consist on training multiple independent learners, with an aggregation layer. Examples of this family are bagging (bootstrap aggregating) (Breiman 1996), which combines classifiers trained with bootstrap sampling (Efron and Tibshirani 1993) of the original training sets and random forest (Breiman 2001), which are trees trained with a randomly selected subset of the original features ("feature bagging").

In order to improve the performance of a single machine, we have to train a number of different diverse learners; to do so, we can appeal to one of the following well-known techniques to induce diversity.

- Bootstrap sampling: Given a set of N training data, we generate a new training set for every learner by sampling with replacement from the original set (the same original samples appear more than once, and some samples are not present).
- Feature bagging: Every learner is trained with a subset of the original features.
- Switching or flipping output: The main idea in switching is to randomly change the true class of a portion of training data before training every learner.
- Random initialization: In some learning algorithms, we need to initialize some parameters, like initial weights in neural networks (the nets converge to different local minima).
- Train learners with different data.

In Big Data scenarios, we dispose of a big volume of data which is distributed on multiple storage and processing units (Figure 12.10). This situation is ideal for combining learners; we can train a learner in each processing unit with data available in that unit and consider the output of these learners as features for a new simple learner that represents the ensemble combination. In this context, diversity guaranteed by the fact that data available for every learner are different.

Regarding the combination of the learner elements, we can consider two different strategies: nontrainable aggregation and trainable aggregation.

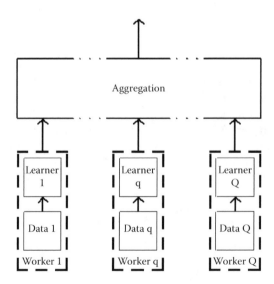

FIGURE 12.10
Ensemble formation in a Big Data scenario. Each worker manages a portion of the data or a subset of features.

Nontrainable Aggregation

Nontrainable aggregation methods are the most popular and fundamental mechanisms, because their computational cost is negligible, making them suitable for Big Data problems. We can look to averaging and majority voting as the most representative aggregation methods.

Trainable Aggregation

In trainable aggregation, we use the learner's outputs as inputs for a new machine to produce the ensemble's output. This type of aggregation provides better results than nontrainable aggregation, but they are more complicated and computationally expensive to train. In general, we need to train the aggregation method using all the available data, but we can overcome this situation by using the same sample selection method as before (data parallelism). Among all available aggregation methods, we can mention the following common approaches:

- Weighted averaging: The combined output is obtained by averaging the outputs of individual learners with different weights. These weights represent individual learner importance. In weighted averaging, the combined output is $O(x) \sum_{t=1}^{T} w_t o_t(x)$, where $o_t(x)$ and w_t are the output and the weight of the t-th learner, respectively. The weights are assumed to be constrained by $w_t \geq 0$ and $\sum_{t=1}^{T} w_t = 1$. It is important to mention that simple averaging is a special case of weighted averaging in which all weights are equal, $w_t = 1/T$.

- Stacking: This is a procedure that entails use of the output of pretrained learners (first-level learners) as the input of a new second-level learner or meta-learner (Wolpert 1992, Breiman 1996, Smyth and Wolpert 1998). The general idea is to train the first-level learners with the original training data set and then generate a new data set to train the second-level learners. This generated data set is formed by the outputs of the first-level learners, which can be regarded as new features. A stacking ensemble can take advantage of heterogeneous learners, i.e., we can use different learning algorithms for first-level learners. In the training phase of stacking, it is recommended to split original data into two portions, one to train first-level learners and the other to train meta-learners. If we were to use the same data to train the two levels, there woud be a high risk of overfitting. Even more, in the Big Data context, the available data allow us to divide data into several partitions.

- Postaggregation: This procedure is similar to stacking but different in the sense that postaggregation also considers as inputs the original data set, a portion of it, or a combination of the first-level outputs as special inputs. In the original postaggregation formulation, the first-level learner outputs are combined by a nontrainable aggregation and used as direct input to a gate-generated functional weight classifier (GG-FWC) (Omari and Figueiras 2013). Figure 12.11 shows a postaggregation scheme using a GG-FWC as a postaggregator unit that generates weights, $w(x)$, that depend on each input datum (Omari and Figueiras 2015).

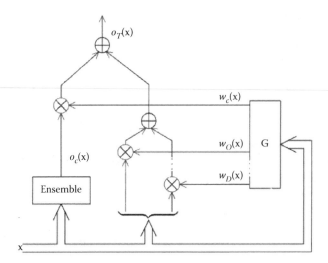

FIGURE 12.11
Postaggregation scheme using a GG-FWC as a postaggregation unit.

References

Agarwal A, Duchi JC. 2011. Distributed delayed stochastic optimization. *Advances in Neural Information Processing Systems* 24:873–881.

Bengio Y. 2009. Learning deep architectures for AI. *Foundations and Trends in Machine Learning* 2(1):1–127.

Bishop CM. 1995. Training with noise is equivalent to Tikhonov regularization. *Neural Computation* 7(1):108–116.

Bottou L. 1991. Stochastic gradient learning in neural networks. *Proceedings of Neuro-Nimes* 91.

Boughorbel ST. 2005. Conditionally positive definite kernels for SVM based image recognition, pp. 113–116. *IEEE International Conference on Multimedia and Expo*. New York: IEEE.

Breiman L. 1996. Stacked regressions. *Machine Learning* 24(1):49–64.

Breiman L. 2001. Random forests. *Machine Learning* 45(1):5–32.

Burges CJC, Schölkopf B. 1997. Improving the accuracy and speed of support vector machines, pp. 375–381. In Mozer MC, Jordan MI, Petsche (ed), *Advances in Neural Information Processing Systems* 9. Cambridge, MA: MIT Press.

Carreira-Perpinan MA, Hinton G. 2005. On contrastive divergence learning. *AISTATS* 10:33–40.

Ciregan D, Meier U, Schmidhuber J. 2012. *IEEE Conference on Computer Vision and Pattern Recognition*. New York: IEEE.

Ciresan DC, Meier U, Gambardella LM, Schmidhuber J. 2010. Deep Big Simple Neural Nets Excel on Handwritten. *CoRR*.

Cortes, C, Vapnik V. 1995. Support–vector networks. *Machine Learning* 20(3):273–297.

Dahl GE, Yu D, Deng L, Acero A. 2012. Context-dependent pre-trained deep neural networks for large-vocabulary speech recognition. *IEEE Transactions on Audio Speech and Language Processing* 20(1):30–42.

Dean J, Ghemawat S. 2008. MapReduce: Simplified data processing on large clusters. *Communications of the ACM* 1:107–113.

Dean J, Corrado GS, Monga R, Chen K, Devin M, Le QV et al. 2012. Large scale distributed deep networks. *Advances in Neural Information Processing Systems* 25:1223–1231.

Deng L, Yu D, Platt J. 2012. Scalable stacking and learning for building deep architectures. *2012 IEEE International Conference on Acoustics Speech and Signal Processing*. New York: IEEE.

Díaz-Morales R, Navia-Vázquez Á. 2016a. Efficient parallel implementation of kernel methods. *Neurocomputing* 191:175–186.

Díaz-Morales, R, Navia-Vázquez Á. 2016b. Improving the efficiency of IRWLS SVMs using parallel Cholesky factorization. *Pattern Recognition Letters* 84:91–98.

Díaz-Morales R, Molina-Bulla HY, Navia-Vázquez Á. 2011. Parallel semiparametric support vector machines. In *Neural Networks (IJCNN), The 2011 International Joint Conference on* 475–481. IEEE.

Efron B, Tibshirani R. 1993. *An Introduction to the Bootstrap*. New York: Chapman & Hall.

Hinton GE. 2002. Training products of experts by minimizing contrastive divergence. *Neural Computation* 14(8):1771–1800.

Hinton GE. 2007. Learning multiple layers of representation. *Trends in Cognitive Sciences* 11(10):428–434.

Hinton GE. 2009. Deep belief networks. *Scholarpedia* 4(5):5947.

Howley T, Madden MG. 2005. The genetic kernel support vector machine: Description and evaluation. *Artificial Intelligence Review* 24(3–4):379–395.

Jolliffe I. 2002. *Principal Component Analysis*. Hoboken, NJ: John Wiley & Sons Ltd.

Kwok JY. 2004. The pre-image problem in kernel methods. *IEEE Transactions on Neural Networks* 15(6):1517–1525.

Le QV. 2013. Building high-level features using large scale unsupervised learning. *2013 IEEE International Conference on Acoustics Speech and Signal Processing*. New York: IEEE.

LeCun YA, Bottou L, Orr GB, Müller K-R. 2012. Efficient backprop, pp. 9–48. *Neural Networks Tricks of the Trade*. New York: Springer.

Lin HT. 2003. A study on sigmoid kernels for SVM and the training of non-PSD kernels by SMO-type methods, pp. 1–32. *Neural Computation*. Cambridge, MA: MIT Press.

Meng XB. 2016. MLlib: Machine learning in Apache Spark. *Journal of Machine Learning Research* 17(34):1–7.

Ngiam J, Coates A, Lahiri A, Prochnow B, Le QV, Ng AY. 2011. On optimization method for deep learning, pp. 265–272. *Proceedings of the 28th International Conference on Machine Learning*. The International Machine Learning Society.

Omari A, Figueiras-Vidal AR. 2013. Feature combiners with gate-generated weights for classification. *IEEE Transactions on Neural Networks and Learning Systems* 24:158–163.

Omari A, Figueiras-Vidal AR. 2015. Post-aggregation of classifier ensembles. *Information Fusion* 26:96–102.

Ooi BC, Tan K-L, Wang S, Wang W, Cai Q et al. 2015. SINGA: A distributed deep learning platform, pp. 685–688. *Proceedings of the 23rd ACM International Conference on Multimedia*. New York: ACM.

Owen S, Anil R, Dunning T, Friedman E. 2011. *Mahout in Action*. Greenwich, CT: Manning Publications Co.

Parrado-Hernández E, Mora-Jimenzez I, Arenas-Garcia J, Figueiras-Vidal AR, Navia-Vázquez Á. 2003. Growing support vector classifiers with controlled complexity. *Pattern Recognition* 36(7):1479–1488.

Rasmussen CE. 2006. *Gaussian Processes for Machine Learning*. Boston: MIT Press.

Recht B, Re C, Wright S, Niu F. 2011. Hogwild: A lock-free approach to parallelizing stochastic gradient descent, pp. 693–701. In *Advances in Neural Information Processing Systems 24*. Cambridge, MA: MIT Press.

Scholkopf B, Smola AJ. 2001. *Learning with Kernels: Support Vector Machines, Regularization, Optimization, and Beyond*. Boston: MIT Press.

Smola AJ. 2001. Sparse greedy Gaussian process regression, pp. 619–625. *Advances in Neural Information Processing Systems 13*. Cambridge, MA: MIT Press.

Smyth P, Wolpert D. 1998. Stacked density estimation, pp. 668–674. In Kearns MJ, Solla SA, Cohn DA (eds), *Advances in Neural Information Processing Systems 11*. Cambridge, MA: MIT Press.

Vapnik V. 2013. *The Nature of Statistical Learning Theory.* New York: Springer Science & Business Media.

Vincent P, Larochelle H, Bengio Y, Manzagol P-A. 2008. Extracting and composing robust features with denoising autoencoders, pp. 1096–1103. *Proceedings of the 25th International Conference on Machine Learning.* New York: ACM.

Walid R, Lasfar A. 2014. Handwritten digit recognition using sparse deep architectures, pp. 1–6. *2014 International Conferenence on Intelligent Systems: Theories and Applications.* New York: IEEE.

Wolpert DH. 1992. Stacked generalization. *Neural Networks* 5(2):241–260.

Xie J, Xu L, Chen E. 2012. Image denoising and inpainting with deep neural networks. *Advances in Neural Information Processing Systems* 25:341–349.

Zinkevich M, Weimer M, Li L. 2010. Parallelized stochastic gradient descent. *Advances in Neural Information Processing Systems* 23:2595–2603.

13

Enhanced Feature Mining and Classifier Models to Predict Customer Churn for an e-Retailer

Karthik B. Subramanya and Arun K. Somani

CONTENTS

Introduction

e-Commerce (electronic commerce, or EC) include the buying, selling of goods and services and the transmitting of funds or data, over an electronic network. These business transactions occur business-to-business (B2B), business-to-consumer (B2C), consumer-to-consumer (C2C), and consumer-to-business (C2B). The terms e-commerce and e-retailer are often used interchangeably in our chapter. We are primarily interested in e-retail business, which is a form of e-commerce that allows consumers to directly buy goods or services from a seller over the internet by using a Web browser or a mobile app. It is projected that in the year 2017 the online e-retail industry will grow to upwards of $600 billion dollars. While most of these e-retailers operate on a B2C business model, a B2B model or a combination of both is also common. Many businesses have migrated from owning a brick-and-mortar shop alone to include an e-retail business to cater to the needs of the customer and to keep up with the competition, while others operate only via the e-commerce route.

Customer loyalty is an important driver to many e-retailers, as the cost of acquiring a new customer is significant in comparison to the cost of retaining one (Farquhar and Panther 2008). Unlike a brick-and-mortar shopping experience, which involves a look and feel, location advantage, and human interaction component, among others, the e-retail business model comes packaged in a single mobile app or website, from the landing page to exit. Therefore, it is an important priority for these companies to entice the customer with a great line of products, pricing, attractive offers, recommendations, personalization, etc., to create a desirable shopping experience. In order to provide the best personalized shopping experiences, these organizations need to invest in a well-structured data pipeline that serves as a backbone of any analytical or data science models, which in turn act as a foundation for providing a desirable shopping experience for the customer.

Customer churn models are applicable to many industries, like the financial, telecom, and automobile industries, to name a few (Wei and Chiu 2002, Kumar and Ravi 2008, Xie et al. 2009). We have developed our own customer churn predictive model for e-commerce that leverages some of the advantages that a Big Data infrastructure brings to an organization. Our work is well tailored to suit the industry model.

The customer churn problem is modeled as a binary classifier problem (Alpaydin 2014), where the output of the classifier is a Boolean output. A nonzero 1 indicates a possible churner, and a 0 indicates a loyal customer. This problem is one of the most common machine-learning problems that has been solved with the help of classifier algorithms. To solve it, we chose a sample set of customers for our study who were similar to each other in terms of their size, spending, behavior, demographics, etc. We refer to this sample set as a given segment of customers.

In order to come up with the best predictors, we have built separate custom classifier models for every segment of customers.

Enterprise Data Pipeline (Hadoop Stack)

The adoption of Big Data pipelines and data lakes is becoming increasingly common across organizations with large customer footprints. The commercial use of Hadoop Stack started in the early 2000s, driven by a strong desire to leverage data through analytics and data science. A large number of open source initiatives from the developer community, organizations, and academicians focused on contributing additional tools and software to improve the Hadoop Stack have helped immensely. This platform has now matured into a highly functional Big Data stack that can serve enterprise-scale operations and be fault tolerant.

Stages of the Hadoop Pipeline

From an e-commerce and retail organizational perspective, different components of the Hadoop ecosystem can be broadly categorized into four different stages of the data pipeline, as shown in Figure 13.1. In the interest of promoting open source software, we restrict our discussion here to a few tools that are fully open source for both commercial and academic purposes. By no means does this list cover all of the available tools on the market.

Source

The data sources that contribute to the Big Data pipeline are not essentially part of the pipeline. It is, however, important to understand what kind of data sources one deals with, including the nature of the data as defined by its volume, variety, and velocity. For an e-commerce and retail industry, valuable data sources worthy of harnessing include

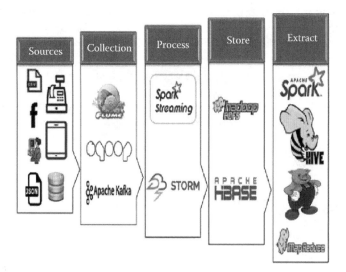

FIGURE 13.1
Data pipeline for retail e-commerce.

transactional data from the point of sale, online and mobile channels, customer data, customer relationship management systems, clickstream logs, social media data, survey and marketing campaign data, customer interaction data, etc., to name a few important ones. The formats of these data vary widely, from unstructured textual data to highly structured data from relational data stores. Having all of these data from different channels in a single environment helps an organization have what is popularly referred as the 360° view of the customer, so that the organization may better understand and serve its customers.

Collection

Collection is the first stage of the Hadoop pipeline. Various tools available in the Hadoop Stack are used to ingest data in real time, using streaming or through a batch process. Apache Kafka (https://kafka.apache.org/) is a popular distributed publish-subscribe messaging system that is commonly used to push data into the pipeline in real time and which can further be used to support online machine learning applications, like fraud detection, clustering applications, recommendations, customer identification, etc. Other tools, like Apache Flume (http://flume.apache.org/), are built more specifically for collecting and aggregating large amounts of nonrelational data from storage servers, server logs, etc., and they digest this information for the Hadoop distributed file system (HDFS). Tools like Apache Sqoop (http://sqoop.apache.org/) are designed to efficiently transfer bulk data from traditional relational databases into HDFS (Shvachko et al. 2010).

Process

The second stage in the Hadoop pipeline is categorized as the process, where any form of computation or transformation happens to the data that are flowing through the cluster. Spark streaming (https://spark.apache.org/) and Apache Storm (https://storm.apache .org/) are widely used tools that perform these computations in real time to support applications downstream before they persist on a disk or are stored in a database. This process stage can involve a wide variety of operations, including filtering, aggregation, joins, normalization, denormalization, changing data format, schema, etc. For use cases that do not involve real-time processing, we might use batch tools, like MapReduce, Apache Hive (http://hive.apache.org/), Pig Latin (Olston et al. 2008), etc., to perform data transformation from a staging area before it can permanently persist. These tools are further discussed in detail below in descriptions of the later stages.

Store

The third stage in the Hadoop pipeline is defined as store, where the data are set to persist at the disk level (HDFS) or in a database. The biggest advantage of a Hadoop data lake is that a lake provides a single environment to store a variety of data and, at the same time, provides fault tolerance. Simultaneously, it is very economical to scale up the volume compared to legacy systems. The form in which the data finally reside is mainly decided based on how the data get retrieved by users and applications which use the data. Efficient data modeling is required to ensure that persisting data fully serve the end users. Many sharding techniques and different data formats like ORC,

Paraquet, Avro, etc. are used to ensure good performance for data retrieval, handling high volumes of data, changing schema, etc. We may also use a distributed No-Sql database, like HBase, to support highly efficient data fetch and updates for applications using these data.

Extract

The final stage in the Hadoop pipeline is the extract stage, when all of the data that have persisted through previous stages are made available to the end user applications, which may range from various visualization software packages, data-querying tools like Hive and Pig Latin, and machine learning libraries like Spark-MLlib (https://spark.apache.org/), Mahout (http://mahout.apache.org/), and Sci-kit (Pedregosa et al. 2012). The end goal of the data pipeline is to effectively serve business analysts and data scientists, who can effectively use these data for various applications. This stage may also involve extraction, transformation, and loading operations performed on these data, due to the heavy computing power available in the cluster and the results exported to other systems.

Existing Models for Customer Churn

Customer churn models have previously been well researched and applied in several industries. Yu et al. (2011) proposed an enhanced singular vector machine (ESVM) framework that they claim scaled well over large-scale data and had the ability to handle nonlinear data effectively. Miguéis et al. (2013) and Camanho and e Cunha (2013) used multivariate regression splines (MARS) as a classification technique to detect customer churn. Coussement and den Poel (2009) and Chen et al. (2012) used several user behavioral metrics through e-mail sentiment mining and longitudinal behavioral data to aid classifiers to make accurate predictions for customer churn. The model proposed by Sundarkumar and Ravi (2015) also used significant qualitative customer behavior data to drive fraud detection in insurance claims by using a one-class SVM (OCSVM) for classification. Linear and nonlinear classifiers like SVM, logistic regression, artificial neural networks (ANN), and tree-based Ensemble classifiers, and their variants are predominant choices of classifiers used by researchers for predicting customer churn.

We observed a significant gap in the feature mining process in previously published work. They all failed to effectively represent the e-commerce business model. The choice of feature set to drive churn prediction is mostly restricted to a list of conventional customer data, which have a huge share of static features along with sales data. Some of the recent work (Chen et al. 2012) published on customer churn has focused on behavioral features. The feature set, however, is still narrow and restricted to only a handful metrics, like recency and frequency factors. They all fall short of capturing the complete customer behavior footprint for a customer during their life cycle. The reason for this limitation in the feature mining process can be attributed partly to technology limitations in data capturing and the rest to the volume of the data with which it is meant to deal.

E-commerce businesses are driven mainly on digital channels, which are centered around, but not limited to, online website and mobile applications. These channels act as a single window between the organization and the customer during the entire relationship. The shopping activity or the online interactions, labeled as a browse session, generate valuable metrics and footprints for customer interactions with the online retailer. The data on sales generated by these online sessions, categories of products brought, etc., are more easily contained in volumes that mainly qualify as conventional quantitative features for our feature matrix. The user click activity, browse path behavior, and overall Web interaction generates several terabytes of data every single day for an e-commerce retailer operating on a large scale.

These valuable user behavior data were previously ignored by researchers for feature mining due to the lack of distributed data ingestion, storage, and computing technologies. These data can now be easily extracted through a feature mining process involving a Big Data pipeline. The click activity, popularly called clickstream, in conjunction with customer sales drive several data products on e-commerce websites under a broader category of recommendations called user personalization. Our proposed work aims to develop a generic framework and make it available for organizations and academic communities for predicting customer churn in an e-commerce business setting by using comprehensive feature mining approaches.

Customer Churn Model

We have already discussed in detail the data pipeline used by e-commerce to power Big Data applications. We now briefly discuss how this pipeline supports our customer churn prediction model. Although we restrict our discussion purely to the customer churn model, the steps followed below are applicable to any predictive modeling applications.

Phase 1: Feature Mining

This step involves extracting what we perceive is a right feature set for predicting customer churn. This may involve querying several locations within the data lake, denormalizing data, and deriving features, etc., so that the information is easily consumed by machine learning libraries for building the predictor model.

Phase 2: Data Science Model Building

This step focuses on feature engineering related to the feature set and implementation of the predictor models on the underlying feature set to develop a better model for customer churn.

Phase 3: Cross-Validation, Business Action, and Performance Tuning

The final step in processing is to evaluate the accuracy of prediction results and perform A-versus-B tests between the best-performing models. Once predictions of a model are implemented by providing preferential treatment to churning customers and results have been monitored, suitable performance enhancements or tuning may be performed, based on the results of the treatment acquired back in the data lake (Figure 13.2).

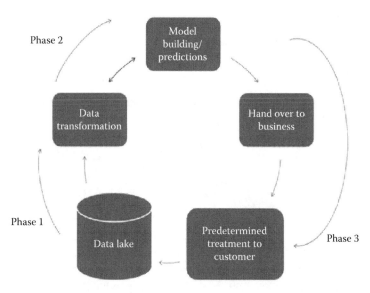

FIGURE 13.2
Customer churn model life cycle.

Feature Engineering

Feature Mining

A novel contribution of our work is to the systematic definition and mining of an extensive feature set to enable effective predictions of customer churn. We use a combination of several unstructured and structured customer data sets to extract several static, categorical and quantitative features, extensively capturing the customer footprint across their life cycle. This feature set, represented in Table 13.1, may be broadly classified into seven different categories.

Demographic Features

These features represent customer-specific demographic features that indicate the geographical location of the customer and the size and type of industry vertical.

Customer Information

These features represent profile information that may contain details like business tier of the account, type of contract with the e-retailer, number of registered users, number of billing accounts, number of shipping accounts, etc.

Customer Sales

These features represent aggregates for revenue, buying behavior, and periodicity including metrics for the latest trends in buying. These are conventional features that have been used in the past for building feature matrix.

TABLE 13.1

Feature Variables for the Customer Feature Matrix

Category	Feature	Description
Demographic Features	Customer base size	Size of customer base
	Vertical	Type of industry to which customer belongs
	Location	Billing address of customer
Customer Information	Age	Age of customer with the organization
	Customer tier	Business tier in which the customer is enrolled
	Registered users	Number of registered users enrolled by customer account
Customer Sales	Annual sales	Annual sales to the customer
	Year-to-date sales	Year-to-date sales to the customer
	Spending slope	Plot of spending over time
	Total returns	Total value of goods returned by customer
	Total orders	Total number of orders placed by customer
	Total rebate	Total rebates offered to the customer
	Year-over-year sales	Year-over-year drop or rise in sales
Product Sales	Total products	Total count of unique products sold
	Category 1 sales	% wallet spent on category 1 products
	Category 2 sales	% wallet spent on category 2 products
	Category n sales	% wallet spent on category n products
Sale Frequency	Frequency of orders	Avg. frequency at which orders are placed
	Frequency of visits	Avg. frequency at which user visits site
	Days since last visit	Number of elapsed days since last visit
	Avg. visits/month	Avg. number of visits/month/user
Behavioral Data	No. of active users	Number of active users on the account
	Active user ratio	Ratio of active/registered users
	Avg. page visits	Avg. number of page visits in a session
	Avg. product views	Avg. number of products viewed in a session
	Avg. session length	Avg. length of sessions by user
	Cart/view ratio	Ratio of cart addition over product views
	Cart/buy ratio	Ratio of cart addition over purchases
	Avg. abandoned cart value	Avg. worth of products abandoned in cart
	Abandon/buy ratio	Ratio of worth of cart abandoned over purchases
	Email click rate	Response to email marketing campaigns
Experience	Out of stock	Number of times user had a product go out of stock
	Exit at checkout	Number of times user had an issue at checkout
	Null results	Number of times product search yielded null results

Product Sales

These features aggregate customer buying patterns at the category level for every product, thus enabling discovery of any specific product categories driving customer churn.

Frequency

These features look at several conventional and longitudinal features related to customer shopping behavior and periodicity.

Behavioral

The behavioral features are extracted from customer interactions with the online channel. They contain features that indicate how customers spend time on the website, including their most recent session lengths, cart activities, including instances of cart abandonment, page navigations, product views, etc. Most of the features captured under behavioral features are unconventional features and hence have to be mined from clickstream logs.

Experience

These features define customer experience metrics, outlining shopping experiences on the website, and are also mined from clickstream logs. Some of the features defining user experiences are the number of instances where a user comes across an out-of-stock product or has difficulty in checking out a cart and placing an order, etc. The underlying hypothesis in mining these features is that over a period of time, bad shopping experiences may drive a customer away from a business.

Feature Selection

Feature selection algorithms are used to rank the prominent features influencing customer churn and to make sure the noisy features without relevance are ignored. We propose baseline methods for filtering the feature set before using univariate feature selection methods and regularization.

Feature selection (Kira and Rendell 1992, Guyon and Elisseeff 2003) refers to the process of selecting a subset of relevant features from a pool of features that are initially available. This process reduces the number of irrelevant features as input to the model and therefore reduces the data acquisition and computation cost. Second, it yields more accurate results and avoids problems of overfitting the model. Feature selection when looked at as a pre-processing step to machine learning has been very effective in reducing dimensionality and irrelevant data, thus increasing learning accuracy and improving result comprehensibility. The final goal of feature selection is to have a minimum number of features that is sufficient to capture all of the trends and variations in the output. It is important to select the right feature set before implementing an effective algorithm. The important factors to consider when removing a feature from the feature vector include the noisy nature of the feature, variance, and correlation among factors. The target of building a feature matrix is not solely to accumulate a number of features, but also to actually gather features that have a sizable impact on the outcome of the classifier.

Baseline Methods

Before employing any feature engineering techniques on the feature matrix, imputer methods are used to account for the missing values and to filter the outlier values from the distribution. The feature matrix is then normalized to aid faster convergence of classifier algorithms. If a correlation test shows that there are features that are highly correlated, then one of the features is removed from the feature set. An example is when there exists a high correlation among different product categories, because customers often buying from one of the categories are likely to buy from another related category. At the same time, features that have no correlations with the output are good candidates to get rid of, since they have no impact on the output event.

Imbalance in Class Label Outputs

An important observation from the data sets is the imbalance in data. On average, about 5 to 10% of customers churn on a year-on-year basis, depending on the segment of customers. This imbalance in distribution consisting returning and/or nonreturning customers is a good recipe for learning algorithms to classify a large number of customers under the returning category and to still attain high overall accuracy. Several works were carried out in the past (Burez and den Poel 2009) that specifically focused on handling imbalance in the data that led to skew the predictions of the model. We employed an in-depth cross-validation technique based on the k-fold, confusion matrix, and receiver operating characteristic (ROC) curve methods to arrive at the best algorithm to rule out such a bias in our model. Weights assigned to the feature vectors are inversely proportional to class frequencies in the input data, as shown in Equation 13.1. Here, $n_{samples}$ is the total number of samples in the data set, n_{class} represents the total possible class outcomes from the output labels, which in our case is 2. The count of occurrence, Y_i, represents the total number of occurrences of samples belonging to a given class whose weights we are interested in calculating.

$$Weight\ of\ Class\ Y_i = \frac{n_{Samples}}{N_{Classes} * Num\ of\ Y_i} \tag{13.1}$$

F-ANOVA

The F-analysis of variance (F-ANOVA) test (Saeys et al. 2007), a univariate feature selection method applied to continuous distributions, is used to predict how well a given distribution (X) predicts the class label we are interested in finding. The F value for every feature matrix is calculated, and features are then ranked according to F score to determine their effectiveness in predicting customer churn.

$$F = \frac{MS_R}{MS_E} \tag{13.2}$$

In Equation 13.2, MS_R (the mean square regression) and the MS_E (the mean square error) are critical. While MS_R indicates the between-group variability, MS_E represents the within-group variability. The statistical tests that assign feature significance with the independent variable determine if the between-group variability is higher than the within-group variability. Figure 13.3 shows how different features impact customer churn by ranking them based on F-score.

Regularization

Regularization (Ng 2004) is normally employed to penalize sparse features, especially when dealing with sparse data and when trying to avoid overfitting. The result of using L1-norm regularization yields features with nonzero coefficients, indicating that these features were not penalized. We use coefficients from regularized logistic regression to determine if the extended set of a feature set we have formulated has a significant impact on the outcome variable, as shown in Table 13.2. Through the above feature selection tests, important features affecting customer churn are determined. This step serves as a direct input to the

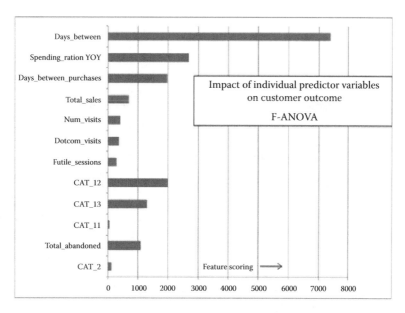

FIGURE 13.3
Feature ranking using the F-ANOVA test.

TABLE 13.2

Results of L1 Regularization of Feature Matrix Binomial
Classifier

Coefficient	Feature Variable
0.164	CAT 2
0.345	CAT 5
0.796	CAT 6
−2.066	CAT 12
−1.316	CAT 13
0.098	CAT 16
−1.161	CAT 17
−0.145	FUTILE SESSIONS
−0.145	NUM VISITS
0.124	TOTAL REBATE
0.285	DOTCOM VISITS
4.470	DAYS BETWEEN PURCHASES
0.939	RATIO CART ABANDONED
0.556	SPENDING SLOPE

organization to look into individual features to see how each of these can be improved to reduce the churn rate. The tests also confirm that for some of the nonconventional features proposed through this work that have been mainly extracted through clickstream logs, longitudinal behaviors have a significant impact on customer churn. This in turn increases the efficiency of predictor models (explored in the next section). Some of these features include the following: total futile sessions, cart abandonment, number of visits to other online channel, spending slope, ratio of cart items abandoned versus items shopped, etc.

Binomial Classifier

A mix of linear, nonlinear, and tree-based ensemble classifiers is employed to evaluate which classifier has the best performance on the data set. The cross-validation techniques determine the best-performing algorithm on the data set. The classifiers discussed below provide the best efficiency. It comes as no surprise that they are popularly used in many predictive applications. All classifiers were implemented using the sci-kit Learn (Pedregosa et al. 2012) Python library, which provides a comprehensive set of both supervised and unsupervised algorithms for machine learning. Some of the classifiers used by earlier researchers for this application included logistic regression, decision trees, Ensemble methods, Bayesian analysis, SVM, etc. Since our predictor models are all widely used by researchers, we refrained from getting into the mathematical details of the models and only discuss the algorithms that returned the best results for the problem. We divided our data into three splits, training, test, and validation, in a ratio of 6:2:2. This ratio is more commonly used by researchers after they have empirically determined the best split.

SVM

The goal of SVM (Scholkopf and Smola 2001) is to find the optimal separating hyperplane that maximizes the margin of the training data by dividing the n-dimensional space into two regions. The methodology can be applied successfully to many linear and nonlinear classification problems. SVM offers several choices of kernel functions for implementation to best fit our training data. We used a linear-kernel function with SVM.

Logistic Regression with L1 Norm

Logistic regression (Alpaydin 2014) is a discriminative classifier that learns a direct map from input x to output y by modeling posterior probability. It uses a logistic function to model the losses, which in turn are minimized by using a gradient descent. Adding regularization to logistic regression reduces overfitting by removing sparse features from the feature set. We used L1-norm-regularized logistic regression for this application.

Gradient-Boost Ensemble

Ensemble learning involves a combination of several models to solve a single prediction problem. It works by generating multiple simpler classifiers which learn and make predictions independently. Those predictions are then combined into a single prediction that should be as good as or better than the prediction made by any one classifier. The gradient boosting (Friedman 2001) classifier combines a set of weak learners and delivers an improved prediction accuracy. The outcome of the model at instance t is weighed based on the outcome of the previous instant, t–1. Shortcomings in predictions are identified by negative gradients. At each step, a new tree is fit to negative gradients of the previous tree.

Cross-Validation

From the confusion matrix shown in Figure 13.4, there are exactly four possible outcomes from a binomial classifier model. The total number of positive instances in the

FIGURE 13.4
Confusion matrix for a binary classifier.

matrix is T = FP + TP, and the total number of negative instances is F = TN + FN. The most common evaluation metrics are overall accuracy, the true-positive rate, and the false-positive rate.

$$Accuracy = \frac{TP + TN}{N + P}$$

The true-positive rate (also known as the hit rate, or the precision) is the proportion of positive instances that a classifier captures.

$$Precision = \frac{TP}{P}$$

The recall is the ratio of the number of positive instances (TP) over the sum of true positives (TP) and false negatives (FN).

$$Recall = \frac{TP}{TP + FN}$$

The false-positive rate (also known as the false-alarm rate) is the proportion of negative instances that a classifier wrongly flagged as positive.

$$FP\,rate = \frac{FP}{N}$$

More than the accuracy, we are interested in increasing the TP rate of our classifier. A customer who is a returning customer but was wrongly classified as nonreturning by the classifier thus falls into the false-positive quadrant and has a lesser impact than an abandoning customer wrongly classified as a returning customer, who would fall into the false-negative quadrant. In the latter case, we would ignore a potential customer who might abandon the company in the near future.

Table 13.3 shows the accuracy and other indicators for all three classifiers used to predict customer churn. As is evident from the table, the gradient boost machines (GBM) classifier outperformed SVM to give the highest accuracy and precision after *k*-fold splitting and hyperparameter tuning. Running this algorithm on a feature set which has already undergone feature pruning leads to an incremental gain in efficiency of more than 5%. The precision score for the GBM model is above 75%, which indicates that we identified every three of four churning customers from a data set that was highly skewed towards nonchurning customers. This is a huge leap over results with the earlier models that were

TABLE 13.3

Classifier Models with the F-ANOVA Feature Selection

Classifier	TN	FN	FP	TP	Accuracy	Precision	Recall
Support vector machines	5520	968	68	259	0.85	0.79	0.211
Gradient boost	6903	590	53	274	0.917	0.838	0.317

built on conventional data sources, as they attained an overall accuracy of 75% with poor precision scores.

k-Fold Strategy for Cross-Validation

We used 5-fold CV by randomly splitting the training dataset (D) into five mutually exclusive subsets (D1, D2, D3, D4, D5) of approximately equal size. Each classification model will be trained and tested five times, where each time 't'ε {1, 2, 3, 4, 5}. It was trained on all except one fold (D, Dt) and tested on the remaining fold (Dt). The accuracy and AUC measures were averaged over the particular measures of the five individual test folds which we shall see in the further section

Receiver Operating Characteristics Curve

When TP rate is plotted as against FP rate, one obtains a receiver operating characteristics (ROC) graph (Bradley 1997). Each classifier is represented by a point on ROC graph. A perfect classifier is represented by point (0, 1) on ROC graph which classifies all positive and negative instances correctly with 100% TP rate and 0% FP rate. The major goal of churn prediction is to detect churn. Therefore, a suitable classifier is the one having high TP rate and low FP rate given that churn is the positive class. Such classifier is located at the upper left corner of ROC graph.

Figure 13.5 shows the ROC curve for Gradient Boost Classifier with *k*-fold cross validation technique. Using *k*-fold strategy folds for different combination of Test, Training

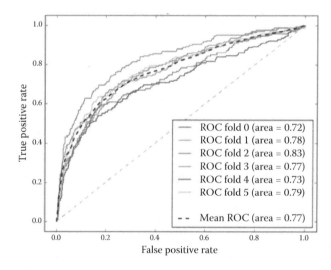

FIGURE 13.5

ROC curve for gradient boost classifier and F-ANOVA-based feature selection.

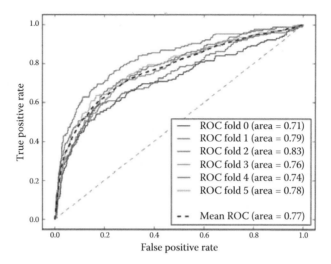

FIGURE 13.6
ROC curve for SVM classifier and F-ANOVA-based feature selection.

has fairly consistent Area under Curve (AUC). The mean ROC as indicated by the plot is 0.77. Once the model is finalized by tuning the hyper-parameters, the area under the ROC Curve can be used to tweak the threshold probability such that we can tune the classifier to return the best predictions for a given quadrant in the confusion matrix.

Similarly, Figure 13.6 shows ROC curve for an SVM Classifier with Linear Kernel on feature set that is an outcome of F-anova test. The probabilistic estimation of classes for an SVM was made available not until recently by the work proposed in (Platt 1999), called the Platt scaling to optimize internal variables to produce a probabilistic score. This tweak in threshold probability identified by TP rate and FP rate populates the graph for the ROC curve. Similar ROC curves can be plotted for other classifiers used in this work.

Conclusions and Future Work

We have presented a Big Data infrastructure that drives an end-to-end pipeline for predicting customer churn in an e-commerce organization. We demonstrated through our results how implicit and longitudinal features obtained through mining of clickstream and web logs, marketing campaigns, etc., act as significant features, along with conventional data from sales histories. These implicit features establish customer behavior and experience, and hence they can be used as features to determine customer churn. Through feature ranking, we showed some of the most influential factors in driving customer churn. Through cross-validation techniques, we established that the gradient boost ensemble classifier, SVM classifier, logistic regression with L1 regularization, are the best models for prediction customer churn.

There is a broad scope for improving data pipelines, as new tools are constantly added into the Hadoop Stack. The feature engineering process and the model-building process could also benefit from exploring other feature selection methods. This activity is continuous and iterative in nature. Improvements to the current classifier results can be brought through further hyperparameter tuning to current best-performing classifiers. Another important avenue worth exploring for addressing customer churn is the application of time series analysis. As a business grows and becomes more complex, there are more data sources, with channels that continuously open up and may hold valuable information. These data need to be captured and harnessed for this or similar applications. Some of the recent advances in convolutional neural networks have made available several libraries in deep learning, including one from Google, called Tensor flow (https://www.tensorflow.org/) and Amazon's Deep Scalable Sparse Tensor Network Engine (https://github.com/amznlabs/amazon-dsstne), that can be used to implement classifiers from existing data sets.

References

Alpaydin E. 2014. *Introduction to Machine Learning*. Cambridge, MA: MIT Press.

Bradley AP. 1997. The use of the area under the ROC curve in the evaluation of machine learning algorithms. *Pattern Recognition* 30(7):1145–1159.

Burez J, den Poel D. 2009. Handling class imbalance in customer churn prediction. *Expert Systems with Applications* 36(3):4626–4636.

Chen Z-Y, Fan Z-P, Sun M. 2012. A hierarchical multiple kernel support vector machine for customer churn prediction using longitudinal behavioral data. *European Journal of Operational Research* 223(2):461–472.

Coussement K, den Poel D. 2009. Improving customer attrition prediction by integrating emotions from client/company interaction emails and evaluating multiple classifiers. *Expert Systems with Applications* 36(3):6127–6134.

Farquhar JD, Panther T. 2008. Acquiring and retaining customers in UK banks: An exploratory study. *Journal of Retailing and Consumer Services* 15(1):9–21.

Friedman JH. 2001. Greedy function approximation: A gradient boosting machine. *Annals of Statistics* 29(5):1189–1232.

Guyon I, Elisseeff A. 2003. An introduction to variable and feature selection. *Journal of Machine Learning Research* 3:1157–1182.

Kira K, Rendell LA. 1992. A practical approach to feature selection, pp. 249–256. *Proceedings of the Ninth International Workshop on Machine Learning*. New York: ACM.

Kumar DA, Ravi V. 2008. Predicting credit card customer churn in banks using data mining. *International Journal of Data Analysis Techniques and Strategies* 1(1):4–28.

Miguéis VL, Camanho A, e Cunha JF. 2013. Customer attrition in retailing: An application of multivariate adaptive regression splines. *Expert Systems with Applications* 40(16):6225–6232.

Ng AY. 2004. Feature selection, L 1 vs. L 2 regularization, and rotational invariance, p. 78. *Proceedings of the Twenty-First International Conference on Machine Learning*. New York: ACM.

Olston C, Reed B, Srivastava U, Kumar R, Tomkins A. 2008. Pig Latin: A not-so-foreign language for data processing, pp. 1099–1110. *Proceedings of the 2008 ACM SIGMOD International Conference on Management of Data*. New York: ACM.

Pedregosa F, Varoquaux G, Gramfort A, Michel V, Thirion B, et al. 2012. Scikit-learn: Machine learning in Python. *Journal of Machine Learning Research* 12:2825–2830.

Platt JC. 1999. Probabilistic outputs for support vector machines and comparisons to regularized likelihood methods, pp. 61–74. *Advances in Large Margin Classifiers*. Cambridge, MA: MIT Press.

Saeys Y, Inza I, Larrañaga P. 2007. A review of feature selection techniques in bioinformatics. *Bioinformatics* 23(19):2507–2517.

Scholkopf B, Smola AJ. 2001. *Learning with Kernels: Support Vector Machines, Regularization, Optimization, and Beyond*. Cambridge, MA: MIT Press.

Shvachko K, Kuang H, Radia S, Chansler R. 2010. The Hadoop Distributed File System, pp. 1–10. *IEEE 26th Symposium on Mass Storage Systems and Technologies*. New York: IEEE.

Sundarkumar GG, Ravi V. 2015. A novel hybrid undersampling method for mining unbalanced datasets in banking and insurance. *Engineering Applications of Artificial Intelligence* 37:368–377.

Wei C-P, Chiu I-T. 2002. Turning telecommunications call details to churn prediction: A data mining approach. *Expert Systems with Applications* 23(2):103–112.

White T. 2012. *Hadoop: The Definitive Guide*. Sebastopol, CA: O'Reilly Media, Inc.

Xie Y, Li X, Ngai EWT, Ying W. 2009. Customer churn prediction using improved balanced random forests. *Expert Systems with Applications* 36(3):5445–5449.

Yu X, Guo S, Guo J, Huang X. 2011. An extended support vector machine forecasting framework for customer churn in e-commerce. *Expert Systems with Applications* 38(3):1425–1430.

Key Terminology and Definitions

AUC: AUC stands for the area under the curve, a metric that calculates the accuracy of a given classifier, depending on how large the area under the plot of the TP rate vs the FP rate is for an ROC graph. The higher the AUC, the better the classifier.

Avro: Apache Avro is a data serialization framework that is schema intensive but neutral to languages. It is mainly used to handle dynamically changing data and wire communications between different Hadoop nodes and services (http://avro.apache.org/).

ETL: the process of extracting data from source systems and bringing them into the data warehouse is commonly called ETL, which stands for extraction, transformation, and loading.

Hadoop Data Lake: data lake is a terminology more commonly used across industries when referring to a Hadoop platform consisting of one or more clusters that store different types of data, both structured and unstructured, relational, object, JSON, sensor, logs, etc. The platform is generally used both for providing cheap storage and also to serve an analytics purpose.

Parquet: Apache Parquet is a columnar storage format available to any project in the Hadoop ecosystem, regardless of the data processing framework, data model, or programming language (https://parquet.apache.org/). It is mostly used when users know in advance the condition on which the data will be retrieved, thereby making the scans extremely fast.

14

Large-Scale Entity Clustering Based on Structural Similarities within Knowledge Graphs

Mahmoud Elbattah, Mohamed Roushdy, Mostafa Aref, and Abdel-Badeeh M. Salem

CONTENTS

Introduction

With the ongoing initiatives aimed at publishing data in a linked data format [1] (e.g., DBpedia, Freebase, and Wikidata), more and more graph-based representations of knowledge have become available. The graph-based representation turns plain strings into "entities" that possess attributes, taxonomy, and relationships to other entities. Viewed this way, linked data can introduce new capabilities and opportunities for exploring data and revealing interesting connections among entities. However, the enormous volumes of such knowledge bases raise new challenges as well, and they require an inevitable need for embracing semisupervised or unsupervised techniques.

In this respect, clustering presents an appropriate method for dealing with immense amounts of data in an unsupervised manner. Clustering has been defined as the segmentation of a heterogeneous population into a number of more homogeneous subgroups [2]. Clustering techniques are widely used for exploratory data analysis, with applications ranging from statistics, computer science, and biology to the social sciences and psychology. Different tasks and purposes can be served by clustering, including:

1. Exploring the underlying structure of data
2. Discovering meaningful patterns
3. Summarizing key characteristics of data

In this chapter, we address entity clustering at scale within one of the largest knowledge bases, Freebase [3]. Initially launched in 2007 by Metaweb Technologies and acquired by Google in 2010, Freebase was developed to serve as an open and collaborative knowledge base [4]. The data in Freebase consist of millions of topics (entities) and tens of millions of relationships between those topics [5]. Recently, the voluminous content of Freebase has been transferred to Wikidata, in what has been described as the "The Great Migration" [6]. The building block of the data model of Freebase is the so-called knowledge graph [7]. Similar to the long-established semantic networks [8], a knowledge graph represents knowledge in patterns of interconnected nodes and arcs. Knowledge graphs have the advantage of being a declarative graph-driven representation of knowledge.

We approach the clustering task from a graph-based standpoint. In particular, homogeneous clusters of entities are segmented based on their graph-based structural similarities. Although we have only endorsed Freebase here, the key idea could be applicable to similar data repositories, such as DBpedia or Wikidata. Broadly, this chapter attempts to clarify the benefits on the theoretical and practical aspects. First, we investigate the validity and applicability of clustering entities based on their structural similarities in knowledge graphs. Second, the computed clusters were employed to gain insights in relation to the underlying structure of Freebase data. Further, the computed clusters can adequately serve as a robust basis for the purpose of topic exploration and discovery. From a practical perspective, we discuss vital issues in relation to scalability while clustering large-scale graphs.

Background: Big Data and Analytics

This section serves as a brief introduction to the world of Big Data. We aimed to highlight the various definitions and characteristics of Big Data. Furthermore, the typical features of modern data analytics are explained.

Definitions of Big Data

Although the Big Data term has been used ubiquitously over the past years, we could not find a universally accepted definition. In fact, the notion of Big Data tends to be very domain dependent, and it can be interpreted quite differently from one context to another. In this regard, numerous studies (e.g., Refs. [9–12]) endeavored to survey the commonly used definitions or to articulate a broader definition for Big Data. For the purpose of this review, we present various definitions that portray Big Data from different perspectives. Table 14.1 lists the proposed definitions in detail.

TABLE 14.1

Proposed Definitions of Big Data

Proposed Definition	Source of Definition
Big Data refers to both large volumes of data with a high level of complexity and the analytical methods applied to them, which require more advanced techniques and technologies in order to derive meaningful information and insights in real time.	UK Government [13]
Big Data is the derivation of value from traditional relational database-driven business decision making, augmented with new sources of unstructured data.	Oracle [14]
Big Data is high-volume, high-velocity, and/or high-variety information assets that demand cost-effective, innovative forms of information processing that enable enhanced insight, decision making, and process automation.	Gartner [10]
According to Intel, Big Data opportunities emerge in organizations generating a median of 300 terabytes of data per week. Intel asserts that the most common data type involved in analytics is business transactions stored in relational databases (this is consistent with Oracle's definition), followed by documents, email, sensor data, blogs, and social media.	Intel [15]
Big Data is the term increasingly used to describe the process of applying serious computing power, i.e., the latest in machine learning and artificial intelligence, to seriously massive and often highly complex sets of information.	Microsoft [16]
Big Data is data which exceed the capacity or capability of current or conventional methods and systems.	National Institute of Standards and Technology (NIST) [17]
The high degree of permutations and interactions within a data set is what defines Big Data. Viewed this way, Big Data is not a function of the size of a data set but of its complexity.	Method for an Integrated Knowledge Environment (MIKE2.0) Project [18]
Big Data refers to data sets whose size is beyond the ability of typical database software tools to capture, store, manage, and analyze.	McKinsey Global Institute [19]

In light of the diversity of definitions used to characterize Big Data, we want to empha-size that there is no absolute definition of Big Data. The understanding of Big Data can therefore depend largely on context, domain, and computation standards. However, most studies generally endorse Big Data in terms of its (i) volume, (ii) complexity, and (iii) technologies.

Characteristics of Big Data

Over the years, many characteristics have been continuously added in order to distinguish Big Data from other simpler scenarios. Below, we present the main viewpoints developed for characterizing the dimensions of Big Data. Furthermore, Figure 14.1 visually summa-rizes the common dimensions of Big Data.

Gartner's Three Vs

In a white paper [20] published by Gartner, Big Data was characterized as having three main attributes. Those three attributes were widely regarded as the common dimensions of Big Data. The three Vs interpretation of Big Data is as follows:

1. Volume: the incoming data stream and cumulative volume of data
2. Velocity: the pace of data used to support interactions and generated by interactions
3. Variety: the variety of incompatible and inconsistent data formats and data structures

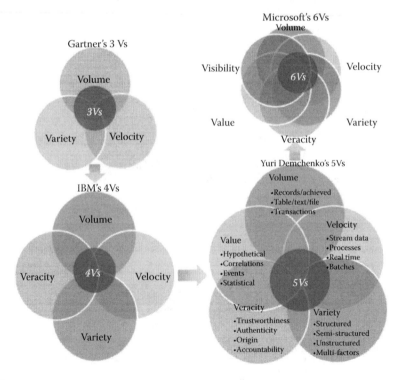

FIGURE 14.1
Various interpretations of Big Data dimensions. (From Wu C et al., arXiv:1601.03115, 2016.)

IBM's Four Vs

IBM added another attribute or V, for veracity, to Gartner's three Vs notation. The reason behind the additional V for the veracity dimension was justified as IBM's clients started to face data quality issues while dealing with Big Data problems [21]. Further studies (e.g., Ref. [22]) added the value dimension along with the IBM four Vs. IBM defined the four Vs as follows [23]:

1. Volume: stands for scale of data
2. Velocity: denotes analysis of streaming data
3. Variety: indicates different forms of data
4. Veracity: implies uncertainty of data

Microsoft's Six Vs

For the purpose of maximizing business value, Microsoft extended Gartner's three Vs into six Vs [24]. The six Vs included additional dimensions for variability, veracity, and visibility. The Microsoft interpretation of Big Data is as follows:

1. Volume: stands for the scale of data
2. Velocity: denotes the analysis of streams of data
3. Variety: indicates different forms of data
4. Veracity: focuses on the trustworthiness of data sources
5. Variability: refers to the complexity of a data set; in comparison with variety, it means the number of variables in a data set
6. Visibility: emphasizes that there is a need to have a full picture of the data in order to make informative decisions

Analytics

Data analytics has become a broad and vibrant domain that includes a diversity of techniques, technologies, systems, practices, methodologies, and applications. Similar to Big Data, various definitions have been developed in order to describe analytics. Table 14.2

TABLE 14.2

Proposed Definitions of Analytics

Definition of Analytics	Reference
The extensive use of data in statistical and quantitative analyses, explanatory and predictive models, and fact-based management to drive decisions and actions. The analytics may be input for human decisions or may drive fully automated decisions. Analytics are a subset of what has come to be called business intelligence.	[25]
Delivering the right decision support to the right people at the right time.	[26]
The scientific process of transforming data into insights for making better decisions.	[27]

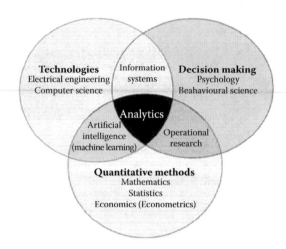

FIGURE 14.2
Taxonomy of disciplines related to the practice of data analytics. (From Mortensen MJ et al., *European Journal of Operational Research* 241:583–595, 2015.)

presents some of the common definitions of data analytics. Moreover, Figure 14.2 portrays the interdisciplinary nature that can be involved within the practice of analytics. According to Ref. [28], these disciplines can fit into one or more of the following categories:

- Technological: refers to the various tools used, including hardware, software, and networks, which together support the efficient processing of large-scale data sets
- Quantitative: refers to applied quantitative approaches to analyzing data, such as statistics, machine learning, econometrics, and Operations Research (OR)
- Decision making: represents an inherently interdisciplinary area, including tools, theories, and practices used to support and understand the decision-making process (e.g., human–computer interactions, visualization in information systems, problem structuring methods in Operations Research/Management Science (OR/MS))

Within different industries, the opportunities enabled by Big Data have led to engender a significant interest in data analytics. Based on the business objectives, data analytics can be classified into four types:

1. Descriptive analytics: What happened?
2. Diagnostic analytics: Why did it happen?
3. Predictive analytics: What will likely happen?
4. Prescriptive analytics: What should be done?

Figure 14.3 [29] illustrates the full spectrum of data analytics. The figure also shows the techniques and the degree of sophistication associated with each type of analytics.

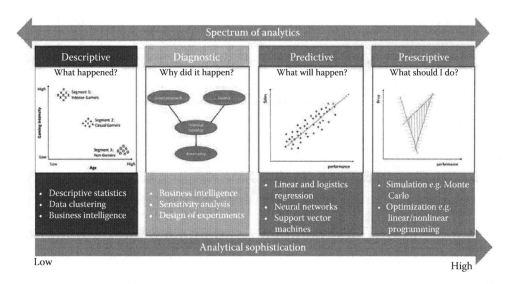

FIGURE 14.3
Spectrum of data analytics. (Modified from Barga R et al., *Predictive Analytics with Microsoft Azure Machine Learning*, 2nd ed., 2015.)

Background: Knowledge Graphs

This section provides a basic understanding of knowledge graphs, whereas our study intensively utilized knowledge graphs extracted from Freebase. In principle, knowledge graphs belong to the category of semantic networks as a method for representing knowledge in a graph-based manner. The composition of a knowledge graph generally includes the following:

- Concepts (i.e., entities or topics): A concept is represented as a node in a knowledge graph. It expresses the existence of a physical or conceptual thing in the real world.
- Predicate (i.e., relationship or connection): A relation between two concepts is expressed by a labelled arc in the knowledge graph.

Figure 14.4 presents a hypothetical example of a knowledge graph that connects two entities (i.e., subject and object) with a single predicate.

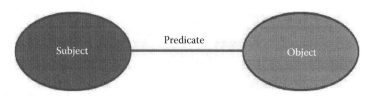

FIGURE 14.4
A simple knowledge graph.

In this simple manner, knowledge graphs aim to provide meaning through graph-based representations (i.e., structures). Knowledge graphs have the capabilities to express or depict deeper semantic layers by using a minimum relation set. For instance, Google has succeeded in exploiting the idea of knowledge graphs in order to enhance search results based on semantic information gathered from a wide variety of sources. Google also refers to its specific implementation of knowledge as their knowledge graph [7].

Motivation: Entity Clustering in Large-Scale Knowledge Graphs

Given a knowledge graph denoted as $G = (V,E)$, V is the set of vertices (entities or topics) and E is the set of edges (connections or relations among entities). We address the problem of computing clusters within the knowledge graph in an unsupervised manner. Furthermore, we investigate the scalability concern, where large-scale knowledge graphs exist. Table 14.3 lists the questions of interest in detail.

Data Description

As mentioned earlier, our study used a subset extracted from the knowledge base of Freebase. Through the following sections, we delineate the specific data model underlying Freebase. Moreover, the data set used by the study is fully described.

Overview

Freebase has been described as a huge collaborative database of cross-linked data [30]. Freebase was initially developed by Metaweb Technologies, before it was acquired by Google. Freebase has the advantage of including a wide diversity of structured data imported from various sources, such as Wikipedia, MusicBrainz, and WordNet [31]. Specifically, it is claimed to comprise about 50 million topics (i.e. entities).

The contents of Freebase have been recently been merged with Wikidata to form a larger knowledge base. The merging process was described by Google as the "The Great Migration" [6]. However, Freebase data are still freely accessible through a downloadable dump, publicly available at Ref. [32]. The data dump was archived as a single tab-separated file of around 250 GB. We used a reduced version of Freebase as described in Ref. [33]. The reduced version contained the basic identifying facts about every topic in Freebase. Likewise, the data were organized into tab-separated files of around 5 GB.

TABLE 14.3

Questions of Interest

Principal Question	Auxiliary Questions
How to partition a knowledge graph into groups so that entities in a group are similar and entities in different groups are dissimilar	Q1) What is the similarity measure that can be used to cluster entities within a large-scale knowledge graph in an unsupervised manner?
	Q2) What is the efficiently scalable algorithm for graph clustering that can deal with large-scale knowledge graphs?
	Q3) How can we precisely measure the quality of computed clusters?

Freebase Data Model

In this section, we aim to explain the data model of Freebase, which defines how knowledge is structured and represented. The Freebase data model is generally broken down into the following components:

- **Topic:** Freebase contains topics about real-world entities, including people, places, and things. A topic may refer to a specific concrete object (e.g., Albert Einstein) or an abstract concept (e.g., Euler's number {e}, Leadership). Freebase adopted the so-called entity reconciliation, where a topic might be associated with many names or acronyms, but each topic should clearly represent one and only one entity or concept. Further, every topic is assigned a globally unique identifier (GUID). Figure 14.5 demonstrates an example where entity reconciliation should be considered.

- **Type:** A type is an object that is used as a conceptual container of properties that are most commonly needed for characterizing a particular aspect of information. In other words, a topic is considered an instance of a type if the topic is associated with that type. Examples of types are "Book Author," "Film Actor," "Location," or "Programming Language." Topics in Freebase can be related to any number of types. However, Freebase types do not support inheritance [34] as opposed to object-oriented or RDF modeling approaches. Figure 14.6 demonstrates the implementation of types in Freebase, with an example of the famous politician Winston Churchill.

- **Property:** A property of a topic denotes a "Has a" relationship between the topic and property value (e.g. London [topic] has a population [property] of ≈8.5 million [value]). It's common that a property is represented as a verb or a verbal phrase (e.g., "Written by" or "Directed by").

- **Domains:** Types are grouped into domains that are similar to sections found in a newspaper (e.g., Arts and Entertainment, Politics). In addition, Freebase includes a special collection of domain names as "Commons," which have met certain standards to be considered well-known topics.

FIGURE 14.5
Example of how Freebase deals with ambiguity and multiplicities of entities. The "University of California Los Angeles" can be mentioned in many different ways. Freebase maps all those different representations into a single entity with a unique ID.

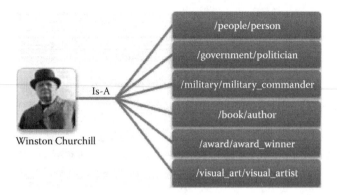

FIGURE 14.6
Example of the multifaceted nature of entities and how Freebase handles them in a flexible manner. In this example, Winston Churchill is a type of "Politician," which belongs to the Government domain, and he is also typed as a Person, which belongs to a different domain (i.e., People domain). However, Winston Churchill is also related to other domains, such as Military Commander, Author, Nobel Laureate, and Visual Artist.

- **Category:** Category is a further bundler of domains into more generic groups. Specifically, Freebase includes nine categories:
    1. Science and Technology
    2. Arts and Entertainment
    3. Sports
    4. Society
    5. Products and Services
    6. Transportation
    7. Special Interests
    8. Time and Space
    9. Commons

Figure 14.7 summarizes the breakdown of the Freebase data model.

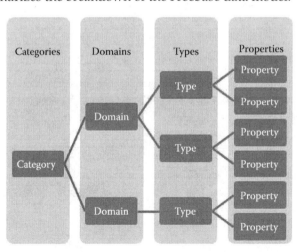

FIGURE 14.7
Hierarchy of the Freebase schema.

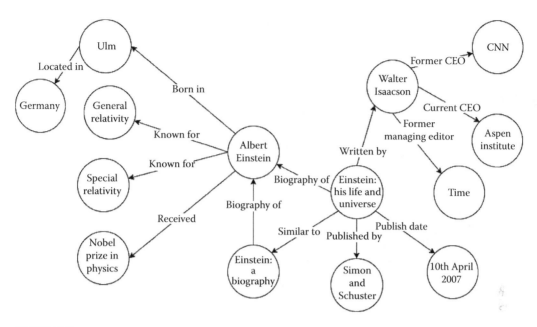

FIGURE 14.8
An illustration of knowledge graphs in Freebase. Triplets (subject-predicate-object) are the building blocks of the graph, where expressive predicates describe relationships among entities, e.g., entities such as "Albert Einstein."

Knowledge Representation in Freebase

As with the widely used RDF model [35], Freebase data can simply be conceived in terms of subject-predicate-object triplets that form a knowledge graph. The knowledge graph of Freebase collectively composes a large-scale directed labeled graph which incorporates around 125 million entities, 4,000 types, and 7,000 properties [14]. Figure 14.8 illustrates an example of how knowledge is represented in Freebase.

Computing Clusters

Data Preprocessing

Due to computing limitations, data have to be partitioned in order to extract an experimental data set. The main limitation is imposed by memory rather than space, whereas a whole knowledge graph should have gone beyond the capabilities of our relatively limited Cloud computing resources.

The data partitioning process in our study included two procedures in order to reduce the number of graph nodes and edges to some extent. First, only four categories of entities were considered. The selected categories were aimed to span cross-disciplinary areas of knowledge, including Science and technology, society, sports, and time and space. Every category comprised a set of narrower domains. Table 14.4 lists the domains within each of the four categories. Second, we only considered the "Is a" predicates within the partitioned graph in order to reduce the number of graph edges.

TABLE 14.4

Domains per Category: Categories Selected to Partition the Freebase Knowledge Graph

Category	Included Domains
Science and Technology	Astronomy, Biology, Chemistry, Computers, Engineering, Geology, Internet, Medicine, Meteorology, Physics
Society	Awards, Celebrities, Conferences and Conventions, Education, Exhibitions, Government, Influence, Language, Law, Library, Organization, People, Projects, Religion, Royalty, and Nobility
Sports	American Football, Baseball, Basketball, Boxing, Cricket, Ice Hockey, Martial Arts, Olympics, Skiing, Soccer, Sports, Tennis
Time and Space	Location, Measurement Unit, Physical Geography, Time, Protected Places, Event

TABLE 14.5

Statistics of the Data Set Used in the Study

Category	Count of Entities (Nodes)	Count of Is-A Links (Edges)
Science and Technology	233,291	276,133
Society	1,652,581	2,112,248
Sports	146,875	177,387
Time and Space	688,302	1,487,158
Total	2,721,049	4,052,926

Nevertheless, with graph partitioning, the extracted data set could still qualify as a large-scale graph due to the massive volume of Freebase data. Specifically, the total number of entities reached around 2.7 million, and the number of graph edges was more than 4 million. The entities are represented as nodes in the knowledge graph, while the "Is a" links represent edges connecting graph nodes. Table 14.5 presents statistics of the extracted data set used in the study.

Formulation of the Similarity Metric

Clustering aims at finding groups in a data set based on some natural criterion of similarity [36]. Therefore, the unavoidable substantial step is to clearly determine that natural criterion of similarity that can account for the resemblance between entities within the knowledge graph.

Our study embraced the hypothesis that highly connected subgraphs can be as clusters of entities that share a similar graph-based structure, despite dissimilar predicate connections that may exist. The desirable properties of a cluster are to be internally well-connected and externally less connected. The study hypothesis was based on the following four assumptions:

Assumption 1. A knowledge graph (G) represents a nonrandom graph of connected knowledge; therefore, (G) can have an inherent community structure [37].

Assumption 2. Given a knowledge graph, the link-based structure of nodes (entities) can serve as a similarity metric for the purpose of clustering.

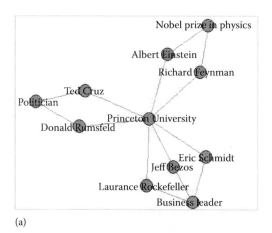
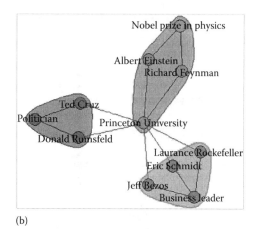

(a)   (b)

FIGURE 14.9

Example of graph-based clustering in a simple knowledge graph. (a) The original knowledge graph, which stretches over three different domains, including science, politics, and business, where Princeton University is a common entity in the graph. The entity connections represent different types of relationships (predicates), such as "Affiliated with," "Graduated from," or "Is-a." However, the edges are considered abstract graph edges. (b) Three well-connected subgraphs that can be considered clusters of entities that share a structural similarity within the knowledge graphs.

Assumption 3. Given a knowledge graph, nodes (entities) are considered to have a similar link-based structure, even though their links represent dissimilar predicates or relations. **Assumption 4.** Given a knowledge graph, detected communities can represent clusters of entities with structural similarity.

The first and principal assumption is derived from the premise that a random graph does not have a community structure [38]. A graph is said to have a community structure when its nodes can be grouped into sets of nodes, such that each set of nodes is densely connected internally and less connected externally [37]. Since knowledge graphs are not randomly constructed, communities can therefore naturally exist. In view of that assumption, the entities in a knowledge graph can be grouped based on the structural similarities, defined by abstract entity connections. Figure 14.9 presents a simple example of a knowledge graph, highlighting clusters of entities that possess similar connections.

Selection of Clustering Algorithm

From the perspective of Big Data, this section addresses another important question: What is a efficiently scalable algorithm for graph clustering that can deal with large-scale knowledge graphs? While dealing with large-scale graphs, the clustering algorithm should be carefully selected. The algorithm should be evaluated not only in terms of clustering quality, but also in terms of scalability. According to Ref. [39], scalability is a broad concept that encompasses four types of scalability, as follows:

1. Load scalability

2. Space scalability

3. Space–time scalability

4. Structural scalability. In our case, the main concern was placed for space–time scalability, meaning that a clustering algorithm should continue to function gracefully as the graph size increases by orders of magnitude.

In this respect, the study endeavored to review the most recognized methods used for graph clustering. We took avail of two exhaustive surveys [40,41] in order to facilitate the review process. Table 14.6 provides a concise overview of the families of graph clustering algorithms and the principal idea behind them. More importantly, Table 14.7 presents a comparative analysis of representative graph clustering algorithms in terms of computational complexity.

In light of that review, it turned out that only very few algorithms struck a balance between clustering quality and scalability, despite the ample algorithms for graph clustering. In particular, only the Louvain [42] and Infomap [43] algorithms proved to provide high scalability with respect to computational complexity. Eventually, we decided to use the Louvain algorithm, since it is obviously the least computationally demanding algorithm. The Louvain algorithm belongs to the optimization-based algorithms family, whereas it follows a strategy that seeks graph clusters with maximal modularity.

The Louvain algorithm is based on two steps. First, each node is initially assigned to a different community, such that there are initially as many communities as there are nodes. For each node, the algorithm evaluates the gain in modularity if a node is placed in the community of one of its neighbor nodes. The node is actually moved to another community only if there is a gain in modularity (Equation 14.1). This process is iteratively applied

TABLE 14.6

Main Categories of Graph Clustering Algorithms

Category of Algorithms		Principal Idea	Examples
Hierarchical Clustering	Divisive Algorithms	Top-down clustering by iteratively splitting clusters, removing edges connecting vertices with low similarity	[37,44,45]
	Agglomerative Algorithms	Bottom-up clustering by iteratively merging nodes and communities based on similarity	[46–48]
Spectral Clustering		Clusters computed using the eigenvalues and eigenvectors of its Laplacian matrix as a measure of vertex similarity	[49–52]
Optimization-based Clustering		Based on the maximization of an objective function, a normalized cut [53], and modularity function [44]	[42,54–56]

TABLE 14.7

Computational Complexity of Graph Clustering Algorithms

Category of Algorithms	Algorithm (reference)	Computational Complexity[a]
Hierarchical Clustering	Ravasz algorithm [47]	$O(n^2)$
	Link clustering [57]	$O(n^2)$
	Girvan-Newman [37]	$O(n^3)$
Spectral Clustering	Spectral clustering [51]	$O(n^3)$
Optimization-based Clustering	Greedy modularity [58]	$O(n^2)$
	Optimized greedy modularity [59]	$O(n\log^2 n)$
	Louvain [42]	$O(m)$
	Infomap [43]	$O(n\log n)$

Source: Adapted from Barabási AL, 2013. *Philosophical Transactions of the Royal Society of London A* 371(1987): 20120375, 2013.

[a] An uppercase letter O is used in complexity theory and computer science to describe the asymptotic behavior of function. For example, $O(n^2)$ means that the worst-case running time of a function $f(n)$ is $O(n^2)$ [60].

to all nodes until no further changes in the community can be performed to increase modularity [42].

$$\Delta Q = \left[\frac{\sum_{in} + k_{i,in}}{2m} - \left(\frac{\sum_{tot} + k_i}{2m} \right)^2 \right] - \left[\frac{\sum_{in}}{2m} - \left(\frac{\sum_{tot}}{2m} \right)^2 - \left(\frac{k_i}{2m} \right)^2 \right] \qquad (14.1)$$

where Σ_{in} is the sum of the weights of the links inside C, Σ_{tot} is the sum of the link weights of all nodes in C, k_i is the sum of the weights of the links incident to node i, $k_{i,in}$ is the sum of the weights of the links from i to nodes in C, and m is the sum of the weights of all the links in the network.

The second step of the algorithm includes building a new graph whose nodes are the communities identified during the first step. The weights of the edges connecting the new nodes are given by the sum of the weights of the edges between nodes in the corresponding two communities [61]. Once the second step is completed, the two steps can be reapplied, calling their combination a pass. The number of communities decreases with each pass. The passes are repeated until there are no more changes in communities and maximum modularity has been reached.

The Louvain algorithm has the advantage of providing a fair compromise between clustering quality and computational complexity which is essentially linear in the number of graph edges. The excellent performance of the Louvain algorithm has been widely recognized in the literature [41,59,62,63]. For instance, one study [63] used the Louvain algorithm in order to efficiently portion very large social network comprising more than 2 million nodes and 38 million edges.

Clustering Experiments

This section elaborates on the practical aspects of the study. We utilized the iGraph package [64] within R language. The iGraph package is one of the most widely used tools for manipulating graphs and analyzing networks. With respect to scalability, the package is acknowledged for handling large-scale graphs efficiently [64,65]. Equally important, iGraph supports a broad diversity of community detection algorithms, including the Louvain algorithm, which we decided to adopted, as explained above.

The knowledge graph was constructed based on the extracted experimental data set. The graph nodes corresponded to entities, and edges represented the Is-A links. The graph nodes were labeled with unique identifiers by simply generating autonumber values.

Since the graph of interest comprised millions of nodes and edges, the R script used for constructing the graph had to be produced in a fully automated manner. A simple C# program was developed for that purpose. The R-script generator worked by reading the list of nodes and edges from flat files and then producing the target executable script. Specifically, the generated R-script was designed as a function doing the following, in sequence:

1. Create graph nodes
2. Create graph edges
3. Compute clusters and return them as a data frame object
4. Compute graph modularity

The source code of the script generator and the generated R-script are accessible through our GitHub repository [66].

The code snippet below presents a simplified example of the R-script generated:

```
g <- graph.empty(directed = FALSE) #Creating an empty undirected graph
g <- g+vertices("101","102","103","104","105") # Adding 5 nodes in the
graph, where every node has its unique ID
g <- g+vertices("201","202","203","204","205") # Adding another 5 nodes
to the graph
# Adding edges to the graph, an edge is defined by a pair of nodes as below
g <- g+edges("101","205","101","103","103","205","205","202","101","202")
g <- g+edges("104","204","105,"104","204","105","104","201","104",203",
"102","204","105","205")
clusters<- multilevel.community(g) #Calling the Louvain algorithm for
community detection
mod <- modularity(clusters) # Computing modularity [37]
```

On the other hand, a Cloud-based execution was unavoidable, as the graph size should exceed the memory limits of usual commodity PCs. We used the Azure Machine Learning system [67] in order to process the large-scale graph. The generated R-script was uploaded to the Azure Machine Learning studio, which flexibly supports executing R and Python scripts as well. The whole script was executed in around 40 minutes. This practically demonstrated the outstanding computational efficiency of the Louvain algorithm. Table 14.8 provides a summary of the computed clusters.

TABLE 14.8

Summary of Computed Clusters

Cluster no.	Size	Sample Entities
1	7,403	Massena Public Library, Iowa City Public Library, Nelson County Public Library
2	7,726	Sekar Language, Parawen Language, Yeskwa Language
3	957,583	Cathal Dunne, Karen Gundersheimer, Thomas Lofaro
4	38,903	Paute River, Vasilievsky Island, Suldenbach, Masaya Volcano
5	320,207	First Industrial (Michigan) Partnership, Heart University, Nova Publications Ltd
6	60,417	Iowa Sports Hall of Fame, Wild Justice, Black Belt Jones
7	122,451	Clarke Abel, Fitzroy Square, Driscoll Bridge
8	7,922	Sulfone, Nickel58, Silver99
9	1,342	British Summer Time, Nativity Fast, World Asthma Day
10	258,159	Lennoxville Massacre, Jose Escuredo, Konstantin Loktev
11	46,140	Peoples Party, Nelson Allen, Eightieth Texas Legislature
12	402	Pound, Point, Megawatt
13	153,853	Parsons College, University of Miyazaki, Oxford Elementary School
14	28	Scalar Boson, Charm Quark, Strong Interaction
15	153,314	Viral Nucleocapsid, Diamond Jubilee, Javan Tiger
16	523,961	Salisbury Heights, Chester,Ranchester
17	44,799	Farrell Spence, Stiff Gins, Manny Manuel
18	15,377	1279 uganda, 5088 tancredi, 25340 segoves
19	1,108	Hurricane Ophelia, Typhoon Olive, Tropical Storm Carrie

Results and Discussion

Evaluation of Cluster Quality

The community detection process identified 19 densely connected clusters of entities within the knowledge graph. The quality of the computed clusters was measured in terms of modularity and cluster density. Modularity [37] represents a quality measure over the entire graph clustering, which has become a standard evaluation criterion for graph clustering quality.

The modularity of a cluster is a scalar value that ranges between –1 and 1 and measures the density of interlinks connecting nodes inside a cluster compared to intralinks connecting communities. The modularity (Q) is calculated as shown in Equation 14.2. The modularity over the 19 clusters of the knowledge graph reached around 0.69, which is considered relatively high, since the maximum possible value is 1.0 [68].

$$Q = \frac{1}{2m} \sum_{i,j} \left[A_{ij} - \frac{K_i K_j}{2m} \right] \delta(C_i, C_j) \tag{14.2}$$

where A_{ij} represents the weight of the edge between i and j, $K_i = \sum_j A_{ij}$ is the sum of the weights of the edges attached to vertex i, C_i is the community to which vertex i is assigned, the δ function $\delta(u, v)$ is 1 if $u = v$ and is 0 otherwise, and $m = \frac{1}{2} \sum_{i,j} A_{ij}$ is the number of edges in the graph.

Furthermore, we evaluated the density of each cluster individually. The density of a cluster was measured based on induced subgraph density. The graph density was typically defined as the ratio of the number of edges to the number of vertices of the graph [69]. In this manner, the density of a cluster was computed as presented in Equation 14.3 below. Figure 14.10 is a histogram of the density distribution within the computed clusters. Apparently, the density of the clusters can be considered an indication that the clusters are internally well-connected. Overall, it can be confidently concluded that the computed graph clusters were of good quality.

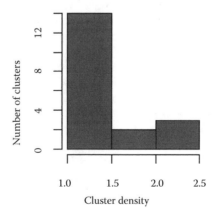

FIGURE 14.10
Histogram of the density of clusters computed based on the subgraph density for each cluster.

$$density(C) = \frac{|E(C)|}{|C|} \tag{14.3}$$

Where C represents a subgraph (cluster), $E(C)$ is the subset of edges, and C is the subset of vertices.

Cluster Analysis

Further observations were drawn by analyzing the structure of clusters. In particular, we aimed to investigate how entities were organized within the computed clusters in comparison to the original Freebase-defined categories. In order to focus the analysis process, the questions below were endorsed:

1. Do computed clusters relatively blueprint the original grouping of the Freebase categories?
2. Do clusters comprise entities largely relating to a single category?
3. What can be inferred in cases when a cross-category cluster exists?

Generally, it turned out that most of the clusters comprised a subset of entities belonging mainly to one of the four included categories: (i) Science and Technology, (ii) Society, (iii) Sports,

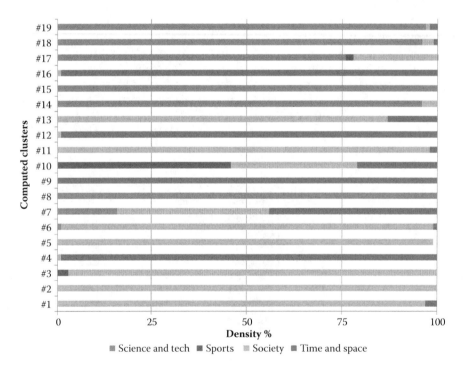

FIGURE 14.11
Density of entities inside clusters with respect to the original categories. The variety of colors indicates that a cluster contains entities belonging to different categories of Freebase. We observed that some communities (#7, 10, 13, and 17) represented highly cross-category clusters.

TABLE 14.9

Structure of Computed Clusters with Respect to the Original Freebase Categories

| Cluster no. | Approximate Density (%) of Categories within Computed Clusters | | | | Cluster Size |
	Science and Tech	Sports	Society	Time and Space	
1	0.0	0.0	97.0	3.0	7,403
2	0.0	0.0	100.0	0.0	7,726
3	0.0	3	97.0	0.0	957,583
4	0.0	0.0	1.0	99.0	38,903
5	0.0	0.0	99.0	0.0	320,207
6	1.0	0.0	98.0	1.0	60,417
7	16.0	0.0	40.0	44.0	122,451
8	100.0	0.0	0.0	0.0	7,922
9	0.0	0.0	0.0	100.0	1,342
10	0.0	46.0	33.0	21.0	258,159
11	0.0	0.0	98.0	2.0	46,140
12	0.0	0.0	1.0	99.0	402
13	0.0	0.0	87.0	13.0	153,853
14	96.0	0.0	4.0	0.0	28
15	100.0	0.0	0.0	0.0	153,314
16	0.0	0.0	1.0	99.0	523,961
17	76.0	2.0	22.0	1.0	44,799
18	96.0	0.0	3.0	1.0	15,377
19	97.0	0.0	1.0	2.0	1,108

Note: The gray highlighted rows signify highly cross-category clusters.

and (iv) Time and Space. This suggests that some computed clusters can be conceived as a form of coherent subcategories within the larger categories, such as the Society category.

On the other hand, a few clusters interestingly featured a pronounced cross-category structure comprising a mixture of entities relating to different categories. These could translate into what can be described as "latent" connections among entities. We called these connections latent because they were not explicitly observed in the basic grouping defined by the categories of Freebase. Figure 14.11 provides a visual summary of the clusters structure. In addition, Table 14.9 delineates the characteristics of clusters.

Future Work: Exploitation of Clusters for Topic Exploration

The discovered clusters can be effectively employed for the purpose of topic exploration and discovery. Specifically, the computed clusters can be used along with the defined grouping of entities provided by Freebase, as explained earlier in this chapter. On one hand, the Freebase-defined categories represent an explicit grouping of entities, which is based on a natural classification of entities with obvious similarity of relational attributes (e.g., grouping of persons who are characterized as politicians or actors.). On the other hand, the computed clusters can be regarded as an implicit grouping of entities that are considered unobservable relations based on the link-based structure similarity within knowledge graphs. Figure 14.12 illustrates the incorporation of both of the entity groupings, which can be used for further applications (e.g., topic exploration, visualization).

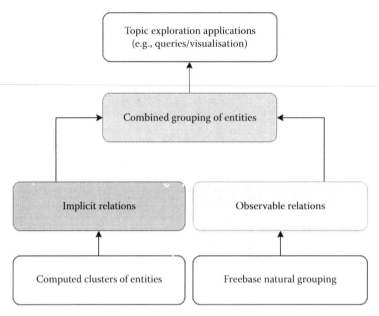

FIGURE 14.12
Utilization of clusters for topic exploration.

Related Work

The problem of finding coherent clusters has been the focus of considerable research effort in many contexts and across various disciplines. Examples are ranging from machine learning, data mining, and network science to biology or social sciences. A plethora of methods were developed to deal with clustering problems. Broadly, data clustering via two approaches has been endorsed:

1. **Relational Clustering:** Data are organized into groups based on a specific attribute similarity (e.g., euclidean distance). The k-means algorithm is a good example, and it is one of the most widely used, as reported in the published literature.

2. **Graph-Based Clustering:** Data are clustered based on link-based structure similarities, in contrast to the vertex similarities in relational clustering. Natural graph clusters can be computed using community detection algorithms [40,41].

With respect to the scope of the study, we aimed to review studies adopting the graph-based clustering methods with a focus on knowledge graphs. In Ref. [70], search results clustering (SRC) was endorsed as they used a representation of texts as graphs of concepts or topics. The nodes (topics) represented Wikipedia pages identified by means of topic annotations applied to search results, and the edges denoted the relatedness among topics. The study proposed an algorithm that used the spectral properties and labels of a topics graph. Also, a study [71] proposed a graph-based semantic model for representing document content. Their method relied on the use of DBpedia for acquiring knowledge about entities and their semantic relations, and then computing the semantic similarity of documents. Likewise, Ref. [72] exploited DBpedia for clustering Web search results. Further recent studies include Refs. [43] and [73].

In view of the related studies, we argue that the literature possibly lacks a number of issues, to the best of our knowledge. First, the validity of clustering knowledge graphs based on a graph-based approach needs to be explicitly discussed. In particular, the assumption that a knowledge graph can have an underlying community structure [37] should be examined. Subsequently, a following assumption that the link-based structure of entities can serve as a similarity metric can be considered. Those assumptions are also discussed. Second, studies generally do not deal with large-scale knowledge graphs; therefore, the scalability issue was not explicitly addressed. Furthermore, the Freebase data were not utilized, though they represent a much richer knowledge base than DBpedia, for example.

Methodology Limitations

The computed clusters should always be considered a suggested grouping of entities, which is bounded to the data set extracted from the study. In this regard, the following limitations should be taken into account:

1. Only four categories of Freebase entities were considered
2. Only the Is-A links were included in the graph produced in the study. More accurate and comprehensive clusters could be identified in cases of covering more categories of entities and including more types of entity connections.

Conclusions

The graph-based representations of knowledge can provide extended opportunities for data exploration and reinterpretation of existing data. Our study embraced an approach for clustering entities based on structural similarities within a knowledge graph. In this manner, entities are grouped by matching their linked-based structures rather than relational attributes. As an exemplar of graph-based knowledge bases, a subset of Freebase data was utilized. Specifically, the data set was used to construct a large-scale knowledge graph covering four categories of entities, including Science and Technology, Society, Sports, and Time and Space.

Using the Louvain algorithm for graph clustering, the study suggested 19 clusters of entities. The computed clusters were examined for good coherence, based on measures of graph modularity and cluster density. Furthermore, the clusters were claimed to be interpretable and revealed relationships among entities. On one hand, most clusters represented homogeneous partitions of entities belonging to a specific category of Freebase. On the other hand, a few clusters featured a remarkable variety of entities relating to different categories. Thus, clusters can reveal latent connections among entities that are not explicitly observed. For one future research direction, the computed clusters can be utilized as a basis for topic exploration and discovery applications.

References

1. Bizer C, Heath T, Berners-Lee T. 2009. Linked data: The story so far, pp. 205–227. Semantic Services, Interoperability and Web Applications: Emerging Concepts. Hershey, PA: IGI Global.
2. Aldenderfer MS, Blashfield RK. 1984. Cluster analysis. Series on Quantitative Applications in the Social Sciences, 07-044. Irvine, CA: Sage University.
3. http://www.freebase.com/
4. Bollacker K, Evans C, Paritosh P, Sturge T, Taylor J. 2008. Freebase: A collaboratively created graph database for structuring human knowledge. Proceedings of the ACM SIGMOD International Conference on Management of Data. New York: ACM.
5. Bollacker K, Tufts P, Pierce T, Cook R. 2007. A platform for scalable, collaborative, structured information integration. Intl. Workshop on Information Integration on the Web. New York: ACM.
6. Tanon TP, Vrandečić D, Schaffert S, Steiner T, Pintscher L. 2016. From Freebase to Wikidata: The great migration, pp. 1419–1428. Proceedings of the 25th International Conference on World Wide Web. New York: ACM.
7. Singhal A. 2012. Introducing the knowledge graph: things, not strings. https://googleblog.blogspot.com/2012/05/introducing-knowledge-graph-things-not.html.
8. Shapiro SC. 1992. Encyclopedia of Artificial Intelligence, 2nd ed. Hoboken, NJ: Wiley Interscience.
9. Ward JS, Barker A. 2013. Undefined by data: A survey of big data definitions. arXiv:1309.5821.
10. Beyer MA, Laney D. 2012. The importance of 'big data': A definition. Stamford, CT: Gartner.
11. Gandomi A, Haider M. 2015. Beyond the hype: Big data concepts, methods, and analytics. *International Journal of Information Management* 35(2):137–144.
12. De Mauro A, Greco M, Grimaldi M. 2015. What is big data? A consensual definition and a review of key research topics. AIP Conference Proceedings 1644(1):97–104.
13. https://www.gov.uk/government/uploads/system/uploads/attachment_data/file/389095/Horizon_Scanning_-_Emerging_Technologies_Big_Data_report_1.pdf.
14. Dijcks JP. 2012. Big Data for the enterprise. Oracle white paper. Redwood City, CA: Oracle.
15. Peer Research Report: Big Data Analytics-Intel http://www.intel.com/content/www/us/en/big.
16. Howie T. 2013. The Big Bang: How the Big Data explosion is changing the world [blog]. Microsoft UK Enterprise Insights. http://blogs.msdn.com/b/microsoftenterpriseinsight/archive/2013/04/15/big-bang-how-the-big-data-explosion-is-changing-theworld.aspx.
17. NIST Big Data Working Group (NBD-WG). http://bigdatawg.nist.gov/home.php.
18. Big Data Definition—MIKE2.0, the open source methodology for Information Development. http://mike2.openmethodology.org/wiki/Big Data Definition.
19. Manyika J, Chui M, Brown B, Bughin J, Dobbs R, Roxburgh C, Byers AH. 2011. Big data: The next frontier for innovation, competition, and productivity. New York: McKinley Global Institute.
20. Laney D. 2001. 3D data management: Controlling data volume, velocity and variety. META Group Research Note 6:70.
21. Zikopoulos PC, deRoos D, Parasuraman K, Deutsch T, Corrigan D, Giles J. 2013. Harness the Power of Big Data—The IBM Big Data Platform. New York: McGraw Hill.
22. Demchenko Y, De Laat C, Membrey P. 2014. Defining architecture components of the Big Data ecosystem, pp. 104–112. 2014 International Conference on Collaboration Technologies and Systems. New York: IEEE.
23. IBM Big Data & Analytics Hub. Available at http://www.ibmbigdatahub.com/infographic/four-vs-big-data, accessed on 15/01/2017.
24. Wu C, Buyya R, Ramamohanarao K. 2016. Big Data analytics = machine learning + Cloud computing. arXiv:1601.03115.
25. Davenport TH, Harris JG. 2007. Competing on Analytics: The New Science of Winning. Cambridge, MA: Harvard Business Press.

26. Laursen G, Thorlund J. 2010. Business Analytics for Managers: Taking Business Intelligence beyond Reporting, vol. 40. Hoboken, NJ; John Wiley & Sons.

27. Liberatore M, Luo W. 2011. INFORMS and the analytics movement: The view of the membership. *Interfaces* 41(6):578–589.

28. Mortenson MJ, Doherty NF, Robinson S. 2015. Operational research from Taylorism to terabytes: A research agenda for the analytics age. *European Journal of Operational Research* 241(3):583–595.

29. Barga R, Fontama V, Tok WH, Cabrera-Cordon L. 2015. Predictive Analytics with Microsoft Azure Machine Learning. New York: Springer Science + Business Media Finance.

30. Arrison T, Weidman S (eds.). 2010. Steps Toward Large-Scale Data Integration in the Sciences: Summary of a Workshop. Washington, DC: National Academies Press.

31. Bollacker K, Cook R, Tufts R. 2007. Freebase: A shared database of structured general human knowledge, pp. 207. AAAI, '07 Proceedings of the 22nd National Conference on Artificial Intelligence, vol. 2. Menlo Park, CA: AAAI.

32. Google. Available at https://developers.google.com/freebase/

33. Amazon. Available at https://aws.amazon.com/datasets/freebase-simple-topic-dump/, accessed on 10/01/2017.

34. O'Reilly T. 2014. Freebase will prove addictive. O'Reilly Radar. http://radar.oreilly.com /2007/03/freebase-will-prove-addictive.html.

35. Lassila O, Swick RR. 1999. Resource Description Framework (RDF) Model and Syntax Specification. Cambridge, MA: W3C.

36. Duda RO, Hart PE. 1973. Pattern Classification and Scene Analysis, vol. 3. New York: Wiley.

37. Girvan M, Newman ME. 2002. Community structure in social and biological networks. *Proceedings of the National Academy of Sciences USA* 99(12):7821–7826.

38. Erdos P, Renyi A. 1959. On random graphs. I. Publicationes Mathematicae 6:290–297.

39. Bondi AB. 2000. Characteristics of scalability and their impact on performance, pp. 195–203. Proceedings of the 2nd International Workshop on Software and Performance. New York: ACM.

40. Schaeffer SE. 2007. Graph clustering. *Computer Science Review* 1(1):27–64.

41. Fortunato S. 2010. Community detection in graphs. *Physics Reports* 486(3):75–174.

42. Blondel VD, Guillaume J-L, Lambiotte R, Lefebvre E. 2008. Fast unfolding of communities in large networks. *Journal of Statistical Mechanics Theory and Experiment* 10:P10008.

43. Aker A, Kurtic E, Balamurali AR, Paramita M, Barker E, Hepple M, Gaizauskas R. 2016. A graph-based approach to topic clustering for online comments to news, pp. 15–29. European Conference on Information Retrieval. CITY: Springer International Publishing.

44. Newman MEJ, Girvan M. 2004. Finding and evaluating community structure in networks. *Physical Review E* 69(2):026113.

45. Radicchi F, Castellano C, Cecconi F, Loreto V, Parisi D. 2004. Defining and identifying communities in networks. *Proceedings of the National Academy of Sciences USA* 101(9):2658–2663.

46. Pons P, Latapy M. 2006. Computing communities in large networks using random walks. *Journal of Graph Algorithms and Applications* 10(2):191–218.

47. Ravasz E, Somera AL, Mongru DA, Oltvai ZN, Barabási AL. 2002. Hierarchical organization of modularity in metabolic networks. *Science* 297(5586):1551–1555.

48. Donetti L. 2004. Detecting network communities: A new systematic and efficient algorithm. *Journal of Statistical Mechanics Theory and Experiment* 2004(10):P10012.

49. Chung FR. 1997. Spectral Graph Theory, vol. 92. Providence, RI: American Mathematical Society.

50. Qiu H, Hancock ER. 2006. Graph matching and clustering using spectral partitions. *Pattern Recognition* 39(1):22–34.

51. Ng AY, Jordan MI, Weiss Y. 2002. On spectral clustering: Analysis and an algorithm. *Advances in Neural Information Processing Systems* 2:849–856.

52. Donath WE, Hoffman AJ. 1973. Lower bounds for the partitioning of graphs. *IBM Journal of Research and Development* 17(5):420–425.

53. Shi J, Malik J. 2000. Normalized cuts and image segmentation. *IEEE Transactions on Pattern Analysis and Machine Intelligence* 22(8):888–905.
54. Clauset A, Newman M, Moore C. 2004. Finding community structure in very large networks. *Physical Review E* 70(6):066111.
55. Wu F, Huberman BA. 2004. Finding communities in linear time: A physics approach. European *Physical Journal B* 38(2):331–338.
56. Newman ME. 2006. Finding community structure in networks using the eigenvectors of matrices. *Physical Review E* 74(3):036104.
57. Ahn YY, Bagrow JP, Lehmann S. 2010. Link communities reveal multiscale complexity in networks. *Nature* 466(7307):761–764.
58. Newman ME. 2004. Fast algorithm for detecting community structure in networks. *Physical Review E* 69(6):066133.
59. Lancichinetti A, Fortunato S. 2009. Community detection algorithms: A comparative analysis. *Physical Review E* 80(5):056117.
60. Cormen TH. 2009. Introduction to Algorithms. Cambridge, Massachusetts: MIT Press.
61. Arenas A, Duch J, Fernández A, Gómez S. 2007. Size reduction of complex networks preserving modularity. *New Journal of Physics* 9(6):176.
62. Barabási AL. 2013. Network science. *Philosophical Transactions of the Royal Society of London A* 371(1987):20120375.
63. Pujol JM, Erramilli V, Rodriguez P. 2009. Divide and conquer: Partitioning online social networks. arXiv:0905.4918.
64. Csardi G, Nepusz T. 2006. The iGraph software package for complex network research. *InterJournal Complex Systems* 1695(5):1–9.
65. Kolaczyk ED, Csárdi G. 2014. Statistical Analysis of Network Data with R, pp. 1–5. New York: Springer.
66. GitHub. Available at https://github.com/Mahmoud-Elbattah/Knowledge_Graphs_Clustering.
67. Barga R, Fontama V, Tok WH, Cabrera-Cordon L. 2015. Predictive Analytics with Microsoft Azure Machine Learning. New York: Springer Science + Business Media Finance.
68. Newman ME. 2004. Analysis of weighted networks. *Physical Review E* 70(5):056131.
69. Goldberg AV. 1984. Finding a Maximum Density Subgraph. Berkeley, CA: University of California.
70. Scaiella U, Ferragina P, Marino A, Ciaramita M. 2012. Topical clustering of search results, pp. 223–232. Proceedings of the Fifth ACM International Conference on Web Search and Data Mining. New York: ACM.
71. Schuhmacher M, Ponzetto SP. 2014. Knowledge-based graph document modeling, pp. 543–552. Proceedings of the 7th ACM International Conference on Web Search and Data Mining. New York: ACM.
72. Schuhmacher M, Ponzetto SP. 2013. Exploiting DBpedia for web search results clustering, pp. 91–96. Proceedings of the 2013 Workshop on Automated Knowledge Base Construction. New York: ACM.
73. Chang S, Dai P, Hong L, Sheng C, Zhang T, Chi H. 2016. AppGrouper: Knowledge-graph-based interactive clustering tool for mobile app search results. New York: ACM.

15

Big Data Analytics for Connected Intelligence with the Internet of Things

Mohammad Samadi Gharajeh

CONTENTS

Introduction

The growth of Big Data has happened for various reasons, including the increase of storage capacities, increase of processing power, and data availability. Big Data is gathered from a wide variety of resources, such as social networks, digital images, and sensors. In addition, Big Data analytics are the strategy of analyzing the huge volumes comprising Big Data. It enables users to evaluate a large amount of the transmitted data that traditional systems would be unable to handle. Big Data analytics tools involve some significant advantages, such as cost savings, competitive advantages, and new business opportunities. These advantages can be used to increase the connected intelligence with the Internet of Things (IoT).

In this chapter, I discuss the important features of IoT, including the IoT paradigm, its main elements, popular applications, and security challenges. In addition, various definitions of the intelligence process are considered. Big Data analytics for intelligence of IoT are described based on a review of data storage and processing modules, the key devices of intelligence in IoT, the fundamental mechanisms for Big Data analytics, and Big Data analytics methods for connected intelligence with IoT. Finally, some of the Big Data as well as Big Data analytics methods to enhance the intelligence level of IoT are evaluated in terms of different simulations.

Iot Paradigm

Figure 15.1 illustrates an overall view of the IoT paradigm according to the convergence of different visions (Atzori et al. 2010). It consists of three visions: thing-oriented vision, internet-oriented vision, and semantics-oriented vision. Thing-oriented vision is composed of two independent categories. The first category contains everyday objects, wireless sensors, and actuators, near-field communications (NFC), and wireless identification and sensing platforms (WISPs). Everyday objects involve the people, animals, and things which can be managed by IoT tools. Wireless sensors and actuators sense data phenomena (e.g., temperature) to monitor desirable environments. NFC is defined as contactless communication between smart devices (e.g., smartphones and tablets). WISP is a radiofrequency identification (RFID) device that supports sensing and computing operations. The second category includes RFID (Finkenzeller 2003), unique, universal, ubiquitous identifier (UID), spimes (Sterling 2005), and smart items. RFID uses radio waves to read and also

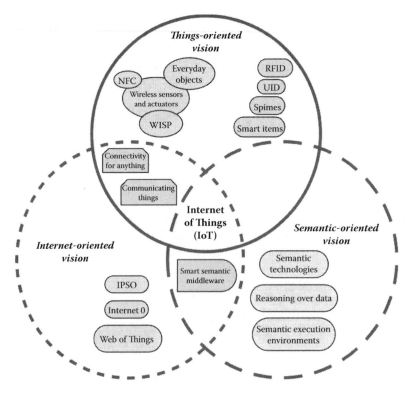

FIGURE 15.1
A schematic of the IoT paradigm regarding the convergence of different visions.

capture information stored on tags attached to various objects. UID provides numeric or alphanumeric information about a single entity within the IoT system. spime represents an invention for modern objects that can be followed via space and time throughout their lifetime. Smart items are the easiest tools for running any environment into a smart home. Internet-oriented vision includes IP for Smart Objects (IPSO) (Dunkels and Vasseur 2008), Internet 0 (Gershenfelo et al. 2004), and the Web of Things (Pfisterer et al. 2011). IPSO indicates an organization promoting the Internet Protocol (IP) in "smart object" communications. Internet 0 contains a low-speed physical layer that is designed to direct the IP of various things over desirable areas.

The Web of Things includes a concept and strategy to incorporate information on everyday physical objects into the Web, completely. Semantic-oriented vision involves semantic technologies, reasoning over data, and semantic execution environments. Semantic technologies encode the meanings from data and content files separately in order to enable machines and people to understand and share various data at the time of execution. Reasoning over data includes some of the intelligence- and knowledge-based methods to infer new happenings according to prior experiences. Semantic execution environments offer some services for discovering, composing, selecting, mediating, and invoking semantic Web services. Two elements (connectivity for anything and communicating things) are placed in the coverage area between thing-oriented vision and internet-oriented vision, as well as smart semantic middleware, which participates in the coverage area between internet-oriented vision and semantic-oriented vision. Connectivity for anything means that things are connected to each other, and "communicating things" indicates that the things transmit various messages to other objects throughout the network.

Main Elements of IoT

As shown in Figure 15.2, IoT consists of five main elements: RFID, wireless sensor networks (WSNs), addressing schemes, data storage and analytics, and visualization (Tilak et al. 2002, Buyya et al. 2009, Gubbi et al. 2013). RFID technology is used in the embedded communication paradigm that activates the design of microchip systems for wireless data communications. It can, automatically, identify anything that holds an electronic barcode. RFID tags have various applications in race timing, attendee tracking, materials management, access control, tool tracking, library systems, etc. WSNs consist of low-energy,

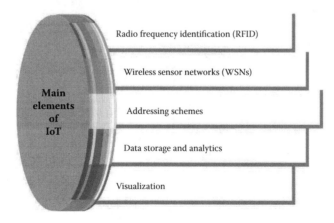

FIGURE 15.2
Overall view of the IoT elements.

low-cost, and large-scale wireless sensor nodes. A sensor network incorporates a gateway that offers wireless connectivity back to the wired world and distributed wireless nodes. Any node can detect and sense phenomena data (e.g., temperature) in order to transmit the sensed data to a certain center (e.g., a base station) (Gharajeh 2016, Gharajeh and Alizadeh 2016, Gharajeh and Khanmohammadi 2016). Traffic control, environmental monitoring, and medical usages are some of the applications which can be designed and implemented by WSNs. Addressing schemes indicate that anything can be uniquely identified through the internet. A unique address is assigned for anything to determine the four critical features for the IoT network: uniqueness, reliability, persistence, and scalability (Honle et al. 2005, Zorzi et al. 2010). Data storage and analytics are the major requirements in the IoT environment that should be stored and intelligently used for smart monitoring and actuation. Furthermore, data can be collected by novel fusion algorithms (Aggarwal et al. 2013). Visualization is required for IoT applications to allow the defined interactions between users and the environment. It can be provided to users via three-dimensional screens to give users more information about the network in meaningful ways (Jin et al. 2014).

Popular Applications of IoT

The popular applications of IoT can be grouped into five domains, as illustrated in Figure 15.3: transportation and logistics, health care, smart environments, personal and social, and futuristic. The transportation and logistics domain involves logistics, assisted driving, mobile ticketing, environmental monitoring, and augmented maps. It represents that advanced vehicles (e.g., cars and trains) that are equipped with sensors, actuators, tags, and processing power to transmit important information to defined centers (e.g., traffic control sites). The health care domain can be categorized mostly into tracking of objects and people (e.g., staff and patients), identification and authentication of people, automatic data collection, and sensing. It indicates that IoT applications can be extended for medical departments (e.g.,

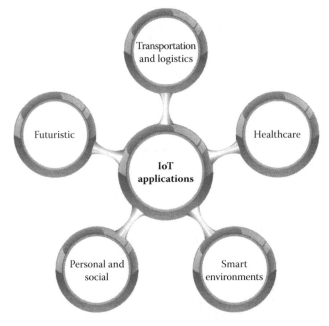

FIGURE 15.3
The five well-known applications of IoT.

hospitals) to gather operational information on patients and personnel. The smart environments domain represents the intelligence feature of contained objects that can be employed to constitute smart offices, industrial plants, etc. It includes comfortable homes and offices, smart museums and gyms, and industrial plants. The personal and social domain (which includes social networking, historical queries, losses, and thefts) enables IoT users to interact with other people in order to build and maintain social relationships. Finally, the futuristic applications domain already have been implemented or can be deployed in a short or medium period of time via available technologies. Robot taxi, city information models, and enhanced game rooms are the main applications of this domain (Atzori et al. 2010).

Security Challenges in the IoT Network

Security challenges of IoT are grouped in three categories: data confidentiality, privacy, and trust. The main issues of each category are shown in Figure 15.4 (Miorandi et al. 2012, Rose et al. 2015). Data confidentiality indicates a basic issue in IoT scenarios and means that only authorized entities can access and modify the collected data (Suo et al. 2012). Generally, the confidentiality indicates that information stored on a system is protected against unintended or unauthorized access. Identity management systems, data stream access controls, and confidentiality-preserving aggregation methods are some applications in this category. The privacy category specifies the rules for individual users authorized to access the available data (Coen-Porisini et al. 2010). It is someone's right to protect their personal matters and relationship secrets. A general privacy model, role-based systems, enforcement mechanisms, and data governance are some of the considerable issues defined in this category. Trust involves a large number of different contexts having various meanings. It indicates a complex opinion about which no agreement exists in the information and computer science environments (Blaze et al. 1996). This category is emerging in various applications, such as object identity management systems, trust negotiation mechanisms, and negotiation language.

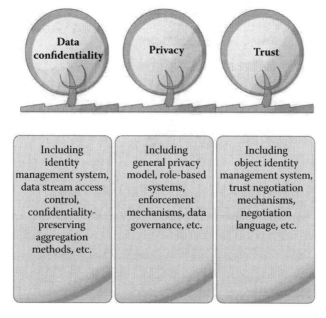

FIGURE 15.4
Graphical representation of security challenges in IoT.

A Brief Description of the Intelligence Definition

Intelligence is considered one of the most important topics in all scientific fields. Furthermore, artificial intelligence is one of the most difficult and significant disciplines in technology. In the last decades, academic and engineering groups have focused on natural intelligence and artificial intelligence to facilitate some of the existing engineering systems (Russell et al. 1995, Korb and Nicholson 2010, Deary et al. 2010, Copeland 2015). There are three approaches for defining artificial intelligence, via its many different understandings. The first approach stems from 1943, and it simulates the structure of the cortex in the human brain; it is therefore named the structuralism approach (Rumelhart 1990). The second approach, presented in 1956, simulates the functions of logical thinking in the human brain and thus is called the functionalism approach (Nilsson 1980). The third approach is from 1990, and it simulates the behavior of intelligent beings and hence is denoted the behaviorism approach (Brooks 1991). Artificial intelligence research includes three major problems: it has had less success in methodology, its limitations regarding sources of research, and its ignoring of some fundamental issues (Zhong 2010). Here, we describe a model of systematic intelligence formation from natural intelligence, foundations of human–computer interactions, and intelligent frameworks within IoT.

A Model of Systematic Intelligence Formation from Natural Intelligence

In the last decades, various significant intelligent models have been presented regarding use of natural intelligence in scientific areas. Figure 15.5 illustrates a model of intelligence formation from the view of natural intelligence. In general, it consists of six steps: information acquisition, information transferring and processing, knowledge extraction, strategy

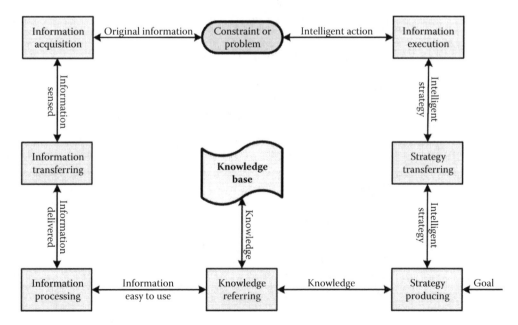

FIGURE 15.5
Model of systematic intelligence formation based on natural intelligence.

(intelligence) production, action generation, and feedback and optimization. Information acquisition is considered the first step of any intelligent system and is the means of gaining the necessary information about problems, constraints, and available solutions. The step of information transferring and processing entails transfer of the information collected in the acquisition with a fidelity to defined point. This process aids to process the information for producing an easy-to-use version of the gathered information. In knowledge extraction involves the corresponding knowledge to be formed based on cognition or other measures. Strategy (intelligence) production represents the knowledge and information that must be reformed into strategy under the guidance of the main goal in order to solve the problem effectively. Action generation focuses on converting the strategy into an action to solve the problem and achieve the goal. This step is used in the model because the strategy cannot solve the problem practically. Finally, feedback and optimization return the difference between the results of the previous step and the goal to the first step. It causes the information, knowledge, and strategy to be improved gradually (Zhong 2010).

Foundations of Human–Computer Interactions

Human–computer interactions consist of three broad foundations: principles, practice, and people. Principles are defined as the intellectual theories, models, and empirical investigations of human–computer interactions. Some of the principles are derived from a number of related disciplines, and others are considered core knowledge of this interaction. Practice is the second foundation and provides practical guidance to practitioners in the interaction design environment. People are the third foundation, as they inspire the interaction field and perhaps most essentially the interaction community for practitioners, researchers, and educators (Dix 2016). The main foundations and features of human–computer interaction are illustrated in Figure 15.6.

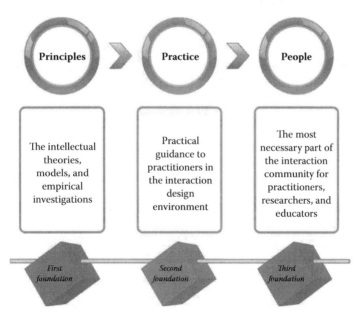

FIGURE 15.6
The main foundations of human–computer interactions.

Health, education, and well-being are some of the specific changes and challenges in human–computer interactions. They look at systems growing together to allow Big Data techniques to determine the trends for individual advices. For example, in this era learning analytics have been applied in higher education to estimate the likelihood that students will provide the learning assistants (Thimbleby 2013). Related to this challenge, many of the trends end up with strong social challenges for human–computer interactions. This challenge is very considerable if the applications are deployed through the procedures that are essential or socially expected as part of "normal" life. These applications are classic and screen-based information systems that contain many features of eGovernment and businesses such as Uber and airBnB (Liebowitz and Margolis 2016).

Intelligent Frameworks in IoT

Various intelligence frameworks have been presented in the IoT era by researchers in recent years. Figure 15.7 illustrates some of the significant intelligent frameworks in IoT: intelligent fault prediction system, an intelligent robot as a service, intelligent decision–support systems and smart built environments, and an intelligent resource inquisition framework. An intelligent fault prediction system for IoT was previously presented by Xu et al. (2012); the system is based on the investigation of current research on fault prediction. It is applied for main mechanical equipment groups in order to improve the working efficiency and also intelligent level of fault prediction. This system consists of a four-layer functional architecture that offers comprehensive condition monitoring, computer intelligent information processing, and reliable information transmission for fault prediction. Chen and Hu (2013) discussed the architectures, interfaces, and behaviors of intelligent electromechanical devices connected to Cloud systems. A robot as a service is considered in a case study to describe the main features of the internet of intelligent things, including autonomous, mobile, sensing, and action taking.

Extension of the centralized Cloud computing environment into a decentralized system is the main goal of this work. The work described by Kaklauskas and Gudauskas (2016) focused on intelligent decision–support systems and issues related to the IoT for smart built environments. They outlined the general theory, including IoT's definition, characteristics, and components. Furthermore, they evaluated various examples and applications of IoT in the built environment. An intelligent resource inquisition framework, called IRIF-IoT, was presented by Bharti et al. (2017); they outlined the existing challenges via its

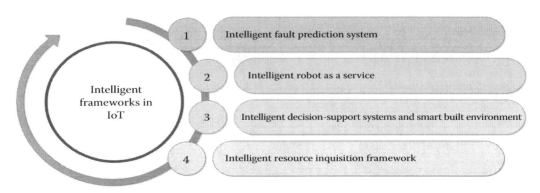

FIGURE 15.7
The four considerable intelligent frameworks in IoT.

three layers, including perception, discovery, and application. It links resources through the usage of semantic description and ontology as well as accessing information via Web terminals for users.

Big Data Analytics for Intelligence in the IoT

In the last decade, Big Data analytics generated very great interest worldwide. It includes processing of high-volume, high-velocity, and/or high-variety information to enable high-performance decision making, wisdom discovery, and process optimization via new forms of processing (Beyer and Laney 2012). Big Data is derived from various data sources, in very large amounts, and often in real time. This considerable trend comes from the vast diffusion and adoption of social media tools, mobile devices, and the IoT. Since Big Data analytics and IoT involve a great potential to transform various academic projects and industries, many scholars and managers have attempted to understand these concepts and utilize the business benefits through the combination of Big Data analytics and IoT.

The main potential of Big Data analytics and IoT has been assessed in very few experimental studies. However, the behavioral, organizational, and business-related usages of Big Data analytics for IoT applications have not been addressed completely. The available frameworks to study the impact of Big Data analytics on IoT issues can be categorized into four levels: society, industry, organization, and individual (Riggins and Wamba 2015). The use of Big Data analytics in IoT entails high uncertainty related to privacy and trust; in addition, the use of Big Data and business analytics in IoT health care applications could enable primitive containment of health hazards and save extended medical costs. The subsequent subsections discuss various topics related to Big Data analytic and IoT, including data storage and processing modules, the key devices of intelligence in IoT, the fundamental mechanisms for Big Data analytics, and Big Data analytics methods for connection to intelligence within the IoT.

Data Storage and Processing Modules

An architecture for indoor/outdoor chronic patient monitoring and dependent care was presented by Páez et al. (2014) and it was designed based on Big Data and IoT. It is composed four main elements: a smart mobile device, an interoperability and messaging platform, a website platform, and a module for finding health-related information. The smart mobile device is used by patients with chronic disease and dependent individuals; it gets the data from sensors of vital signs and then transmits this information via the mobile network 3G/HDSPA or internet. The interoperability and messaging platform is designed to deliver the information to all assigned actors in the system via technological advances in communication (e.g., mail). The website platform enables both family caregivers and social workers to find the associated patient information through a desktop computer and/or from mobile devices. The module for finding health-related information allows users to use a Web search interface based on natural language medical terms. Figure 15.8 illustrates principal components of the data storage and processing modules considered in the presented architecture. Because the large amounts of data are processed in the systems, the authors used NoSQL databases (Pokorny 2013) instead of the classical SQL relational databases on the server side. Moreover, a RIAK database (http://basho.com/riak/) was

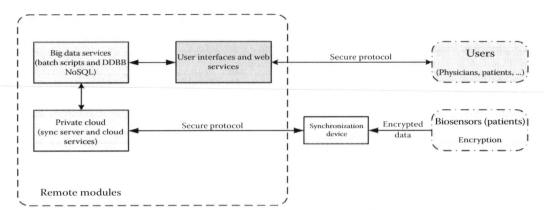

FIGURE 15.8
Data storage and processing modules of chronic patient monitoring.

used to evaluate the system performance, as this is a scalable, distributed, and open source key value nonrelational database.

The Key Devices of Intelligence in IoT

Through the use of IoT in our world, the next-generation internet will promote interactions among objects, humans, and environments. An embedded intelligence about humans, the environment, and society can be illustrated via the interaction between humans and IoT. As shown in Figure 15.9, intelligence can be found in IoT via different devices, such as surveillance cameras, smart indoor artifacts, wearable sensors, mobile phones, smart vehicles, and smart cards. A surveillance camera is the main part of a static sensing infrastructure. It is an early type of static sensor and is widely used in urban environments (e.g., public spots in the city). Smart indoor artifacts are used in daily living environments, which can be improved by inexpensive and tiny sensors (e.g., RFID tags). The simple activities of various objects will be detected by using one smart artifact. Wearable sensors are mounted on different parts of a human's body to make possible the human-centric sensing system.

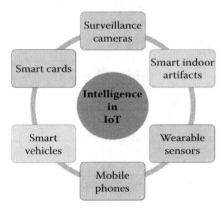

FIGURE 15.9
Some of the popular devices that provide intelligence for the IoT.

The sensors can sense body information, including human activity, social situations, daily routines, etc. Mobile phones are used in IoT applications to grant portable and promising activities to the previous devices. They are equipped with various tiny sensors, such as Bluetooth, Wi-Fi, GPS receivers, accelerometers, cameras, and ambient light. Following development of mobile phones, smart vehicles and smart cards are used in urban environments to deploy public transportation systems (Guo et al. 2013).

The Fundamental Mechanisms for Big Data Analytics

Big Data analytics evaluates a large volume of varied data. It considers several new issues to process the raw data: discovery, iteration, flexible capacity, mining and predicting, and decision management. Discovery indicates that the obtained different information should be figured out via a process of exploration stages. Iteration often leads a cycle process down a path that turns out to be a dead end. Because of the iterative nature in Big Data analysis, problems will be solved by spending more time and utilizing more resources. Since it is not clear how the data elements associate with each other, mining and predicting can be applied to discover the existing patterns and relationships and this can yield the insights that a user seeks. When Big Data analytics are used to drive many operational decisions, the procedures to automate the implementation of all the defined actions should be determined carefully. Big Data analysis requirements are categorized into three groups: minimize data movement, use existing skills, and attend to data security. Minimize data movement leads to conservation of computing resources (e.g., memory). It makes more sense to store the high volumes of data in the same place. Although new skills are required to process new data sources, the existing skill set should be considered and applied by the services too. Therefore, a combination of training, hiring, and new tools would address the problems that occurr. Many corporate applications need data security to protect their gathered data. They apply a reliable set of administration policies and security controls to define robust data security. Figure 15.10 shows the main fundamental mechanisms for Big Data analytics (Oracle 2013, Hu et al. 2014).

Big Data Analytics Methods for Connected Intelligence with IoT

This section reviews three methods that use Big Data or Big Data analytics for optimal intelligence in IoT. These methods apply the combination of Big Data analytics and IoT to design smart environments (e.g., smart cities). The following statements describe the main motivations and features of the methods.

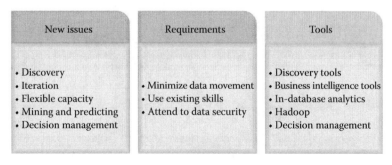

FIGURE 15.10
Graphical representation of the fundamental mechanisms for Big Data analytics.

A context-aware dynamic discovery of things (CADDOT) model was presented by Perera et al. (2014) that used Big Data in smart environments. It discovered sensors deployed in a specified location, despite their heterogeneity, by using the developed tool SmartLink. This tool builds a direct communication between the sensor hardware side and Cloud-based IoT middleware platforms. As shown Figure 15.11, the CADDOT model for configuration of things in the IoT paradigm consists of eight phases: detect, extract, identify, find, retrieve, register, reason, and configure. The detect phase indicates that sensors are used to actively search open wireless access points (e.g., Wi-Fi and Bluetooth). This process is performed to enable the sensors to be connected without any authorization, because they do not have any authentication details in this phase. In the extract phase, the SmartLink tool fetches information from the sensors detected in the previous phase. In the identify phase, SmartLink transmits all the information collected from the newly detected sensors toward the Cloud. Cloud-based IoT middleware discovers the data stores by using the collected information to identify the complete profile of the source sensors. The find phase is used to seek a matching plug-in (also called drivers) after identifying the sensors with unique identifiers. In the retrieve phase, SmartLink retrieves the full set of information that can be provided by the sensors (e.g., schedules and sampling rates). After all the information about a certain sensor has been obtained, the registration process takes place in the Cloud, in the register phase. The reason phase is a significant part of the model in the sensor configuration, so that it offers an efficient sensing strategy. In the configure phase, sensors and Cloud-based IoT software platforms are configured based on the strategy offered in the reason phase.

A smart e-health gateway was presented by Rahmani et al. (2015); it provided multiple higher-level services, such as real-time local data processing, local storage, and embedded data mining, via the bridging points. It contained various challenges ubiquitous to health care systems, including energy efficiency, reliability issues, scalability, etc. The large deployment of ubiquitous health monitoring systems (especially in clinical environments) can be offered by a successful implementation of smart e-health gateways. The system architecture of an IoT-based health monitoring system that can be applied in smart

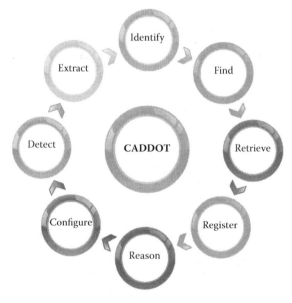

FIGURE 15.11
Eight phases of the CADDOT model for configuration of things in the IoT paradigm.

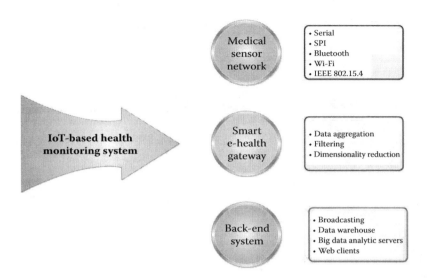

FIGURE 15.12
Main components of the system architecture for an IoT-based health monitoring system.

hospitals involves three components: a medical sensor network, a smart e-health gateway, and a back-end system. A schematic of this system and its elements are shown in Figure 15.12. The medical sensor network is based on the ubiquitous identification, sensing capability, communication capacity, biomedical information, and context signals. Its data are collected from the body or room used for treatment and medical diagnosis. Smart e-health gateways offer various communication protocols and are the touching points between a sensor network and the local switch or internet. The back-end system is composed of two remaining components, a local switch and a Cloud computing platform. It involves broadcasting, data warehouse, Big Data analytic servers, and Web clients as a graphical user interface for the final visualization and apprehension process.

A combined IoT-based system for urban planning and building smart cities was presented by Rathore et al. (2016); they used Big Data analytics to achieve their defined goals. Their system included various types of sensors, such as smart home sensors, weather and water sensors, vehicular networking, smart parking sensors, and surveillance objects. Moreover, the system was composed of a four-tier architecture: a bottom tier 1, intermediate tier 1, intermediate tier 2, and top tier. Bottom tier 1 is used to control IoT sources, data generation, and collections. Intermediate tier 1 is applied to manage all types of communication between sensors, relays, base stations, and the internet. Intermediate tier 2 conducts data management and processing by using the Hadoop framework. Finally, the top tier is used to control applications of the data analysis and results. In addition, the system's implementation entails various elements, including data generation and collecting, aggregation, classification, filtration, computing, preprocessing, and decision making. The authors implemented the system by using Hadoop with Spark, voltDB, and Storm or S4 for real-time processing of the IoT data to generate the expected responses. The implementation stage was carried out to establish the defined smart city. Furthermore, the offline historical data were evaluated on Hadoop by using the MapReduce program to carry out urban planning for future development. Smart homes, smart parking weather, pollution, and vehicle data sets are generated by IoT data sets to conduct the analysis and evaluation processes. Main components and specifications of the proposed system are illustrated in Figure 15.13.

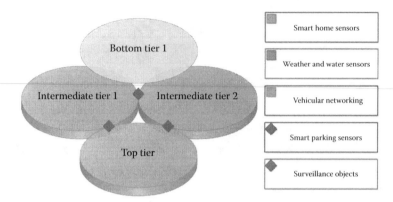

FIGURE 15.13
Elements of urban planning and building of smart cities based on IoT and Big Data analytics.

Evaluation Results

This section evaluates the performance of the IoT- and Big Data analytics-based intelligent methods presented above. Table 15.1 represents the evaluation results of thje CADDOT model (Perera et al. 2014), which was evaluated for the time taken to perform the following steps: (1) set up the sensor, (2) initiate the connection between the sensor and the SmartLink tool, (3) initiate communication between the sensor and SmartLink, (4) fetch sensor identification information, (5) get the complete profile of the sensor, (6) configure the sampling rate, (7) configure the communication frequency, (8) configure the sensing schedule, (9) configure the network and authentication details, and (10) connect to the secure network by using authentication details. The results indicate that the times taken obtained by the Bluetooth protocol were less than those for the TCP and UDP protocols in the initial connection, initial communication, and connection to the secure network.

TABLE 15.1

Time Taken for Steps in the CADDOT Model

	Time for Step (sec [logarithmic scale])		
Step	Wi-Fi (TCP)	Wi-Fi (UDP)	Bluetooth
1	6	6	13
2	8	8	4
3	5	5	3
4	0.3	0.32	0.4
5	0.3	0.32	0.4
6	0.3	0.32	0.4
7	0.3	0.32	0.4
8	0.3	0.32	0.55
9	0.3	0.33	0.55
10	6	6	0

Source: Modified from Perera C et al., *Big Data and Internet of Things: A Roadmap for Smart Environments*, pp. 215–241, 2014.

TABLE 15.2

Comparison of Results for the LZO and LZ4 Algorithms in the Smart e-Health Gateway

No. of Nodes	No. of Analog Channels	Compression Time (msec)		Decompression Time (msec)	
		LZO Algorithm	LZ4 Algorithm	LZO Algorithm	LZ4 Algorithm
1	8	18	60	23	40
2	8	20	60	19	50
5	8	23	50	27	60
10	8	30	40	37	40
50	8	30	40	40	40

Source: Modified from Rahmani A-M et al., *Proceedings of the 12th Annual IEEE Consumer Communications and Networking Conference*, pp. 826–834, 2015.

Furthermore, the times for steps 4 to 9 achieved via UDP and Bluetooth were longer than those for TCP.

Table 15.2 summarizes results of the LZO and LZ4 algorithms used by the smart e-Health gateway (Rahmani et al. 2015). The results indicate that the LZO algorithm has a low compression time compared to the LZ4 algorithm in all states of the number of nodes and number of analog channels. Moreover, decompression times obtained by the LZ4 algorithm were longer than those obtained by the LZO algorithm in most simulation cases. All of the results demonstrated that the efficiency of the LZO algorithm was better than that of the LZ4 algorithm, according to the comparison results.

Table 15.3 represents evaluation results related to the system for urban planning and building smart cities based on IoT and Big Data analytics (Rathore et al. 2016) in terms of processing time and throughput. The results show that the processing time of the presented system increased proportionally when data set size increased in the simulation process. Furthermore, the system throughput was enhanced by increasing the data set size in the obtained results. The authors claimed that the performance of their system was better than other systems according to the comparison results. Moreover, the authors indicated that the system throughput was also directly proportional to the data set size, because of the parallel processing nature of the Hadoop system. This is the big achievement of the presented system: that the system throughput will be enhanced with an increase in data set size.

TABLE 15.3

Performance Results of the System for Urban Planning and Building Smart Cities Based on IoT and Big Data Analytics

Data Set Size (MB)	Processing Time (msec)	Throughput (MBp)
78	28,000	3
150	30,000	5
301	40,000	7
450	60,000	8
1,228.8	130,000	9
1,843.2	180,000	10
3,276.8	230,000	14
5,345.28	280,000	19

Source: Modified from Rathore MM et al., *Computer Networks* 101:63–80, 2016.

Conclusions and Future Work

Big Data analytics is the process of using large data sets for discovering hidden patterns, market trends, unknown correlations, and other essential business information. In addition, the IoT consists of the objects which are interconnected to each other via the internet of computing devices to send and receive data. The combination of Big Data analytics and the IoT under an intelligence framework can build smart models to facilitate our lives. This chapter has presented a brief description of the IoT network, including main elements of IoT, popular applications of IoT, and security challenges in the IoT network. Next we presented various definitions of the intelligence process. A model of systematic intelligence formation from natural intelligence was described, foundations of human–computer interactions were considered, and several intelligent frameworks in IoT were fully explained. We discussed Big Data analytics for intelligence of IoT by review of data storage and processing modules, the key devices of intelligence for the IoT, the fundamental mechanisms for Big Data analytics, and of Big Data analytics methods for connected intelligence with IoT. Finally, we evaluated the performance of smart methods developed for Big Data analytics and connected intelligence with IoT.

Big Data analytics can be used in other computer networks similar to the IoT network. The use of Big Data analytics in Cloud computing (Demirkan and Delen 2013, Khan et al. 2015) and smart grids (Simmhan et al. 2013) should be considered in future work.

References

Aggarwal CC, Ashish N, Sheth A. 2013. The Internet of Things: A survey from the data-centric perspective, pp. 383–428. In Aggarwal CC (ed.), *Managing and Mining Sensor Data*. Berlin: Springer Verlag.

Atzori L, Iera A, Morabito G. 2010. The Internet of Things: A survey. *Computer Networks* 54(15):2787–2805.

Beyer MA, Laney D. 2012. *The importance of 'big data': a definition*. Stamford, CT: Gartner. https://www.gartner.com/doc/2057415/importance-big-data-definition/.

Bharti M, Saxena S, Kumar, R. 2017. Intelligent resource inquisition framework on Internet-of-Things. *Computers and Electrical Engineering* 58:265–281.

Blaze M, Feigenbaum J, Lacy J. 1996. Decentralized trust management, pp. 164–173. In *Proc. IEEE Symposium on Security and Privacy*, Oakland, CA. New York: IEEE.

Brooks RA. 1991. Intelligence without representation. *Artificial Intelligence* 47(1):139–159.

Buyya R, Yeo CS, Venugopal S, Broberg J, Brandic I. 2009. Cloud computing and emerging IT platforms: Vision, hype, and reality for delivering computing as the 5th utility. *Future Generation Computer Systems* 25(6):599–616.

Chen Y, Hu H. 2013. Internet of intelligent things and robot as a service. *Simulation Modelling Practice and Theory* 34:159–171.

Coen-Porisini A, Colombo P, Sicari S. 2010. Privacy aware systems: From models to patterns, pp. 232–259. In Mouratidis H (ed.), *Software Engineering for Secure Systems: Industrial and Research Perspectives*. Hershey, PA: IGI Global.

Copeland J. 2015. *Artificial Intelligence: A Philosophical Introduction*. New York: John Wiley & Sons.

Deary IJ, Penke L, Johnson W. 2010. The neuroscience of human intelligence differences. *Nature Reviews Neuroscience* 11(3):201–211.

Demirkan H, Delen D. 2013. Leveraging the capabilities of service-oriented decision support systems: Putting analytics and big data in cloud. *Decision Support Systems* 55(1):412–421.

Dix A. 2016. Human computer interaction, foundations and new paradigms. *Journal of Visual Languages and Computing* doi:10.1016/j.jvic.2016.04.001.

Dunkels A, Vasseur JP. 2008. *IP for Smart Objects*. White paper no. 1, vol. 1. Internet Protocol for Smart Objects Alliance. http://www.dunkels.com/adam/dunkels08ipso.pdf/.

Finkenzeller K. 2003. *RFID Handbook*. New York: John Wiley & Sons.

Gershenfelo N, Krikorian R, Cohen D. 2004. The Internet of Things. *Scientific American* 291(4):46–51.

Gharajeh MS. 2016. Avoidance of the energy hole in wireless sensor networks using a layered-based routing tree. *International Journal of Systems Control and Communications* 7(2):116–131.

Gharajeh MS, Alizadeh M. 2016. OPCA: Optimized prioritized congestion avoidance and control for wireless body sensor networks. *International Journal of Sensors Wireless Communications and Control* 6(2):118–128.

Gharajeh MS, Khanmohammadi S. 2016. DFRTP: Dynamic 3D fuzzy routing based on traffic probability in wireless sensor networks. *IET Wireless Sensor Systems* 6(6):211–219.

Gubbi J, Buyya R, Marusic S, Palaniswami M. 2013. Internet of Things (IoT): A vision, architectural elements, and future directions. *Future Generation Computer Systems* 29(7):1645–1660.

Guo B, Zhang D, Yu Z, Liang Y, Wang Z, Zhou X. 2013. From the internet of things to embedded intelligence. *World Wide Web* 16(4):399–420.

Honle N, Kappeler U-P, Nicklas D, Schwarz T, Grossmann M. 2005. Benefits of integrating meta data into a context model, pp. 25–29. *Proc. 3th IEEE International Conference on Pervasive Computing and Communications Workshops*. New York: IEEE.

Hu H, Wen Y, Chua T-S, Li X. 2014. Toward scalable systems for big data analytics: A technology tutorial. *IEEE Access* 2:652–687.

Jin J, Gubbi J, Marusic S, Palaniswami M. 2014. An information framework for creating a smart city through Internet of Things. *IEEE Internet of Things Journal* 1(2):112–121.

Kaklauskas A, Gudauskas R. 2016. Intelligent decision-support systems and the Internet of Things for the smart built environment, pp. 413–449. In Pacheco-Torgal F, Rasmussen ES, Granqvist CG, Ivanov V, Kaklauskas HA, Makonin S (eds.), *Start-Up Creation: The Smart Eco-Efficient Built Environment*. Sawston, Cambridge, United Kindgom: Woodhead Publishing.

Khan Z, Anjum A, Soomro K, Tahir, MA. 2015. Towards cloud based big data analytics for smart future cities. *Journal of Cloud Computing*, 4(2):1–11.

Korb KB, Nicholson AE. 2010. *Bayesian Artificial Intelligence*, 2nd ed. Boca Raton, FL: CRC Press.

Liebowitz SJ, Margolis SE. 2016. Network externalities (effects). *New Palgraves Dictionary of Economics and the Law*. Stuttgart, Germany: MacMillan.

Miorandi D, Sicari S, De Pellegrini F, Chlamtac I. 2012. Internet of Things: Vision, applications and research challenges. *Ad Hoc Networks* 10(7):1497–1516.

Nilsson NJ. 1980. *Principles of Artificial Intelligence*. Berlin: Springer-Verlag.

Oracle. 2013. *Big Data Analytics: Advanced Analytics in Oracle Database*. An Oracle white paper. http://www.oracle.com/technetwork/database/options/advanced-analytics/bigdataa.

Páez DG, Aparicio F, de Buenaga M, Ascanio JR. 2014. Big Data and IoT for chronic patients monitoring, pp. 416–423. In Hervás R, Lee S, Nugent C, Bravo J (eds.), *Ubiquitous Computing and Ambient Intelligence: Personalisation and User Adapted Services*, vol. 8867. Berlin: Springer-Verlag.

Perera C, Jayaraman PP, Zaslavsky A, Christen P, Georgakopoulos D. 2014. Context-aware dynamic discovery and configuration of 'things' in smart environments, pp. 215–241. In Bessis N, Dobre C (eds.), *Big Data and Internet of Things: A Roadmap for Smart Environments*. Berlin: Springer-Verlag.

Pfisterer D, Römer K, Bimschas D, Kleine O, Mietz R, Truong C, Hasemann, H, Kröller A, Pagel M, Hauswirth M. 2011. SPITFIRE: Toward a semantic web of things. *IEEE Communications Magazine* 49(11):40–48.

Pokorny J. 2013. NoSQL databases: A step to database scalability in web environment. *International Journal of Web Information Systems* 9(1):69–82.

Rahmani A-M, Thanigaivelan NK, Gia TN, Granados J, Negash B, Liljeberg P, Tenhunen H. 2015. Smart e-health gateway: Bringing intelligence to internet-of-things based ubiquitous healthcare systems, pp. 826–834. *Proc. 12th Annual IEEE Consumer Communications and Networking Conference*. New York: IEEE.

Rathore MM, Ahmad A, Paul A, Rho S. 2016. Urban planning and building smart cities based on the Internet of Things using Big Data analytics. *Computer Networks* 101:63–80.

Riggins FJ, Wamba SF. 2015. Research directions on the adoption, usage, and impact of the internet of things through the use of big data analytics, pp. 1531–1540. *Proc. 48th IEEE Hawaii International Conference on System Sciences.* New York: IEEE.

Rose K, Eldridge S, Chapin L. 2015. *The internet of things: An overview.* The Internet Society. https://pdfs.semanticscholar.org/6d12/bda69e8fcbbf1e9a10471b54e57b15cb07f6.pdf/.

Rumelhart DE. 1990. Brain style computation: Learning and generalization, pp. 405–420. In Zornetzer SF, Davis JL, Lau C (eds.), *An Introduction to Neural and Electronic Networks.* San Diego: Academic Press.

Russell SJ, Norvig P, Canny JF, Malik JM, Edwards DD. 1995. *Artificial Intelligence: A modern approach,* vol. 2. Upper Saddle River, NJ: Prentice Hall.

Simmhan Y, Aman S, Kumbhare A, Liu R, Stevens S, Zhou Q, Prasanna V. 2013. Cloud-based software platform for big data analytics in smart grids. *Computing in Science & Engineering* 15(4):38–47.

Sterling B. 2005. *Shaping Things.* Mediaworks pamphlets. Cambridge, MA: MIT Press.

Suo H, Wan J, Zou C, Liu J. 2012. Security in the internet of things: A review. *Proc. IEEE International Conference on Computer Science and Electronics Engineering,* vol. 3, pp. 648–651. New York: IEEE.

Thimbleby H. 2013. Reasons to question seven segment displays, pp. 1431–1440. *Proc. SIGCHI Conference on Human Factors in Computing Systems.* New York: ACM.

Tilak S, Abu-Ghazaleh NB, Heinzelman W. 2002. A taxonomy of wireless micro-sensor network models. *ACM SIGMOBILE Mobile Computing and Communications Review* 6(2):28–36.

Xu X, Chen T, Minami M. 2012. Intelligent fault prediction system based on internet of things. *Computers and Mathematics with Applications* 64(5):833–839.

Zhong Y. 2010. Advanced intelligence: Definition, approach, and progress. *International Journal of Advanced Intelligence* 2(1):15–23.

Zorzi M, Gluhak A, Lange S, Bassi A. 2010. From today's intranet of things to a future internet of things: A wireless- and mobility-related view. *IEEE Wireless Communications* 17(6):44–51.

Key Terminology and Definitions

Big Data: Big Data presents a high volume, high velocity, and high variety of information advantages. High volume means the amount or quantity of data; high velocity indicates the rate at which data are created; high variety represents the different types of data. Big Data requires new technologies and techniques to capture, store, and analyze the data to allow improved decision making into discovery optimization. There are many data sources (e.g., customer e-mail) that can be analyzed by Big Data efficiently. Big Data can be used in Web browsing data to capture various types of customers' behaviors.

Intelligence: in all cultures, intelligence means the ability to learn from prior experiences, solve existing problems, and utilize a knowledge base to adapt to new situations. The intelligence contains a potential capacity to make some solutions based on previous experiences based on different characteristics, such as creativity and interpersonal skills. Furthermore, it involves some mental abilities, which enable anyone to adapt to, shape, or select one's environment. Any intelligent system can deal with people, objects, and symbols via various mental skills. It also acts purposefully, thinks rationally, and deals effectively with the environment.

Internet of Things: the Internet of Things (IoT) enables various devices and systems to use leveraged data gathered by RFID, sensors, and actuators in physical objects. It can offer some potential capabilities to improve efficiency, security, health, education, and various aspects of daily life. Enterprises will be able to improve productivity and decision making in manufacturing, retail, agriculture, and other fields. The device-to-device communications, device-to-Cloud communications, device-to-gateway model, and back-end data-sharing model are the four communications models of IoT. Note that IoT needs IPv6 to generate true end-to-end internet connectivity.

16

Big Data-Driven Value Chains and Digital Platforms: From Value Co-creation to Monetization

Roberto Moro Visconti, Alberto Larocca, and Michele Marconi

CONTENTS

Introduction

Big Data is the term for any gathering of high-volume information sets from multiple sources; Big Data is so expensive, fast changing, and complex that it can become hard to process. The processing difficulties cover investigation, catch, duration, inquiry, sharing, stockpiling, exchange, perception, protection infringement, and quantification of financial value. The explosive growth of data in almost every industry and business area has been driven by the rapid development of the Web, the Internet of Things (IoT), and Cloud computing (Jin et al. 2015).

Traffic among different websites fuels the creation of Big Data, with file sharing, streaming media through social networks, interacting devices such as IoT sensors, use of mobile apps, science data, emails, digitalizers, texts, geometries, sounds, antennas, voice data, videos, posts, blogs, and other connecting sources through several different devices. Combinations of different data sources are also relevant, as they add value through data fusion. A networked domino effect, driven by scalable data systems connected through digital platforms, spreads information in real time.

Literature about Big Data is also growing and is too wide and heterogeneous to be properly quoted or even synthesized. Big Data surveys have been included, for instance, in reports published by Aruna and Anusha (2016), Chen and Zhang (2014), Chen et al. (2014),

Khan et al. (2014), and Lugmayr et al. (2016). The definition of Big Data used here was coined by Ward and Barker in 2013.

Within this framework, many crucial issues for Big Data analytics and their use for effective business planning are still underinvestigated. In particular, the interaction between value chains and Big Data, especially if leveraged by networking applications, needs further scrutiny.

In this chapter, we show that:

1. Value chains are the strategic backbone of business modeling and planning.

2. Big Data-driven value chains have an underexploited and misunderstood added value, especially with data fusion, which combines heterogeneous information that would otherwise remain uncorrelated and forgotten.

3. Networking digital platforms leverage Big Data-driven value chains, exponentially increasing their potentialities even in terms of value co-creation.

4. Monetization is both the final step of value chains and the key input/output component of financial planning. It cashes in on resources that can remunerate stakeholders and can be reinvested in analytics and technological improvements.

Big Data-Driven Value Chains

Value chains, even in traditional terms and irrespective of either Big Data or networks, are the strategic backbone of business modeling and planning, as they indicate the targets of corporate goals.

In particular, a Big Data-driven value chain is represented by several consequential steps, such as data creation, search and capture, storage, querying, analysis, sharing and transfer, visualization, and customization. Each step, codified by software algorithms, is part of an incremental and flexible value chain. Every step adds value that has to be shared among its contributors (providers, intermediating platforms, users, etc.) to value co-creation. This chain produces different stages of information that are embedded in traditional value chains that become Big Data driven.

A Big Data value chain is based on the following strategic steps (synthesized in Figure 16.1):

1. Creation (data capture)

2. Storage (warehousing)

3. Processing (data mining, fusion, and analytics)

4. Consumption (sharing)

5. Monetization

	1. Creation (Data capture)	2. Storage (Data warehouse)	3. Processing (Data mining and fusion)	4. Consumption (Visualization and sharing)	5. Monetization (Business plan)
Volume	++++	+++	+++	+	+
Velocity	+++	+++	+++	++	+
Variety	+++	+	+++++	++	+
Veracity	+	+	++++	++++	++
Value	+	+	++	+++	+++++

FIGURE 16.1
This Big Data chart follows a consequential value chain approach, and for each step, evidence of big data features is given. Sign + , ++ … graduate the importance of these characteristics.

Each step of the value chain is linked to Big Data's "Five Vs" (volume, velocity, variety, veracity, and value). What matters most is interactions of the Five Vs, whose impacts along the value chain change from step to step, as shown in Figure 16.1.

Figure 16.1 shows an impact decrease along the value chain for the early Vs (volume, and velocity) and a correspondent increase for the last V (value). Variety and veracity acquire importance with the processing phase, and their impacts are optimized (with data mining fusion and with data visualization and sharing) and then transferred to maximize value during monetization.

In particular, larger quantities of data are routinely produced from an increasing number of sources. At this stage, data value is low because data are unstructured, uncorrelated, and the stakeholders deemed to capture the data have a low capacity to evaluate their veracity.

Data warehousing hardly increases Big Data value, because it is concerned with storing data regardless of their type (variety with only one +) and validity. Several data-processing resources are allocated to drastically solve issues on data volume (mining only the essential data) and variety (fusing several types of data). Although processing increases Big Data value, its outputs are not yet ready for immediate use.

The fourth stage of the value chain addresses the exchange of Big Data processing outputs via adoption of communication (sharing platform) and representation (data visualization) technologies. Here, volume, velocity, and variety are already simplified; however, the veracity is still partially unsolved. Finally, the last stage of the value chain maximizes value through a synthesis of the first four Vs.

Therefore, Big Data drives value generation that can be revealed by:

- (Radical) innovation;
- Market expansion (new products or services toward new markets);
- Differentiation and branding (optimization);
- Shortened supply chain and processing speed, thus favoring cost reductions;
- Better forecasting and consequent risk reduction.

Cost reduction is brought about by many factors and in different phases along the product and service life cycle, like ofcptimized logistics or just-in-time production, and stock management. For manufacturing, the IoT can have a tremendous impact on cost reduction, for example, by lowering maintenance costs for tools and machines, higher product conformity, production cycle optimization, etc. Risk reduction is also significantly impacted by Big Data analysis, as it better defines key elements of business planning, such as production processes or sales and marketing strategies.

One milestone for value creation is represented by the challenging step that takes unstructured and uncorrelated data to hidden causal interpretation of Big Data linkages detected by data-mining techniques.

Value can also be destroyed by incomplete chains, with either missing steps or insufficient development. Since the potential for upgrade is theoretically unlimited, value bottlenecks are ubiquitous and need constant monitoring and fixing.

Pivotal elements of these networks are digital platforms that work as nodes of the network. Below, we discuss the function and importance of digital platforms for value creation; we also describe further upgrades that occur when Big Data-driven value chains are linked with other chains through digital networks.

Creation (Data Capture)

Creation of Big Data is increasing day by day in volume, velocity, and variety of data sources. For example, Earth Observation generates terabytes of geolocated images hourly with increasing spatial, temporal, and spectral resolutions (Benediktsson et al. 2013). Sensor observation services produce more data from the "sensor web" and "citizen sensors" (Goodchild 2007). Social networks, such as Twitter and Facebook, generate Big Data and are transforming social sciences. Business interactions (e.g., credit card transactions and online purchases) generate large-volume, high-velocity, and highly unstructured (variety) data sets.

This exponential increase in volume, velocity, and variety seems limited only by the technological capacity to capture data automatically, without human involvement. Such technologies include, but are not limited to, bar codes, radio frequency identification, biometrics, magnetic stripes, optical character recognition, smart cards, and voice recognition programs.

IoT continuously generates data streams on space and time from interconnected devices. Applications of this can be very different, such as industrial production lines, urban traffic management, telemedicine, and home automation.

Achieving geographical and chronological localization of Big Data at this early stage adds value. Captured information can be detected from (i) how data flow in space and in time, (ii) where storage and computing resources are located, and (iii) detecting proactively the location of access of users at different places and times. Kozuch et al. (2009) demonstrated that location-aware applications outperform those with no location-detection capability by factors of 3 to 11.

Storage (Data Warehousing)

Increasing the volume and velocity of Big Data is a challenge for common computer storage capacity. Like the large volume of data, which could be decreased by filtering redundant data, the velocity of Big Data creation and obsolescence require storage systems able to scale up quickly. New methods based on Cloud technologies allow storing a large volume of data and enhance Big Data velocity through Cloud computation resources. Moreover, Cloud technologies guarantee higher security levels against fault and data loss and have a greater sharing potential. However, Cloud storage introduced a new limitation: a bandwidth capacity bottleneck in relation to the large volume of data. Furthermore, Cloud storage raises concerns about data security, including the protection of commercial and financial information and strategic and sensible data, intellectual property, and personal privacy (Chen and Zhang 2014), thus requiring the development of sophisticated services for cybersecurity.

Efficient data warehousing should be based on algorithms for data maintenance, security, accessibility, and veracity control, allowing the maximization of added value at this stage.

Processing (Data Mining and Fusion)

Data processing is strongly linked with all five Vs of Big Data. At the processing stage, data volume is still large and the velocity of processing is a key factor. Data processing connects different kinds of data (e.g., pictures, text, video, etc.), resolving the variety of Big Data (with data fusion and interoperability, as described below); at the same time, it establishes protocols to confirm data veracity.

Data processing concerns data discovery and integration of heterogeneous data, veracity assurance, reuse and preservation over time, and capture of value. The NoSQL (Not Only SQL, like SimpleDB, Google BigTable, Apache Hadoop, MapReduce, MemcacheDB, and Voldemort) database (Gessert et al. 2016) is a current approach for large and distributed data management. The main Big Data platforms implement this approach to overcome the scarce elasticity of the standard relational database management approach. NoSQL is schema free and enables modifications of the data structure without rewriting tables, being flexible to store heterogeneous data.

Several scientific methods have been applied to Big Data analysis:

- Statistical methods have been used to explore causal relations and correlations among Big Data. Reduction algorithms, such as principal component analysis and other nonlinear techniques, are used to reduce Big Data volumes, minimizing the loss of information;

- Data mining is a collection of tools (e.g., clustering analysis, classification, regression, association rule learning) that are able to extract patterns from data;

- Machine learning is a subdomain of artificial intelligence which is aimed at producing algorithms that allow computers to develop behaviors based on empirical data and discovery of knowledge;

- An artificial neural network is a set of techniques applied, for example, in pattern recognition and image analysis. However, the learning process of this technique over Big Data is time- and memory-consuming;

- Social network analysis is an emerging technique that has been adopted to study social relationships and social media. It represents the social system according to the network theory (see below).

Generally, a combination of two or more of these techniques is used to analyze Big Data. For example, Walmart uses statistical techniques and machine learning to discover configurations among their large amount of transaction data. These configurations help to design better pricing strategies and advertising campaigns, enhancing their competitiveness.

These techniques present difficulties in managing the volume of Big Data due to huge workloads requested within limited runtimes. Currently, the strategies are based on (i) sampling Big Data populations in smaller samples, (ii) developing reduction algorithms for removing potential irrelevant, redundant, noisy, and misleading data (Zhai et al. 2014), and (iii) designing parallel and distributed processing approaches by using Cloud computing technologies. One of the aims of these techniques is to determine Big Data veracity. It has crucial importance for data processing and, although often underreported, it is a threat, especially when working on unstructured data.

There are two issues related to data veracity:

1. Data validation. Data specialists need to apply best practices to ensure that data are captured, stored, and replicated correctly. There are some technical solutions for data validation. However, unstructured data are more challenging to manage because of their unexpected behavior and changing nature.

2. For unstructured data (e.g., text messages, especially from social networks), there can be a threat of false information being deliberately shared, as happened with TripAdvisor when it was realized that many reviews were untrue and had been written intentionally to damage competitors.

Working on a false data set can create irreversible problems for many business aspects. First, it can seriously damage the reputation of the service or product provider. As a consequence, the trust among community members for the brand can be eroded with significant economic and potential legal consequences. Second, working on an incorrect data set means that the Big Data analysis will probably lead to untrue observations, resulting in the creation of wrong new data products, marketing and communication strategies, client profiling, etc.

Data validation has also an impact on operational costs, influencing time-to-market and human resources costs. Companies wishing to leverage data analytics results should, therefore, see data auditing as one of the pillars of their Big Data business strategy. Big Data auditing stands out as a new field of action. Metadata are an essential element to detect the integrity of data provenance and thus to validate Big Data and their value. A challenging task concerns the development of algorithms that automatically generate metadata to describe Big Data and relevant processes (Oguntimilehin and Ademola 2014).

Consumption (Sharing)

Data must be visualized, communicated, and shared with stakeholders. At this stage of the value chain, variety should be processed to be transformed into value. The visualization of Big Data processing outputs uncovers hidden patterns and reveals unknown correlations to improve the decision-making process (Nasser and Tariq 2015). Consequently, a new scientific discipline, data visualization, addresses effective knowledge representation. According to Chen and Zhang (2014), both aesthetic form and functionality are necessary to convey the knowledge to the widest possible audience.

Big Data sharing is consistent with value co-creation among different stakeholders, along the value chain, from data creation to monetization. The synthesis produced by data visualization tools is a key element that transforms the information revealed by Big Data processing, understood only by specialists scientists, into knowledge accessible to all stakeholders. Current Big Data visualization tools still have poor performance levels in terms of scalability and response time. Representation of uncertainty is also complex and not at all achieved (Yingcai et al. 2012). New data visualization paradigms and frameworks are strongly claimed by the Big Data community and need the training of professionals with strong mathematical skills combined with communication and figurative arts expertise.

A specific application of data visualization is related to the representation of geolocalized information, traditionally achieved using a geographic information system (GIS). For example, human mobility patterns can be plotted geographically to capture quickly where people are and in which moment. However, traditional GIS software is unable to properly visualize Big Data, mainly because the information reported on a map is too dense to be understood by a map reader and thus be transformed into knowledge. Therefore, traditional GIS software should be merged with the Big Data processing tools described above and rethought as data visualization tools.

Big Data consumption, amplified by sharing, typically takes place within IT networks, such as the Web. Diffusion and usage foster monetization: sharing is a value co-creation driver, derived from feedback and joint use. Sharing can also be interpreted in terms of network theory; this is described below.

Assembling Value via Heterogeneous Data Fusion and Interoperability

Data fusion explores complex and evolving relationships among data, resolving conflicts from a collection of heterogeneous sources, linking different records, and looking for data veracity. Different sources of uncorrelated and spurious data in different formats (e.g., numeric, text, video, audio) are hard to combine but can generate an unexploited added value. Interoperability concerns information exchange and communication among different systems (cross-domain information) through their IT interfaces and is scaled up by Big Data through data fusion.

Data fusion between different sets of structured and unstructured data creates a new data set, i.e., a new data product for sale. Analytically, the challenge is to see correlations in this new data set. The goal of data fusion is to combine relevant information from two or more data sources into a single source that provides a more accurate description than any of the individual data sources; this is achieved by capturing the (hidden) commonalities between several data sets with countless combinations.

Data should be conveniently transformed to become interdisciplinary, computationally ready, and born-connected. Big Data creation and processing require digital platforms that can read, write, and exchange information with suitable formats and protocols, a key element in system design.

Big Data can generate a competitive advantage with revolutionary data analysis through increasingly sophisticated algorithms, and can yield incremental value with excess revenues and cash flows. Data fusion and interoperability of uncorrelated information are a major value driver. These added values remunerate the stakeholders that rotate around the digital platform, with scalable benefits that are transmitted and shared in the whole network. Applications concern several trendy industries, such as mobile health or e-commerce.

For example, the use of sensor data in the increasingly popular fitness and health mobile wearable devices creates a stream of heterogeneous data that are conveniently integrated to reveal the correlation between activities and lifestyle. Singular streams of data have a value that is multiplied by data fusion. When these data and their analyses are shared on data-driven social platforms, the value of data fusion is further amplified.

Some new products and services are the result of data fusion. For example, shared economy (peer-to-peer exchange) platforms, such as AirBnB and Uber, are based on the integration of location-based data with freely shared customer data. Cloud storage allows data scalability, and analytical tools predict customer needs and match supply and demand. As a result, new data products are created, and time to market becomes minimal.

Data fusion, therefore, represents a new business model; firms may have proprietary data and can marry that data with public data or data from another firm to create a whole new perspective on customers or markets. People-centered ecosystems and mass collaboration platforms are valuable sources for acquiring data for fusion and for sharing output. From this perspective, variety is the most promising uncharted area in Big Data (Wienhofen et al. 2015).

Data integration is critical for achieving value from Big Data through integrative data analysis and cross-domain collaborations (Christen 2014). Dong and Divesh (2015) summarized the data integration challenges of schema mapping, record linkage, and data fusion; metadata is essential for tracking these mappings to make the integrated data sources "robotically" resolvable and to facilitate large-scale analyses. However, as mentioned above (in the discussion on veracity of Big Data), efficiently and automatically creating metadata from Big Data is still a challenge.

Intermediating Digital Platforms

Digital platforms are the virtual marketplace where products and services are exchanged by buyers and sellers, often through B2B, B2C, or C2C e-commerce transactions. As such, digital platforms are the virtual places where data are exchanged and collected, thus feeding the high volume of information that will be analyzed with data mining. While horizontal platforms fit all sectors, vertical platforms are specialized and use more customized Big Data; an example is given by vertical advertising, which segments potential customers according to their characteristics.

Digital platforms can be:

- Websites (such as e-commerce platforms), where the content is created by the seller of the product or service; the platform can be offered as a service by a third party (for example, eBay) or it can be owned by the seller itself (for example, an airline);
- Social networks, where the content is produced by all members of the community ("proconsumer");
- Mobile Apps, which are rapidly overtaking websites and can cover all functions of websites and social networks but with the great advantage of real-time geolocalized data;
- Closed digital platforms offered as a marketplace by device producers to app developers to sell their products (for example, Google Play for Android);
- Intranets, such as closed group company networks;
- Machine networks (IoT), i.e., machines and computers that exchange data automatically without human intervention (for example, industrial robots or smart cities sensors).

Value chains perform an intermediating function through digital platforms, and they interact with Big Data-driven supply chains of products and services. Websites and mobile apps are somehow similar to a traditional marketplace, where supply and demand meet with a seller presenting a well-defined product to the buyer. As in traditional marketplaces, word of mouth plays an important role also in digital platforms; those who can merge structured data (i.e., product descriptions) with unstructured data, such as reviews or comments, can facilitate the transaction by providing real-time detailed information to match supply and demand.

However, the role of an intermediating digital platform is much more than a simple interface. It acts as a digital business analyst and product broker and:

- Gathers information on the market (accurate, real-time, and on a massive scale);
- Advises buyers on the most suitable products and best offers;
- Advises sellers on market demands;
- Runs targeted (vertical) advertising campaigns;
- Can "guess" potential interest in new products (as discussed below); and
- Has the power to move the market.

All these characteristics can be enhanced by Big Data. Digital platforms can, however, be impermeable interfaces: transactions between buyers and sellers are mediated by the digital platform, which in fact is the sole owner of the data being exchanged and the data products being created. This "ownership" may cause legal issues if it surreptitiously expropriates the property rights of intermediating entities, with asymmetric monetization of the proceeds. The input and output on digital platforms are summarized in Table 16.1.

Digital platforms are complex and dynamic interfaces that collect both active and passive data, as well as external and internal data, and thus they have to be designed accordingly. Key features that digital platforms must achieve are:

- Real-time collection of geolocalized data;
- Correct definitions of parameters. An insightful data analysis requires information that describes well the trade dynamics and the buyer's profile. This means that IT specialists need to work with market specialists to collect the right data in the right format;
- Data analysis that is able to highlight trends and create new data products (which can be sold as a new product or service to existing customers, used to improve internal operations, or sold to third parties). Data collection without processing algorithms is valueless (Figure 16.1);
- Sufficient flexibility to identify and then develop potential new data products for sale; this translates into responsive business plans;
- Capacity to customize offers to a single buyer, leveraging individual information gathered both actively and passively. Accurate profiling of buyers and identification of social circles are also important;
- Real-time matching of supply and demand.

Social networks are specifically interesting for Big Data analysis, because they offer unrivaled unstructured data from which correlations and trends can emerge. Characteristics of social network platforms are:

- Great spatial and temporal accuracy, through M-app geolocalization in real time;
- Great potential for vertical marketing, since users share all kinds of information and companies can customize communication and vertical advertising.

In social networks, some community members have more "pull" than others, i.e., they are influencers. Pyramidal networks with a central platform, like Facebook, differ from

TABLE 16.1

Input and Output Data for Digital Platforms

Input	Output
Product or service (seller)	New data product
Personal data (buyer)	Pattern, trends, and correlations for sales, marketing and product development
Spatio-temporal data (buyer)	Customized offers
Data collected by sensors (IoT)	Customized advertising
Community information (social networks)	Community suggestions
Transactional data	Operational data

peer-to-peer networks, such as WhatsApp. Network analysis can detect the community leaders, whose heavier nodes have the capacity to create closer links (shorter edges).

Linking Big Data with Network Theory

Value chains based on traditional databases become networked when they are linked to other chains through value-adding networks. Value chains networks are more resilient and able to cope with risks of failure, enabling alternatives. Networked value chains fueled by Big Data stand out as the best value-maximizing option, as illustrated in Figure 16.2.

Network theory is the study of graphs as a representation of (a)symmetric relations among discrete objects. A network can be defined as a graph in which nodes and/or edges (defined below) have attributes (e.g., names). Network theory is a branch of network science, an academic field which studies complex networks such as Telecommunications (TLC) (teachable language comprehender) networks, ICT (information and communications technology) networks, biological networks, cognitive and semantic networks, and social networks; network theory considers distinct elements or actors represented by nodes (or vertices) and the connections between the elements or actors as links (or edges).

Degree, correlations, clustering, and centrality provide information on single nodes, their immediate surroundings, and their position with respect to the overall network (Caldarelli and Catanzaro 2012). These features matter even for Big Data, which can be seen as networked informative nodes. Edging Big Data correlated to nodes disseminates massive information in real time.

The topology of networks, which is so important for their interpretation, is based on computing the edge "betweenness" that finds the edges through which most of the shortest paths pass. Even this characteristic can be referred to Big Data as it is a key informative nexus between different edges.

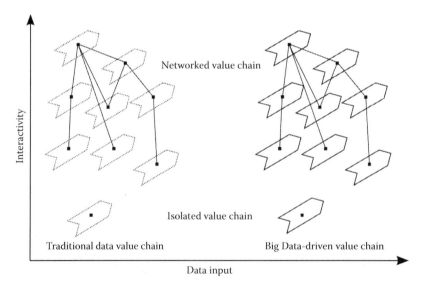

FIGURE 16.2
Interactivity of Big Data-driven value chains is enhanced by massive data inputs that reduce information asymmetries. (From Visconti, RM, 2017, Public private partnerships, big data networks and mitigation of information asymmetries, *Corporate Ownership & Control* 14(4).)

Websites and the internet can be interpreted in terms of network science, represented by relations among vertices and their connecting edges. Social networks, continuously fueled by Big Data collection and processing, show the dynamic relationships among social entities (persons, groups, etc.). Along the value chain, they develop in particular the sharing phase. Big Data processing of social network contents is quite complicated, since wording is semantically hard to interpret and classify. The analysis of links within a network is a subset of network analysis that explores the associations among objects or nodes, such as websites.

Networks are concerned with a disordered pattern of many different interactions, characterized by processing massive amounts of data. Since networks are patterns of interaction and connectedness, they play a fundamental role in any step of progressive value chains. Even if Big Data has hardly been linked to network theory in the existing literature, this passage to big network data seems important, since it helps us understand their intrinsic workings within the value chain described.

Networks are concerned with Big Data at each stage of the value chain. During the creation (data capture) phase, different data can be considered nodes (vertices) that are collected and then linked in the processing phase. Big Data storage is performed by a network of repositories in the Cloud. Even during the processing phase, the involved stakeholders adopt algorithms derived from network theory to explore and solve Big Data complexity. Big Data consumption takes place through sharing, again linking nodes of users. Finally, monetization is eased by optimal sharing of information and economic interaction among Big Data users; networking is, for instance, concerned with the aforementioned B2B, B2C, and C2C e-commerce applications.

Networks play several roles in Big Data analysis at the same time, behaving as:

- Sharing structures. Edges are the vehicles through which information travels (social networks, email systems, data exchange, etc.) and are also viewed in physical terms (e.g., telecom networks);

- Storage tools. Data are stored in database (nodes) clusters, such as HDFS (Hadoop distributed files system);

- Processing infrastructure. Large data volumes are conveniently processed in the data clusters where they are stored, making processing faster. Also, shared computing can perform more efficiently and economically than individual supercomputers;

- New data product. Big Data analysis highlights hidden correlations and trends that can be described by network theory (for example, identification of a new community, or a subset of an existing community, by using community detection algorithms); and

- Multiplying economic factor. The value of new data products can grow exponentially if channeled through well-profiled community networks. Also, predictive analysis of network dynamics can lead to increased profits and risk reduction, cost reduction, and operational optimization.

Network theory can help identify leaders within digital communities: influencers are heavier nodes that have the capacity to create stronger and shorter edges, for example, through more frequent interaction or quantity of data exchanged.

Understanding structural network aspects such as closeness, centrality, or degrees can be of great of value for marketing and communication strategies. Big Data combined with network theory models can afford detailed profiling of both individual community members and the communities (and their subsets). Profiling can also include community dynamics such as causality, clustering, network interconnectivity, network convergence or splitting, etc.

Big Data-Driven Business Planning

Business modeling with strategic value chains is the core component of effective planning. This general statement applies also to Big Data-driven and networked value chains, such as those illustrated in Figure 16.2. Business planning is central for any monetization-driven strategy, since it consists of a numerical formulation of the business plan that embodies cash flow forecasts.

Many companies are developing new business models specifically designed to create additional value by extracting, refining, and capitalizing on data (Hartmann et al. 2016). Big Data represents a powerful, albeit underexploited, source of information for descriptive, prescriptive, and predictive analytics concerned with models for forecasting future events based on observing past ones. This information needs to be collected, processed, and made available to users through the value chain described in above. Value-enhancing business process reengineering and decision making can be fueled by Big Data.

Information and knowledge extracted from Big Data matters for business planning in many complementary ways: due to its velocity, it allows a mark-to-market update and refresh of forecasts that flexibly adapt to changing market conditions, whereas data volume makes estimates more precise and less volatile, reducing the risk of uncertainty and making massive analysis possible.

Big Data influences predictive analytics and business planning through many complementary aspects (Jin et al. 2015, Hartmann et al. 2016), such as:

- Uncertainty modeling;
- Probability (statistical) theory (nondeterministic algorithmic theory);
- Signal processing;
- Computer programming;
- Data engineering;
- Pattern recognition and visualization;
- Hypotheses updating and fine-tuning in real time, due to Big Data velocity.

Big Data processing (data mining) is becoming a core input of business planning (for example, incorporating temporal and geospatial customer activities in the model). Firms that embed Big Data and aggregate information in their models can gain a competitive advantage in understanding market trends with scale, precision, and velocity. According to Muhtaroglu et al. (2013), "Companies which can adapt their businesses well to leverage Big Data have significant advantages over those that lag this capability. The need for exploring new approaches to address the challenges of Big Data forces companies to shape their business models accordingly."

Social networks, e-commerce transactions, and other sources are rich data mines that shed light on the lifestyles, beliefs, outlook, and preferences of geo-tagged customers, up to the point of inspiring new brands, products, and services.

For business firms, passive data capture provides an opportunity to learn about customers and markets to reduce risk in business decisions and to achieve segmentation that enables customized advertisements and customer offers. Given that each customer is analyzed precisely, unique and personalized messages can be deployed to them. Firms can selectively decide who to contact through digital platforms that process Big Data with precise segmentation and geographically oriented strategies. Passive data capture allows firms to share data with customers through feedback loops and provide customer-added convenience. Individuals who use mobile devices and are active on social networks are highly measurable and should expect even more sensors to become available on smartphones and devices such as watches, glasses, and other body sensors (Walker 2015). Data capture, especially from unaware individuals, can however raise privacy concerns and prevent previous feedback and value co-creation strategies. As mentioned before, this can happen through intermediating digital platforms.

Business planning and business model canvas represent a formal statement of business targets and strategies to reach them, showing in numerical terms the value of these goals. Big Data strategies are mainly focused on:

1. Performance management, which involves understanding the meaning of Big Data in company databases using predetermined queries and multidimensional analysis.

2. Data exploration that makes heavy use of statistics to experiment and get answers to new questions. This approach leverages predictive modeling techniques to foresee user behavior based on their previous business transactions and preferences.

3. Social analytics (metrics) that measure the vast amount of existing nontransactional data. Much of these data are present on social media platforms. Social analytics measure three broad categories: awareness, engagement, and word-of-mouth or reach.

Decision science involves experiments and analysis of nontransactional data, such as consumer-generated product ideas and product reviews, to improve the decision-making process. Unlike social analyzers, who focus on social analytics to measure known objectives, decision scientists explore social Big Data as a way to conduct "field research" and to test hypotheses. Data-driven decision making applies to business planning strategies. Big Data can optimize:

1. Sales planning and revenue streams. After comparisons of massive data, enterprises can optimize their prices, predict consumer behavior, and analyze trends by segregating the relevant information of the targeted audience.

2. Operations. Enterprises can improve their operational efficiency and satisfaction, optimize their labor force, cut operational costs, and avoid excessive production.

3. Supply chain (smart logistics). Big Data can foster inventory and logistics optimization and supplier coordination, shortening the supply chain and making it more resilient to external shocks.

Thus, higher economic and monetary margins are a natural result of these optimization strategies.

Use and mining of Big Data heralds a new wave of productivity growth and consumer impetus (Jin et al. 2015), increasing windows of opportunity as data can be turned into products with better-aimed marketing, discovering unknown customer needs. Data and data-driven products can answer economic questions, giving more precise insights about value, use, risk, utility, characteristics, markets, customer behavior analytics, performance, policy decisions, etc. Data-driven business models are based on both internal and external data, and their key activities are represented by data generation and acquisition, processing, aggregation, analytics, visualization, and distribution, following a pattern consistent with the value chain. Big Data predictive modeling can be incorporated into business planning, creating value through appropriate implementation strategies that leverage information value.

Monetization Strategies

Big Data monetization deals with generating and cashing revenues from (un)structured Big Data sources, capturing created value through business intelligence and analytics. According to Najjar and Kettinger (2013), "data monetization is when the intangible value of data is converted into real value, usually by selling it. Data may also be monetized by converting it into other tangible benefits or by avoiding costs. Three current IT trends are enabling businesses to achieve the previously elusive goal of data monetization: Big Data, business intelligence and analytics, and Cloud computing. Potential buyers of an organization's data include a direct supplier, an upstream supply chain partner, a data aggregator, an analytics service provider, or even a competitor."

While monetization is still an underinvestigated issue, its importance is growing, since it is the key for proper remuneration of value-adding strategies. Data monetization, according to Najjar and Kettinger (2013), requires high technical data capabilities (the hardware, software, and network capabilities that enable the collection, storage, and retrieval of data) and high analytical capabilities (the mathematical and business analytical knowledge needed to exploit the data).

Multiple streams of monetization can occur when different strategies are combined. Synergistic data fusion driven by multidisciplinary and multicriteria analysis can bring scalable value. Analysis of monetization strategies is consistent with the aim of this chapter, since it represents the key component, in financial terms, of value co-creation policies.

Strategies for monetizing Big Data (Walker 2015) include:

1. Leveraging data for internal operations, keeping them proprietary (data are a worthy asset to protect).
2. Entering new businesses, even with versioning (product differentiation).
3. Licensing (rent, lease, or temporarily grant) proprietary data exclusively to selected clients, charging usage or subscription fees.
4. Trading data (even to business partners, for shared benefits).
5. Selling premium data products (to asset owners, other interested parties, etc.) and leveraging data subscription models (data vending and Big Data as a service available through digital platforms).

6. Making data (freely) available to many stakeholders.

7. Sharing data with partners.

8. Leveraging data for advertisement opportunities (with selective, vertical advertisement).

9. Developing new data products and services created from data fusion.

As stated above, all stakeholders take part in value co-creation. Monetization also involves all participants in the Big Data value chain, even though this could happen in unconventional ways.

In fact, if for companies producing, managing, or using Big Data the monetary reward can be evident, it is less so for netizens, i.e., the millions of users who create a substantial part of the data. It is often said that "if you do not pay for a product, you are the product," with a negative emphasis on the exploitation of unaware netizens in favor of IT companies. However, the sharing economy, based on the free exchange of user data, gives back to the users products that are clearly worthy to them, for example, connectivity with friends and family (social and emotional value, as well as inexpensive communication), the possibility to network for professional purposes, access to services that enable them to save time and money (e.g., car sharing), and information exchange (e.g., to make more informed decisions on some product purchases).

At the same time, by willingly sharing more personal data, users contribute to improve volume, velocity, variety, and veracity of data, enriching the value chain and eventually enabling the production of better data products in a sort of self-improving and self-fueling Big Data cycle. Artificial intelligence and self-learning algorithms can boost this process.

At the individual level, sharing personal data can also contribute to the veracity of a personal digital profile, which in turn could be useful for some platforms based on endorsement or verification. Use of data for the continuous improvement of internal operations and interactions with decision makers can bring cost and risk reductions and customer service improvements. Misunderstood risks, tracked in real time, can be identified and minimized with Big Data.

Monetization has to include the consideration of data as an asset to exploit to produce innovation and new data products and services. Monetization strategies have to target the right stakeholders to charge for data utilization, i.e., vendors and advertisers are typically more willing to pay than users. Allowing users to access data for free removes a major obstacle to their participation in data collection and sharing, boosting scalability in digital platforms. Data can strongly improve decisions, making them more accurate and timely, thus incorporating an added value that can be monetized.

Conclusions

This chapter has shown that Big Data can be conveniently embedded in traditional value chains, especially if linked to networking digital platforms. In such cases, scalability is boosted and value is levered. Monetization represents the last step of integrated value chains and cashes in resources that can be reinvested in analytics and technological improvements; it is a key parameter for effective planning. Hence, optimal business modeling and planning should consider Big Data as a worthy asset.

As value chains are composed of subsequent steps, it is possible to consider them both holistically and separately; in the latter case, each step can be combined with other (external) chains within flexible value co-creation networks.

Data fusion is among the main value drivers, since it combines heterogeneous information that would otherwise remain uncorrelated and unexploited. Finding value in data sets and leveraging Big Data information within network systems is a challenging option embedded in most trendy strategies based on improved forecasting, resource optimization, and capacity planning.

Challenging opportunities deriving from Big Data analytics involve both academics and practitioners, jointly engaged in interpreting and designing unprecedented business models and innovative sectors. These concerns, for example in social media, nurture customers via personalized experiences on the Web that also capture all data about users or members. Without Big Data, these experiennces would simply not exist. Data-intensive scientific recovery, also known as Big Data problems, is a new scientific paradigm where Big Data is used in order to test and back new scientific theories (Chen and Zhang 2014).

New research avenues may conveniently address underinvestigated issues, such as:

- Value co-creation between platform intermediaries, data sources, and users;
- Big Data's influence on long-term sustainability, which is so crucial for effective business planning;
- The impact of social networks on Big Data, since they represent an impressive, growing, and complex source of data;
- The impact of Big Data and computational (data) science on data-intensive scientific research and business plan simulations;
- The impact of algorithms on Big Data and other networked value chains, consistent with networks, as digital numbering brings to value measurement and monetization.

The last research target seems particularly challenging but also rewarding. Should it become possible to represent Big Data-driven networked value chains with algorithms, it would then be feasible to measure and manage value creation and monetization.

References

Aruna Sri PSG, Anusha M. 2016. Big Data survey. *Indonesian Journal of Electrical Engineering and Informatics* 4(1):74–80.

Benediktsson JA, Chanussot J, Moon WM. 2013. Advances in very-high-resolution remote sensing. *Proceedings of the IEEE* 101(3):566–569.

Caldarelli G, Catanzaro M. 2012. *Networks: A Very Short Introduction*. Oxford: Oxford University Press.

Chen CLP, Zhang C. 2014. Data-intensive applications, challenges, techniques and technologies: A survey on Big Data. *Information Sciences* 275:314–347.

Chen M, Mao S, Liu Y. 2014. Big Data: A survey. *Journal of Mobile Networks and Applications* 19(2):171–209.

Christen P. 2014. Privacy aspects in Big Data Integration: Challenges and opportunities. *Proceedings of the First International Workshop on Privacy and Security of Big Data*. LOCATION: ACM.

Dong XH, Divesh S. 2015. Big Data integration. *Synthesis Lectures on Data Management* 7(1):1–198.

Gessert F, Wingerath W, Friedrich S, Ritter N. 2016. NoSQL database systems: A survey and decision guidance. *Computer Science Research and Development*. Special issue paper. *Computer Science Research and Development*. Berlin: Springer-Verlag.

Goodchild MF. 2007. Citizens as sensors: The world of volunteered geography. *GeoJournal* 69(4):211–221.

Hartmann PM, Zaki M, Feldmann N, Neely A. 2016. Capturing value from big data: A taxonomy of data-driven business models used by start-up firms. *International Journal of Operations and Production Management* 36(10):1382–1406.

Jin X, Wah BW, Cheng X, Wang Y. 2015. Significance and challenges of Big Data research. *Big Data Research* 2(2):59–64.

Khan N, Yaqoob I, Hashem IAT, Inayat Z, Ali WKM, Alam M, Shira M, Gani A. 2014. Big Data: Survey, technologies, opportunities, and challenges. *Scientific World Journal* 2014:712826.

Kozuch MA, Ryan MP, Gass R, Schlosser SW, O'Hallaron D, Cipar J, Krevat E, López J, Stroucken M, Ganger GR. 2009. Tashi: Location-aware cluster management, pp. 43–48. *Proceedings of the First Workshop on Automated Control for Datacenters and Clouds*, June 19 2009, Barcelona, Spain. New York: Association for Computing Machinery.

Lugmayr A, Stockleben B, Scheib C. 2016. A comprehensive survey on Big Data research and its implications: What is really "new" in Big Data? It's cognitive Big Data! *PACIS Proceedings*, paper 248. http://aisel.aisnet.org/pacis2016/248.

Muhtaroglu F, Pembe C, Demir S, Obali M, Girgin C. 2013. Business model canvas perspective on Big Data applications. *IEEE International Conference on Big Data*, Santa Clara, CA. doi:10.1109/BigData.2013.6691684.

Najjar MS, Kettinger WJ. 2013. Data monetization: Lessons from a retailer's journey. *MIS Quarterly Executive* 12(4):213–225.

Nasser T, Tariq RS. 2015. Big Data challenges. *Journal of Computer Engineering and Information Technology* 4(3):1–10.

Oguntimilehin A, Ademola EO. 2014. A review of Big Data management, benefits and challenges. *Journal of Emerging Trends in Computing and Information Sciences* 5(6):433–438.

Visconti, RM. 2017. Public private partnerships, big data networks and mitigation of information asymmetries. *Corporate Ownership & Control* 14(4).

Walker R. 2015. *From Big Data to Big Profits*. Oxford: Oxford University Press.

Ward JS, Barker A. 2013. Undefined by data: A survey of Big Data definitions. Working paper, Cornell University Library. https://arxiv.org/pdf/1309.5821v1.pdf.

Wienhofen LWM, Mathisen BJ, Roman D. 2015. Empirical Big Data research: A systematic literature mapping. arXiv:1509.03045.

Yingcai W, Guo-Xun Y, Kwan-Liu M. 2012. Visualizing flow of uncertainty through analytical processes. *IEEE Transactions on Visualization and Computer Graphics* 18(12):2526–2535.

Zhai Y, Ong YS, Tsang IW. 2014. The emerging "big dimensionality." *IEEE Computational Intelligence Magazine* 9(3):14–26.

17

Distant and Close Reading of Dutch Drug Debates in Historical Newspapers: Possibilities and Challenges of Big Data Analysis in Historical Public Debate Research[*]

Berrie van der Molen and Toine Pieters

CONTENTS

Introduction

In recent years, large amounts of data with great humanistic and historical relevance have become available to researchers. Digitized archives of socioculturally relevant material, such as newspapers, historical records, and material native to the digital sphere (e.g., online forums and social networking sites), are expanding at a fast rate. It is evident that this material can be of vital value to the humanities; in the digital humanities (DH), scholars argue that Big Data allows scholars in the humanities and history to ask new, different questions (e.g., Guldi and Armitage 2014) or predict that tools will answer such new questions eventually (Scheinfeldt 2010). Nicholson (2013) suggested that history might be in the process of a digital turn. Big Data is a buzzword and it has been for over a decade. This is also apparent from the continuing emergence of many projects devoted to developing tools fit for specific data sets. Unfortunately, tools are often not sustained beyond their initial projects, preventing a more elaborate network of DH tools (Snelders et al. 2017). The focus on new projects and tools means that the exploration of new approaches, driven by the profitable urge for the new, takes priority over sustaining and elaborating on existing methodological approaches characterized by the critical engagement and contextual awareness crucial to humanities research.

---

[*] We would like to thank Dr. Jasmijn van Gorp (UU) for her fruitful comments.

In DH, a clear shift toward interpretation has been apparent since the second digital humanities manifesto (http://manifesto.humanities.ucla.edu/2009/05/29/the-digital-human ities-manifesto-20/). Early research on Big Data in DH tended to present digital results as end results with intrinsic humanistic or historic relevance, but scholars are moving away from this perspective (Bod 2013, Drucker 2016). We argue that continuity with the humanities methodological tradition can help us formulate what humanities scholars and historians should hope to gain from DH. We advocate a research approach that combines the potential of searchable data sets with a critical humanistic perspective. Instead of focusing on (asking or answering) new questions, we want to benefit from the available DH knowledge and experiences while building sustainable technological solutions for our ongoing historical research on the topic of public drug debates in the Netherlands.

In this chapter, we work towards such an approach with a twofold aim. First, we underline the potential of Big Data for historical public debate research by introducing our research approach. Second, we demonstrate our approach with research conducted on public debates in Dutch newspapers between 1945 and 1990 regarding amphetamine. We combine distant reading techniques (Moretti 2013) with close reading (actual reading) of the empirical material to analyze public debates focused on amphetamine and their interaction with drug regulation in the Netherlands. We underline important directions for the development of new technologies within DH. This will stimulate productive collaboration between humanities scholars of different disciplines and computer scientists.

This chapter consists of three parts. In the first part, we describe the relation between public debate research and DH by drawing on secondary literature and existing work. In the second part, we outline our own methodological approach and provide a research demonstration in which we use the text-mining tool Texcavator (https://www.escience center.nl/project/texcavator, http://dig.hum.uu.nl/texcavator/). Finally, we provide two important challenges (sustainable research infrastructures and cross-media public debate research) for future research in the field, along with our research ambitions and intentions for use and development of the text-mining tool AVResearcherXL (http://dig .hum.uu.nl/avresearcher-xl/).

Big Data and Digital Humanities

Big Data can help scholars get a grasp on historical public debates, and we argue that a sustainable approach should be based on combining distant reading techniques with close reading of the historical material.

Public Debate Research

Historical public debate research can benefit from a Big Data approach, because it enables access to large bodies of significant cultural texts. Computers can be used to search and analyze Big Data sets; this is is called distant reading (Moretti 2013), in which the properties of a data set are "read," generating valuable information. In our research on public drug debates, we use advanced search and visualization tools to mine relevant digitized historical data sets, such as newspaper and television archives. This means that the material can be researched bottom-up instead of top-down, because of keyword search, which is of great value for historical research (Nicholson 2013).

Text mining may have the capacity to determine "what the significant themes in public debates within a specific historic time frame actually were" (van Eijnatten et al. 2013). Distant reading techniques can help us gain insight into a corpus; we can find out where we should be looking and we can establish better search strategies based on initial results. From a humanities perspective, or to be more precise, from our historical perspective, it is imperative to keep an eye on the actual sources. In DH, the call for a more critical and reflexive stance towards digital methods has been heard for some time (Borgman 2009, Mahrt and Scharkow 2013). Boyd and Crawford (2012) warned about Big Data's supposed objectivity, stating that "interpretation is at the center of data analysis" and thus forces scholars to take account of the involved methodological processes. Drucker (2016) stressed that visualization techniques are essentially representations that pass off as presentations, whereas visualization is a process of remediation and translation. It has been argued that the adoption of a Big Data approach in a discipline risks blindly reproducing old assumptions because of the explicit "new" association with Big Data (Barnes 2013). The adoption of DH techniques thus forces us to be critical and it presents us with a number of challenges. In historical research, Zaagsma (2013) described the challenge for historians to use hybrid approaches integrating traditional and digital methods. Noordegraaf (2016) suggested that the challenge is to adapt tools and techniques to the needs of humanities scholars, instead of fearing that Big Data-based techniques may have no place in the inherently complex analysis of culture. We position ourselves similarly: we use DH techniques to strengthen our interpretative capacity.

Bod (2012) stressed the importance of critical reflection and interpretation in his coinage of the term "humanities 3.0." In Bod's view, the humanities are closer to science than is often assumed: he (re)formulated the humanities as a pattern-seeking discipline (Bod 2015). He argued that the humanities have been concerned with recognizing patterns in cultural and social domains. Although we agree with his focus on critical reflection, we adopt a different perspective on the humanities' essence. The history of science teaches us that science itself is not a linear, pattern-seeking, independent quest for world description (e.g., Kuhn's 1962 writings on scientific revolutions [Kuhn 2012]). Instead, what is the truth in science is often contested, undergoing change and influenced by social processes. In order to keep that perspective on science and on knowledge in general, we need the contextual awareness and critical perspective of the humanities. So, instead of attempting to reformulate the humanities as a science of the arts and culture, we choose to define humanities by its dependence on critical reflection and contextual awareness based on expertise. This enables original insights and challenges to existing assumptions.

In the process of using quantitative methods, an important part of DH research, we then need to keep two related things in mind. First, we need to remain critical of our methods; we should always be wary of basing qualitative claims on quantitative observations. Van Eijnatten et al. (2013) wrote that DH is unable "to produce a historical narrative authored by a craftsman whose evocation of the past depends on individual erudition, scholarship, insight, talent, and the ability to tell a story." Leaving this interpretative process to computer processing is dangerous, because it is precisely the ability to reflect that helps us to observe meaningfully. Patterns or trends found by using distant reading techniques should not be accepted as evidence-based research results; however, they should support our interpretive capacity. Second, DH methods should help us to make better informed interpretations of sociocultural phenomena of the past; we need to draw explicitly on historical contextual awareness to interpret search results. Digital search results do not automatically provide relevant answers to the "so what?" research question, but they may help us to identify and ask more informed and significant research questions (Bron et al.

2016). Historical or humanistic expertise enables researchers to refine and reframe questions; in our case study on public debates regarding amphetamine we are knowledgeable interpreters of the data, because we understand the sociocultural context of drugs in The Netherlands and we have knowledge of the legislative drug history of the Netherlands.

Our strategy to benefit responsibly from Big Data's potential in our historical research is to consistently combine distant reading techniques with close reading, or actual reading. This ensures that throughout the analysis process, the researcher maximizes critical awareness of the empirical material. In his review of opportunities and challenges for digitized newspaper archive analysis, Bingham (2010) insisted that what he called "blunt" keyword search needs to be combined with analysis of entire newspapers. Walma's (2015) research on public perceptions of morphine in Dutch newspapers showed that close reading of search results helped to enrich the understanding of public debates and helped to formulate user-centered design requirements for text-mining tools. Below, we outline our strategy, in which we continuously alternate between distant reading and close reading.

Dutch Historical Newspapers as Big Data

For our ongoing historical enquiry into public perceptions of drugs in postwar Netherlands, we research the approximately 11 million digitized newspaper pages of the Royal Dutch Library (www.delpher.nl). With the text-mining tool Texcavator, we seek to trace public debates in this data set, essentially treating historical newspapers as Big Data.

We want to improve our understanding of the historical interaction between public debates, policy decision making, and regulation in The Netherlands. Our research on public drug debates is part of a research project called "The Imperative of Regulation," in which the history of Dutch drug regulation is researched from several perspectives. Of course, public debate is only a single factor that interacts with drug regulation. In the NWO project, different factors were researched in different subprojects (http://www.nwo .nl/onderzoek-en-resultaten/onderzoeksprojecten/i/46/13546.html). Our specific aim is to gain an understanding of the historical role of public perceptions of drugs in relation to drug regulation. Here, we proceed with a research demonstration of amphetamine use in order to show the possibilities and historical benefits of our distant/close reading approach.

Discourse Analysis and Governmentality

Our research is interdisciplinary: we seek to combine a historical perspective with theoretical and methodological approaches from media studies. Although our interpretation of the empirical material is informed mainly by the historical knowledge of drugs and drug regulation in The Netherlands, we have a particular theoretical understanding of the meaningful relation between the text and its sociocultural context, as is usual in media studies.

Although public debate research is a suitable term for the discussion of particular topics in national media, it does become somewhat problematic in the context of Big Data research. Debate is not an accurate term for an artificially generated collection of newspaper articles that is a result of our distant reading efforts. It would suggest that we accept the quantitative distant reading process as an interpretive agent. We therefore decided to regard these "debates" (search results) as a means to analyze the "discursive formation" of drugs at a particular time. Discourse can be understood as the culturally constructed, historically specific conditions of truth (Foucault 1998). That is to say that, in relation to our national case study in The Netherlands, at each particular time, a particular culturally defined truth or understanding of amphetamine use has existed. In the Foucauldian understanding of discourse, it is intimately related to a specific conception of power. Power exists everywhere in society where there is interaction between humans, and it is defined by discursive conditions. Hypothetically, if discourse on a particular drug is overwhelmingly positive (for instance, because it is considered to have enormous medical potential), there will be public outrage about criminalization of the substance. Should the drug start to be associated more with criminal activity, for instance in newspapers, criminalization of the substance would start to look acceptable to a population. Power relations are thus structured by discursive conditions in this understanding. Perceiving the public perception of drugs in this way helps us to understand it in relation to regulation. Although, as we argue in this section, we think discourse analysis is a highly suitable theoretical framework, our methodological approach can be combined with different theoretical frameworks (depending on the topic and research question).

Discourse analysis can then be used to understand a sociocultural meaning of a particular topic at a particular time. This is a useful approach to understand the public perception of a drug, because it attempts to distill from all the different material an overall cultural conception. It also means that the relevance of the articles is not necessarily related to the number of relevant words appearing. The aim is to understand this discursive formation of a particular topic. Small remarks or passing mentions of amphetamine may be just as informative as grand debates involving amphetamine. This makes it a particularly suitable framework for our approach that treats digitized newspapers as Big Data: the historical argument does not depend on individual articles but on the overall understanding of the time period. The assumption is that reading the subset gives pointers to the discursive formation of a topic beyond the subset, as every hit reveals a little bit of information about what could be said about a particular drug at a particular time. The high probability that we will fail to include all relevant articles due to optical character recognition issues (technical) or underlying assumptions in the search process (subjective) should not have a significant effect on the overall impression of the discursive formation of the topic.

For our perception of the relation between public discourse and regulation, we draw on the theoretical framework of governmentality as Michel Foucault described it in *Security, Territory, Population* (2007). There is no empirical connection between the spheres of public perception and regulation, which are in themselves difficult to pinpoint. We approach regulation as governmental actions, as interventions in the milieu: the set of natural and artificial givens. "The milieu appears as a field of intervention in which ... one tries to affect, precisely, a population" (Foucault 2007). Public debate can be considered an artificial part of this milieu, with newspapers being elements where traces of the public debate can be found. If we want to understand the connection between how amphetamine use is constructed in the public debate and amphetamine regulation, we need to compare the discursive formation of amphetamine in these two spheres. In this research demonstration on amphetamine use and regulation, we have drawn on secondary literature for our understanding of developments in drug regulation (Blom 2015, de Kort 1995). What happens when amphetamine use moves from a more medical discursive formation to a mostly criminal discursive formation? Is it possible to find changes in the discursive formation of amphetamine use preceding regulation, or does the public perception of amphetamine use change following regulation? (Note that this approach is not concerned with individual agency in the first place, as that would require a stronger focus on specific actors and types of newspapers. We remain on a more general, national level of discourse.)

Zinberg (1984) influentially stated that a thorough understanding of drugs (use or abuse) needs to take into account the specific drug (intoxicant), set (associated user[s]), and the (physical and social) setting at all times. These are elements on which we focus in our analysis of public debates. How do different associated sets and settings develop in the public perception of amphetamine use? Before we get to our research demonstration, we will explicate the methodological steps that constitute our "leveled approach."

A Leveled Approach

In our explorative historical, leveled approach, we can define three different levels (Figure 17.1), where we go from distant reading techniques on the macro level to close reading of the articles on the micro level (Van der Molen et al. 2017). We use this approach to trace and analyze relevant empirical material in the digitized newspaper data set. Crucially, we keep navigating between the research levels, thus treating the tools as signposts to indicate the most relevant material in need of close reading. (Combining distant and close reading is common practice in DH; we emphasize the need to make explicit the steps between distant and close reading and the continuous navigation between the two analysis methods.) This also addresses the challenges associated with keyword search in historical research (Huistra and Mellink 2016): by adapting the query in the research process based on new information, we minimize the risk of not ending up with the most relevant subset. The approach works in text-mining tools that offer timeline graphs, word cloud functionalities, and document viewing. Text-mining tools like Texcavator and AVResearcherXL, which work on the specific newspaper Delpher data set, both offer these. The research below was conducted using Texcavator.

On the macro level, we tackle the overall specified period with a drug query. We then use the timeline visualization functionality to make continuous series of subperiods, based on word frequency patterns found by looking at the peaks and valleys on the timeline. Texcavator creates subsets for every year. Here, on what we call the meso level, we

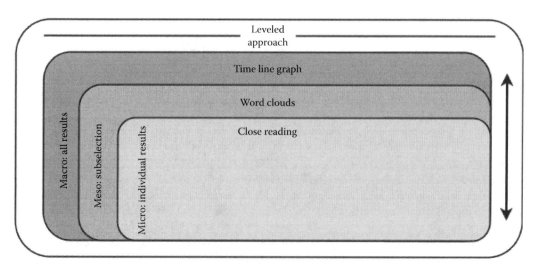

FIGURE 17.1
Schematic overview of the leveled approach.

compare the different word clouds. The strongly associated terms in these word clouds might indicate bursts of attention regarding the drug. We consequently adapt the query by adding terms from the word clouds (the selection of terms depends both on our findings so far and our informed research interest), singling out results related to particular topics and in particular time frames. This is what we call the micro level, and on this level we read the actual articles in order to understand the historical and cultural significance of the debates. Throughout this process, which we repeat several times in iterative cycles, we accumulate information, enabling us to formulate informed and enriched research questions.

The quantitative techniques used throughout the analysis process serve to support or inform our qualitative research. In interpreting the search results, we depend on our historical understanding of the context and the theoretical framework described above.

Research Demonstration: Public Perception of Amphetamine in Dutch Newspapers

With our theoretical and methodological framework, we are now equipped to mine the newspaper data set with Texcavator. Note that we do not set out with an initial research question; we start the iterative research process with our topic (amphetamine) and historical contextual knowledge. Taking these into the empirical material helps us to formulate informed questions along the way, as will become apparent below. Although this research demonstration is full of historical observations and qualitative interpretation, it should not be read as research results. Instead, we hope that describing the steps we take in approaching the empirical material and the moments of interpretation are made explicit. The actual research process is more iterative than is apparent from our description here. For clarity's sake, this section reads in one overall direction (from distant to close reading), but in practice we need to navigate between the two reading types repeatedly to be able to formulate and answer detailed research questions. Moreover, the figures we have included in this research demonstration do not function as research results; they merely illustrate the process.

Amphetamine was discovered in 1887 (de Kort 1995). Originally it was perceived as a scientifically developed miracle drug, and it was successfully positioned as an antidepressant in the 1940s, but it was also used as a performance enhancer and prescribed as a diet pill (Rasmussen 2008). De Kort (1995) suggested that the widespread use of amphetamine among soldiers in World War II possibly played a role in its postwar prevalence in The Netherlands. In the 1950s, amphetamine was often prescribed by doctors as an antidepressant or as part of weight loss treatment in The Netherlands (de Kort 1995). Its use spread beyond the medical context, and the substance proved to be addictive, prompting a regulatory response (de Kort 1995). In 1968, some types of amphetamine became prescription-only drugs, and in 1969 further regulation of the sales and the stocking of amphetamines was enacted under the Wekaminenbesluit (Pieters 2005). In the 1976 modification of the Dutch Opium Law, a distinction was made between drugs with unacceptable harmfulness (List I) and less harmful drugs (List II) (Blom 2015). Amphetamine was included on List I, classified as a hard drug and putting an end to amphetamine use beyond strictly medical contexts. The amphetamine-type drug methylphenidate is currently the most widespread treatment form for attention deficit hyperactivity disorder (it is marketed under the brand name Ritalin) (Chan et al. 2016).

We do not have a "so what?" research question yet at this point. As is apparent from our short introduction to amphetamine, its regulatory framing changed drastically. Our aim is to understand how the discursive formation of amphetamine changed in Dutch newspapers throughout this time period. We started with distant reading of materials from the relevant time frame, using Texcavator, hoping to find as many newspaper articles mentioning amphetamine as possible. The query that we used included the following terms: am*etami*, wekami*, benzedri*, perviti*, me*ylam*etami*, isophan, neopharmedri*, preludin*, fencamfamin*, and actedron*. This query incorporated different spelling variations and brand names that we know were used during (part of) the period between 1945 and 1990. (The different names and variations of the terms may have differing connotations in the public sphere. We want to emphasize that combining them does not mean that we intend to downplay the importance of these differences; during this stage of our analysis, we actually hoped to find leads for understanding different parts of the truth construction at different moments in time.) Entering this query generated a timeline graph, which allowed us to view developments in coverage of amphetamine in Dutch newspapers (relative to the overall data set) (Figure 17.2).

In Figure 17.3, we have combined the most cooccurring words for every year between 1945 and 1990. Every column represents a year, with the most frequently cooccurring word listed at the top and decreasing frequencies as the output proceeds to the bottom. Naturally, we were looking for particular elements because of our historical research interest: we wanted to understand the interaction between regulation and public discourse. Therefore, we went through these words and assigned different colors to different categories (see the Figure 17.3 legend). This is an interpretive process: words often have more than one meaning and could fit in different categories, or they may not fit into the assigned category sometimes (e.g., staat, meaning both state and stands [as a verb] in Dutch). It does help to get an impression of the predominant themes of the context of amphetamines in newspapers. We continued to go back and forth between the macro and meso levels; we looked at the coverage and obtained a first impression about the meaning of this coverage by looking at the developments of the different categories. Already at this stage of the research, we scanned individual search results in document view, which helps to avoid confusion while maintaining a sense of the empirical material not based merely on the distant reading results. Thus, we alternated between distant and close reading.

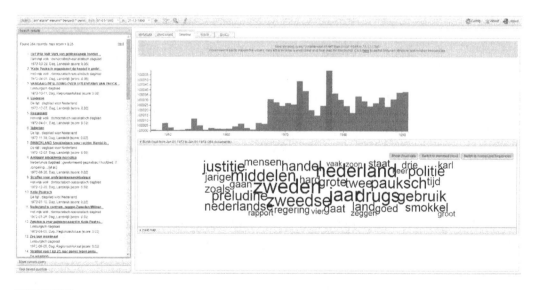

FIGURE 17.2
Texcavator output. The display shows the timeline graph for the amphetamine combined query between 1945 and 1990 and the word cloud for the year 1972.

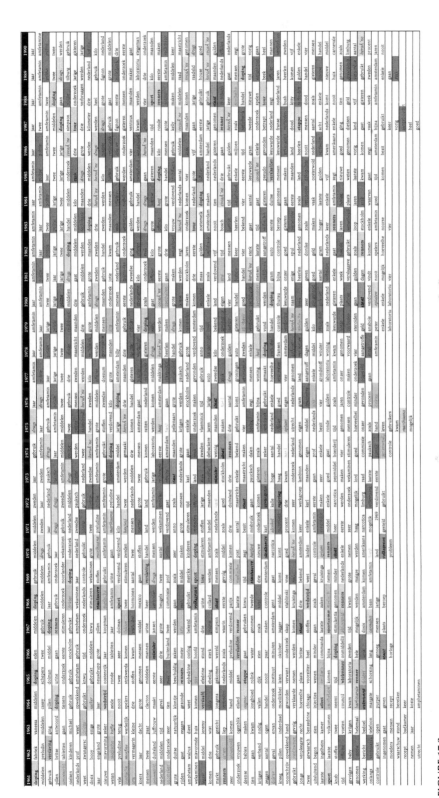

FIGURE 17.3
Detail of our overview of the most frequently cooccurring words per year, displaying 1961–1990. Legend: dark gray shading, criminal; light gray shading, medical; in bold font, sports; in italic font, other intoxicants; in bold-italic font, governmental.

The main initial observation was that the medical terms became less predominant after 1969. From the early 1970s, a rapid increase in criminal/judicial terms was seen, and to the end of the overall period criminal terms appeared to be used to characterize the debates the most. This is in line with what we would expect historically: in 1968, amphetamine regulation began. Moreover, a concentration of governmental terms appears from 1964 until 1977. This is precisely the time frame in which the regulations happened, and this is therefore also unsurprising.

At this point, we were able to formulate an informed research question about the data set. We wanted to understand how the discursive formation of amphetamine changed in public debates, because legislation in the period changed the status of amphetamine from an over-the-counter drug to a "hard" drug. The assumption would then be that amphetamine had two distinct medical framings (as a medicine and as a harmful drug), with a transition period. The question we formulated was "How did the medical component of the discursive formation of amphetamine change between 1945 and 1990?" The question was based on the assumption that this medical component (or element of the debate) must have changed over time, but it is open to any qualitative outcome following further iterative distant and close reading cycles.

Having established a specific question, we adapted our initial query. We added all the medical terms we found in the word clouds to the original query to narrow the selection of articles, as follows: +(am*etami*, wekami*, benzedri*, perviti*, me*ylam*etami*, isophan, neo-pharmedri*, preludin*, fencamfamin*, actedron*) +(dokter*, dokter arts*, arts medisch psychi-atri*, internist apothe*k* geneesmiddel*, patiënt* medicijn*, medicament*). This query yields all articles that include (i) at least one of the amphetamine names/variations and (ii) at least one of the most frequently cooccurring medical terms. The number of results generated was 1,170 (Figure 17.4). We have thus far attempted to cover as many articles mentioning amphetamines as possible and, subsequently, we have attempted to reduce this subset to articles with a medical term. It is certain that we have not found all articles that fit these criteria, but we do know that we have selected all articles that mention any of the medical terms occurring in the 50 most frequently used words in each of the years.

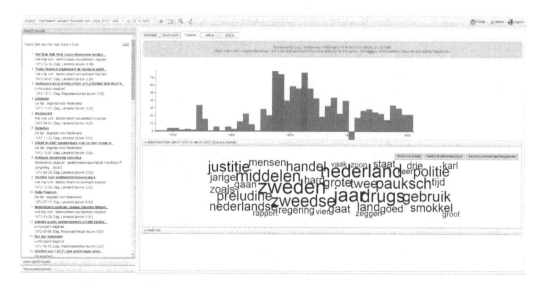

FIGURE 17.4
Texcavator output. The display shows the timeline graph for the *medical* amphetamine combined query between 1945 and 1990.

We did not want to go directly to a close reading of the 1,170 results at this stage; instead, we developed a more informed perspective before we decided which results we would read. The two timeline graphs helped. One shows us the concentrations of amphetamine debates, and the other shows us the prevalence of amphetamine debates with a medical term. For both of them, the relative prevalence (the number of results in relation to the overall number of articles that year) is a guide. We were interested in the role of medical discourse in the period, taking into consideration the regulatory changes of 1969 and 1976.

We formulated five questions based on a combination of interpretations of the visualization techniques and historical knowledge of drug regulation. The questions are not results of the quantitative queries; they are questions grounded in our historical understanding of the time period as a response to the quantitative results we obtained. Answering the questions demands close reading of the search results. We answered each of the questions by reading the articles for the respective years (less than 100 for each of the mentioned years). Most importantly, we considered how we could interpret these answers as they related to drug regulation: How did the role of the medical discourse in public debates on amphetamine as a part of the Dutch milieu change in this period? That is the question that ties together the answers to all of these other questions. We will go through these questions in chronological order.

1. *What is the meaning of the medical component in the articles in the years 1954 and 1955, especially considering the strong presence of other drugs (alcohol, opium, and morphine) in that time period?*

The appearance of medical terms here was not surprising, as this was the period where amphetamine functioned as a more or less innocent over-the-counter drug. The word *arts* (doctor) appeared much more often than it did in previous and successive years, which was interesting. We also saw a relative increase in the number of articles mentioning amphetamines compared to the frequencies in previous and subsequent years (Figure 17.2). The highly frequent appearance of other drugs in the articles was surprising, however, since there was no immediate reason to believe that amphetamine would be mentioned in other drug debates. Close reading of the articles showed that the cooccurence with other intoxicants (alcohol, morphine, and opium) was the result of two types of reports. First, there was an ongoing discussion about a number of court cases in which doctors who were said to have been driving drunk used the argument that they were under the influence of Pervitine (the brand name of an amphetamine) as their defense. Second, there were reports on two medical professionals who stole drugs (morphine or opium) from pharmacies. One of them, a nurse, was reported to have been an opiate addict, but she was also reported to have stolen amphetamine. The other, a doctor, was reported to be a morphine addict who asked the apothecary for Pervitine while stealing morphine from the pharmacy stock.

Both types of reports indicated that amphetamines were in a gray area: they appeared in the context of sociocultural problems related to other intoxicants, but their reputation did not yet put them at the heart of addiction debates. Looking at these early cases with a long-term perspective, however, it is telling that amphetamines were already appearing in close proximity to regulated intoxicants in public debates. Moreover, although it was not considered an addictive substance yet, we could in retrospect identify the reports of medical staff stealing drugs as cases of iatrogenic amphetamine addiction. The discursive formation of amphetamines at the time did not accommodate this conclusion, naturally. In relation to the first reports (about the doctors driving under the influence of Pervitine), we also saw public unrest about existing legislation, with government officials commenting that the situation in which substances endangering road safety needed to be regulated. There was, in that sense, a call for regulation of amphetamine in as far as it posed a risk to others. Conclusively, although there was no clear medical distrust of amphetamine at this time, its mention did appear in close proximity to mentions of other intoxicants as early as the mid-1950s.

2. *What is the meaning of the medical component in the articles in the years 1961 and 1962?*
   Are there reasons to link this to the apparently sudden appearance of doping-related terms?

Just under a decade passed since the observations of the previous question, but the discursive formation of amphetamine seems to have changed noticeably in this time period. It is worth noting that upon close reading, it turned out that one large article appeared with several duplicates in the result list of the year 1961. This did not affect the interpretation of the individual articles, but it underlines the importance of going to the source material before making qualitative claims based on quantitative results. We found a rise of doping-related terms from this period onward. Upon reading the actual articles, however, we saw that doping was just one of the reasons why discursive formation regarding amphetamine changed. One prominent debate is indeed the doping debate, with commentators complaining that in cycle racing, using one of the "-ines" (including amphetamine) has become the rule rather than the exception. The use of amphetamine in sports is related to a concern with the origins and availability of nonmedical amphetamine. In neighboring countries, amphetamine has become available only by prescription. In the Netherlands, amphetamine can still be bought at pharmacies, although there is a growing concern about uses that are not medically dictated, with articles warning about pill addictions and linking use of the drug by young people as well. On May 4, 1961, the *Nederlandse Vereniging van Fabrikanten van Pharmaceutische Producten* even published a letter responding to the unrest about the "pill chaos." We found several articles reporting pharmacology Professor Booy's plea to make amphetamine a prescription-only drug. For 1962, we also noted several articles about the risks of deformation of children as a consequence of use of Preludine (another amphetamine brand name) during pregnancy. Here as well, the pharmaceutical industry did respond in an attempt to rebuke these claims.

Over the course of a few years, public unrest about (different types of) amphetamine seems to have risen steeply. Concerns about doping in cycle racing were not the only concerns. We also saw that amphetamine was starting to lose its strong connection to medical use; instead, it was starting to appear as a performance enhancer in sports and as a stimulant used gratuitously by young people. The substance thus appeared in relation to a very different set and settings than in the 1950s. Although by this time there was an ongoing discussion about including amphetamine in the Opium Law (de Kort 1995), there was no legislative change regarding amphetamine until the change to prescription-only drug status for several types of amphetamines in 1968 and stricter control on sales and possession of amphetamines under the *Wekaminenbesluit* of 1969.

3. *What is the meaning of the attention burst for amphetamine in medical discourse in 1972,*
   and how can this be understood in the historical context of the regulatory transition?

The articles from 1972 are mostly directly related to the call for amphetamine regulation. As we observed from the word cloud for the year, there was a large presence of the words *Zweden* (Sweden) and *Pauksch*, the name of an infamous amphetamine smuggler since 1971. Articles feature called for repercussions against the amphetamine trade, as the fear existed that the Netherlands was turning into an amphetamine trade hub because other European countries profited from the Netherlands' different regulatory context; penalties for amphetamine production and trade were much lower in the Netherlands. It is telling that also in the public debate there was more public unrest about the amphetamine trade than amphetamine use, which is in line with the Netherlands' dual-track policy. Amphetamine appeared mostly in a criminal setting because of this international trade, meaning that this setting dominated the discursive formation, which could have helped to make the inclusion of the substance under the Opium Law in 1976 seem a natural decision.

4. *What is the meaning of the medical resurgence in the years 1979 and 1980? How was it related to the recent regulation in 1976?*

In 1979, we see that the discursive formation of amphetamine changed drastically and in line with what could be expected from our observations under question 2. In an article from *Nieuwsblad van het Noorden* from May 28, 1979, a doctor was accused of prescribing *een gevaarlijke kuur* (a dangerous treatment) to 11 patients. The treatment included amphetamine. In articles that were related to doping, we see that these articles mainly mentioned amphetamine in relation to anabolic steroids. Having come under scrutiny at this time period, they are in contrast with amphetamine use being considered more similar to medication (than the latter) (e.g., *Het Vrije Volk*, August 17, 1979). It seems, then, that the medical terms appearing in conjunction with amphetamine in these years were used to define amphetamine as having no place in medicine anymore. Amphetamine is now regularly linked to drug addiction; in doping discussions, the risk of addiction is usually mentioned as the biggest danger related to the use of amphetamine (along with the danger to others, which is especially interesting as a development from our observations under Question 1). We also saw several reports of pharmacy raids in this time period. In 1980, discussions on how to improve the safeguarding of drugs in pharmacies appeared, where amphetamines were usually mentioned in one breath with opiates, citing increasing drug thefts. A rise in the theft of amphetamine was not surprising: the substance had been available rather easily at pharmacies until a decade before.

There are still a few traces of the medical reputation (obviously amphetamine did remain in use in some capacity). A doctor commenting on the unrest regarding doping in *De Volkskrant* from September 22, 1979 reminisced that he understood that athletes could possibly feel that amphetamine doping was not outrageous, considering doctors also prescribed the substance as part of weight loss treatments. Another trace of the medical reputation can be found in relation to doping: in *Het Vrije Volk* from October 11, 1980, a doctor commented on the use of anabolic steroids and that, providing amphetamine is administered professionally, amphetamine is more innocent than anabolic steroids.

Amphetamine is gradually losing its medical reputation and mentions of it appear mostly in criminal and doping debates. Amphetamine is generally thought of addictive and dangerous. There are a few exceptions in which it has been remarked that under the right medical circumstances use of the substance could be acceptable.

5. *Although medical terms regarding amphetamine seemed to fade from prominence early in the 1980s, there was one mention of the term "medische" (medical) in 1988. What was the role of the medical component just over 10 years after regulation, at a time when amphetamine debates seemed to be mostly defined in criminal terms?*

The articles found in 1988 no longer placed amphetamine in a medical context. There are some cases of iatrogenic addiction, where pharmacists steal from the stock, and some passing remarks about amphetamine addicts. The bulk of the articles at this time was again related to doping discussions. Questions arose concerning the cost of the ever-increasing doping controls, with discussions on whether doping was such a grief misstep. There was no unrest directly related to amphetamine either; reports on smuggling of amphetamine were reported in a matter-of-fact tone. A number of articles reported on the inclusion of ecstasy/XTC (e.g., *Nieuwsblad van het Noorden*, December 29, 1988), an amphetamine derivate, on List I in an amendment of the Opium Law. These articles have a similarly nonsensationalizing tone. A report on the inclusion of amphetamine in the kit of alpinists (*Limburgsch Dagblad*, April 2, 1988) mentioned that there was, according to the alpinist, no need to be secretive about this part of his outfit, implying it was a legitimate emergency option for alpinists.

Compared to the discursive formation of amphetamine in 1979–1980, we saw that it was no longer framed as an explicitly dangerous drug. Reports of smuggling and use were formal but consistently placed the drug in the criminal sphere. The drug appears to be uncontroversial as an illegal drug by this time, with the medical cooccurring terms no longer connecting amphetamine to a medical setting. This is a very different discursive formation compared to the first time periods we analyzed.

Regulation and Public Perception of Amphetamine

In this research demonstration, we showed how our research approach enabled us to reformulate our research questions between iterative cycles. This process was a result of distant reading techniques and close reading based on our historical understanding of the context of the material.

Focusing on the articles featuring medical terms helped us to improve our understanding of the transition in the public perception of amphetamine. Already in the 1950s, mention of amphetamine appeared in close proximity to that of other intoxicants. It was not connected to addiction debates and remained in the medical setting. This already changed before its inclusion on List I of hard drugs in 1976: in the early 1960s, it was starting to be connected to a different set and setting, to younger people and to athletes as possibly dangerous performance enhancers. Before the end of the 1970s, the general view was that amphetamine is harmful and addictive unless used under professional medical supervision. Later, in the 1980s, a decade after regulation, there was hardly any medical framing in discussions. However, we also noticed that it was no longer framed as particularly dangerous. Public unrest subsided, once it was more firmly rooted as a controlled illegal drug. Having developed this improved understanding of the medical components in the amphetamine debates, we can now ask more precise questions about discussions related to doping or crime as well as about early signals of yet another shift in the 1990s towards the medical sphere once again (Pieters 2005). Throughout this research demonstration, we have hinted at other elements of the discourse (e.g., criminal, legislative). The results discussed in this demonstration should be understood as part of a more comprehensive analysis of amphetamine. The criminal and legislative components would need their own respective research cycles in order to paint the full picture.

Modularity and the Cross-Media Challenge

Looking ahead, we suggest two directions for development in the field of public debate research. First, we underline the importance of creating a sustainable research environment; second, we stress the urgent need for solutions to the cross-media challenge for

Big Data public debate research. We elaborate on why these are important and state how we intend to contribute with the development of the text-mining tool AVResearcherXL (Figure 17.5).

One of the main challenges in DH is to deal with the speed at which technologies change. Generally, the field is defined by a revolutionary imperative. Research projects attract funding by emphasizing their original and groundbreaking potential; relevance is often expressed in terms of leaps forward and change. A result of this eagerness to be at the forefront of technological possibilities is that such projects often revolve around the implementation of new, project-specific tools. Although this means that projects generate powerful tools, it also means that these tools are often tailored to very specific aims. Often, these tools are not embedded permanently in existing research infrastructures, meaning that they are eventually abandoned. This was one of the main conclusions of the recent congress, *Historical Newspapers as Big Data*, held at the Dutch Royal Library (https://www.kb.nl/nieuws/2017/historisch-onderzoek-in -digitale-kranten-verslag-van-het-big-data-congress). Funding for the necessary technological maintenance and modernization of such tools is difficult to attract and often not even applied for, since projects focusing on new tools are more likely to attract funding over less revolutionary project proposals. This needs to change in order to warrant a sustainable research environment that continuously builds on previous achievements.

Within the research infrastructure CLARIAH, the decision was made to move to a modular approach in media studies (http://www.clariah.nl/werkpakketten/focusgebieden /media-studies). Instead of thinking in terms of project-specific tools, there has been a shift to thinking in terms of functionalities as part of an overall research environment, called Media Suite. We believe that Big Data-fueled public debate research needs to move in this direction as well. Our intention is to develop the text-mining tool AVResearcherXL as a component in the CLARIAH Media Suite. AVResearcherXL is a CLARIAH recipe tool that enables cross-media comparisons of NISV's iMMix catalogue (radio and television) and KB's Delpher (newspapers) by means of word clouds, bar charts, timelines, and result lists (Huurnink et al. 2013; Van Gorp et al. 2015). The tool was primarily developed to be a distant reading tool for media researchers, to discern patterns in media representations. We intend to extend AVResearcherXL's applicability to research on public debates. Its embedment in the Media Suite will make it easy to incorporate and combine other distant

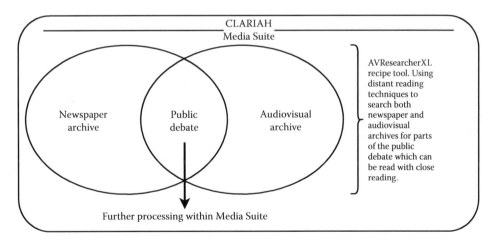

FIGURE 17.5

Schematic overview of our development intentions for use of the text-mining tool AVResearcherXL within the CLARIAH Media Suite.

reading techniques or data sets, ensuring that new DH strategies can be incorporated in the distant/close reading research approach.

As historians, our interest in public debate analysis tools goes beyond singular data sets or media. Research methods and tools need to accommodate that. However, tools are often developed for one media type or data set. In order to truly understand Dutch public debates in the postwar period, television and radio cannot be left out. Television was introduced in The Netherlands in the early 1950s and reached a mass audience in the 1960s (Prenger 1993). Since we are at the cutting edge of media studies and cultural history, we want to maximize the historical potential of this public debate research methodology. In other words, we need a tool that can accommodate our distant and close reading approach across media, which is what we intend AVResearcherXL to be.

We have found that a cross-media approach to public debates highlights methodological differences between textual and audio-visual (AV) data (Van der Molen et al. 2017). This is not just an issue that relates to historical use of the current AVResearcherXL recipe; it relates to important concerns about medium specificity and source criticism. In the newspaper archive, the actual words are "read" in a distant reading approach, but similar distant reading of AV material is difficult. AV data have specific properties (framing, editing, mise-en-scene, etc.) that affect the discursive formation of drugs which cannot be read by means of distant reading. This is a challenge that is further complicated by access and intellectual property right contexts that differ between data sets.

Both the modular approach and the cross-media approach fit our ambition to develop a durable public debate research method based on alternating between distant and close reading. By building a modular environment, new distant reading techniques can be added to the research infrastructure to create new innovative analysis methods. Focusing on cross-media functionalities is a necessity in light of the diverse media landscape; if our current research approach were to be used for recent or contemporary public debate research, much more extensive cross-media research combinations would be indispensable. Our research on postwar drug debates in The Netherlands is also in urgent need of such functionalities.

Conclusions

Digital humanities methods and tools should reinforce the humanities by allowing researchers to ask enriched questions and by helping researchers find empirical material for critical interpretation. We argue that combining distant reading techniques with close reading of the material in iterative cycles is an expedient strategy to answer this need.

In our research demonstration, we showed that our approach is effective for public debate analysis that relies on Dutch newspapers as Big Data. We were able to signalize and interpret changes in the (medical part of the) discursive formation of amphetamine, finding that amphetamine already appeared in close proximity to mentions of other intoxicants in the 1950s, and that it started to be connected to a different set and setting of young people and athletes as performance enhancers in the early 1960s. By the time it was fully regulated in 1976, the change in public perception of amphetamine from medicine to harmful drug had already occurred. Moreover, our demonstration provided leads for follow-up questions, which we will take up in our ongoing research on drug debates in the Netherlands.

We identified two important challenges in public debate research: there is an urgent need for both more sustainable research environments and also options for cross-media analysis. Dealing with these challenges is directly relevant to our drug debate research. In our intended development of the text-mining tool AVResearcherXL we expect to contribute to overcoming both challenges; the tool will be integrated into the modular Media Suite of CLARIAH, ensuring sustainability, and it will enable public debate research with simultaneous mining of textual and AV data sets. By explicating our needs as domain users and explicating our research approach, we can keep working on creating a methodology that utilizes Big Data analysis as an enrichment of interpretative research on historical public debates.

References

Barnes TJ. 2013. Big data, little history. *Dialogues in Human Geography* 3(3):297–302.

Bingham A. 2010. The digitization of newspaper archives: Opportunities and challenges for historians. *Twentieth Century British History* 21(2):225–31.

Blom T. 2015. *Opiumwetgeving en drugsbeleid*. Deventer: Wolters Kluwer.

Bod R. 2012. Het Einde van de Geesteswetenschappen 1.0. University of Amsterdam Digital Academic Respository. http://www.oratiereeks.nl/upload/pdf/PDF-1433Weboratie_Rens_Bod_-_def.pdf.

Bod R. 2013. Who's afraid of patterns? The particular versus the universal and the meaning of humanities 3.0. *BMGN Low Countries Historical Review* 128(4):174–180.

Bod R. 2015. *A New History of the Humanities: The Search for Principles and Patterns from Antiquity to the Present*. Oxford, United Kingdom: Oxford University Press.

Borgman CL. 2009. The digital future is now: A call to action for the humanities. *Digital Humanities Quarterly* 3(4).

Boyd D, Crawford K. 2012. Critical questions for Big Data. *Information Communication Society* 15(5):662–679.

Bron M, Van Gorp J, de Rijke M. 2016. Media studies research in the data-driven age: How research questions evolve. *Journal of the Association for Information Science and Technology* 67(7):1535–1554.

Chan JYC, Dennis TA, Macleod MA. 2016. The over-prescription of ritalin for suspected cases of ADHD. *Journal of Health Sciences* 2(2):35–40.

de Kort M. 1995. *Between Patient and Delinquent*. Hilversum: Uitgeverij Verloren.

Drucker J. 2016. Graphical approaches to the digital humanities, pp. 238–250. In S. Schreibman S, R. Siemensand R, Unsworth J. (eds.), *A New Companion to Digital Humanities*. Malden, MA: Wiley/Blackwell.

Foucault M. 1998. *The Will To Knowledge. The History of Sexuality*, vol. 1. London: Penguin Books.

Foucault M. 2007. *Security, Territory, Population: Lectures at the College De France, 1977–78*. New York: Picador.

Guldi J, Armitage D. 2014. *The History Manifesto*. Cambridge University Press.

Huistra H, Mellink B. 2016. Phrasing history: Selecting sources in digital repositories. *Historical Methods* 49(4):220–229.

Huurnink B, Bronner A, Bron M, van Gorp J, de Goede B, van Wees J. 2013. *AVResearcher: Exploring Audiovisual Metadata*. DIR 2013. Dutch-Belgian Information Retrieval Conference, Delft.

Kuhn TS. 2012. *The Structure of Scientific Revolutions*, 4th ed. Chicago: University of Chicago Press.

Mahrt M, Scharkow M. 2013. The value of Big Data in digital media research. *Journal of Broadcasting and Electronic Media* 57(1):20–33.

Moretti F. 2013. *Distant Reading*. Brooklyn, NY: Verso Books.

Nicholson B. 2013. The digital turn. *Media History* 19(1):59–73.

Noordegraaf J. 2016. Computational research in media studies. Methodological implications. *KWALON* 21(1):52–59.

Pieters T. 2005. Een eeuw omgang met "moeilijk en druk" gedrag. *Signaal* 53:12–27.

Prenger M. 1993. Uitglijden over de beeldbuis. Nederlandse politici op de televisie in de jaren vijftig en zestig. In: *Jaarboek Mediageschiedenis 5*. Amsterdam: Stichting Mediageschiedenis.

Rasmussen N. 2008. *On Speed: The Many Lives of Amphetamine*. New York: NYU Press.

Scheinfeldt T. 12 May 2010. Where's the beef? Does digital humanities have to answer questions? *Found History* http://foundhistory.org/2010/05/wheres-the-beef-does-digital-humanities-have -to-answer-questions/.

Snelders S, Pim H, Jaap V, de Rijke M, Toine P. 2017. A digital humanities approach to the history of culture and science. In: Odijk J, Hessen A. (eds.). *CLARIN in the Low Countries*. LOCATION: Ubiquity Press. (In press.)

van der Molen B, Buitinck L, Pieters T. 2017. The leveled approach. using and evaluating text mining tools AVResearcherXL and Texcavator for historical research on public perceptions of drugs. arXiv:1701.00487.

van Eijnatten J, Pieters R, Verheul J. 2013. Big Data for global history: The transformative promise of digital humanities. *BMGN Low Countries Historical Review* 128(4):58–77.

van Gorp J, de Leeuw JS, van Wees J, Huurnink B. 2015. Digital media archaeology: Digging into the digital tool AVResearcherXL. *Journal of European Television History and Culture*. http://dspace .library.uu.nl/handle/1874/321428.

Walma L. 2015. Filtering the "news": Uncovering morphine's multiple meanings on Delpher's Dutch newspapers and the need to distinguish more article types. *Tijdschrift Voor Tijdschriftstudies* 38:61–78.

Zaagsma G. 2013. On digital history. *BMGN Low Countries Historical Review* 128(4):3–29.

Zinberg NE. 1984. *Drug, Set, and Setting: The Basis for Controlled Intoxicant Use*. London: Yale University Press.

Index